lonely planet

S0-AZB-106

Jordan

Paul Greenway
Damien Simonis

LONELY PLANET PUBLICATIONS
Melbourne • Oakland • London • Paris

Handwritten annotations:

- Asks people to get up?
  Come to the mosque
  to pray (2)
- Come the successful - to win(2)
- God is the biggest (iz)
  There
  (is no other God(1)

079·709·824

9/24/00: Jordanian Dinar = $1 = .71

$871
× 0.71
————
618.41
+ 3%
————
636.96
— 30
————
806.96

JORDAN

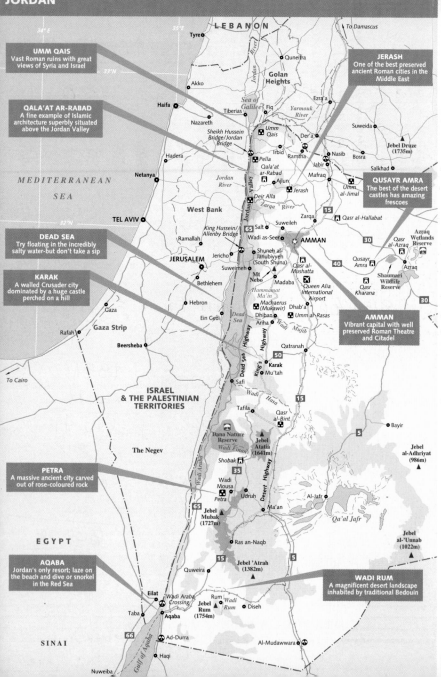

UMM QAIS
Vast Roman ruins with great views of Syria and Israel

QALA'AT AR-RABAD
A fine example of Islamic architecture superbly situated above the Jordan Valley

DEAD SEA
Try floating in the incredibly salty water–but don't take a sip

KARAK
A walled Crusader city dominated by a huge castle perched on a hill

PETRA
A massive ancient city carved out of rose-coloured rock

AQABA
Jordan's only resort; laze on the beach and dive or snorkel in the Red Sea

JERASH
One of the best preserved ancient Roman cities in the Middle East

QUSAYR AMRA
The best of the desert castles has amazing frescoes

AMMAN
Vibrant capital with well preserved Roman Theatre and Citadel

WADI RUM
A magnificent desert landscape inhabited by traditional Bedouin

LEBANON

To Damascus

Tyre

Akko

Haifa

Nazareth

Hadera

Netanya

MEDITERRANEAN SEA

Tel Aviv

Ramallah

JERUSALEM

Bethlehem

Hebron

Gaza

Rafah

Gaza Strip

Beersheba

To Cairo

ISRAEL & THE PALESTINIAN TERRITORIES

The Negev

EGYPT

Eilat

Taba

SINAI

Nuweiba

Quneitra

Golan Heights

Sea of Galilee

Tiberias

Fiq

Yarmouk River

Ezra'a

Suweida

Jebel Druze (1735m)

Der'a

Ramtha

Nasib

Bosra

Jabir

Salkhad

Umm Qais

Irbid

Pella

Qala'at ar-Rabad

Ajlun

Jerash

Mafraq

Umm al-Jimal

QUSAYR AMRA

Qasr al-Hallabat

Sheikh Hussein Bridge/Jordan Bridge

Deir Alla

Zarqa River

Salt

Suweileh

Zarqa

AMMAN

Azraq Wetlands Reserve

Qasr al-Azraq

West Bank

Jordan River

Jericho

Suweimeh

King Hussein/Allenby Bridge

Wadi as-Seer

Shuneh al-Janubiyyeh (South Shuna)

Qasr al-Mushatta

Qasr al-Azraq

Qasr Kharana

Qusayr Amra

Azraq

Shaumari Wildlife Reserve

Ein Gedi

Dead Sea

Mt Nebo

Madaba

Hammamat Ma'in

Machaerus (Mukawir)

Dhiban

Aria

Dhab'a

Umm ar-Rasas

Queen Alia International Airport

Qatranah

Safi

Karak

Mu'tah

King's Highway

Wadi Hasa

Bayir

Tafila

Qasr al-Bint

Dana Nature Reserve

Wadi Feinan

Jebel Atata (1641m)

Jebel al-Adhriyat (986m)

Shobak

Wadi Mousa

Petra

Udruh

Ma'an

Al-Jafr

Qa'al Jafr

Jebel al-'Unnab (1022m)

Jebel Mubak (1727m)

Ras an-Naqb

Quweira

Jebel 'Atrah (1382m)

Desert Highway

Wadi Araba Crossing

Wadi Araba

Rum Wadi Rum

Jebel Rum (1754m)

Diseh

WADI RUM

Aqaba

Ad-Durra

Al-Mudawwara

Haqi

Gulf of Aqaba

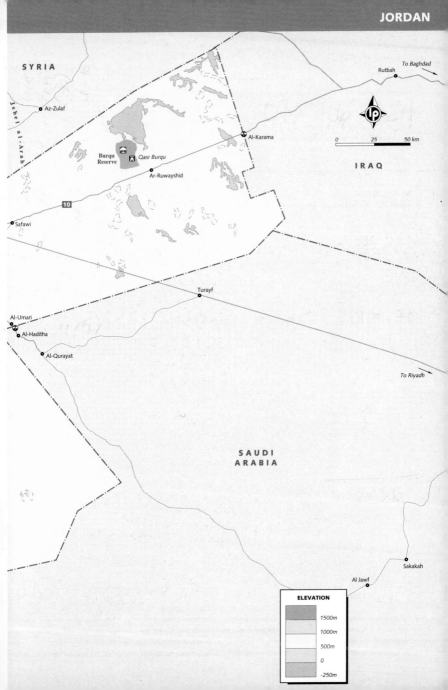

Jordan
4th edition – March 2000
First published – October 1987

Published by
Lonely Planet Publications Pty Ltd A.C.N. 005 607 983
192 Burwood Rd, Hawthorn, Victoria 3122, Australia

Lonely Planet Offices
Australia PO Box 617, Hawthorn, Victoria 3122
USA 150 Linden St, Oakland, CA 94607
UK 10a Spring Place, London NW5 3BH
France 1 rue du Dahomey, 75011 Paris

Photographs
All of the images in this guide are available for licensing from
Lonely Planet Images.
email: lpi@lonelyplanet.com.au

Front cover photograph
A guide and his horse, Petra (Simon Bracken)

ISBN 0 86442 694 1

Contents – Text

2 Contents – Text

Contents – Maps

3

The Authors

Paul Greenway

Paul caught his first tropical disease in 1985 and has had the travel bug ever since. Gratefully plucked from the blandness and security of the Australian Public Service, he is now a full-time traveller and writer. Paul has contributed to several Lonely Planet guides, such as *South India* and *Indonesia*, and has written guides to a diverse number of countries, such as *Mongolia, Iran* and *Bali & Lombok*.

During the rare times he is not travelling (or writing, reading and dreaming about it), Paul tries to write and record some tuneless ditties, eats and breathes Australian Rules football, and will do anything (like going to Mongolia and Iran) to avoid settling down.

Damien Simonis

With a degree in languages and several years' reporting and subediting on several Australian newspapers (including the Australian and the Age), Sydney-born Damien left the country in 1989. He has lived, worked and travelled extensively throughout Europe, the Middle East and North Africa. Since 1992, Lonely Planet has kept him busy with *Jordan & Syria, Egypt & the Sudan, Morocco, North Africa, Italy*, the *Canary Islands, Spain* and *Barcelona*. He has also written and snapped for other publications in Australia, the UK and North America. When not on the road, Damien resides in splendid Stoke Newington, deepest north London.

FROM PAUL

I would like to thank many people, particularly everyone who wrote to Lonely Planet with ideas, comments and criticisms. In Jordan, a huge thanks to the indefatigable Tamam Koudeih, who constantly went out of his way to help me for no personal reward. Thanks also to Kamal I Twal of the National Society for Preservation of the Heritage of Madaba and its Suburbs; Nofa Nasser of the Jordan Tourism Board; Aysar Akrawi of the Petra National Trust; Qusay Ahmad and Rana Shaheen of the Royal Society for the Conservation of Nature; Bruce Pollock of the Global Environment Facility in Aqaba; and, finally, to Osama Musa, my Sudanese friend at Rum. Finally, thanks to Ruth Kent of the Jordan Information Bureau in London.

Back home in Adelaide, South Australia, thanks to Mum, Gill, Graham, Tom and Amelia, Dad and Judy; and to Richard and Janet Allen for being such great friends.

At Lonely Planet, thanks to Geoff Stringer for sending me to Jordan, and apologies to all the long-suffering and unsung editors, cartographers and designers who had to battle with my manuscript and maps.

This Book

This book was based on the Jordan chapters from the 3rd edition of *Jordan & Syria*, written by Damien Simonis and Hugh Finlay. The Hiking section in the Activities chapter was adapted and expanded from information provided by Tony Howard and Di Taylor in the 3rd edition of *Jordan & Syria*.

From the Publisher

This book was edited in Lonely Planet's Melbourne office by Julia Taylor with assistance from Sarah Mathers and Dan Goldberg. Brett Moore coordinated the design and mapping with assistance from Heath Comrie and Shahara Ahmed. Quentin Frayne organised the Language chapter; Simon Bracken and Indra Kilfoyle designed the cover. Thanks to Peter Ward of Peter Ward Book Exports for his assistance with bookshop information.

THANKS
Many thanks to the travellers who used the last edition and wrote to us with helpful hints, advice and interesting anecdotes. Your names appear in the back of this book.

Foreword

ABOUT LONELY PLANET GUIDEBOOKS

The story begins with a classic travel adventure: Tony and Maureen Wheeler's 1972 journey across Europe and Asia to Australia. Useful information about the overland trail did not exist at that time, so Tony and Maureen published the first Lonely Planet guidebook to meet a growing need.

From a kitchen table, then from a tiny office in Melbourne (Australia), Lonely Planet has become the largest independent travel publisher in the world, an international company with offices in Melbourne, Oakland (USA), London (UK) and Paris (France).

Today Lonely Planet guidebooks cover the globe. There is an ever-growing list of books and there's information in a variety of forms and media. Some things haven't changed. The main aim is still to help make it possible for adventurous travellers to get out there – to explore and better understand the world.

At Lonely Planet we believe travellers can make a positive contribution to the countries they visit – if they respect their host communities and spend their money wisely. Since 1986 a percentage of the income from each book has been donated to aid projects and human rights campaigns.

Updates Lonely Planet thoroughly updates each guidebook as often as possible. This usually means there are around two years between editions, although for more unusual or more stable destinations the gap can be longer. Check the imprint page (following the colour map at the beginning of the book) for publication dates.

Between editions up-to-date information is available in two free newsletters – the paper *Planet Talk* and email *Comet* (to subscribe, contact any Lonely Planet office) – and on our Web site www.lonelyplanet.com. The *Upgrades* section of the Web site covers a number of important and volatile destinations and is regularly updated by Lonely Planet authors. *Scoop* covers news and current affairs relevant to travellers. And, lastly, the *Thorn Tree* bulletin board and *Postcards* section of the site carry unverified, but fascinating, reports from travellers.

Correspondence The process of creating new editions begins with the letters, postcards and emails received from travellers. This correspondence often includes suggestions, criticisms and comments about the current editions. Interesting excerpts are immediately passed on via newsletters and the Web site, and everything goes to our authors to be verified when they're researching on the road. We're keen to get more feedback from organisations or individuals who represent communities visited by travellers.

Lonely Planet gathers information for everyone who's curious about the planet – and especially for those who explore it first-hand. Through guidebooks, phrasebooks, activity guides, maps, literature, newsletters, image library, TV series and Web site we act as an information exchange for a worldwide community of travellers.

Research Authors aim to gather sufficient practical information to enable travellers to make informed choices and to make the mechanics of a journey run smoothly. They also research historical and cultural background to help enrich the travel experience and allow travellers to understand and respond appropriately to cultural and environmental issues.

Authors don't stay in every hotel because that would mean spending a couple of months in each medium-sized city and, no, they don't eat at every restaurant because that would mean stretching belts beyond capacity. They do visit hotels and restaurants to check standards and prices, but feedback based on readers' direct experiences can be very helpful.

Many of our authors work undercover, others aren't so secretive. None of them accept freebies in exchange for positive write-ups. And none of our guidebooks contain any advertising.

Production Authors submit their raw manuscripts and maps to offices in Australia, USA, UK or France. Editors and cartographers – all experienced travellers themselves – then begin the process of assembling the pieces. When the book finally hits the shops, some things are already out of date, we start getting feedback from readers and the process begins again ...

WARNING & REQUEST

Things change – prices go up, schedules change, good places go bad and bad places go bankrupt – nothing stays the same. So, if you find things better or worse, recently opened or long since closed, please tell us and help make the next edition even more accurate and useful. We genuinely value all the feedback we receive. Julie Young coordinates a well travelled team that reads and acknowledges every letter, postcard and email and ensures that every morsel of information finds its way to the appropriate authors, editors and cartographers for verification.

Everyone who writes to us will find their name in the next edition of the appropriate guidebook. They will also receive the latest issue of *Planet Talk*, our quarterly printed newsletter, or *Comet*, our monthly email newsletter. Subscriptions to both newsletters are free. The very best contributions will be rewarded with a free guidebook.

Excerpts from your correspondence may appear in new editions of Lonely Planet guidebooks, the Lonely Planet Web site, *Planet Talk* or *Comet*, so please let us know if you *don't* want your letter published or your name acknowledged.

Send all correspondence to the Lonely Planet office closest to you:

Australia: PO Box 617, Hawthorn, Victoria 3122
USA: 150 Linden St, Oakland, CA 94607
UK: 10A Spring Place, London NW5 3BH
France: 1 rue du Dahomey, 75011 Paris

Or email us at: talk2us@lonelyplanet.com.au

For news, views and updates see our Web site: www.lonelyplanet.com

HOW TO USE A LONELY PLANET GUIDEBOOK

The best way to use a Lonely Planet guidebook is any way you choose. At Lonely Planet we believe the most memorable travel experiences are often those that are unexpected, and the finest discoveries are those you make yourself. Guidebooks are not intended to be used as if they provide a detailed set of infallible instructions!

Contents All Lonely Planet guidebooks follow roughly the same format. The Facts about the Destination chapters or sections give background information ranging from history to weather. Facts for the Visitor gives practical information on issues like visas and health. Getting There & Away gives a brief starting point for researching travel to and from the destination. Getting Around gives an overview of the transport options when you arrive.

The peculiar demands of each destination determine how subsequent chapters are broken up, but some things remain constant. We always start with background, then proceed to sights, places to stay, places to eat, entertainment, getting there and away, and getting around information – in that order.

Heading Hierarchy Lonely Planet headings are used in a strict hierarchical structure that can be visualised as a set of Russian dolls. Each heading (and its following text) is encompassed by any preceding heading that is higher on the hierarchical ladder.

Entry Points We do not assume guidebooks will be read from beginning to end, but that people will dip into them. The traditional entry points are the list of contents and the index. In addition, however, some books have a complete list of maps and an index map illustrating map coverage.

There may also be a colour map that shows highlights. These highlights are dealt with in greater detail in the Facts for the Visitor chapter, along with planning questions and suggested itineraries. Each chapter covering a geographical region usually begins with a locator map and another list of highlights. Once you find something of interest in a list of highlights, turn to the index.

Maps Maps play a crucial role in Lonely Planet guidebooks and include a huge amount of information. A legend is printed on the back page. We seek to have complete consistency between maps and text, and to have every important place in the text captured on a map. Map key numbers usually start in the top left corner.

Although inclusion in a guidebook usually implies a recommendation we cannot list every good place. Exclusion does not necessarily imply criticism. In fact there are a number of reasons why we might exclude a place – sometimes it is simply inappropriate to encourage an influx of travellers.

Introduction

Squeezed between Iraq, Saudi Arabia and Israel and the Palestinian Territories, Jordan has had a short but tumultuous history – yet it's probably the safest and most stable country in the region. It has until recently had one leader for over 45 years; Islamic extremism and militancy are nonexistent.

Jordan is home to the Bedouin, many of whom still live a traditional lifestyle in the desert. Men wearing full flowing robes and leading herds of goats and sheep across the modern highways are a common sight. Visitors may spend a lot of time enjoying the endless cups of tea and coffee offered by these hospitable people.

The capital, Amman, is a modern, thriving city built on many small hills or *jebels*. It is home to several very good museums and art galleries, and some excellent hotels and restaurants. Aqaba is Jordan's resort town, much visited by Jordanians and Saudis, and offers the country's only diving and snorkelling sites, and swimming beaches. Other attractions are the ancient cities of Jerash and Umm Qais, while the incredible red sandy jebels of Wadi Rum always impress. The Dead Sea is the lowest point on earth, and swimming – or more correctly, floating – in the salty water is a unique experience. The area is slowly being developed for tourism, as are the natural thermal springs and waterfalls at Hammamat Ma'in.

Undoubtedly, the highlight of Jordan, and one of the most spectacular sights in the entire Middle East, is the ancient Nabataean city of Petra. Carved out of rock in the 6th century BC, it is remarkably well preserved and has delighted ancient travellers, writers and painters – and more recently the producers of the film *Indiana Jones and the Last Crusade*.

Much to the chagrin of the tourist authorities, most people only come to Jordan for a short time. However, there are enough attractions – landscapes, hiking, castles, nature reserves, bird life and cafes – to keep most visitors happy for at least two weeks. Now realising the importance of tourism to

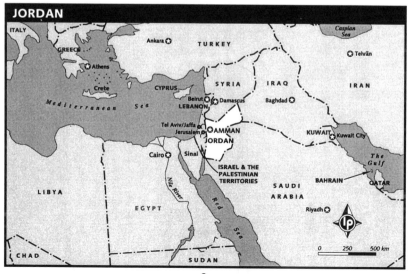

Jordan's floundering economy, the authorities are busy building new roads, hotels and tourist facilities. The mass pilgrimage of Christians and others to Jordan and Israel to celebrate the Birth of Christ in 2000 will further open up tourism.

Unlike some countries in the region, Jordan welcomes visitors with open arms. Visas are normally available on arrival, travelling is reasonably cheap and often good value, and there is a wide range of hotels in most major towns and tourist sites. Don't miss an opportunity to try the local cuisine, whether it be sitting down to a formal banquet or squatting around a communal bowl of rice and meat with a Bedouin family in their desert tent. Alternatively, western delights are easy to find in the larger towns.

Jordan is easy to get around independently because English is widely spoken and the country is compact; it's possible to see everything on day trips from only four towns. Most attractions are accessible by public transport, and renting a car, or chartering a taxi, is straightforward.

Many people come to Jordan on a side-trip from Israel, through one of three open borders, or as a stopover along a fascinating jaunt between Turkey and Egypt, via Syria. But, simple to reach from Europe by air and with connecting flights from the USA, Canada, Australia and New Zealand now easier to arrange, it's never been a better time to visit. Jordan is certainly worth an exclusive trip; definitely worth more than the few days most travellers allow.

Facts about Jordan

HISTORY

Although the modern state of Jordan is a creation of the 20th century, the area it encompasses can claim to have one of the oldest civilisations in the world. The region was never strong enough to form an empire itself, and it was for the most part a collection of city states, but its strategic position ensured that all the great early civilisations passed through. The Egyptians, Assyrians, Babylonians, Hittites, Greeks, Romans, Arabs, Turks and Crusaders all helped to shape the history of the region. They traded, built cities and fought their wars here, leaving behind rich cultural influences.

Ancient History

Evidence of human habitation in the area dates back about 500,000 years, but little is known until the Neolithic Age. Archaeological finds from Jericho (on the other side of the Jordan River, in the Palestine National Authority), and Al-Beidha (near Petra), positively dated at around 9000 BC, have revealed extensive villages where inhabitants lived in mud and stone houses, bred domestic animals, made pottery and used sophisticated agricultural methods.

'Ain Ghazal, another ancient village from the Neolithic Age (and far larger than Jericho), was 'discovered' recently when a highway was being built to Amman; some items from the site are now on display in the National Archaeological Museum in Amman.

The Chalcolithic (or Copper) Age (4500-3300 BC) saw the beginning of copper smelting. Sheep and goats were reared and crops, such as olives, wheat and barley, were introduced. Materials such as basalt and mud were used for buildings, and irrigation systems were first implemented.

The remains of buildings and implements used for copper smelting can be found at Khirbat Finan (in the Dana Nature Reserve), and village ruins from the Chalcolithic Age are dotted throughout the Jordan Valley and Irbid.

The Bronze Age signalled the common making of crafts, such as pottery and jewellery, and permanent settlements at the Citadel (in modern-day Amman), and in the southern desert regions. Foreigners introduced the idea of mixing copper and tin, creating bronze, a hardier material for making domestic implements and weapons.

The Early Bronze Age (3000-2100 BC) saw occupation of the Jordan Valley by the Canaanites, a Semitic tribe. They grew crops such as wheat and olives, raised sheep and goats, and used more sophisticated methods of irrigation. Along with other tribes in the area, the Canaanites discovered the virtue of building defensive walls against invaders. The Middle Bronze Age (2100-1500 BC) saw the development of trade with neighbouring powers in Syria, Palestine and Egypt. The Late Bronze Age (1500-1200 BC) saw the decline of Egyptian influence and created opportunities for the tribes in the surrounding regions, such as the Hebrew-speaking people who later became known as the Israelites.

During the Iron Age (1200-330 BC), Jordan was divided into three: the Edomites settled in the southern region; the Moabites, near Wadi Mujib; and the Ammonites on the edge of the Arabian Desert with their capital at Rabbath Ammon (the site of present-day Amman). This is the period detailed in the Bible that saw the rule of the great Israelite kings David and his son Solomon. By David's death, in 960 BC, he ruled the principalities of Edom, Moab and Ammon and, at the time of Solomon's rise to the throne, Israel entered its golden age with great advancements in trade. However, by about 850 BC, the time of Ahab, the seventh king of Israel, the now-divided empire was defeated by Mesha, king of Moab, who recorded his victories in stone, the famous Mesha Stele, in the Moabite capital of Dhiban (see the boxed text 'A Stele at Twice the Price' in the King's Highway chapter).

The Greeks, Nabataeans, Romans & Byzantines

In 333 BC, Alexander the Great stormed through Jordan on his way to Egypt. After his death in 323 BC, Alexander's empire was parcelled up among his generals: Ptolemy I gained Egypt, Jordan and parts of Syria, while Seleucus established the Seleucid dynasty in Babylonia. Many people in Jordan now spoke Greek, and cities were renamed accordingly, eg Amman became Philadelphia. In 198 BC, the Seleucid ruler Antiochus III defeated Ptolemy V, and took control of western Jordan. Around this time, the Jews gradually re-established themselves and by 141 BC controlled much of northern Jordan.

In southern Jordan, the Nabataeans rose to prominence with the establishment of their major city, Petra, a testimony to their brilliant architectural abilities. Originally a nomadic tribe, their strength lay in the control of trade routes and almost exclusive knowledge of desert strongpoints and water supplies. Heavy duties imposed on goods transported on the trade routes, and protection money to keep bandits at bay, made them comparatively wealthy.

The Nabataeans never really possessed an 'empire' in the common military and administrative sense of the word, but rather, from about 200 BC they established a 'zone of influence' that stretched throughout the region. Parts of the Nabataean kingdom in Jordan were unsuccessfully attacked by the Roman general Pompey in 64 BC, but further attacks by Herod the Great were more harmful and by his death in 4 BC the Nabataeans were much reduced in stature. By the time of the Nabataean King Rabbel II, the Nabataeans had lost much of their commercial power – Palmyra to the north was presenting increasing competition as the major trade route – and the remaining remaining Nabataean land was peacefully incorporated into the Roman Empire on Rabbel's death in 106 AD.

The Sassanians (or Sassanids) from Persia (modern-day Iran) briefly occupied parts of eastern Jordan in about 260 AD, while the Byzantines occupied the rest. Under Byzantine occupation, Christianity became the official religion of Jordan as the Byzantine emperor Constantine had converted to Christianity in the early 4th century AD. This was a period of prosperity and stability, marked by changes in language, arts and traditions. Many churches were constructed (often over the remains of ancient temples) and were usually decorated with elaborate mosaics.

In the early 7th century, the Sassanians again re-occupied parts of Jordan. Although the Byzantine emperor Heraclius forced them into a peace agreement Syria in 628, it was the beginning of the end for Byzantine rule in the region.

The Advent of Islam

After Prophet Mohammed's death in 632, his followers, the Muslims, began to exert power in the region. They lost their first battle against the Byzantines at Mu'tah (near Karak) in 629 but defeated them in 636 under Khaled ibn al-Walid at the Battle of Yarmouk. Islam quickly became the major religion, and Arabic became the major language, of the region. The capital of their empire was in the holy city of Medina (in modern-day Saudi Arabia).

By 323 BC Alexander the Great's empire stretched from Greece to India.

The ascension of Ali, the fourth caliph (successor) to the Prophet Mohammed, caused the schism between the Sunni and Shi'ite factions (see Religion later in this chapter). The Syrian governor, Mu'awiya, succeeded Ali in 661 and established the Umayyad dynasty, based in Damascus.

The comparatively benevolent Umayyads built such great monuments as the Umayyad Mosque in Damascus, and the Mosque of Omar and the Dome of the Rock in Jerusalem. The Umayyads' great love of the desert led to the construction of the 'desert castles' (in eastern Jordan). Nevertheless, it was also a time of almost unremitting internal struggle.

In 747 an earthquake devastated much of Jordan, weakening the Umayyad's hold on power. They were overthrown by the Abbasids, in 750. The Abbasids followed a stricter form of Islam, and were far less tolerant of Christianity than the Umayyads. Based in distant Baghdad, the Abbasids were perpetually fighting the Fatimid dynasty in Egypt and Seljuks from Turkey; as a result, Jordan was virtually ignored.

In 969 the Cairo-based Fatimids wrested control of Palestine, Transjordan and southern Syria from the Abbasids. In 1037 the Seljuk Turks took over what remained of the Abbasid territory and within the next 50 years also took over Transjordan.

The Crusaders

In 1095 Pope Urban II sought a 'holy war' as revenge for the ongoing destruction of churches and to protect pilgrim routes to the Holy Land. The Crusaders captured Jerusalem in 1099, slaughtering countless inhabitants and causing devastation. They probably would not have lasted long if the region had not been so divided.

The Crusaders took control of most of Jordan by about 1115, and built fortresses (which can still be seen today) at Karak, Shobak and on Pharaoh's Island, just offshore from Aqaba. As a minority, their hold was always tenuous, and could only survive if the Muslim states remained weak and divided, which they obligingly did until the late 12th century.

In the 12th century, Nur ad-Din (literally 'Light of the Faith'), son of a Turkish tribal ruler, was able to unite all of Syria, and most Arabs in the region, to defeat the Crusaders in Egypt. His campaign was completed by Salah ad-Din ('Righteousness of the Faith'), who overthrew the Fatimid rulers in Egypt, recaptured Palestine and occupied most of the Crusader strongholds in Jordan. The Damascus-based Ayyubids, members of Salah ad-Din's family, parcelled up his empire on his death in 1193, and the Crusaders recaptured much of their former territory along the coast. The main remnant of Ayyubid rule in Jordan is the magnificent castle at Ajlun.

The Mamluks, the name given to a vast group of boys taken from foreign lands to serve as slaves and soldiers for the Ayyubids, gained so much power that they eventually overthrew their masters in 1250. From their bases in Cairo and Damascus they defeated the first wave of rampaging Mongolian forces in 1258, invaded Jordan and finally expelled the Crusaders. The Mamluks rebuilt the castles at Karak, Shobak and Ajlun, which they used as lookouts and as a series of staging posts for carrier pigeons transporting messages. The Mongols under Tamerlane then destroyed much of the Mamluk Empire around 1400.

The Ottoman Turks

The Ottoman Turks took Constantinople in 1453, and defeated the Mamluks in Jordan in 1516. The Ottomans concentrated on other cities, such as the holy city of Jerusalem and the commercial centre of Damascus, and Jordan again declined in importance. However, the Ottomans did build the Hejaz Railway linking Damascus with the holy city of Medina, via Amman (see the boxed text 'The Hejaz Railway' in the Getting There & Away chapter).

The dynasty declined in influence and power after the incursions, and brief occupation of Jordan, by the Egyptians in the 1830s. The Egyptians were eventually defeated with the unexpected assistance of several European powers.

[Continued on page 18]

BIBLICAL JORDAN

As Christianity was the dominant religion in Jordan from the late 4th century to the early 7th, there are a number of sites of relevance to Christians, as well as to others. Almost 100 places in Jordan are mentioned in the Bible, but often with different names, eg the Citadel in Amman was known as Rabbath Ammon, Karak was Kir Moab, and Madaba was Medeba.

In tandem, the authorities of Jordan and Israel are heavily promoting tourism to both countries in 2000 (and 2001) to celebrate the Birth of Christ. More information is available from the Jordan Tourism Board (JTB) offices in Amman and overseas – see the Tourist Offices section in the Facts for the Visitor chapter for details.

Major Biblical Sites

'Ain Musa or Ayoun ('Ain) Musa
Then Moses raised his arm and struck the rock twice with his staff. Water gushed out, and the community and their livestock drank. (Numbers 20:11)
The exact location of where Moses struck the rock is open to debate: it's either 'Ain Musa (north of Wadi Mousa, near Petra), or Ayoun ('Ain) Musa, near Mt Nebo. (See Petra and King's Highway chapters, respectively.)

Anjara
'Lady of the Mountain' is a cave where baby Jesus and the Virgin Mary stopped on their way between Galilee and Jerusalem. The place is mentioned a few times in the Bible, but not by name.

Near the cave is a 19th century Roman Catholic church and a wooden statue of Mary and Jesus – both built for pilgrims. The area is likely to be developed in time for the pilgrimage, and is only a couple of kilometres south of Ajlun.

Dead Sea
... while the water flowing down to the Sea of the Arabah was completely cut off ... (Joshua 3:16)
The Sea of Arabah, also known as the Salt Sea, is mentioned several times in the Bible.

Jebel Haroun
Remove Aaron's garments and put them on his son Eleazar, for Aaron will be gathered to his people: he will die there. Moses did as the Lord commanded: they went up to Mount Hor in the sight of the whole community. (Numbers 20:26-27)

Mt Hor is believed to be Jebel Haroun in Petra. It is also a holy place for Muslims. (See Hiking in the Petra chapter.)

Inset: Mosaic segment, St Georges church, Madaba (See the King's Highway chapter for details; photo by Olivier Cirendini)

Jebel Umm al-Biyara

He [the Judaean king, Amaziah] was the one who defeated ten thousand Edomites in the Valley of the Salt and captured Sela in battle ... (2 Kings 14:7)

The village on top of Umm al-Biyara mountain in Petra is deemed to be the ancient settlement of Sela – but this is also disputed, and it may be elsewhere in the Petra region. (See Hiking in the Petra chapter.)

Khirbat al-Wahadneh

This is the birthplace, in ancient Gilead, of Elijah. Nearby is a hill, Tell Mar Elias, where Elijah *went up to heaven in a whirlwind.* (2 Kings 2:11)

Lot's Cave

He and his two daughters ... settled in the mountains ... and lived in a cave. (Genesis 19:30)

The cave where Lot and his daughters lived for years after Lot's wife turned into a pillar of salt is thought to be just off the Dead Sea Highway, not far from Safi. (See the Dead Sea Highway section of the Northern & Western Jordan chapter.)

Machaerus

The King was sad, but because of his oaths and his dinner guests he gave orders that her request be granted, and had John beheaded in the prison. (Matthew 14:9-12)

John the Baptist had claimed that Herod Antipas' marriage to his

BIBLICAL SITES OF JORDAN

1 Umm Qais
2 Tell Mar Elias
3 Anjara
4 Khirbat al-Wahadneh
5 Tell al-Kharrar
6 Ayoun ('Ain) Musa
7 Mt Nebo
8 Madaba
9 Machaerus
10 Karak
11 Lot's Cave
12 'Ain Musa
13 Sela & Jebel Umm al-Biyara
14 Jebel Haroun

brother's wife, Herodias, was unlawful. So, at the request of Salome, Herodias' daughter, John was killed. His tomb has never been found, however. (See the Mukawir section in the King's Highway chapter.)

Mt Nebo

Go up into ... Mount Nebo in Moab, across from Jericho, and view Canaan, the land I am giving the Israelites as their own possession. There on the mountain that you have climbed you will die. (Deuteronomy 32:49-50).

Mt Nebo is a particularly holy place because it is where Moses died – although his tomb has never been found. (See the Mt Nebo section in the King's Highway chapter.)

Tell al-Kharrar

Then Jesus came from the Galilee to the Jordan to be baptised by John. (Matthew 3:13)

Tell al-Kharrar (also known as Wadi Kharrar and Al-Maghtas) is 'Bethany beyond the Jordan' where Jesus was baptised by John the

VALERIE TELLINI

Left: The magnificent Siyagha mosaic can be viewed today at the Moses Memorial Church, Mt Nebo. (See the King's Highway chapter for details.)

Pilgrimage Sites

The Vatican has designated five places in Jordan as official 'Pilgrimage Sites'. If you don't have the time to actually attend the pilgrimages on these dates in 2000, don't worry – the sites will become permanently open to visitors, and are likely to be further developed in the future.

Tell al-Kharrar	7 January & 26 October
Anjara	10 June
Khirbat al-Wahadneh	21 July
Machaerus	25 August
Mt Nebo	1 September

Baptist. It is also where Jesus *went back across the Jordan to the place where John had been baptising to escape persecution from Jerusalem* (John 10:40). (See the Tell al-Kharrar section of the Northern & Western Jordan chapter.)

Umm Qais

When he [Jesus] arrived at the other side in the region of the Gadarenes, two demon-possessed men coming from the tombs met him. (Matthew 8:28-34)

Umm Qais was known as Gadara in the Bible, and in other ancient scriptures.

Right: Founded around the 3rd century BC, Umm Qais prospered in Roman times and was the seat of a bishopric until the 7th century.

INDRA KILFOYLE

[Continued from page 13]
WWI

During WWI Jordan was the scene of fierce fighting between the Ottoman Turks, who had German backing, and the British, based in Suez (Egypt). By the end of 1917 British and Empire troops occupied Jerusalem and, a year later, the rest of Syria. Their successes would not have been possible without the aid of the Arabs, loosely formed into an army under Emir Faisal, who was Sherif (ruler) of Mecca and had taken up the reins of the Arab nationalist movement in 1914. The enigmatic British colonel, TE Lawrence known as 'Lawrence of Arabia' (see the boxed text in the Southern Desert chapter), helped coordinate the Arab Revolt and secure supplies from the Allies.

In June 1916 the Arabs joined the British drive to oust the Turks, following British assurances that they would be helped in their fight to establish an independent Arab state. This was one month after the British and French had concluded the secret Sykes-Picot Agreement, whereby 'Syria' (modern-day Syria and Lebanon) was to be placed under French control and 'Palestine' (a vaguely defined area including modern Israel, the Palestine National Authority and Jordan) would go to the British.

This betrayal was heightened by the 1917 Balfour Declaration, a letter written by the British Foreign Secretary, Arthur Balfour, to a prominent British Jew, Lord Rothschild. It stated that:

His Majesty's Government view with favour the establishment in Palestine of a National Home for the Jewish people, and will use their best endeavours to facilitate the achievement of this object, it being clearly understood that nothing shall be done which may prejudice the civil and religious rights of existing non-Jewish communities in Palestine, or the rights and political status enjoyed by Jews in any other country.

After WWI

At the end of the war, Arab forces controlled most of modern Saudi Arabia, Jordan and parts of southern Syria. The principal Arab leader, Emir Faisal, set up an independent government in Damascus at the end of 1918, a move at first welcomed by the Allies. His demand at the 1919 Paris Peace Conference for independence throughout the Arab world was not so kindly greeted.

The British later came to an agreement with Faisal, giving him Iraq and having his elder brother, Abdullah, proclaimed ruler of the territory that came to be known as Transjordan (formerly part of the Ottoman province of Syria), lying between Iraq and the East Bank of the Jordan River. This angered Zionists, because it effectively severed Transjordan from Palestine and reduced the area of any future Jewish national home.

Abdullah made Amman his capital. Britain recognised the territory as an independent state under its protection in 1923, and a small defence force, the Arab Legion, was set up under British officers – the best known of whom was Major JB Glubb (Glubb Pasha). A series of treaties between 1928 and 1946 led to almost full independence, and Abdullah was proclaimed king in 1946.

The Palestinian Dilemma

Transjordan's neighbouring mandate of Palestine now became a thorn in Britain's side. The Balfour Declaration, and subsequent attempts to make the Jewish national home a reality, were destined for trouble from the start. Arabs were outraged by the implication that they were the 'intruders' and the minority group in Palestine, where they accounted for about 90% of the population.

Persecution of Jews under Hitler in the 1930s accelerated the rate of Jewish immigration to Palestine and violence between Jews and Arabs increased. In 1939 a White Paper was drawn up calling for the creation of a bi-national state. This was rejected by both sides, however, and during WWII both sides cooperated with the British.

After the war, the conflict reached its highpoint. In 1947, the UN voted for the partition of Palestine and on 14 May 1948 the State of Israel was proclaimed. The British Mandate finished but as troops withdrew from the area, Arab armies marched into Palestine. Highly trained Israeli forces proved too strong for the illequpped Arab volunteers and by mid-1949 armistices had been signed.

King Abdullah harboured dreams of a 'Greater Syria' to include all the modern states of Syria, Lebanon, Transjordan and what is now Israel in a single Arab state (later to include Iraq, as well). For this, he was suspected by his Arab neighbours of pursuing different goals from them in their fight with the new state of Israel.

At the end of hostilities, Jordanian troops were in control of East Jerusalem and the West Bank. In response to the establishment of an Egyptian-backed Arab Government in Gaza in September 1948, King Abdullah proclaimed himself King of All Palestine. In April 1950, he formally annexed the territory, despite paying lip service to Arab declarations backing Palestinian independence and expressly ruling out territorial annexations. The new Hashemite Kingdom of Jordan won immediate recognition from the governments of Britain and the US. However, the first wave of Palestinian refugees virtually doubled Jordan's population.

King Abdullah was assassinated outside the Al-Aqsa Mosque in Jerusalem in July 1951. His son Talal ruled for a year, then his grandson Hussein came to power. In 1956, Hussein sacked Glubb Pasha (by now Chief of Staff of the Jordanian Army). After elections that year, the newly formed Jordanian government broke ties with the UK, and the last British troops left Jordan by mid-1957. Hussein staged a coup against his government, partly because it had tried to open a dialogue with the Soviet Union.

With the (temporary) union of Egypt and Syria in 1958, King Hussein feared for his own position and tried a federation with his Hashemite cousins in Iraq. This lasted less than one year because the Iraqi monarchy was overthrown and British troops were sent in to Jordan to protect Hussein.

In February 1960, Jordan offered citizenship to all Palestinian Arab refugees and, in defiance of the wishes of the other Arab states for an independent Palestine, insisted that its annexation of Palestinian territory be recognised. Despite Jordan's opposition to this, the Palestine Liberation Organiza-tion (PLO) was formed in 1964 with the blessing of the Arab League to represent the Palestinian people. The Palestine National Council (PNC) was established within the PLO as its executive body – the closest thing to a Palestinian government.

At about the same time, an organisation called the Palestine National Liberation Movement (also known as Al-Fatah) was established. One of the stated aims of both the PLO and Al-Fatah was to train guerrillas for raids on Israel. Al-Fatah emerged from a power struggle for control of the guerrilla organisations as the dominant force within the PLO, and its leader, Yasser Arafat, became chair of the executive committee of the PLO in 1969.

The Six Day War

With aid from the USA and a boom in tourism – mainly in Jerusalem's old city – the early 1960s saw Jordan's position improve dramatically. Things changed with the outbreak of the Six Day War.

The build-up to the war had been severe Israeli warnings about increasingly provocative Palestinian guerrilla raids into Israel from Syria. The Syrians stepped up the raids once President Nasser of Egypt promised support in the event of an Israeli attack. When the Syrians announced that Israel was massing troops in preparation for an assault, Egypt responded by asking the UN to withdraw its Emergency Force from the Egypt-Israel border, which it did. Nasser then closed the Straits of Tiran (the entrance to the Red Sea) effectively nullifying the port of Eilat. Five days later, Jordan and Egypt signed a mutual defence pact; Israel knew it was alone and surrounded.

On 5 June 1967, the Israelis dispatched a pre-dawn raid that wiped out the Egyptian Air Force on the ground, and in the following days clobbered Egyptian troops in the Sinai, Jordanian troops on the West Bank and stormed up the Golan Heights in Syria.

The outcome for Jordan was totally disastrous: it lost the whole of the West Bank and its part of Jerusalem, which together supplied Jordan with its two principal sources of income (agriculture and tourism), and resulted in yet another massive wave of Palestinian refugees.

After this defeat, the Palestinians became more militant and although there was tacit agreement with the Jordanian government that they would operate freely out of their bases in the Jordan Valley, they also expected immunity from Jordan's laws. The country became increasingly unsettled.

Clearly this couldn't last and the showdown came in September 1970 in an incident that became known as 'Black September'. The PLO hijacked four commercial aircraft and flew three of them to northern Jordan, holding passengers and crew hostage. This was part of a campaign in which thousands died as the guerillas took control of the northern strip of Jordan.

Although the hostage crisis was resolved, and a cease-fire put in place at the end of the month, fighting soon resumed. The Jordanian army went in with force, and during a brief civil war ending in July 1971, wiped out all resistance. The guerillas were forced to recognise Hussein's authority and the Palestinians had to choose between exile or submission.

In October 1974 King Hussein reluctantly agreed to an Arab summit declaration recognising the Palestinian Liberation Organization (PLO) as the sole representative of the Palestinians and its right to set up a government in any liberated territory, nullifying Jordan's claims to the West Bank.

In November 1989 the first full parliamentary elections since 1967 were held in Jordan, and women were allowed to vote for the first time. Four years later, most of the political parties were legalised and allowed to participate in parliamentary and municipal elections.

Although the Islamic Action Front occupies many of the 80 lower house seats, royalist independents together still constitute a large majority, which continued to assure that King Hussein remained in power.

The Gulf War
Dependent on Iraq for about 25% of its trade and most of its oil imports, Jordan found itself caught between a rock and a hard place when Saddam Hussein invaded Kuwait in 1990. Support among Palestinians in Jordan for Saddam, who promised to link the Kuwait issue to their own and force a showdown, was at fever pitch.

King Hussein had little choice but to side with Saddam against the majority of the Arab states and the multinational force sent to eject Saddam from Kuwait. The monarch played the game with typical dexterity. Although tending to side publicly with Baghdad, he maintained efforts to find a peaceful solution and complied with the UN embargo on trade with Iraq. This last step won him the sympathy of western financial bodies and, although US and Saudi aid was temporarily cut, along with Saudi oil, loans and help were forthcoming from other quarters, particularly Japan and Europe.

Peace with Israel
In July 1988, seven months after the beginning of the Intifada – the Palestinian revolt in the West Bank and Gaza – King Hussein announced that all of Jordan's administrative and legal ties with the West Bank, along with the development program, were to be cut.

With the signing of the PLO-Israeli declaration of principles in September 1993, which set in motion the process of establishing an autonomous Palestinian authority in the Occupied Territories, Jordan appeared to have definitively abandoned all claims to the area. Since renouncing its claims to the West Bank in 1988, the territorial question was virtually removed as an obstacle to peace with Israel.

Compared with its northern neighbour Syria, Jordan, through the savvy King Hussein, long displayed greater flexibility in its attitude to Israel and the peace process. On 26 October 1994 Jordan and Israel signed a peace treaty which provided for the dropping of all economic barriers between the two countries and close cooperation on security, water and other issues.

The unknown element is how the Palestinians, sandwiched between the two sides, will fare; they have long feared that any cooperation between Jordan and Israel would ultimately undermine any nascent Palestinian state. The clause in the treaty recognising the 'special role of the Hashemite Kingdom of Jordan in the Muslim holy shrines in Jerusalem' sounded alarm bells in Palestinian circles. The treaty made Jordan very unpopular with the region's people and governments alike, and severely strained relations with countries such as Syria and Libya.

The King is Dead, Long Live the King

While King Hussein was in the USA for cancer treatment, Hassan bin Talal (Hussein's brother and Crown Prince for 34 years), was in charge. Just before his death, Hussein returned to Jordan, stripped Hassan of power and unexpectedly announced that Hussein's son, Abdullah bin Hussein (see the boxed text) would be the new king.

Hussein died in February 1999. After an official mourning period, Abdullah was enthroned as King Abdullah II on 9 June 1999. Prince Hamzah, the 18-year-old son of Queen Noor and King Hussein, is the very popular Crown Prince.

Queen Noor, who retains her title of 'Queen', has been surprisingly absent from Jordan since Hussein's death: neither she nor Prince Hamzah were at Abdullah's enthronement ceremony, and she spent most of 1999 travelling overseas as part of her charity work. There have been no obvious threats to King Abdullah's power, and he feels safe enough to travel overseas frequently.

Throughout mid-1999, Abdullah visited important leaders in the region, including Jordan's old foes, Syria and Libya. He also went to Paris, Washington and London to ensure financial support from major western allies, and successfully obtained US$300 million of aid from the USA. Abdullah plans to continue his father's pragmatic relationship with Israel and, with the almost simultaneous change in leadership in Israel, the chances for peace in the Middle East are promising.

GEOGRAPHY

Jordan is a tiny country with a very strange shape (see the boxed text 'Winston's Hic-

King Abdullah II

Abdullah was born on 30 January 1962 to King Hussein's second (British) wife, Princess Mona. He studied in the USA and, like his father, attended Sandhurst in the UK and other military academies in the USA. He was promoted to lieutenant in the Jordanian Army at 22, and became head of Jordan's Special Forces in 1998 after he was involved in the successful (and televised) capture of two assassins.

Abdullah is a keen sportsman, pilot and rally driver; he enjoys western food and speaks perfect English. He is married to Queen Rania, a glamorous Palestinian dedicated to children's and women's charities, and has two young children, Prince Hussein and Princess Iman.

cup'). The total area is 91,860 sq km – slightly smaller than Portugal or the US state of Virginia. When King Hussein renounced claims to the West Bank (5600 sq km) in 1988, the country reverted back to the same boundaries as the former Transjordan.

Jordan can easily be divided into three major regions: the Jordan Valley, the East Bank plateau, and the desert. Distances are short – it's only 430km from Ramtha, on the Syrian border in the north, to Aqaba, in the far south. From Aqaba to the capital, Amman, it's 335km.

Jordan Valley

The dominant physical feature of the country is the fertile valley of the Jordan River. Forming part of the Great Rift Valley of Africa, it rises just over the Lebanese border and continues the entire length of Jordan from the Syrian border in the north, past the salty depression of the Dead Sea, and south down to Aqaba and the Red Sea. The 251km-long river is fed from the Sea of Galilee (Lake Tiberias), the Yarmouk River and the valley streams of the high plateaus to the east and west.

The Dead Sea (see the boxed text in the Northern & Western Jordan chapter for more information) is the lowest point on earth, and

the highly saline soils of this central area of
the Jordan Valley support little vegetation.

East Bank Plateau

The East Bank plateau is broken up only by
gorges cut by Wadi Zarqa, Wadi Mujib and
Wadi Hasa (*wadi* is the Arabic word for a
valley formed by an often dry watercourse;
some wadis begin to flow again when there
has been substantial rainfall).

This area contains the main centres of
population: Amman, Irbid, Zarqa and Karak.
It also contains the sites of major interest to
visitors: Jerash, Karak, Madaba and Petra.
The plateau ends at Ras an-Naqb, from
where a fairly rapid drop leads down to the
Red Sea, and port and resort town of Aqaba.

The Desert

About 80% of Jordan is desert, mostly in the
south and east. The volcanic basalt of the
north (the bottom end of the area known as
the Hauran in Syria) gives way to the south's
sandstone and granite, which sometimes
produces amazing sights. The area known as
Wadi Rum is one of the most fantastic
desertscapes in the world, and boasts Jebel
Rum (1754m), the highest peak in Jordan.

CLIMATE

For such a small country, Jordan has an extraordinary range of climates. The weather
in the Jordan Valley is extremely oppressive
in summer – it feels like you're trapped in
an airless oven. Daily temperatures are well
in excess of 36°C and have been recorded

as high as 49°C. Rainfall is low: under
200mm annually.

Average daytime maximum temperatures
in **Amman** range from 12.6°C in January to
32.5°C in August. Snow in Amman is not
unheard of, and even Petra gets the occasional fall. The area around **Aqaba** has
much warmer, drier weather, with average
daytime maximum temperatures of around
20°C in January and 38°C in August.

The climate in the **desert** is extreme: summer temperatures can reach into the high
40s yet there are days in winter when cold
winds howl down from central Asia. Rainfall is negligible: less than 50mm per year.

Weather forecasts for Amman, the Jordan
Valley, the southern desert, northern Jordan
and Aqaba are all listed in the two English-
language daily newspapers published in
Amman, the *Arab Daily* and *Jordan Times*.

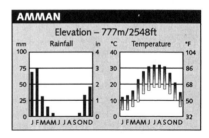

ECOLOGY & ENVIRONMENT

The biggest environmental problem in Jordan is a lack of water, caused by a growing
population, rising living standards in the
cities, heavy exploitation for agriculture, and
wastage (see the boxed text 'Water Works'
under Economy later in this chapter).

Effects of Tourism

While a substantial recent increase in the
number of tourists has brought in badly
needed foreign currency for government and
private businesses, very little is being spent
on environmental protection. Jordan is developing its tourist industry by attracting foreign
investment, but most of the funds are used to
build more hotels, roads and tourist facilities
– at the expense of the environment.

Tourism has caused a rapid increase in demand for precious water, pollution from cars and industries, as well as damage to unique sites, such as Jerash and Petra (see the boxed text 'Tourism in Petra' in the Petra chapter for details). Despite the documented damage to the environment around Hammamat Ma'in and Wadi Mousa (near Petra) from hotel construction, more hotels are being built, and the damage to Wadi Rum from jeep tours is serious. Other problems are vandalism at archaeological sites; damage to artwork from flash photography; rubbish left at hot springs and baths; and the recent inclination to hold huge festivals and sound-and-light shows at the ancient cities of Jerash and Petra.

See the Impact of Tourism section under Society & Conduct later in this chapter for more information.

Marine Life

The reefs off the coast at Aqaba are a treasure trove of marine life, but every year thousands of tonnes of phosphates are dumped at the port at Aqaba (see the boxed text 'Red Sea Marine Peace Park' in the Southern Desert chapter for more information). The Dead Sea is also slowly dying (see 'The Dead Sea' boxed text in the Northern & Western Jordan chapter.)

Desertification

Like most countries in the region, desertification (the seemingly unstoppable spread of the desert to fertile, inhabited and environmentally sensitive areas) is a very serious problem. According to the Royal Society for the Conservation of Nature (RSCN), millions of hectares of fertile land in Jordan have become infertile and uninhabitable desert. This means there are now less pastures for livestock and crops (paradoxically, overgrazing is also a cause), reduced land for native animals and plants, and an unhealthy and unattractive landscape for the Jordanian people (and tourists).

Desertification is usually caused by human factors, eg overgrazing, deforestation, 4WD jeeps and other off-road vehicles (like at Wadi Rum) – as well as wind erosion and drought.

The governments of Jordan and other affected countries such as Egypt and Tunisia are looking into the problem.

Useful Organisations

For further information on the ecology and environment of Jordan, contact the following organisations:

Jordan Royal Ecological Diving Society (JREDS)
 (☎ Aqaba 03-202 2995; ☎/fax Amman 06-567 9142, email jreds@nets.com.jo)
Royal Society for the Conservation of Nature
 (☎ Amman 06-533 7931, fax 534 7411, email tourism@rscn.org.jo) PO Box 6354, Amman 11183

FLORA

Jordan boasts over 2500 species of wild plants and flowers (including about 20 species of orchid), but due to desertification, urban sprawl and pollution at least 10 have become extinct over the past 100 years.

Spring is the best time to see wildflowers, and Wadi as-Seer, near Amman, is especially beautiful. The pine forests of the north give way to the cultivated slopes of the Jordan Valley where cedar, olives and eucalyptus are dominant. In the very few tropical areas, such as the Dana Nature Reserve, acacia (more commonly found in Australia) thrive. In the deserts, cacti are about the only plants that grow, unless there is some heavy rain.

The national flower of Jordan is the Black Iris (not to be confused with the hideous number of black plastic bags stuck to tiny shrubs all over the countryside).

FAUNA

Jordan is not renowned for its quantity and variety of wildlife, and visitors will count themselves very fortunate to see anything more than a few domesticated goats and camels. The eastern and southern deserts are home to the desert and red foxes, sand rat, mountain and desert hare, and several species of rodent, namely the jerboa (with long legs for jumping), shrew and gerbil. More menacing are the species of wolf and the Asiatic jackal.

The Jordan Valley, and the forested and sparsely inhabited hills of northern Jordan, are home to the ill-tempered wild boar, marbled polecat, stone marten, jungle cat, crested porcupine and ibex, as well as species of mongoose, hyrax and hedgehog. In the uncommon wet and swampy areas, such as the Jordan Valley and Azraq wetlands, there are several species of otter.

For information about underwater wonders in the Gulf of Aqaba, refer to 'Diving & Snorkelling' in the Activities chapter.

Birdlife

About 365 species of bird have been recorded in Jordan. Commonly seen around the eastern and southern desert regions are the many species of lark, vulture, eagle and partridge. For a desert region, Dana Nature Reserve boasts an extraordinary number of bird species, including warbler, partridge, vulture and falcon. The Azraq Wetlands Reserve and the Burqu area (both in eastern Jordan) attract a huge number of migratory water bird species, such as heron and egret. Around the Dead Sea, the Dead Sea sparrow and quaintly named Tristam's grackle can be seen. Other species which live in Jordan are the Palestine sunbird, hoopoe and Sinai finch (see the boxed text below). Aqaba is also home to a variety of migratory birds, but nothing is done to protect them, and their habitats are being eroded by urban development and desertification.

Jordan's National Bird

The Sinai finch *(Carpodacus synoicu ssynoicus)* is Jordan's national bird. It thrives in the few areas where there is water, such as the Jordan Valley, but has learnt to adapt to drier and rockier areas of southern Jordan (but not the harsh deserts).

The bird was first found in Petra in the early 20th century, but now also lives in the Dana Nature and Wadi Mujib reserves, as well as the Sinai peninsula of Egypt (after which it was named). The male is a distinctive pink, but the female is grey or brown. Adults are small (about 16cm long), and the female produces up to five eggs a year.

Endangered Species

About 20 species of animals have become extinct in the past 100 years. Some were hunted and poached (especially after WWII, when weapons were more common), including species of lion, cheetah and gazelle, and the Syrian brown bear, onager (wild ass) and Arabian leopard. (The last known leopard was killed in the area now known as Dana Nature Reserve in 1986, although there have been unsubstantiated sightings since.)

The reasons for the number of extinct species – and the continuing threat to animals and birds – are manifold: poor land management, such as deforestation, and pumping water from vital areas such as the Jordan River, Dead Sea and the Azraq wetlands; urban sprawl, including Palestinian refugee camps; weak environmental laws; unremitting use of pesticides, especially near water sources in the Jordan Valley; air and water pollution; and overgrazing.

Officially endangered are the Northern Middle East wolf and South Arabian grey wolf (both are often shot to protect livestock); lynx (always popular for hunters); striped hyena; Persian squirrel; and the Persian, darcas, goitred and mountain gazelles. Endangered birdlife include the marbled duck; imperial and less spotted eagles; houbara bustard; lesser kestrel; and bluenecked ostrich.

Several species of animals have been successfully re-introduced to Jordan after becoming extinct, however, and are being bred in captivity, such as the Arabian oryx, onager and Nubian ibex. (See the Shaumari Reserve section of the Eastern Jordan chapter.)

NATIONAL PARKS & RESERVES

About 20 years ago the Jordanian government established 12 protected areas, totalling about 1000 sq km. While environmental agencies waited for funds and battled with bureaucracy, some potential reserves were abandoned because they had suffered appalling ecological damage from deforestation, overgrazing and water extraction.

The limited resources of the RSCN (see the boxed text on page 26) are used to maintain and develop the six reserves listed

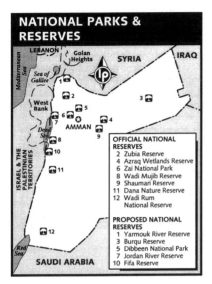

NATIONAL PARKS & RESERVES

OFFICIAL NATIONAL RESERVES
2 Zubia Reserve
4 Azraq Wetlands Reserve
6 Zai National Park
8 Wadi Mujib Reserve
9 Shaumari Reserve
11 Dana Nature Reserve
12 Wadi Rum National Reserve

PROPOSED NATIONAL RESERVES
1 Yarmouk River Reserve
3 Burqu Reserve
5 Dibbeen National Park
7 Jordan River Reserve
10 Fifa Reserve

below. These represent about 1% of Jordan's total land area – a small percentage compared with the land allocated in Saudi Arabia (9%) and the USA (11%).

Azraq Wetlands Reserve (12 sq km) This new reserve is home to about 300 species of bird, plus a few buffalo, semi-wild horse, jackal and jerbil. Camping is not allowed, but there are hotels nearby. Walks on designated trails are permitted. It's easy to reach from Azraq town. See the Eastern Jordan chapter for details.

Dana Nature Reserve (320 sq km) This reserve is home to a diverse ecosystem, including about 600 species of plants, about 200 species of birds, and 33 species of animals. Pre-set tents are available, and there are hotels in nearby Dana village. Nothing is cheap, however, and it's not easy to reach. Short walks and long-distance hiking is possible. See the King's Highway chapter for details.

Shaumari Reserve (22 sq km) This small but unfortunately disappointing reserve is specifically for reintroduced Arabian oryx, blue-necked and red-necked ostriches; subgutu rosa and darcas gazelle; and onager. Nearly 250 species of birds have also been identified. Camping is allowed just outside the reserve, and it's not hard to reach from Azraq town. Hiking is not permitted. See the Eastern Jordan chapter for details.

Wadi Mujib Reserve (212 sq km) This vast reserve is mainly used for the captive breeding of Nubian ibex. Camping is allowed in designated areas, but hiking is not allowed without permission from the RSCN. It's not easy to reach, however. See the King's Highway chapter for details.

Wadi Rum National Reserve (540 sq km) This popular tourist area will soon become a national reserve, but the RSCN's plans for the reserve are currently unclear. Camping and hiking are currently allowed, but regulations will undoubtedly change soon. See the Southern Desert chapter for details.

Zai National Park A small and dense pine forest, close to Amman, with great views and a government-owned restaurant. See the Amman chapter for details.

Zubia Reserve (12 sq km) This small and disappointing reserve was established to protect native fauna, including the roe deer. It's not set up for tourism, however, and unfortunately is not worth visiting. Camping is allowed where designated, but hiking is not. It's also very difficult to find. See the Northern & Western Jordan chapter for details.

In addition, the RSCN and the Jordanian government hope to create five new protected areas (their exact names are not confirmed at this stage).

Burqu Reserve (400 sq km) After the debacle in the Azraq wetlands (see the boxed text 'What Happened to the Wetlands?' in the Eastern Jordan chapter for details), the desert lake at Burqu needs urgent protection. See the Eastern Jordan chapter for more details.

Dibbeen National Park (8 sq km) This is one of the last pine forests left in Jordan, and home to endangered species such as the Persian squirrel. See the Northern & Western Jordan chapter for more details.

Fifa Reserve (27 sq km) This area alongside the Dead Sea has rare subtropical vegetation, and is home to migratory water birds.

Jordan River Reserve (5 sq km) Based around the Tell al-Kharrar religious site (see the Northern & Western Jordan chapter for details), this is the only section of the Jordan River which has not been ecologically damaged in some way.

Yarmouk River Reserve (30 sq km) Because of its proximity to the Israeli border, this area has remained undeveloped and is home to many natural features of the forest including water birds, endangered gazelle and otter.

Royal Society for the Conservation of Nature (RSCN)

The RSCN was established in 1966, and is now Jordan's major environmental agency. It aims to protect the local environment in six official reserves and hopes to establish several more in the future. The RSCN is also heavily involved in saving several species of animals, plants and birds from extinction, and has successfully re-introduced species such as the Arabian oryx, Nubian ibex and onager, and two species of ostrich.

The RSCN's other activities include conducting public awareness programs among Jordanians, especially children; sponsoring about 800 environmental clubs throughout the country; educating and training guides; promoting ecotourism; fighting against poaching and hunting; lobbying against development and mining; and promoting programs such as the Wadi Dana Project, in which people are involved in maintaining their culture and heritage.

The RSCN publishes the excellent *Al-Reem* magazine (JD2.500; free to members) every three months in Arabic and English. If you don't want to become a member, consider 'adopting' an animal from an endangered species which costs from JD30 to JD60 per year. For contact details, see Useful Organisations under Ecology & Environment earlier this chapter.

GOVERNMENT & POLITICS

Jordan is officially called the Hashemite Kingdom of Jordan (HKJ), or *Al-Mamlakah al-Urdunniyah al-Hashimiyah* in Arabic. The Hashemites were named after Hashem, the great-grandfather of the Prophet Mohammed, to whom King Abdullah (the founder of modern Jordan) claimed descent.

The 1952 constitution states that Jordan is a hereditary constitutional monarchy with three levels of power. The first level is the king, who is vested with wide-ranging powers, eg he appoints judges, approves amendments to the constitution, declares war and is Commander of the Armed Forces. He approves and signs all laws, although his power of veto can be overridden by a two-thirds majority of both houses of the National Assembly.

Secondly, the 80-member lower house is elected by all citizens (men and women) of Jordan over the age of 18, but the prime minister, president and 40 members of the Senate are appointed by the king. The prime minister, or the king through the prime minister, appoints a Council of Ministers who are subject to the approval of parliament. The Council is responsible for general policy and the various government departments.

Thirdly, some minor power is given to the 305 local councils throughout Jordan. Jordan now has 22 registered parties, including a communist party and the Islamic Action Front (IAF), which is the largest and most powerful. The IAF has connections with the fundamentalist Muslim Brotherhood (which is outlawed in some neighbouring countries), and the IAF's opposition to the peace treaty with Israel causes disquiet. In fact, elections are sometimes boycotted by the IAF and other parties because of the Jordanian government's relationship with Israel.

Although municipal and parliamentary elections are supposed to occur every four years, the polls in November 1989 were the first held since Jordan lost the West Bank in the Six Day War in 1967. (During that period Jordan had in effect been under martial law.) Voting is not compulsory, but 72% of all voters turned out for 1995's municipal elections.

For administrative purposes, Jordan is divided into 12 *muhafazat* (governorates): Irbid, Ajlun, Jerash, Balqa (west of Amman), Amman, Mafraq, Zarqa, Madaba, Karak, Tafila, Ma'an and Aqaba.

ECONOMY

Many Jordanians happily complain that their country has 'no oil and no water'. While this is a slight exaggeration, Jordan is not able to obtain vital foreign currency by exporting oil (which Jordan had been importing cheaply from Iraq before the Gulf War), and continues to suffer from severe water shortages (see the boxed text 'Water Works' below).

Jordan is also squeezed between several countries with recent political turmoil – namely Lebanon, Israel, the Palestinian territories and Iraq – which has resulted in massive numbers of refugees fleeing to Jordan, and political sanctions against important trading partners. However, considering that Transjordan (as it was known) in 1948 was a country of about 400,000 mostly poor Bedouin, the transformation in the past 50 years or so has been remarkable.

Like most countries in the region, Jordan suffers from high unemployment, unsettled refugees, poverty, nepotism and corruption. It also relies very heavily on foreign aid, and has one of the highest foreign debts per capita in the world – currently about 100% of the gross domestic product (GDP). This foreign debt is a result of unrestrained increases in population, forcing necessary increased

infrastructure; poor financial management by the government; and an arms build up in the region.

Currently, about 30% of the government's expenditure is used to pay off massive debt. Since becoming king, Abdullah II has been visiting western allies to ensure that the foreign aid continues, and to ask for the easing (successful), and the eradication (unsuccessfully), of the burden of debt.

Gulf War

Jordan was one of the main economic victims of the Gulf War in 1990-91, but it managed to weather the storm far better than expected. One UN assessment put the total cost to Jordan of the war from mid-1990 to mid-1991 at more than US$8 billion. The UN naval blockade of Aqaba, which was aimed at enforcing UN sanctions against Iraq, cost Jordan around US$300 million a year in lost revenue between 1991 and 1994.

Water Works

According to experts, Jordan uses about 30% more water than it receives from natural sources. It has endured droughts for five consecutive years: the one in 1998/9 was the worst in 50 years, and cost an estimated US$200 million in lost and damaged agriculture and livestock.

One major problem is simply mismanagement: Jordan's farmers consume two-thirds of the water (and often inefficiently), so crops such as eggplant and corn are sometimes banned because they require so much water. According to one report, half the water consumed in Amman is lost in leakage.

Jordan's only sources of water are the Jordan and Yarmouk Rivers, and subterranean aquifers – already in many cases over-exploited, such as in Azraq (see the boxed text 'What Happened to the Wetlands?' in the Eastern Jordan chapter).

In 1964, Israel diverted most of the Jordan River to feed irrigation canals in that country, but no water is being diverted back to Jordan (as promised under a joint agreement) until it is able to build adequate treatment plants. Current treatment plants are sometimes unable to effectively treat algae and some bacteria, and a scandal in 1998 about foul-smelling and foul-tasting water in Amman resulted in the mass (forced) resignation of several high-level members of government.

To meet the never-ending demand for water, a pipeline was laid in 1995 to carry 30 million cubic metres a year from the Sea of Galilee (Lake Tiberias) to Jordan's King Abdullah Canal, and in 1998 Jordan had to beg ingloriously for water from Syria (an old foe). Both Jordan and Israel have recently allocated millions of Jordanian dollars to water projects, such as the joint Israeli-Jordanian Wihdeh Dam on the Yarmouk River. Another idea is the construction of a series of canals, desalination plants and hydroelectric power stations that would link the Red Sea with the Dead Sea (see the boxed text 'The Dead Sea' in the Northern & Western Jordan chapter for details).

A quarter of Jordan's pre-war trade had been with Iraq, and for a while Jordan was obliged to seek other sources of oil (80% of which was being delivered from Baghdad prior to the war). Later, Amman was allowed to take Iraqi oil as direct debt repayment, but only as long as no cash changed hands.

Until the Gulf War, a very important source of income had been remittances from Jordanians and Palestinians working in the Gulf States. By early 1992, most had left the Gulf States, and about 300,000 settled in Jordan. The loss of remittances was initially seen as a heavy blow, but the 'returnees' brought US$500 million home with them, and actually helped unleash an unprecedented boom, stimulating economic growth to a staggering 11% in 1992.

Agriculture

Agriculture, which makes up 6 to 7% of Jordan's GDP, is concentrated in the Jordan Valley, where ambitious irrigation schemes, like the King Abdullah Canal and several dam projects, make cultivation possible on thousands of hectares. Modern methods (`plasticulture' and greenhouses) have greatly increased productivity, and Jordan exports much of the fruit, vegetables and cereals that are its most important crops. On the highlands forming the eastern edge of the Jordan Valley, crops such as tobacco, wheat, barley and beans are grown, as well as olives, tomatoes and watermelons.

Scarce water supplies, however, are a constant threat, and farmers are sometimes ordered not to plant crops because there's not enough water to go around. Jordan is home to about three million sheep and goat, but there is simply not enough pasture to feed them, so a lot of feed is now imported. The authorities are trying to encourage farmers to earn an income in some other way, while closing some pastoral lands to alleviate overgrazing and the subsequent problem of desertification.

Two possible answers to the problem are to introduce other types of feed, such as spineless cacti, which require little water, and to recycle sewerage as a water source for irrigation.

Industry

Industry accounts for about 26% of Jordan's GDP. Phosphate mining, carried out from vast reserves at Wadi Hasa and Shidiya (near Ma'an) is a major export, as is potash from near the Dead Sea. Mining companies are hoping to mine areas of the Dana Nature Reserve, which have been rich in copper for thousands of years, but the Jordanian government has reluctantly not granted any mining licences (thanks to pressure from environmental agencies). Local manufacturing ranges from cement and batteries to toys, beer and matches.

Oil is yet to be found in commercially viable quantities, and the government is placing greater hope in natural gas. Big reserves were found in the north-east of the country in 1987-88, and now meet about 17% of Jordan's energy needs.

As a way of encouraging foreign investment, the Jordanian government has introduced a reduced corporate tax rate, and provided other incentives, but so far the interest shown from overseas investors has been less than the government had hoped.

Tourism

Tourists first started to trickle into Transjordan in the 1920s, but only since the 1994 peace agreement with Israel has tourism been taken seriously by the government as a significant contribution to the Jordanian economy.

Tourism now counts for about 10% of the GDP, and is the second largest source of foreign currency (after industry). Tourism generates a total annual income of about JD564 million (about US$794 million), and employs about 15,000 people. In 1998, 1.2 million people visited Jordan – up from 858,000 only four years before. However, about 60% of visitors are from neighbouring countries, staying with friends and families and not spending much money. In fact, about 10% of all visiting Arabs come to Jordan solely for high-quality and low-cost medical care.

Jordan is small and has a limited, although fascinating, number of attractions, so tourists do not generally stay very long. As an example, the average number of nights that a tourist stays in Israel is 18; eight in Egypt; but only four in Jordan. The total number of tourists to Jordan also fluctuates remarkably, depending on regional politics. Any war or political strife in the Middle East (which is all too common), regardless of the distance from Jordan, means a significant drop in tourist numbers. The open border with Israel means that many Israelis come, but often only on day trips to Aqaba or Petra.

Tourism is fairly one-dimensional, and still tends to focus on Jordan's archaeological marvels. To encourage more tourists to come, and to stay longer than a few days, the authorities are trying to promote events such as the Jerash Festival, and Christian pilgrimages. (The Jordanian tourist authorities are hoping that about 1.3 million western tourists will come to Jordan to celebrate the Birth of Christ in 2000.)

Foreign governments have accepted the importance of tourism to the Jordanian economy. The Japanese recently announced an offer of technical assistance and soft loans, to develop a tourist bus system around central Amman (how this will happen is anyone's guess!); to line Sahat al-Malek Faysal al-Awal St in Amman with outdoor cafes; and to create more museums in Salt, Karak and along the Dead Sea.

POPULATION & PEOPLE

The population in 1998 was about 4.75 million, a substantial increase from about 600,000 in the 1950s. In an effort to reduce the expected population of eight million in 2024, the Jordanian National Population Commission is hoping to halve the birth rate through the promotion of family planning.

About 80% live in urban centres, eg about 1.7 million live in the capital, Amman, and a further 650,000 in and around nearby Zarqa. Irbid in the north is the second largest city, and has about 500,000 inhabitants.

Approximately 98% of the population are Arabs; the other 2% are Circassians or Chechens, and a mixture of European and US expatriates.

The Bedouin

These desert dwellers – *bedu* means 'nomadic' – number several hundred thousand, but while some have opted for city life, most have settled down to cultivate crops rather than drive their animals across the desert in search of fodder.

The estimated 40,000 or so truly nomadic Bedouin are provided with services such as education and housing, but both are usually passed up. They camp for a few months at a time in one spot and graze their animals. All over the east and south of Jordan are the black goat-hair tents *(beit ash-sha'ar)*; often three or four together. Such tents are generally divided into a *haram* for the women and another section for the menfolk. The latter is the public part of the home, where guests are treated to tea/coffee, and sit to discuss the day's events.

A Bedouin family is a close-knit unit. The women do most of the domestic work; the men are traditionally the providers and warriors. With little warring to do these days, the average Bedouin man can find himself distinctly underemployed. Most continue to wear traditional dress, including a dagger – a symbol of a man's dignity. The women tend to dress in more colourful garb, but rarely do they veil the face: instead, facial tattoos are displayed.

The Bedouin are renowned for their hospitality, and it's part of their creed that no traveller is turned away. The thinking is simple: today, you're passing through, and they have something to offer; tomorrow they may be passing your camp and you may have food and drink – which you would offer before having any yourself. Such a code of conduct made it possible for ancient travellers to cross the desert, despite the hostile natural environment.

However, if tourists continue to pass through in large numbers, outsiders can no longer expect to be regaled with such hospitality. In places where tourists are common, eg Wadi Rum and Petra, you may be charged for tea or coffee – and certainly for food and accommodation.

Arabs

Arabs are descended from various tribes that migrated to the area over the centuries from all directions. About 92% are Sunni Muslims; and there are tiny populations of Shi'ite and Druze (see Religion later in this chapter).

Palestinians About 60% of the population are Palestinians (many still registered as refugees) who fled, mostly from the West Bank, during the wars of 1948 and 1967. Since the Gulf War in 1990, some 300,000 Palestinians have returned from the Gulf States to join their Jordan-based counterparts.

All Palestinians have been granted the right to Jordanian citizenship, and many have exercised that option. Palestinians play an important part in the political and economic life of Jordan, and although many occupy high positions in government and business they continue to dream of a return to an independent Palestine. This is partly the reason why so many continue to live in difficult conditions in the 30 or more refugee camps that dot the landscape. UN agencies are responsible for refugee welfare, and provide health and education services.

Circassians & Chechens

The Circassians fled persecution in Russia in the late 19th century to settle in the Jordan Valley, becoming prosperous farmers. There are now about 30,000 Circassians – living mainly in Wadi as-Seer and Na'ur (both near Amman) – but intermarriage has made them virtually indistinguishable from Arabs.

Historically and ethnically related to the Circassians is the small (about 4000) Shi'ite community of Chechens, the only other recognised ethnic minority in Jordan.

EDUCATION

Jordan is one of the better educated Arab countries: about 87% of Jordanians are literate, and about 97% of children attend primary school. There are three kinds of schools – government, private and missionary – but about 70% of pupils attend government schools. UN agencies run schools for refugee children. School is compulsory from the ages of five to 14.

Of the seven state-owned universities, three of the largest are the University of Jordan (Web site www.ju.edu.jo) in northern Amman, Yarmouk University (Web site www.yu.edu.jo) in Irbid, and Mu'tah University (Web site www.mutah.edu.jo), south of Karak. There are also 13 private universities, including the American University of the Middle East which recently established a campus near Amman. Although the universities are attended by about 100,000 students, these include a large number of foreign students from the Palestinian territories and elsewhere in the Middle East, so the demand for spaces from Jordanian students still exceeds supply.

ARTS

While the region has been home to various important forms of music, literature and arts for centuries, the comparatively modern country of Jordan could not boast much in the way of contemporary arts and literature until the last 25 years.

Music & Dance

Arab music reflects a synthesis of indigenous and western influences. The popular music takes some time to get used to, and for many its attraction remains a mystery. Others, however, are eventually caught up in its own particular magic – which is probably a good thing, because you'll hear it in one form or another wherever you go.

The Bedouin have long had their own musical traditions, simple but mesmerising. The sound of men chanting at a distant wedding, drifting across the desert on a still night, is haunting. Up close, the musical side of the evening's festivities are clearly rooted in ancient traditions. A row of men will, arm in arm, gently sway backwards and forwards engaged in what appears to be an almost trance-like chant. They are singing to a lone, veiled woman who dances before them with restrained but unmistakable sensuality.

The music in the streets of Amman today, however, has precious little to do with timeless desert traditions. The most common and popular style of music focuses on a star performer backed by anything from a small quartet to a full-blown orchestra. The kind of orchestras that back these singers are a curious mix of east and west, although the sounds that emanate from them are anything but western. Western-style instruments such as violins, the piano and many of the wind and percussion instruments predominate, next to local instruments such as the *oud* (lute).

The Performing Arts Center in Amman was established in 1987 under the auspices of the Queen Noor Foundation to 'develop the value and understanding of contemporary music and dance by local Jordanians'. The subsequent interest in modern music and dance resulted in the first western musical – *The Wizard of Oz* – performed in Jordan in Arabic, and the opening of the Theatre Arts School with over 50 students being trained in theatre, music, dance and writing. Foreign governments, and NGOs, such as the British Council in Amman, continue to sponsor all forms of art in Jordan.

Literature

Classical Literature & Poetry The Quran itself is considered as the finest example of classical Arabic writing. In fact, it underwent several transformations before the final, and current, version was settled upon.

Al-Mu'allaqaat, which predates the Quran and the advent of Islam, is a widely celebrated collection of early Arab poetry. Prior to Islam, a poet was regarded by Arabs as having knowledge forbidden to ordinary people, supposedly acquired from the demon. Al-Mu'allaqaat means 'the suspended', and refers to traditions according to which the poems were hung for public view, possibly on the walls of the Qaaba in Mecca.

As the Middle Ages drew to a close, and the fractious Arab world came to be dominated by other forces (most notably the Ottoman Turks), Arabic literature also faded, stagnating in a classicist rut dominated by a complex and burdensome poetical inheritance until well into the 19th century.

One of the few classical Jordanian poets was Mustafa Wahbi al-Tal, also known as Irar. Born in Irbid in 1899, he was renowned for his incisive and humorous poems about Arab nationalism and anticolonialism.

Contemporary Literature & Poetry

Modern literary genres such as the novel have only fairly recently taken off in Jordan, largely due to increased contact with Europe and a reawakening of Arab 'national' consciousness in the wake of the Ottoman Empire's putrefaction.

Egyptians (such as the Nobel Prize-winning Naguib Mahfouz), Lebanese and, to a lesser extent, Palestinians, seem to dominate Middle Eastern literature, but there are now a number of renowned Jordanian writers and poets. Ramadan al-Rawashdeh has published collections of short stories, such as *The Night*. His novel *Al-Hamrawi* won the Naguib Mahfouz Arabic Novel Prize, and more recently he published *The Shepherds' Songs*. Rifka Doudeen, one of an emerging number of female authors, has published a collection of short stories called *Justifiable Agony*, and a novel, *The Outcast*. Another popular Jordanian writer is Yousef Dhamra.

Many Jordanian writers and poets are Palestinians who often graphically relate their first-hand experiences in the Arab-Israeli conflicts. For example, Taher al-Edwan's *The Fact of Time,* telling the story of a Palestinian family fleeing to Amman in 1948, is regarded as an important Jordanian novel.

Very few of these titles are available in languages other than Arabic, but the best place to look for an English translation is the Amman Bookshop in Amman.

Painting

That Islam frowns on the depiction of living beings does not mean that everyone took the hint. Long-standing artistic traditions in Asia Minor, Persia and further east – including Spain and other parts of Europe, eg Sicily – held by the Muslims could not be so completely swept away. While the greatest riches of this kind are to be found in illustrated manuscripts mostly coming from Turkey, parts of Iraq and further east, good examples can still be seen in Jordan today.

The Umayyad rulers, who comprised the first real dynasty after the demise of the Prophet Mohammed, left behind a series of so-called 'desert castles' across the eastern desert of Jordan; traces of frescoes can be

Contemporary Art

One of the first Jordanian painters to gain any international recognition was the redoubtable Fahrenasa Zeid (the great-great aunt of King Abdullah II), who exhibited works in the galleries of Europe and the USA in the 1910s and 1920s. However, it really wasn't until the creation of the Jordan Artists' Association in 1978, and the opening of the country's first art gallery (the Jordan National Gallery of Fine Arts) two years later, that contemporary art in Jordan was taken seriously.

Many Jordanian artists are Palestinians who fled the West Bank during the two wars with Israel: Adnan Yahya specialises in gut-wrenching paintings of Palestinian persecution; Ahmad Nawash is famous for his distinctive stick figures in pastel colours; and another famous Palestinian-Jordanian painter is Ibrahim abu-Rubb.

Other popular contemporary Jordanian painters include Suha Shoman, Yaser Duweik, Ali Jabri, Mohanna Durra and Rafiq Lahham. Lahham is a pioneer of modern Jordanian art. His

work, which is reproduced here, incorporates traditional Islamic architectural forms, reflecting the built environment of the Middle East. He uses an eclectic mix of styles, with some of his most appealing work incorporating kufic script along with abstract elements and a striking use of colour. A new female artist is Samar Haddadin, whose paintings and drawings capture religious harmony. The Jordanian sculptor, Larissa Najjar, specialises in sandstone sculptures with different colours and unusual designs. Also renowned for her sculptures is Samaa Tabaa.

Works by these and other Jordanian artists can be seen in the numerous art galleries and cultural centres of Amman (particularly Darat al-Funun, and the Jordan National Gallery of Fine Arts), as well as galleries in Madaba, Salt and Fuheis.

The three works featured on pages 32-3 are by Jordanian artist Rafiq Lahham.

found on the walls of most of these – but none so extraordinary as in Qusayr Amra, where not only kings are depicted on the walls, but also a nude woman bathing – certainly not what one might have expected from the more austere rulers of Islam.

The boxed texts in the Madaba section of the King's Highway chapter have information about the ancient (and contemporary) art of mosaics.

Handicrafts
Jewellery Excavations show that jewellery made from copper and gold was worn as far back as the 8th century BC.

Throughout the region, jewellery was used for dowries (these days less common) and as an indicator of wealth, and many believed that some types of jewellery had healing powers or brought good luck. Silver has also been supplanted in popularity by gold, most of which is imported from overseas.

The Bedouin make traditional silver jewellery with old coins or precious or semiprecious stones, such as red agate. Popular among Jordanians are bracelets, mostly made of gold, called *mabroomeh*; chokers; and necklaces called *hjab* and *kirdan*, often made with precious stones or decorated with inscriptions from the Quran. Rings are often elaborate, and are also worn by men.

Weaving Weaving, to furnish tents, create saddle-bags and make ornaments, was always an important part of the Bedouin lifestyle. These days, an estimated 2000 or more Palestinian and Bedouin women are involved in the manufacture of *mafrash* rugs, carpets, *idel* bags and other goods under the guidance of several Jordanian charity organisations. (See Shopping in the Facts for the Visitor chapter, and the boxed text 'The Bani Hamida Story' in the King's Highway chapter, for more information.)

Home-made looms are still used for simple items, but workshops in the village are now more common. Weavers use sheep and goat wool, dyed the dark colours preferred by the Bedouin; while some natural dyes from the Jordan Valley are used, most dyes are chemically based and imported.

Traditional Dress Traditional women's clothes are elaborate, and vary considerably from one end of Jordan to another. However, unless you're invited to a traditional ceremony, or a special event, you're unlikely to see many traditional costumes in Jordan.

In Ma'an, which has always had close ties with Syria (because of the Hejaz Railway), women's dresses are very colourful; while in Jerash and Ajlun, the long men's and women's *shirsh* features an embroidered neckline, cuffs and sleeves. In Karak and Salt, men and women often wear a woollen belt called an *ub*. Materials are sometimes imported from Syria, such as *dubeit* (black cotton), but synthetics from Asia are now common.

SOCIETY & CONDUCT
Jordan is a typically Arab country, with very hospitable people. Jordanians are usually willing to forgive foreigners who innocently break the numerous etiquettes; see Dos & Don'ts later in this chapter to get an idea of how to avoid giving offence.

Traditional Culture
Welcome! You could be forgiven for thinking that 'welcome' is the first word of English learned by Jordanians. At every turn you'll hear it, and it seems to leave as many travellers perplexed as enchanted. Behind this simple word and makeshift translation lies a whole series of social codes.

One of the most common greetings in Arabic is *ahlan wa sahlan*. The root words means 'people' or 'family' *(ahl)* and 'ease' *(sahl)*, so translated loosely the expression means 'be as one of the family and at your ease'. A nice thought, and one that ends up simply as 'welcome' in English. Among Arabs, it's used to mean anything from 'hello' to 'you're welcome' (after thanks).

There is, however, a lot more to it. The Arab traditions of hospitality and kindness are based on the harsh realities of life in the desert and have been virtually codified in social behaviour. As a rule, strangers were given shelter and food as a matter of course (see the boxed text 'The Bedouin' earlier in this chapter).

Accepting an offer to join people in a meal or a cup of tea/coffee can be a wonderful way to learn more about the country (and its people) you're travelling in. Some visitors may feel bad accepting what is often very generous treatment; offering small gifts or mementos can be a good way around this.

Sometimes people will insist that you join them – but nine times out of 10 this is not the case. Rather than curtly saying 'no', the way to avoid any kind of invitation that you feel disinclined to accept is to refuse politely with your right hand over your heart – you may have to do it several times. Adding something noncommittal like 'perhaps another time, *in sha'allah*' (if God wills it) is a perfectly suitable, ambiguous and, most importantly, inoffensive way to turn down unwanted offers.

In the Home Many families, especially in smaller towns and rural areas, remain traditional in terms of divisions within the house. Should you be invited into one, it's worth bearing a few things in mind. As a rule various parts of the house are reserved for men, and others for women. This becomes particularly apparent when guests are present.

Given that the most likely reason for you being in someone's home is to eat, remember that meals are generally eaten on the floor, everyone gathered around several trays of food shared by all. Single men invited to eat or stay over at a house will be taken to a room reserved for men, or perhaps a mixed dining area. Depending on how conservative your hosts are, you may be directly served by the women or simply observe them bringing food and drink to the men, who then deal with you, the guest. Do not offer food, or take food from a communal plate, with your left hand (see the boxed text 'Body Language').

Foreign women will more often than not be treated as an honorary 'male'. In the case of a couple, a foreign woman may be welcome to sneak off to hang around with the Jordanian women and then come back to see how the 'men's world' is getting on. In

Body Language

Arabs gesticulate a lot in conversation, and some things can be said without uttering a word. Jordanians often say 'no' by raising the eyebrows and lifting the head up and back. This is often accompanied by a 'tsk tsk' noise, which can be a little off-putting if you're not used to it.

Shaking the head from side to side means 'I don't understand'. Stretching out the hand as if to open a door and giving it a quick flick of the wrist is equivalent to 'what do you want?', 'where are you going?' or 'what is your problem?'.

If an official holds out their hand and draws a line across their palm with the index finger of the other hand, they're pointing out that they want to see your passport, bus ticket or other document.

A foreign man asking directions should not be surprised to be taken by the hand and led along by another man; it's quite natural. Women should obviously be more circumspect about such an action from a Jordanian man.

A right hand over your heart means 'no, thanks' When you've had enough tea, put your hand over the cup, and say *da'iman* ('always').

As the left hand is associated with toilet duties it's considered unclean, so always use your right hand when giving or receiving something.

this sense, a foreign woman can find herself in the unique position of being able to get an impression of home life for both sexes.

More traditional families are often quite hierarchical at meal times, too. The grandparents and male head of the house may eat in one circle, the latter's wife and the older children and other women in the family in another, and the small children in yet another. Usually, outsiders eat with the head of the household.

Dress Immodest dress is still a major source of irritation to locals and can often lead to trouble for women (see the Women

Women in Jordan

Compared to some neighbouring countries, particularly Saudi Arabia, women in Jordan do enjoy more freedom and privileges: they have access to a full education; they can vote (a few women have become members of parliament); many work in male-dominated industries and businesses; and they can drive cars.

Jordan is secular, and freedom of religion is part of the constitution. Unlike some neighbouring Muslim countries, polygamy (by men) is rare; segregation is uncommon (except in some homes and restaurants, and all mosques); divorce is allowed for women (but it still carries a stigma); there are no restrictions about dress codes; and female infanticide and female circumcision are extremely rare.

Arranged marriages and dowries are still common, but parents often do not enforce a wedding against their daughter's wish. A 'woman's honour' is still valued in traditional societies, and sex before marriage can still be dealt with harshly by other members of her family. According to a recent report, 'honour crimes' make up a staggering 25% of all solved murders in Jordan, and the (mostly male) judges and juries are not unsympathetic to the (male) murderers.

Women in more traditional societies are starting to gain some financial independence, prestige and self-respect through a number of Jordanian charity organisations (mentioned in the Shopping section of the Facts for the Visitor chapter).

Travellers section in the Facts for the Visitor chapter for more information).

Do dress appropriately: men can get around in shorts without eliciting much of a response, but women are advised to wear knee-length dresses or pants and to cover the shoulders. Both sexes should always be well covered when entering mosques.

If you have crossed from Eilat to Aqaba, for instance, remember that there is great cultural difference between the two places.

Dos & Don'ts

Etiquette is very important in Jordanian (and Arab) culture, and you'll find that Jordanians will respect you more if you follow these few simple rules:

- Stand when someone important, or another guest, enters the room.
- Shake hands with everyone – but only with a Jordanian women if she offers her hand first.
- Do not sit so that the soles of your feet point to anyone.
- Never accept any present or service of any kind without first politely refusing twice.
- Don't engage in any conversation about sensitive topics, eg the Jordanian royal family or Judaism, unless you know the person you're talking to well.
- An unaccompanied foreign man should not sit next to an unaccompanied Jordanian woman in public transport, unless it's unavoidable.
- Remove your shoes when visiting a mosque, or a private house (unless you're specifically told to keep them on).
- Never walk in front of, or interrupt in any way, someone praying towards Mecca.
- Foreign couples should not hold hands, or show any signs of affection, in public.

Impact of Tourism

Although there have been some official studies about the impact of tourism on Jordan's environment, little has been done to determine the damage from tourism to the traditional lifestyles of the Jordanians, particularly the Bedouin. Like most other conservative traditional societies, unrestrained tourism from western countries can create a dichotomy between the host and visiting cultures, often exacerbated by thoughtless westerners who, for example, drink alcohol in public or wear skimpy clothes.

Vast differences between the cultures of the west and Jordan can cause many problems: resentment from locals who have little or no opportunity for improvement; social values to change as young Jordanians pick up unattractive habits from the west, eg swearing, drinking alcohol and taking drugs; and education to suffer as the youth flock to tourist areas in search of a fast buck.

Also, the cost of housing and rent in places like Wadi Mousa (near Petra) and

Aqaba is often high, so locals cannot afford to live where they like; and land is sometimes bought by richer Jordanians solely for speculative purposes. The price for fruit, meat and vegetables is often high in tourist areas, because of the demand for these goods from big-spending, upmarket hotels.

Treatment of Animals

Most visitors to Jordan will witness what they regard as maltreatment of animals – whether it's shepherds whipping their beasts, overloaded camels plodding through the desert or donkeys struggling up hundreds of steps in Petra. These sort of activities may seem cruel by western standards, but the owners rely heavily on their animals to make a living, and are normally sensible enough to keep them healthy.

The Jordanian government, with the aid of several NGOs, has started educating children about the treatment of animals, especially in the poorer regions. In addition, children are being taught about the importance of preserving their environment.

One of the very few animal hospitals and agencies working for animal rights is the Princess Alia Horse Clinic, affiliated with the Brooke Hospital for Animals, in Petra – see the boxed text in the Petra chapter for more information.

RELIGION

Although the population is overwhelmingly Islamic, Jordan is officially secular, and freedom of religion is a statute right of the Jordanian constitution.

Islam

Islam is the predominant religion in Jordan. Muslims are called to prayer five times a day and no matter where you might be, there always seems to be a mosque within earshot. The midday prayers on Friday, when the sheikh of the mosque delivers his weekly sermon, or *khutba*, are considered the most important.

Islam shares its roots with the great monotheistic faiths – Judaism and Christianity – that sprang from the unforgiving and harsh soil of the Middle East, but is considerably younger than both. The holy book of Islam is the Quran. Its pages carry many references to the earlier prophets of both the older religions: Abraham (known in the Quran as Ibrahim), Noah (Nuh), Moses (Musa) and others – but there the similarities end. Jesus is seen as another in a long line of prophets that ends definitively with Mohammed.

The Quran is believed to be the word of God, communicated to Mohammed directly in a series of revelations in the early 7th century. For Muslims, Islam can only be the apogee of the monotheistic faiths from which it derives so much. Muslims traditionally attribute a place of great respect to Christians and Jews who they consider *Ahl al-kitab*, the 'People of the Book'. However, the more strident will claim Christianity was a new and improved version of the teachings of the Torah and that Islam was the next logical step – and therefore 'superior'.

Mohammed, born into a trading family of the Arabian city of Mecca (in present-day Saudi Arabia) in 570 AD, began receiving revelations in 610 AD, and after a time began imparting the content of Allah's message to the inhabitants of Mecca. The essence of it was a call to submit to God's will (*islam* means submission), but not all locals were terribly taken with the idea.

Mohammed gathered quite a following in his campaign against the idolaters of Mecca, and his movement especially appealed to the poorer levels of society. The powerful families became increasingly outraged, and by 622 had made life sufficiently unpleasant for Mohammed and his followers; they fled to Medina, an oasis town some 300km to the north and now Islam's second most holy city. This migration – the Hejira – marks the beginning of the Islamic calendar, year 1 AH or 622 AD.

In Medina, Mohammed continued to preach. Soon he and his followers clashed with the rulers of Mecca, led by the powerful Quraysh tribe, possibly over trade routes. By 630, his followers returned to take Mecca. In the two years until his death, many of the surrounding tribes swore allegiance to him and the new faith.

Mecca became the symbolic centre of the Islamic religion, containing as it did the Ka'aba, which houses the black stone that long had formed the object of pagan pilgrimage and later was said to have been given to Ibraham by the Archangel Gabriel. Mohammed determined that Muslims ('those who submit') should always face Mecca when praying outside the city.

Upon Mohammed's death in 632, the Arab tribes conquered all of what makes up modern Jordan, Syria, Iraq, Lebanon, Israel and the Palestinian territories. By 644, they had taken Egypt and spread into North Africa, and in the following decades crossed into Spain and, for a while, deep into France.

The initial conquests were carried out under successive caliphs, or Companions of Mohammed, of whom there were four. In turn, the caliphs were followed by the Umayyad dynasty, based in Damascus, and the Abbasids, based in the newly built city of Baghdad (in modern Iraq). For more information see the History section earlier in this chapter.

In order to live a devout life, a Muslim is expected to carry out at least the Five Pillars of Islam:

Haj The pinnacle of a devout Muslim's life is the pilgrimage to the holy sites in and around Mecca. Ideally, the pilgrim should go to Mecca in the last month of the year, Zuul-Hijja, and join Muslims from all over the world in the pilgrimage and subsequent feast. The returned pilgrim can be addressed as Haj, and in simpler villages at least, it is not uncommon to see the word Al-Haj and simple scenes painted on the walls of houses showing that its inhabitants have made the pilgrimage.

Sala Sometimes written *salat*, this is the obligation of prayer, done ideally five or six times a day when the muezzins call upon the faithful to pray. Although Muslims can pray anywhere, a strong sense of community makes joining together in a *masjid* (mosque) preferable to most.

Shahada This is the profession of the faith, the basic tenet of Islam: 'There is no God but Allah and Mohammed is his prophet'. *La illaha illa Allah Mohammed rasul Allah.* It's commonly heard as part of the call to prayer, and at other events such as births and deaths. The first half of the sentence has virtually become an exclamation good for any time of life

or situation. People can often be heard muttering it to themselves, as if seeking a little strength to get through the trials of the day.

Sawm Ramadan, the ninth month of the Muslim calendar, commemorates the revelation of the Quran to Mohammed. In a demonstration of the Muslims' renewal of faith, they are asked to abstain from sex, and from letting anything (including cigarettes) pass their lips from dawn to dusk every day of the month. For more information about Ramadan, see the Public Holidays & Special Events section of the Facts for the Visitor chapter.

Zakat Giving alms to the poor was, from the start, an essential part of Islamic social teaching and, in some parts of the Muslim world, was later developed into various forms of tax as a way of redistributing funds to the needy. The moral obligation towards one's poorer neighbours continues to be emphasised at a personal level, and it's not unusual to find notices, exhorting people to give, posted up outside mosques.

Sunnis & Shi'ites In its early days, Islam suffered a major schism that divided the faith into two streams, the Sunnis and Shi'ites. The power struggle between Ali (the last of the four caliphs and Mohammed's son-in-law) and the Umayyad dynasty in Damascus lay at the heart of the rift that tore asunder the new faith's followers.

The succession to the caliphate had from the first been marked by intrigue. Ali, the father of Mohammed's sole male heirs, lost his struggle and was assassinated, paving the way to the caliphate for the Umayyad leader Mu'awiya. The latter was related to Ali's predecessor, Othman, in whose murder some believed Ali was implicated.

Those who recognised Mu'awiya as caliph (which were the majority) came to be known as the Sunnis, who would become the orthodox bedrock of Islam. The Shi'ites, on the other hand, recognise only the successors of Ali. Most of them are known as Twelvers, because they believe in 12 imams (religious leaders), the last of whom has been lost from sight, but will appear some day to create an empire of the true faith. The rest are called Seveners, because they believe seven imams will succeed Ali.

The Sunnis divided into four schools of religious thought, each lending more or less importance to various aspects of doctrine.

Islamic Customs When a baby is born, the first words uttered to it are the call to prayer. A week later this is followed by a ceremony in which the baby's head is shaved and an animal is sacrificed. The major event of a boy's childhood is circumcision, which normally takes place sometime between the ages of seven and 12.

Marriage ceremonies are colourful and noisy affairs. One of the customs is for all the males to drive around the streets in convoy making as much ballyhoo as possible. The marriage ceremony usually takes place in either the mosque or the home of the bride or groom. After that the partying goes on until the early hours of the morning, often until sunrise.

Before praying, Muslims must follow certain rituals. They must wash their hands, arms, feet, head and neck in running water before praying. All mosques have a small area set aside for this purpose. If they're not in a mosque and there is no water available, clean sand suffices, and where there is no sand, they must still go through the motions of washing.

Then they must cover their head, face Mecca (all mosques are orientated so that the *mihrab*, or prayer niche, faces the right way) and follow a set pattern of gestures and genuflections. Outside of the mosques, Muslims can pray anywhere, and you regularly see them praying by the side of the road or in the street; many keep a small prayer rug handy for such times.

In everyday life, Muslims are prohibited from drinking alcohol, eating pork (as the animal is considered unclean) and keeping dogs, and must refrain from fraud, usury, slander and gambling.

Druze The Druze religion is an offshoot of Shi'ite Islam and was spread in the 11th century by Hamzah ibn Ali and other missionaries from Egypt who followed the Fatimid caliph, Al-Hakim. The group derives its name from one of Hamzah's subordinates, Mohammed Darazi, who had declared Al-Hakim to be the last imam and God in one – but most Egyptians found the bloody ruler to be anything but divine. When Al-Hakim

died in mysterious circumstances, Darazi and his companions had to flee Egypt.

Most members of the Druze community now live in the mountains of Lebanon, although there are some small Druze towns around the Syria-Jordan border. Their distinctive faith has survived intact mainly because of the secrecy that surrounds it. Not only is conversion to (or from) the faith prohibited, but only an elite, known as *uqqal* ('knowers'), have full access to the religious doctrine, the *hikmeh*.

The hikmeh is contained in seven holy books that exist only in handwritten copies. One of the codes it preaches is *taqiyyeh* (caution), under which a believer living among Christians, for example, can outwardly conform to Christian belief while still being a Druze at heart. They believe that God is too sacred to be called by name, is amorphous and will reappear in other incarnations. Although the New Testament and the Quran are revered, they read their own Scriptures at *khalwas* (meeting houses) on Thursdays.

Christianity

Statistics on the number of Christians in Jordan are often wildly contradictory. They are believed to account for 5 to 6% of Jordan's population. Most live in Karak, Madaba, Salt, Fuheis, Ajlun and Amman – all with a bewildering array of churches representing the three major branches of Christianity in Jordan: Orthodox, Catholic and (to a far lesser extent) Protestant.

About two-thirds of Christians in Jordan are Greek Orthodox. This church has its liturgy in Arabic, and is the mother church of the Jacobites (Syrian Orthodox), who broke away in the 6th century, and the Greek Catholics, who split off in the 16th century. Coptic Orthodox, with a pope and most coreligionists in Egypt, are also represented in Jordan.

The other third are Greek Catholics, or Melchites, under the authority of the patriarch who resides in Damascus. This church observes a Byzantine tradition of married clergy being in charge of rural parishes, while diocesan clergy are celibate.

LANGUAGE

Arabic is the official language in Jordan. Anyone working in the tourist industry will speak good English, and the majority of other Jordanians can speak passable English. Almost all town and street signs throughout the country are also helpfully in English. Some locals also speak a little French or German, and will be delighted to practise it with native speakers visiting from Europe.

Although it is not necessary to learn Arabic to travel around Jordan, any effort you make to communicate with the locals in their language will be well rewarded. No matter how far off the mark your pronunciation or grammar might be you will usually get the cheerful response (just about always with a big smile): 'Ah, you speak Arabic very well!'

Turn to the Language section at the back of this book for further details. It provides useful information regarding the development of Arabic and an explanation about pronunciation, as well as listing some vital words and phrases.

Facts for the Visitor

SUGGESTED ITINERARIES
One week is the minimum required to truly explore Jordan on any form of transport; one month is ideal. And don't forget: even if you use public transport most of the time, it's still worth hiring or chartering a vehicle for a few days to visit remote places.

Public Transport
Using any available form of public transport (and occasionally hitching when public transport is infrequent or nonexistent), the following itineraries are well worth considering:

Three Days
   Amman/Jerash (one day) and Petra (two).
One Week
   Amman (one); Jerash and Umm Qais (one); Madaba & Karak (one); Petra (two); Wadi Rum (one); and Aqaba (one).
Two Weeks
   Amman (two); Jerash and Umm Qais (one); desert castles (one); Dead Sea (one); Madaba and around (two); Karak (one); Petra (three); Wadi Rum (two); and Aqaba (one).
One Month
   Follow the schedule listed above for two weeks, with one or two extra days in each place, and allow some extra time to dive/snorkel in Aqaba; trek/rock climb in Wadi Rum, Petra or northern Jordan; visit one or two national reserves; and explore more remote sites like Machaerus castle at Mukawir, and Shobak castle.

Rented Car or Chartered Taxi
Renting a private car is a popular option (see the Car & Motorcycle section in the Getting Around chapter for more information). However, it's not cheap and is impractical if you spend a few days exploring vast sites like Petra and Jerash, which can only be explored on foot. Chartering a service (public) taxi or private taxi with a driver is potentially better value because the taxi can be chartered one hour or one day at a time.

The following suggested itineraries do not include visits to Amman, Madaba, the Dead Sea Rest House at Suweimeh, Wadi Rum, Aqaba, Petra and Jerash because they are all easy to reach by public transport.

Three Days
   Day 1: North of Amman – Ajlun, Dibbeen National Park, Umm Qais, Al-Himma (Mukheiba), Pella and Deir Alla.
   Day 2: Amman to Wadi Mousa (near Petra), via the King's Highway – Madaba, Mt Nebo, Hammamat Ma'in, Mukawir, Wadi Mujib, Karak, Dana Nature Reserve and Shobak castle.
   Day 3: Wadi Mousa (near Petra) to Amman, via the Dead Sea Highway – Al-Beid (Little Petra), Rum village, Aqaba, Lot's Cave and the Dead Sea.
One Week
   It's easy to see everything in Jordan by rented car or chartered taxi in one week, and there's little point renting or chartering a vehicle for any longer. Follow the schedules listed above for three days, and allow extra time to visit places near Petra, Diseh (near Wadi Rum), the Dead Sea and Aqaba. Alternatively, add an extra day to visit the desert castles, Umm al-Jimal and one or two national reserves.

PLANNING
When to Go
The best time to visit Jordan is in the spring (March to May) and autumn (September to November) seasons, when the daytime temperatures aren't going to knock you flat and the winds aren't too cold (see the Climate section in the Facts about Jordan chapter for further information).

If you visit in summer be well prepared, and come with a hat, sunscreen and other protective clothing. At this time the entire country boils, nowhere more than around Wadi Rum and the eastern desert. The humidity can also become quite suffocating, especially along the Jordan River.

Despite this, July and August is the peak tourist season, and the number of tourists visiting the major sites can be daunting. The tourist authorities usually plan festivals (such as the exciting Jerash Festival) for July/August.

HIGHLIGHTS

Archaeological Sites
Petra (p 206)
Petra is the greatest site in Jordan, and one of the most spectacular in the whole of the Middle East. Allow at least two days. There is plenty of accommodation in nearby Wadi Mousa. But the bad news is the horrendous entrance fee.

Jerash (p 144)
This vast, and remarkably well preserved, Roman city is second only to Petra as a 'must-see'. It's very easily accessible from Amman, and can be combined with visits to other sites in northern Jordan, eg Ajlun and/ or Umm Qais.

Karak (p 197)
Arguably the most interesting and spectacular castle, palace or fort. Nothing very much is labelled or explained, but the setting is truly superb.

Umm Qais (p 156)
These ruins of another vast ancient city offer wonderful views over the Jordan Valley to Israel and Syria.

Museums & Galleries
National Archaeological Museum (p 123)
The main museum in the capital is compact and informative, and located in the ruins of the ancient Citadel.

Museum of Jordanian Heritage (p 154)
Probably the best museum in Jordan, it's easy to reach from Amman and is in the middle of the vibrant Yarmouk University in the northern city of Irbid.

Darat al-Funun (p 125)
A short walk from Downtown Amman, this art gallery has various interesting exhibitions and a charming outdoor cafe.

Landscapes & Natural Features
Wadi Rum (p 232)
Wadi Rum offers the most stunning desert landscapes in Jordan. Camping, hiking and jeep tours are currently allowed. Acknowledged as one of the world's foremost desert climbing areas.

The Dead Sea (p 163)
Although not nearly as developed and enticing as the western coast of the Dead Sea in Israel, there's enough salt, sea and mud for an enjoyable day trip from Amman.

Wadi Mujib (p 194)
This vast valley stretches from the Dead Sea Highway to the King's Highway and beyond, and part of it is now being developed as a national park.

Hammamat Ma'in (p 190)
Although slightly forlorn and a bit tacky in parts, the waterfall and swimming pool are popular with locals, and it's only a short trip from Madaba.

Activities
Diving & Snorkelling (p 257)
Although generally not as good as some of the sites along the Sinai peninsula in Egypt, Aqaba has enough coral and marine life to satisfy most divers; the best can also be enjoyed by snorkellers.

Hiking & Rock Climbing (p 236)
Anyone with some fitness and experience can enjoy trekking and rock climbing among the hills of Wadi Rum. Guides are normally available, and often necessary.

For Something a Bit Different...
Jeep Tours (p 238)
Bedouin drivers offer trips around the remarkable Wadi Rum in battered old jeeps.

Archaeological Digs (p 79)
Anyone with a specific interest, and plenty of time, can often join an archaeological dig.

Camel Treks (p 239)
For a taste of the (old) Bedouin lifestyle, camel treks can be organised from Wadi Rum to Wadi Mousa (near Petra) and Aqaba.

Winter is not a complete washout. It can be bitterly cold throughout most of the country, and snow is not unheard of in Amman and Petra, but once you come off the high plateaux and head down to Aqaba and the Red Sea, it becomes very pleasant. In fact, Aqaba is quite a hit with deep-frozen northern Europeans during winter.

Ramadan is a time when visitors should not eat, drink or smoke in public during the day for one month, so it's not the best time to visit, although some travellers cannot avoid coming at this time. Eid al-Fitr, the great celebration after the end of Ramadan, can last several days. Although this is a fun time to visit, it's best to stay put for a few days because buses are heavily booked, service taxis and private taxis are less frequent and hotel rooms are sometimes hard to find, especially in Aqaba. The Public Holidays & Special Events section later in this chapter has more information about travelling around Jordan during Ramadan.

What Kind of Trip

Because Jordan is small, and has a limited, but fascinating, number of attractions, two weeks is enough to take in all the main sights, and perhaps finish off with some relaxing diving, snorkelling and swimming in Aqaba. In fact, Jordan is so compact that it's easy to base yourself in a handful of towns – ie Amman, Madaba, Karak, Wadi Mousa (near Petra) and Aqaba – and take day trips to all the major attractions.

Some people prefer to join an organised tour around Jordan, or one that combines Jordan with Syria or Israel, but this is obviously much more expensive, and less flexible, than travelling around independently. Jordan is easy to get around under your own steam: public transport is frequent and chartered taxis are easy to arrange; English is widely spoken at places tourists are likely to go; staff at tourist offices, and the tourist police, are usually eager to help; and Jordanians are normally happy to assist in any way.

Maps

For most visitors, the maps in this guidebook will be more than sufficient, but if you're doing some hiking or intensive exploration, a detailed map of Jordan, such as Lonely Planet's *Jordan, Syria & Lebanon travel atlas,* is a good idea.

The most accurate map of Jordan (and available in the country) is the colourful Map of Jordan, published by Luma Khalaf. It comes in various different forms, and is not particularly easy to find. The Royal Geographic Centre of Jordan publishes a series of decent maps, which are available at major bookshops in the country. Its map of Amman, called Today's Amman, is excellent, as is the hiking map of Petra, but the ones for Jerash, Madaba, Karak and Aqaba are less useful.

Several detailed maps should be available in your own country: Bartholomew's *Israel with Jordan* is OK, but it includes Israel at the expense of eastern Jordan; *Jordan* by Kümmerly & Frey is good, and probably the best if you're driving around Jordan; and the third edition of GEO Project's *Jordan* (1:730,000) also includes an excellent map of Amman.

What to Bring

For most travellers, the backpack remains the best option, and the only one if you end up having to do any walking. On the down side, they do not afford the greatest protection to valuable belongings.

A travel pack is recommended, ie where the straps of the pack can be zipped away when not needed. This combines the carrying ease of a pack with the added strength of a bag. Another alternative is a large, soft zip bag with a wide shoulder strap so that it can be carried with relative ease if necessary. You can also get some tabs sewn on so you can partially protect it from theft with small padlocks.

A hat, sunscreen and sunglasses are essential in summer. A few other handy items are: a Swiss army knife, torch (flashlight), a few metres of nylon cord (for use as a clothesline), some pegs, a universal sink plug, an adaptor for electrical items (if necessary), earplugs (useful if staying near mosques), medical and sewing kits, padlocks, a towel, short-wave radio, canteen, sleeping sheet and/or sleeping bag if you're camping or staying overnight in Wadi Rum (see the Accommodation section later in this chapter).

If you're going in winter, make sure you have plenty of warm clothes and a windproof and waterproof jacket, because some parts of Jordan, particularly the north, can get surprisingly miserable at this time of year. The southern desert region, eg at Wadi Rum, can also get cold at night at any time of the year.

Otherwise, bring a pair of light cotton trousers, a pair of shorts, a few shirts and T-shirts, underwear and socks (at least one heavy pair), a pair of strong walking shoes and a pair of sandals or flip-flops (thongs).

Tampons are not always readily available. You should also bring your own contraceptives and any special medications. Other toiletries are easily found. Refer to the Health section later in this chapter for a list of medical items worth bringing.

RESPONSIBLE TOURISM

About 20 years ago, Jordan started to fully realise the economic importance of tourism, but only recently have the Jordanian government and, more particularly, foreign nongovernment organisations (NGOs) fully realised the impact on the environment from mass tourism. For example, the compound effects of the extraordinary number of people visiting the precious and fragile ancient city of Petra every day, and the near-sighted policies of some government departments, are threatening the future of Petra – which is also a vital source of revenue for the government. (The boxed text 'Petra & Tourism' in the Petra chapter has more information.)

The environmental problems of Jordan may seem insurmountable, but there is a lot we can all do to minimise our impact:

- Leave it as you found it. For as long as outsiders have been searching for, and stumbling over, the ancient monuments of Jordan, they have also been chipping bits off, or leaving their contributions engraved upon them. When visiting historical and archaeological sites, please consider how important it is to leave things alone.

- Don't litter. Discarded rubbish is strewn all across the countryside. Some of the refuse – eg plastic bottles – recycled in many ways, so don't be too quick to point an accusing finger at the locals. However, there's no doubt that inadequate waste disposal, and a scant regard for environmental issues, produce some ugly sights, eg the plethora of black plastic bags stuck to the spindly shrubs all across the landscapes. Please resist the local tendency to ditch rubbish out of the car or bus window.
- Do as requested. Please follow instructions and regulations, eg don't touch the coral off the coast of Aqaba; don't go to areas of national reserves which are off limits; and always dress conservatively.

For more details about the impact of tourism on the environment refer to the Ecology & Environment and Society & Conduct sections in the Facts about Jordan chapter.

TOURIST OFFICES
Local Tourist Offices

The main tourist office in Amman is called the Downtown visitors centre, and staff are very helpful. Less helpful and convenient is the Public Relations office at the Ministry of Tourism & Antiquities in Amman. There's an information counter (☎ 06-445 3200) at Terminal 2 of the Queen Alia international airport, south of Amman, but it is also of little use.

Smaller tourist offices are located at Madaba, Aqaba, Karak, Jerash, Ajlun, Petra and Umm Qais. A new innovation in Jordan is the number of visitors centres springing up, eg at the desert castle of Qusayr Amra in eastern Jordan.

The Jordan Tourism Board (JTB) publishes an array of excellent brochures in English, German, Spanish, Italian and French and sometimes you can even find one in Japanese. The general brochure about Jordan is less useful, but the ones about Amman, the desert castles, Umm Qais, Jerash, Petra, Karak, Mount Nebo, Madaba, Ajlun, Wadi Rum, Aqaba and Petra are informative, pocket-sized and free. Pick one up from a JTB office overseas – or, possibly, a Royal Jordanian Airlines office or Jordanian embassy/consulate – before you leave; or from any tourist office as soon as you arrive in Jordan.

Tourist Offices Abroad

After evaluating the importance of tourism to the Jordanian economy, the Jordan Tourism Board has recently spread its network to include offices in several countries:

France
(☎ 01-45 61 92 58, fax 42 25 66 40)
32 rue de Ponthieu, 75008 Paris
Germany
(☎ 69-9231 8870, fax 9231 8879, email eadam@adam-partner.de) Postfach 160 120, 60064 Frankfurt
UK
(☎ 020-8877 4524, fax 8874 4219, email clare@representationplus.co.uk) Representation House, 11 Blades Court, Deodar Rd, London, SW 152NV
USA
(☎ 202-244 1451, toll-free ☎ 1-877SEEJOR DAN, fax 244 0534, email seejordan@ aol.com) 3504 International Drive NW, Washington DC, 20008

The JTB office in Amman (☎ 06-567 8294, fax 567 8295) is upstairs in the shopping complex at the Ammon Hotel (see Places to Stay in the Amman chapter), but is not a local tourist office. The JTB has a Web site (www.tourism.com.jo), and publishes a free, monthly newsletter in English called *Jordan Travel & Tourism News*. If you cannot visit a JTB office overseas, it's probably best to email (jtb@nets.com.jo) them from wherever you are.

Information is sometimes available from Royal Jordanian Airline offices (such as those in Amsterdam, Berlin, Chicago, Frankfurt, London, Los Angeles, Montreal, New York, Paris, Rome and Sydney). Also try the Jordanian embassies and consulates listed later in this chapter.

VISAS & DOCUMENTS
Passport

Everyone requires a valid passport to travel to Jordan. Check that your passport is valid for at least six months after you arrive in Jordan; otherwise you may not be granted a visa. Keep an eye on the number of pages you have left in the passport. If it's nearly full get a new one before leaving home.

Always carry your passport with you when travelling around sensitive areas, eg near the Israeli border – which means most of the Jordan Valley, the Dead Sea and anywhere along the Dead Sea Highway. Checkpoints are common near all borders, and passport checks are often required.

Visas

Visas are required by all foreigners entering Jordan. These are issued at the border or airport on arrival, or can be obtained from Jordanian embassies and consulates outside the country. There are three ways of obtaining a visa, and where or how you get one depends on: (a) how you enter Jordan – remember that Jordanian visas are not issued at the King Hussein Bridge; and (b) what sort of visa you want, eg a multiple-entry visa or one for longer than 14 days – but don't forget: visa extensions are easy to obtain.

Your first, and most expensive, option is to obtain a visa from the Jordanian embassy or consulate in your home country. A single-entry 14-day visa costs C$65 for Canadians in Ottawa, UK£28 for UK citizens in London, and US$44 for US citizens in Washington. It is necessary to obtain your visa this way if you want a multiple-entry visa or you're going to Jordan on business. All visas issued abroad are valid for three months (ie you must enter Jordan within three months of issue).

Your second option is a single-entry 14-day visa obtained at a Jordanian embassy or consulate in a neighbouring country, eg Syria, Turkey, Egypt or Israel. In Damascus (Syria), Jordanian visas are reportedly very easy to obtain, and cost most nationalities about US$7. (Some readers report to have been deliberately overcharged for their Jordanian visa in Damascus, so get a receipt and make sure the amount charged matches the amount on the visa stamp itself.) In Istanbul and Ankara (Turkey), visas cost about US$10. They are also not difficult to obtain in Cairo (Egypt) and Tel Aviv (Israel), but avoid the latter if you wish to travel elsewhere in the region (see the boxed text 'Travelling To/From Israel'). Bear in mind, however, that some Jordanian

Travelling To/From Israel

Most countries in the Middle East and North Africa (with the exception of Jordan, Egypt and Morocco) will not grant visas, or allow entry, to anyone who has *any* evidence of visiting Israel, or the Palestine National Authority (which includes the West Bank). This includes Israeli exit stamps from any of the three borders with Jordan, ie from Eilat, King Hussein Bridge and Sheikh Hussein Bridge; Israeli exit stamps or Egyptian entry stamps at Rafah and Taba, both on the Israel/Egypt border; and any Jordanian entry stamps at the Israel/Jordan borders.

Even if you do things in a convoluted fashion – eg visit Israel from Egypt, return to Egypt and go to Jordan on the ferry – you run a good chance of acquiring unwanted evidence in your passport. Even if the Israelis do not stamp you in or out, the Egyptians may well do so (at Rafah at least). And then if you apply for a Syrian visa, or cross the Jordan/Syria border, without a Jordanian entry stamp you'll probably be denied a visa or entry.

The only foolproof method is to visit the countries that will not accept evidence of a visit to Israel *before* going to Israel, and then go to countries, such as Egypt and Jordan, which will accept Israeli visas/stamps – and later get a new passport. If you have dual citizenship, try to get two passports, but keep them separate and make sure you get the correct visas and stamps in the right passport.

If none of the above is possible or feasible, cross the border from Jordan to Israel at the King Hussein Bridge, stay only in the Palestine National Authority (ie West Bank), but don't venture further into Israel – and go back to Jordan the same way. But make sure you ask for all Jordanian and Israeli stamps to be placed on a separate piece of paper. People who have crossed from Jordan to the West Bank in small groups have asked for stamps on separate pieces of paper, but have still been caught out; for some reason, Israeli immigration officials may not stamp the first two or three passports, and then spitefully stamp the next few – so it's best to cross individually or in groups of two.

If you get an Israeli or Jordanian exit or entry stamp in your passport, there's little you can do. If you report that your passport is 'lost' to your embassy in any country in the Middle East, it may be met with extreme cynicism, and even rejection. And some countries may also be highly sceptical, and even refuse you a visa or entry, if you have a brand new, unused passport issued in the Middle East.

---

embassies/consulates in the Middle East, except for Cairo, seem less willing to issue anything but single-entry visas.

The third easiest option is to get a single-entry 14-day visa at any border (including if arriving by ferry from Egypt), or at one of the three international airports. It will cost: JD11 for French and Italian citizens; JD15 for Germans; JD16 for Aussies and Kiwis; JD23 for Brits; JD33 for Americans; and JD39 for Canadians.

Visa Extensions A single-entry visa is valid for 14 days after arrival in Jordan, and is stamped with a reminder to visit the police within that period if you wish to stay longer than 14 days. Failure to do so will result in a fine of at least JD1 per day for every day you have overstayed.

One visa extension of two or three months is quick and easy to obtain, and often possible in less then 30 minutes. Extensions are technically possible in major provincial capitals, eg Irbid and Karak, but are best done at Amman or Aqaba (see Visa Extensions in the Aqaba section of the Southern Desert chapter for details). Surprisingly, an extension costs nothing, and no photos or photocopies of passports are needed.

Currently, two offices in Amman provide visa extensions: the Hussein Police Centre and the Muhajireen Police Station (see the Visa Extensions section of the Amman chapter for details of how to get there). Both

Getting Other Visas in Jordan

If you need visas for neighbouring countries in Jordan, these are the conditions. (See Embassies & Consulates in Jordan later in this chapter for addresses.)

Egypt

Requirements for a one-month single-entry visa from the embassy in Amman are one passport photo and JD17 (all nationalities). Visas are valid for three months, and can usually be obtained on the same day (at about 3pm). The embassy in Amman is open 9 am to noon, Sunday to Thursday.

However, the consulate in Aqaba is a much easier place to obtain a visa. A one-month single-entry visa issued within one or two hours (even on the spot if they're not busy) for JD12. The place is often deserted (except at opening times), which is a great contrast to the chaos of the embassy in Amman. The visa section is open from 9 am to 3 pm, every day except Friday.

Most nationalities are issued a visa on arrival in Egypt, including on arrival at Nuweiba, if arriving by ferry from Aqaba (but the Egyptians make a song and dance and demand US dollars); however, it's very important to check whether the visa issued at the Egyptian embassy or consulate, or on arrival at Nuweiba, is for all of Egypt – or just the Sinai peninsula (ie as far as Sharm el-Sheikh). Some visitors have been caught, so check with the Egyptian consulate in Aqaba (which is more approachable and knowledgeable than the embassy in Amman) beforehand.

Israel

Most nationalities do not require Israeli visas; they're normally available at the border. If you go to the embassy in Amman, do not line up with the multitude of Palestinians. Visas can normally be picked up later on the same day. The embassy is open 8 to 11 am, Sunday to Thursday.

Lebanon

A one-month single-entry visa requires one photocopy of your passport details, one passport photo and JD14 (all nationalities). The visa is normally available in 24 hours, but some readers have been 'questioned' about their planned itinerary while in Lebanon. The embassy is open 8 to 11 am, every day but Friday and Sunday.

Syria

It is imperative to note that only foreign residents in Jordan, ie expatriate workers and diplomats, can be issued a Syrian visa at the embassy in Amman. Some readers have received a Syrian visa after obtaining a letter of recommendation (in Arabic) from their embassy in Amman, but this is absolutely a last resort, and is not guaranteed at all.

Visas are not normally available at either Syria/Jordan border (although some Irish and Australians have been successful) so all nationalities should obtain a Syrian visa before arriving in Jordan, eg from Cairo, Istanbul or Ankara.

You will be refused a Syrian visa, and entry to Syria, if there is any indication in your passport of entry to Israel – refer to the 'Travelling To/From Israel' boxed text for more information. The embassy is open 9 to 11 am every day but Friday.

are open every day, except Friday, from 8 am to 2 pm. The people who deal with visa extensions speak good English, and can fill out the small card in Arabic for you. Keep this card with you for the length of your trip and hand it to the immigration authorities when you depart Jordan.

If you are intending to stay longer in Jordan and you require extensions of more than two or three months, you may be sent to the Directorate of Residence, Borders & Foreigners (☎ 196, ext 3392), Suleiman an-Nabulsi St, Amman, which opens from 8 am to 2 pm, Saturday to Thursday.

Travel Insurance

A travel insurance policy to cover theft, loss and medical problems is a good idea. Some policies offer varied rate medical-expense options; the higher ones are chiefly for countries such as the USA, which have extremely high medical costs. There is a wide variety of policies available, so check the small print.

Some policies specifically exclude 'dangerous activities', which can include scuba diving, motorcycling and even trekking. A locally acquired motorbike licence is not valid under some policies.

You may prefer a policy which pays doctors or hospitals directly rather than having to pay on the spot and claim later. If you have to claim later make sure you keep all documentation. Some policies ask you to call back (reverse charges) to a centre in your home country where an immediate assessment of your problem is made.

Check that the policy covers ambulances or an emergency flight home.

Driving Licence

An International Driving Permit may be required if you intend to drive anywhere in Jordan, although most car rental companies do accept your national driving licence instead. For more information, refer to the Car & Motorcycle section in the Getting Around chapter.

Student Cards

Unhappily, International Student Identity Cards (ISIC) and the like are next to useless in Jordan. Many travellers – including many with dodgy student cards – were asking for student discounts from the Department of Antiquities in Amman that the authorities decided not to offer any discounts to any students anywhere in Jordan, including Petra. No amount of impressive paperwork from any government department or university in Jordan or anywhere else around the world will get you a student discount to any archaeological site in Jordan.

Photocopies

It is a wise precaution to keep photocopies of all the data pages of your passport and any other identity cards, even your birth certificate if you can manage it, with you – and with someone you trust at home. Other worthwhile things to photocopy include airline tickets, travel insurance documents with emergency international medical aid numbers, credit cards (and international card loss phone numbers), driving licence, vehicle documentation and any employment or educational qualifications you may need if you're considering work or study. Keep all of this, and a list of the serial numbers of your travellers cheques, somewhere separate from the originals of the documents.

Another option for storing details of your vital travel documents before you leave is Lonely Planet's online Travel Vault. Storing details of your important documents in the vault is safer than carrying photocopies. It's the best option if you will be travelling in a country with easy Internet access. Your password-protected travel vault is accessible online at anytime. Create your own travel vault for free at www.ekno.lonelyplanet.com.

Although theft is not a big problem in Jordan, some spare cash tucked away into a money belt, stuffed into a pair of socks or otherwise concealed, could come in very handy if you lose your wallet or purse.

EMBASSIES & CONSULATES
Jordanian Embassies & Consulates

All of the following are embassies unless otherwise indicated:

Australia
   (☎ 02-6295 9951, fax 6239 7236)
   20 Roebuck St, Red Hill, Canberra, ACT, 2603
Canada
   (☎ 613-238 8091, fax 232 3341)
   100 Bronson Ave, Suite 701, Ottawa, Ontario, K1N 6R4
Egypt
   (☎ 2-349 9912, fax 360 1027)
   6 Al-Juhaini St, Doqqi, Cairo
France
   (☎ 01-46 24 23 78, fax 46 37 02 06)
   80 Blvd Maurice Barres, 92200 Neuilly-sur-Seine, Paris
Germany
   (☎ 228-357 046, fax 353 951)
   Beethovenallee 21, 5300 Bonn 2

Consulate:
(☎ 211-800 85) Poststrasse 7, 4000 Düsseldorf
Consulate:
(☎ 511-323 834) Andraea-Strasse 1, 3000 Hanover
Consulate:
(☎ 089-283011) Barenstrasse 37, 8000 Munich 40
Consulate:
(☎ 711-83977) ASK-Kugellagerfabrik beim Bahnhof, 7015 Stuttgartt-Korntal
Israel
(☎ 3-751 7722, fax 751 7712)
Dan Hotel, 99 Hayarkon St, Tel Aviv; visas issued from 9 am to 1 pm, Sunday to Thursday
Lebanon
(☎ 1-922 500, fax 922 502)
Elias Helou Ave, Baabda, Beirut
Netherlands
(☎ 70-352 5161, fax 354 1046)
Van Stolkweg 1, 2585 JL, The Hague
Syria
(☎ 11-333 4642, fax 333 6741)
Al-Jala'a Ave, Damascus; visas issued from 9 am to 1.30 pm, Saturday to Wednesday
Turkey
(☎ 312-440 2054, fax 440 4327)
Mesnevi, Dedekorkut Sokak No 18, Çankaya, Ankara
Consulate:
(☎ 212-277 9704, fax 241 4331)
Istanbul
UK
(☎ 020-7937 3685, fax 7937 8795)
6 Upper Phillimore Gardens, London, W8 7HB
Web site www.jordanembassyuk.gov.jo
USA
(☎ 202-966 2909, fax 966 3110)
3504 International Drive NW, Washington DC 20008
Web site www.jordanembassyus.org

Embassies & Consulates in Jordan

Most of the foreign embassies and consulates listed below are in Amman (☎ 06); however, the German Honorary Consulate and the Egyptian Consulate are both situated in Aqaba (☎ 03). All of the following contact details are for embassies unless otherwise indicated.

Australia
(☎ 593 0246, fax 593 1260)
Zahran St, between 4th and 5th Circles; open from 7.30 am to 3.30 pm, Sunday to Thursday

Your Own Embassy

It's important to realise what your own embassy – the embassy of the country of which you're a citizen – can and cannot do to help you if you get into trouble.

Generally speaking, it won't be much help in emergencies if the trouble you're in is remotely your own fault. Remember that you're bound by the laws of the country you're in. Your embassy will not be sympathetic if you end up in jail after committing a crime locally, even if such actions are legal in your own country.

In genuine emergencies you might get some assistance, but only if other channels have been exhausted. For example, if you need to get home urgently, a free ticket home is exceedingly unlikely – the embassy would expect you to have insurance. If you have all your money and documents stolen, it might assist with getting a new passport, but a loan for onward travel is out of the question.

Canada
(☎ 566 6124, fax 568 9227)
Abdoun; open 8 am to 4.30 pm, Sunday to Wednesday, and until 1.30 pm on Thursday
Egypt
(☎ 560 5175, visas ☎ 560 5203, fax 560 4082)
Qurtubah St, next to the distinctive Dove Hotel; open 9 am to noon, Sunday to Thursday
Consulate:
(☎ 201 6171) On the corner of Al-Istiqlal and Al-Akhatal Sts in Aqaba, north of the city centre; open 9 am to 3 pm Sunday to Thursday
France
(☎ 464 1273, fax 465 9606)
Mutanabi St, Jebel Amman, between 3rd and 4th Circles; open 9 am to noon, Sunday to Thursday.
Web site www.ambafrance.org.jo
Germany
(☎ 593 0367, fax 593 2887)
31 Benghazi St, south of 4th Circle, Jebel Amman; open 8 am to 11 am, Sunday to Thursday
Consulate:
(☎ 201 3521) In the grounds of Coral Beach Hotel, King Hussein St, Aqaba; open 8 am to midday, Sunday to Wednesday

Israel
(☎ 552 4686, fax 552 4689)
Le Meridien Hotel, Shmeisani; open 8 to 11 am, Sunday to Thursday

Lebanon
(☎ 592 9111, fax 592 9113)
Nile St, Abdoun, near the UK Embassy; open 8 to 11 am, every day but Friday and Sunday

Netherlands
(☎ 593 0525, fax 593 0214)
Jordan InterContinental Hotel; open 9 am to noon, Sunday to Thursday

New Zealand
Consulate:
(☎ 463 6720, fax 463 4349)
Khalas Building, 99 Al-Malek al-Hussein St, Downtown; open 9 am to 1 pm, Sunday to Wednesday

Syria
(☎ 464 1935, fax 465 1945)
Afghani St, between 3rd and 4th Circles – a side street to the right (north) of the Spanish embassy; open 9 to 11 am, every day except Friday

UK
(☎ 592 3100, fax 591 3759)
Abdoun; open 8 am to 2 pm, Sunday to Thursday

USA
(☎ 592 0101, fax 592 0163)
Abdoun; open 8.30 am to 2.30 pm, Sunday to Thursday.
Web site www.usembassy-amman.org.jo

CUSTOMS

The usual goods are prohibited, eg drugs and weapons, but so are 'wireless equipment', which may include a mobile telephone (so keep it hidden), and 'immoral films, tapes (cassettes) and magazines' – but customs inspectors are not tough on this unless the stuff is pornographic. Anything obviously made in Israel – particularly books or magazines written in Hebrew – may be confiscated, but usually only at the Israel/Jordan borders, or after arriving by air from Tel Aviv.

The duty-free allowances for 'nonresidents' (ie tourists) are: 200 cigarettes or 25 cigars or 200g of tobacco; two bottles of wine or one bottle of spirits; and a 'reasonable amount of perfume for personal use'. Visitors are obliged to declare on arrival if they are carrying more than one camera and

gifts worth more than JD200. If so, the items are written on a slip of paper to ensure that you take them out again – or so the theory goes.

There are no restrictions on the import and export of Jordanian and foreign currency.

MONEY
Currency

The currency in Jordan is the Jordanian Dinar (JD) – known as the *gee-dee* among hip young locals and most visitors – which is made up of 1000 fils. You may also hear the terms *piastre* or *qirsh* used, which are both 10 fils – so 10 qirsh equals 100 fils. Sometimes when a price is quoted the unit of currency is omitted, so if you're told that something costs '25', work out whether it's 25 fils, 25 qirsh or 25 dinar! Just to complicate things a little more, 50 fils is sometimes referred to as a *shilling*, 100 fils (officially a *dirham*) as a *barisa*, and a dinar as a *lira*. However, most Jordanians avoid using these terms when dealing with foreigners, and prefer the less complicated 'fils' and 'dinars'.

Coins are 50, 100, 250 and 500 fils, and one dinar. The value of the coins are written in English; the numerals are in Arabic only. Each denomination has two different versions, often a different shape (circular or octagonal), colour (gold, silver or both) and names (eg '500 fils' or 'half-dinar'). Don't worry: even locals get confused. Some taxi drivers, and occasional unscrupulous merchants, sometimes use the confusing array of coins as a way to short-change foreigners, so take care.

Notes come in denominations of JD0.500, 1, 5, 10 and 20. For everyday use, the JD5 note is about as large as you want, but even finding change for a JD3.500 meal with a JD5 note can cause minor chaos in some restaurants. Try to change larger notes as often as possible at larger restaurants, and when paying your hotel bill.

The rates offered by the banks and moneychangers are slightly less than the official rate, ie about US$1 = JD0.7000 fils for cash at a bank or moneychanger, and about US$1 = JD0.6900 fils for travellers cheques at a moneychanger, but far less at a bank. The official exchange rates (and those offered by banks and moneychangers) are fairly consistent, and do not vary much from day to day.

The current exchange rates for most major foreign currencies are printed in the business sections of the English-language daily newspapers, the *Arab Daily* and the *Jordan Times*.

Exchange Rates

country	unit		dinar
Australia	A$1	=	JD0.5400
Canada	C$1	=	JD0.5651
euro	€1	=	JD0.7668
France	10FF	=	JD1.1085
Germany	DM1	=	JD0.3920
Japan	Y100	=	JD0.5892
New Zealand	NZ$1	=	JD0.4370
UK	UK£1	=	JD1.1559
USA	US$1	=	JD0.7100

Exchanging Money

Changing money is very easy in Jordan, and most major currencies are accepted in cash and travellers cheques. US dollars are the most accepted, followed by UK pounds and German Deutschmarks; however, you'll get absolutely nowhere with New Zealand dollars or Irish punts.

Jordanian currencies can sometimes be bought before leaving your home country, or in neighbouring countries (especially Syria), and there are no restrictions about the amount of dinars that can be brought into Jordan. It is possible to change dinars back into some foreign currencies in Jordan, but you'll need to show receipts to prove that you changed your currency into dinars at a bank in Jordan.

As a rule, the most widely recognised travellers cheques are American Express. Some banks, such as the Union Bank, which is a sort of 'agent' for Amex, will change nothing else – but still charges a hefty JD7 fee per transaction.

Cash and travellers cheques can be changed in large hotels (for guests and the public), but rates are always lower than those offered by the banks and moneychangers.

Banks There are banks all over Amman, and several in every major town throughout Jordan. All banks will change cash, and most change travellers cheques – but beware of commissions.

Banks seem to offer slightly better rates than moneychangers for cash, but the rates are not worth worrying about unless you're going to change a huge amount. However, all banks charge a hefty fee for changing travellers cheques – from JD3 per transaction to 10% of the amount changed – so change travellers cheques at a moneychanger.

One irritating demand made by some banks is to see the sales receipts for the cheques before changing them – directly contradicting the standard instructions to keep them separate. Sometimes they will relent; sometimes they won't.

There are small branches of some major banks at the borders and at the airports, but these charge high fees for changing travellers cheques and give lousy rates for cash, so change enough to last until you can reach a moneychanger. Some banks, particularly the Housing Bank, are fussy about the older (and apparently more 'counterfeitable') US dollar notes, and may not even accept them.

Moneychangers Despite offering slightly lower rates for cash than banks, moneychangers do not normally charge commission for travellers cheques – if a moneychanger starts mumbling about commissions, go somewhere else. Moneychanger offices are also smaller and easier to use than banks, and are open for far longer hours – usually every day from about 9 am to 9 pm. They can be found in Amman, Irbid, Wadi Mousa (near Petra) and Aqaba.

Credit Cards There are no local charges on credit card cash advances but the maximum daily withdrawal amount is JD500, whether over the counter or from an automatic teller machine (ATM). Whether you can get this much or not will depend on the conditions pertaining to your particular card, however. All banks have large signs (in English) outside indicating which credit cards they choose to accept.

Visa, which is the most widely accepted card for cash advances and ATMs, is accepted at most branches of the Housing Bank; Arab Bank; Bank of Jordan; ANZ Grindlays; Cairo-Amman Bank; Arab Banking Corporation; Jordan Arab Investment Bank; and the Jordan Investment & Finance Bank.

MasterCard is accepted at most branches of the Arab Bank; Jordan National Bank; British Bank of the Middle East; and Bank of Jordan. Other cards, such as Cirrus and Plus, are also accepted by some of the local banks and ATMs.

The emergency numbers to contact in Amman (☎ area code 06) if you lose your credit card are: American Express (☎ 560 7014); Visa (☎ 568 0554); Diners Club (☎ 567 5850); and MasterCard (☎ 465 5863). Amex has offices in Amman, Aqaba and Wadi Mousa (near Petra), but they do not change Amex travellers cheques (just hold mail for clients).

Most major credit cards are accepted at mid-range and top end hotels and restaurants, travel agents, larger souvenir shops and bookshops. However, always be sure to ask if any commission is being added on top of your purchase price. This can sometimes be as much as 5%; if so, it may be better to get a cash advance and pay with the paper stuff.

International Transfers Some major banks, eg the Arab Bank and Jordan National Bank, can arrange the international transfer of money. The Cairo-Amman Bank is part of the international service offered by Western Union and, at the time of research, the Bank of Jordan had just started a 'swift transfer service' (only in US dollars) with the US-based MoneyGram company. However, fees are high, so obtaining a cash advance with a credit card – and even changing travellers cheques at a bank (despite the commission) – is probably better.

Security

Money is about the most precious stuff you'll have on your trip, so it's worth looking after it. Although theft is not a real problem in Jordan, it's always wise to take basic precautions. Always carry your wallet (if you have one) in a front pocket, and don't have too much cash in it. The bulk of your money, travellers cheques and documents are better off in a pouch worn close to the skin. There are many types of pouch and moneybelts that you can hang around the neck or wear around the waist – most travel equipment shops sell several versions of this sort of thing. The best material in hot places like Jordan is cotton.

It's also sensible to leave some of your money hidden as a separate stash in your luggage (eg rolled up in a pair of thick socks) in case you find yourself in deep trouble at some point.

Costs

Jordan is not the cheapest country in the area to travel around, but it is possible to get by on a really tight budget and, if you spend wisely, good value can be found all over the country – with the exception of anywhere in or around Petra.

The most basic accommodation will generally cost about JD2/4 for a single/double room, but most decent budget places cost about JD5/8/11 for singles/doubles/triples; slightly more in Amman and Wadi Mousa (near Petra). A bed in a shared room ranges from about JD3 to JD5; and sleeping on the roof, about JD2 per person.

Snacks like *felafel* and *shwarma* (see the Food section later in this chapter) cost 250 to 500 fils; other decent meals, about JD1. A cup of tea normally costs about 250 fils; Turkish coffee, from 500 fils. A large 1.5L bottle of mineral water is about 300 fils; and a 650ml bottle of Amstel beer costs up to JD1.500 in a local bar. Public transport is cheap: less than 500 fils per hour of travel in a pubic bus or minibus, and about JD1 per hour in a more comfortable, long-distance private bus.

If you stay in a shared room or sleep on the roof at the cheapest possible hotel, eat nothing but felafel and shwarma and use public transport and/or hitch exclusively, it's possible to get by on about JD5/4 per day travelling as a single/double. In reality, most budget-minded travellers should allow at least JD9/7; about JD12/10 is more reasonable. If you add the cost of occasional chartered taxis, souvenirs, a splurge every now and then on a slap-up meal or a mid-range hotel, and the entrance fee to Petra, the cost per day for a budget-minded traveller is about JD15/12.

Tipping & Bargaining

Tips of 10% are generally expected in the better restaurants, except where a mandatory 'service charge' of 10% has been added. Elsewhere, rounding up the bill to the nearest 250 fils is appreciated by underpaid staff. Hotels in the mid-range and top end categories usually add a service charge of about 10%, plus a 'government tax' of another 10%, thereby adding considerably to the final bill.

Like most countries in the region, almost all prices are negotiable, except public transport (which is set by the government), food in grocery shops and meals and drinks in restaurants where prices are listed on a menu. Bargaining, especially when souvenir-hunting, is essential but shopkeepers are less likely than their Syrian and Egyptian counterparts to shift a long way from their original asking prices.

POST & COMMUNICATIONS
Postal Rates

To the UK and anywhere in Europe, postcards cost 200 fils, and normal-sized letters cost 300 fils. To Australia, New Zealand, the USA and Canada, postcards cost 300 fils, and normal-sized letters, 400 fils. Larger letters – rather than parcels – to the UK and Europe cost 300 fils for the first 10g, and 150 fils for every subsequent 10g; and to Australia, New Zealand, the USA and Canada, 400 fils for the first 10g, and 200 fils per extra 10g.

Parcel post is ridiculously expensive, so Jordan is not the best place from which to send some souvenirs home. To send anything by air to Australia, for example, the first 1kg costs JD12.700, and each subsequent 1kg, JD7.500. To the UK and Europe, the first 1kg is JD9.500, and then JD3.400 per extra 1kg; and to the USA and Canada, JD9.700, then JD5.600.

However, you may wish to avoid paying extra for 'air express'. (In my case, a letter

was sent 'air express' to Australia by sea and took about three months.) Sending things by sea is cheaper, but the costs seem to vary from one post office to another, and from one staff member to another, which does not inspire confidence about the likelihood of it reaching its destination.

Amman is the best place to send parcels from – refer to the Post section of the Amman chapter for more information about sending parcels home, and about grappling with the Customs Office.

Sending Mail

Stamps are available from all post offices, and from many souvenir shops where postcards are sold. All postcards and normal-sized letters can be dropped in any of the obvious post boxes around most towns. Letters posted from Jordan take up to two weeks to reach Australia and the USA; often as little as three or four days to the UK and Europe. Every town has a post office, but you're well advised to send things from major places like Amman, Madaba, Karak, Wadi Mousa (near Petra) and Aqaba.

A wide range of international courier companies, and quite a few homegrown versions, are flourishing in Jordan. Most are based in Amman (☎ 06), such as Federal Express (☎ 567 6062, fax 569 5720, email fedex@go.com.jo), TNT (☎ 565 9423) and DHL (☎ 681 8351).

Receiving Mail

The only reliable post restante services are at the main post office in Amman and Aqaba. If you send anything to a poste restante in another post office it's likely to end up in Amman anyway, so send it there. Note that packages sent to Jordan can end up at the Queen Alia international airport, where you'll have to battle with the Customs Department to determine whether any customs duty is applicable.

Telephone

The telephone system in Jordan has recently been privatised, and is now run by two companies: JPP and Alo. There are no longer any public telephone offices to make calls from, so visitors must either: (a) use a private telephone agency; (b) call from a hotel or shop; or (c) buy a telephone card for one of the 1000 or more pay phones operated by both companies throughout Jordan.

The pay phones operated by JPP accept telephone cards to the value of JD2 (but only good for local calls) and JD10; for Alo telephones, the cards cost JD3 (local calls only), JD5 or JD15. Cards for JPP phones cannot be used in Alo phones, and vice versa, but either can be bought at shops and stalls over the country. Alo phones are more widespread. The blue JPP pay phones, and the green and red Alo pay phones, are labelled in English, and easy to use. Booths with phones operated by both companies are located in tourist spots and around the main squares in larger towns.

Local calls within the same telephone area code cost 100 fils for three minutes. Most shopkeepers and hotel staff will make their telephones available for about 250 fils, and it costs about the same at a private telephone agency.

The major telephone area codes used in Jordan are:

Ajlun, Irbid, Jerash and Umm Qais	☎ 02
Aqaba, Karak, Ma'an, Wadi Mousa (near Petra) and Wadi Rum	☎ 03
Azraq, Dead Sea, Fuheis, Hammamat Ma'in, Madaba, Pella and Salt	☎ 05
Amman	☎ 06
All mobile telephones in Jordan	☎ 079

The cost of overseas calls from Jordan varies: the cheapest rates are between 10 pm and 8 am, and all day Friday and public holidays, when the charges for either company are about JD1.100 per minute to Europe, the USA and Canada; and about JD1.200 to Australia and New Zealand. The most expensive rate (about 25% more) is charged during Jordanian business hours.

Overseas calls can be made at any pay phone operated by JPP or Alo with the appropriate telephone cards, or from private telephone agencies in the central business districts and around tourist spots. Rates at the private agencies do vary, so shop around if you're making a lengthy long-distance call. They range from JD1 to JD1.500 per minute to most western countries, ie most of Europe, Australia, New Zealand, Canada and the USA. Overseas calls from hotels cost substantially more than using a telephone card or a private telephone agency. For example, the smaller hotels charge about JD3 to JD4 per minute for a call to Europe; the bigger hotels often charge more.

When ringing Jordan from overseas, firstly dial the international access code in your country, followed by Jordan's international area code of ☎ 962, then the internal area code (listed earlier) and finally the individual number.

Reverse-charge telephone calls are normally not possible, and the Home Country Direct Dial service is not available. Jordan is covered by the GSM Cellular Network and mobile telephones can be rented for all sorts of different rates from companies such as Mobile Zone (☎/fax Amman 06-581 8294, email thezone@nets.com.jo).

Although telephone directories in English and Arabic are published, along with a Yellow Pages in English, finding either anywhere in Jordan can be very difficult. The libraries in the cultural centres and bigger hotels in Amman might possibly have a copy. Some useful telephone numbers are listed below. All numbers of more than four digits are in Amman; the other numbers listed can be dialled from anywhere in Jordan for free.

Fire Brigade	☎ 461 7101
First Aid & Ambulance	☎ 193
Hotel Complaints	☎ 461 3103
International Directory Assistance	☎ 0132
Local Directory Assistance	
Amman	☎ 121
Elsewhere	☎ 131
Ministry of Foreign Affairs	☎ 464 4361
Police	☎ 191/192
Post Office Information	☎ 121
Price Complaints	☎ 566 1176
Public Transport Complaints	☎ 464 2311
Queen Alia international airport	☎ 445 2700
Traffic Police	☎ 489 6390

Fax

The main post offices in Amman and Aqaba can arrange telegrams, telexes and faxes. The cost for a fax depends on the destination and the time it takes to send it, and is charged at the rates mentioned in the preceding Telephone section. Most hotels in the larger towns also send and receive telexes and faxes for guests, but at higher costs than the post office.

Email & Internet Access

Jordan is now truly part of the 'cyber-world', and boasts eight Internet Service Providers (ISPs). All are based in Amman, which means that using the Internet in somewhere like Aqaba is four times more expensive than in Amman, because of the long-distance rates involved in contacting the ISPs.

Internet Centres in Jordan There are now over 70 Internet centres across Jordan, including Amman, Wadi Mousa (near Petra), Ma'an, Madaba, Aqaba and Irbid. The most competitive rates, and the highest number of Internet centres, are located outside the major universities, eg Yarmouk University at Irbid and the University of Jordan in northern Amman. Costs range from about JD1.500 per hour in Amman and Irbid to about JD8 per hour in Aqaba. These places are not really 'Internet Cafes' as such, although tea, coffee and soft drinks are often available.

Travelling With Your Computer Travelling with a portable computer is a great way to stay in touch with life back home, but unless you know what you're doing it's fraught with potential problems. If you plan to carry your notebook or palmtop computer with you, remember that the power supply voltage in Jordan may vary from that at home, risking damage to your equipment. The best investment is a universal AC adaptor which will enable you to plug in your appliance anywhere without frying its innards. You may also need a plug adaptor for Jordan, which is easier to buy before you leave home.

Also, your PC-card modem may or may not work once you leave your home country – and you won't know for sure until you try.

The safest option is to buy a reputable 'global' modem before you leave home, or buy a local PC-card modem if you're spending an extended time in Jordan. Keep in mind that the telephone socket in Jordan will probably be different from that at home, so ensure that you have at least a US RJ-11 telephone adaptor that works with your modem. You can almost always find an adaptor that will convert from RJ-11 to the local variety. For more information on travelling with a portable computer, see the two Web sites www.teleadapt.com or www.warrior.com.

Major ISPs such as AOL (www.aol.com), CompuServe (www.compuserve.com) and IBM Net (www.ibm.net) have dial-in nodes throughout Europe, but not in Jordan; it's best to download a list of the dial-in numbers before you leave home. If you access your Internet email account at home through a smaller ISP or your office or school network, your best option is either to open an account with a global ISP, like those mentioned above, or to rely on Internet centres to collect your mail.

If you intend to rely on Internet centres, you'll need to carry three pieces of information with you to enable you to access your Internet mail account: your incoming (POP or IMAP) mail server name; your account name; and your password. Your ISP or network supervisor will be able to give you these. Armed with this information, you should be able to access your Internet mail account from any net-connected machine in the world, provided it runs some kind of email software (remember that Netscape and Internet Explorer both have mail modules). It pays to become familiar with this before you leave home.

A final option to collect mail through Internet centres is to open a free Web-based email account such as HotMail (www.hot mail.com) or Yahoo! Mail (www.mail.ya hoo.com). You can access your mail from anywhere in the world from any net-connected machine using a standard Web browser.

INTERNET RESOURCES

The World Wide Web is a rich resource for travellers. You can research your trip, hunt down bargain air fares, book hotels, check on weather conditions or chat with locals and other travellers about the best places to visit (or avoid!).

There's no better place to start your Web explorations than the Lonely Planet Web site (www.lonelyplanet.com). Here you'll find succinct summaries on travelling to most places on earth, postcards from other travellers and the Thorn Tree bulletin board, where you can ask questions before you go or dispense advice when you get back. You can also find travel news and updates to many of our most popular guidebooks, and the sub-WWWay section links you to the most useful travel resources elsewhere on the Web.

Useful Web Sites

Web sites have an annoying habit of coming and going, but the following should provide a useful starting point for researching your trip to Jordan. More specific Web sites are listed in the appropriate sections in the book.

Access to Arabia
  www.access2arabia.com/arabworld/Jordan
  (the best place to start)
Baladna
  www.jordan-online.com
  (excellent for general information, links and chat lines)
Hamas
  www.hamas.org
  (for an alternative view of the Israel-Palestine situation)
Jordan Government
  www.petra.gov.jo
  (about Petra and other major sites)
Jordan Hotels Assocation
  www.johotels.com
  (information and bookings for upmarket hotels)
Jordan Travel Exchange
  www.mideasttravelnet.com/jte
  (airline and travel information and bookings)
Primus' World
  www.cns.com.jo
  (with a useful Jordan Directory)
Webs of Jordan
  www.websofjordan.com.jo
  (sports, history, business etc)

BOOKS

Most books are published in quite different editions by different publishers in different countries. As a result, a book might be a hardcover rarity in one country while it's readily available in paperback in another. Fortunately, bookshops and libraries search by title or author, so your local bookshop or library is best placed to advise you on the availability of the following recommendations.

Lonely Planet

If you're heading to other countries in the region, Lonely Planet also publishes books devoted to Jordan's neighbours in *Syria, Lebanon* and *Israel & the Palestinian Territories*. Travellers contemplating a longer swing through several countries of the Middle East should check out other Lonely Planet titles to the area, particularly the *Middle East* (which also covers Libya, Egypt, Syria, Lebanon, Israel & the Palestinian Territories, Turkey, Iran, Iraq, the Gulf States and Yemen), *Turkey, Iran, Egypt* and *Istanbul to Cairo*. There are also phrasebooks, including (Egyptian) Arabic.

Annie Caulfield's *Kingdom of the Film Stars: Journey into Jordan* is an entertaining, personal account of the author's relationship with a Bedouin man. This is part of Journeys, Lonely Planet's travel literature series.

Guidebooks

We hope that you'll rarely need any more information than this guidebook offers, but you may crave more detailed information about specific archaeological sites or tourist attractions, or want to buy a souvenir book as a memento of somewhere special, eg Petra. Guidebooks to places like Petra and Jerash are mentioned in the relevant sections in the rest of this book.

MG Graphic Formula publishes a series of souvenir-cum-guidebooks, such as the general *Jordan: History, Culture & Traditions*, and more specific ones about Jerash and Petra. They're published in English, French, Dutch, Italian, German and Dutch, and are widely available in Jordan for JD4 to JD6.

The booklets published in English, French and Italian by Al-Kutba in Amman cover Jerash, Amman, Umm Qais, Pella, Madaba and Mt Nebo, the desert castles, Wadi Rum and Umm al-Jimal. They are portable, affordable (JD3) and detailed, and available at most major bookshops in Jordan. Another decent pocket-sized guide is *This Way Jordan* by Jack Altman. It has a distinctive yellow cover, and is published by JPM Publications (JD5). Arabesque also publishes a series of colourful pocket-sized guides (JD5) to Amman, Jerash and Petra.

A few private companies publish ·free booklets for tourists visiting Jordan, but they are all frustratingly very hard to find. *Jordan Today*, published monthly by Info-Media International, features some information about cultural events and entertainment; *Your Guide to Amman*, also published monthly, includes almost nothing but ads for car rental companies and travel agencies; and *Jordan Tourism & The Holy Land*, published annually by Remoon (remoon@usa.com), is one of a series of detailed and informative guides to Jordan (and Israel).

Travel
Most of the early and more contemporary travellers (like many visitors these days) came through Jordan as part of their travels around the Middle East.

In the late 19th century, the archaeologist Selah Merrill set off to the explore what is modern Jordan, the area he called *East of the Jordan*. His book is one of the very few written in the 19th century about this area.

Johann Ludwig (also known as Jean Louis) Burckhardt spent many years in the early 19th century travelling extensively through Jordan, Syria and the Holy Land, disguised as a pilgrim and compiling a unique and scholarly travelogue detailing every facet of the culture and society he encountered along the way. The result is *Travels in Syria and the Holy Land*, which mentions his 'discovery' of Petra (see the boxed text in the Petra chapter for details).

The redoubtable English woman Gertrude Bell wrote a few memoirs including the fairly dated and light-hearted *The Desert and the Sown* about her travels in the region in the early 20th century. She, and other travellers, are also mentioned in James Simmons' *Passionate Pilgrims: English Travellers to the World of the Desert Arabs*.

History & Politics
On Jordan's recent history, there is the somewhat gushing *Hussein of Jordan* by James Lunt. A slightly more serious look at Jordanian history is Kamal Salibi's *The Modern History of Jordan*, spanning from the 1920s to the Gulf Wars. A more academic and dry work is Ma'an Abu Nowar's *The History of the Hashemite Kingdom of Jordan*.

For a look at the country in the wider perspective of its position among shaky neighbours, *Jordan in the Middle East:1948-1985* is an insightful collection of essays edited by Joseph Nevo and Ilan Pappé. *King's Highway* by Graeme Nonnan is a potted history of Jordan, based around the country's historical central positioning.

One of the numerous books about King Hussein – all written before his death in 1999 – is *A Life on the Edge: King Hussein* by Roland Dallas.

Among a couple of general recommended histories of the Arabs is Philip Hitti's *History of the Arabs*, which is something of a classic. A more recent and widely acclaimed work is *A History of the Arab Peoples*, by Albert Hourani. It's as much an attempt to convey a sense of the evolution of Muslim Arab societies as a straightforward history, with extensive treatment of various aspects of social, cultural and religious life.

Contemporary Middle Eastern affairs are treated in *The Modern Middle East*, edited by Albert Hourani, Phillip Khoury and Mary Wilson. Peter Mansfield has written several works, including *The Arabs* and *A History of the Middle East*. A unique approach to the subject is *The Longman Companion to the Middle East Since 1914*, by Ritchie Ovendale, which presents a series of chronologies, biographies and dictionaries of key names and events (a handy reference work).

Readers of French might find Joseph Burlot's *La Civilisation Islamique*, a manageable introduction to the history not only of the Arab world but of all those countries that have come under the sway of Islam. Dominique & Janine Sourdel's *La Civilisation de l'Islam Classique* is a more thorough work on the Islamic world in its glory days, from the 9th to the 12th centuries.

General

Religion Getting a handle on Middle Eastern history and culture, and just to have an inkling of some of the reasoning behind much of what you see in day-to-day life in Jordan, requires at least some knowledge of Islam. One of the better, short, accounts of Islamic belief and practices is *Mohammedanism – An Historical Survey*, by HAR Gibb. The Quran itself might seem daunting, but there are several translations around. AJ Arberry's *The Koran Interpreted* and *The Meaning of the Holy Qur'an* by Abdullah Yusuf Ali are among the better ones.

Culture & Society For a general look at the life of women in Muslim countries, one introduction worth some time is Wiebke Walther's *Women in Islam: From Medieval to Modern Times*.

The World of Islam, by Bernard Lewis, is a cross between a light introduction and a coffee-table size picture book; it's an unwieldy, but highly attractive, tome. For something a little more prosaic, try Professor RM Savory's *Introduction to Islamic Civilisation*.

Photography *High Above Jordan*, an officially sanctioned book of aerial photographs by Jane Taylor, is unexceptional (JD20). One classy glossy is *Journey Through Jordan* by Mohammed Amin, Duncan Willetts and Sam Wiley. For a rare look into the Jordan long gone, Malise Ruthuen's *Freya Stark in the Levant* provides a selection of this remarkable British writer's photographs from the region. Stark travelled all over the Middle East and left behind some 50,000 photos, many dating to the early decades of this century and as yet largely uncatalogued.

Flora & Fauna Anyone interested in the flora of Jordan should pick up the detailed *Wildflowers of Jordan and Neighbouring Countries* by Dawud MH Al-Eisawi, with beautiful illustrations and photographs (all captioned in English). *The Birds of the Hashemite Kingdom of Jordan* by Ian J Andrews is the definitive work about our feathered friends. *Wild Mammals of HK Jordan* by Adnan Y Dajani, and *Mammals of the Holy Land* by Mazin Q Qumsiyeh, are comprehensive and colourful.

Arts & Architecture *Treasures from an Ancient Land*, by the renowned Arabist Pitor Bienkowski, specialises in the pottery, sculpture and jewellery of Jordan.

If you're serious about looking for quality rugs, kilims and the like, it could pay to first consult *Oriental Rugs – A Buyer's Guide* by Essie Sakhai; or the identically titled book by Lee Allane. Books dealing with the intricate and complex artform of Arabic calligraphy include *Calligraphy and Islamic Culture*, by Annemarie Schimmel. On a less exalted level, Heather Colyer Ross looks into popular art forms with her book, *The Art of Bedouin Jewellery*, a useful asset for those contemplating buying up the stuff.

If you're interested in learning more about Muslim religious architecture and its permutations, *The Mosque*, edited by Martin Frishman and Hasan Uddin Khan, is beautifully illustrated and detailed.

Bookshops in Jordan Amman has a good range of bookshops with titles in English (and, occasionally, other languages), but none offer a total selection of available titles. There are also two excellent bookshops in Aqaba; although called 'libraries', the books are for buying, not borrowing.

NEWSPAPERS & MAGAZINES

Jordan maintains a reasonably free media, although the government does exercise its muscle about reports which displease it. According to some journalists in the country, pressure is still exercised from time to time on writers and editors, so the bulk of newspapers (in Arabic and English) all too often push an editorial line curiously similar to the government's position. By regional standards, however, the controls are loose.

Two English-language newspapers are published every day, except for Fridays, in Amman, and are also available in Amman and Aqaba. The *Jordan Times* (200 fils) has a reasonably impartial outlook and gives good coverage of events in Jordan, elsewhere in the Middle East and worldwide; and the tabloid

Arab Daily (400 fils) has interesting art and culture sections on Thursday.

Every day (but Friday) both newspapers list emergency telephone numbers, relevant anywhere in Jordan; telephone numbers for important government departments and pharmacies in Amman, and the hospitals throughout Jordan; the arrival and departure times for all international and domestic flights; and television programs for the English- and French-language Channel 2.

Subtitled 'Jordan's Political, Economic and Cultural Weekly', the *Star* (400 fils) is an English-language tabloid published every Wednesday in Amman, with a supplement in French called *Le Jourdain.*

Of the many local Arabic daily and weekly newspapers printed in Amman, *Ad-Dustour*, *Al-Ra'i* and *Al-Aswaq* are among the more popular.

Some major European daily newspapers, such as the *International Herald Tribune* (surprisingly reasonable value at JD1.250), *The Times* (from the UK) and *Le Monde* from France (JD1.500) are available in bookshops in Downtown Amman, upmarket hotels in the capital, and at the two major bookshops in Aqaba. These newspapers are generally not more than two days old, but it can cost as much as JD6 for a copy of the hefty *Sunday Times* from the UK.

Current issues of international magazines, such as *Der Spiegel* from Germany, and *Time* and *Newsweek*, are available at major bookshops in Amman and Aqaba, but are not cheap.

RADIO & TV

The Jordanian government maintains more control over local radio and television than it does over the newspapers, because the stations are controlled by the state.

Radio Jordan transmits in English on 96.3FM, and 90.0FM in French. Radio Monte Carlo (74.4FM) broadcasts from Paris (via Cyprus), and features news in French and Arabic, and western music later in the day.

If you have a short wave radio, Voice of America, the BBC World Service and most major European stations can be picked up

easily. The BBC alters its programing every six months or so, and the British Council in Amman has the latest information.

Jordan TV offers three channels. Channels 1 and 3 broadcast in Arabic, and Channel 2 features bad Australian soap operas, worse American sitcoms and locally produced news all in English; and documentaries in French. Programs on Channel 2 run every day from about 4 pm to midnight.

International satellite stations, such as the BBC, CNN and MTV are found in the homes of most wealthy Jordanians, all rooms in top end hotels and, often, the lobby of any budget and mid-range hotel. There is no censorship, and dingy bars are sometimes full of local watching a soft-porn channel from northern Europe. The programs offered by the mainstream satellite stations are listed in the *Arab Daily* every day (but Friday).

Jordanians may not like the Israelis, but they don't mind watching Israeli TV, which is relaxed and easy to pick up in southern Jordan. Even if the programs broadcast in Israel have no subtitles in Arabic, any episode of something like *Baywatch* will attract a healthy audience (of men).

PHOTOGRAPHY & VIDEO
Film & Equipment

Most western brands of print and slide film are available throughout Jordan, but at tourist sites (especially Petra) the prices are, of course, horrendous.

In Amman, a roll of Kodak 24/36 print film costs about JD2.650/3.500; Fuji and lesser-known brands are a little cheaper. Developing a roll of 24 prints costs about JD3.850 (if returned on the same day) or about JD3.350 (for the next day); about JD5.400 (same day) or about JD4.700 (next day) for 36 prints. A roll of 36 slide film costs a whopping JD7.900, excluding developing (a roll of 24 slide film is almost impossible to buy). Developing a roll of 24 or 36 slide film (mounted) costs about JD5 (next day).

Technical Tips

The single biggest factor to take into account is light. Try to work it so that you have your back to any sources of light (sunlight or artificial); the idea is to have light falling onto your subject. If the facade of a building you want to photograph is in shadow, try to come back at another time of day when it's lying in sunlight.

The sun shines strong and hard in Jordan. Taking pictures in the middle of the day is virtually a guarantee of ending up with glary, washed out results. Where possible, try to exploit the softer light of the early morning and late afternoon, which enhances subtleties in colour and eliminates problems of glare. If you do need to take shots in bright light use a lens filter. As a rule, 100 ASA film is what you'll need most, although a couple of rolls of 200 ASA and/or 400 ASA can be handy for the odd occasion when the light is not so strong.

Restrictions

Photography in military zones such as 'strategic areas' like bridges, public buildings is forbidden.

Photographing People

Taking pictures of anything that suggests any degree of squalor, even the hectic activity of the marketplace, can offend some people's sense of pride. Sensitivity about the negative aspects of their country leads some Jordanians to become quite hostile about snappers.

A zoom lens is great for taking people shots, usually without being noticed. Some Jordanians, women in particular, object to being photographed, so ask first. Persisting if your snapping is unwelcome can lead to ugly scenes, so exercise caution and common sense. Children will generally line up to be photographed.

Airport Security

All airports in Jordan have X-ray machines for checking luggage. Despite assurances that they are safe for camera film, it's better to keep any unexposed film somewhere where it can be easily removed for examination.

Video

Properly used, a video camera can give a fascinating record of your holiday. As well as videoing the obvious things – sunsets and spectacular views – remember to record some of the ordinary, everyday details of life in the country. Often the most interesting things occur when you're actually intent on filming something else. Remember too that, unlike still photography, video 'flows' – so, for example, you can shoot scenes of the countryside rolling past the train window to give an overall impression that isn't possible with ordinary photos.

Video cameras these days have amazingly sensitive microphones, and you might be surprised how much sound will be picked up. This can also be a problem if there's a lot of ambient noise: filming by the side of a busy road might seem OK when you do it, but viewing it back home might simply give you a deafening cacophony of traffic noise. One good rule to follow for beginners is to try to film in long takes, and don't move the camera around too much. Otherwise, your video could well make your viewers seasick! If your camera has a stabiliser, you can use it to obtain good footage while travelling on various means of transport, even on bumpy roads. And remember, you're on holiday – don't let the video take over your life, and turn your trip into a Cecil B de Mille production.

Make sure you keep the batteries charged, and have the necessary charger, plugs and transformer for Jordan. It's usually worth buying at least a few cassettes duty free to start off your trip, but blank cassettes are available in major towns in Jordan.

Finally, remember to follow the same rules regarding people's sensitivities as for still photography – having a video camera shoved in their face is probably even more annoying and offensive for locals than a still camera. Always ask permission first.

TIME

Around mid-1999, the Jordanian government (after much prevarication over this controversial issue) decided to permanently bring forward the time in Jordan by one hour – ie three hours ahead of Greenwich Mean Time (GMT) – and, at the same time, abolish daylight summer time. This means that sunrise in summer is often about 4.15

am, and the *muezzin* (the official calling the faithful to prayer) starts at about 2.45 am!

There are no time differences within Jordan, so when it's midday in Jordan, the time elsewhere is:

Los Angeles	1 am
New York	4 am
London	9 am
Paris and Rome	10 am
Beirut, Damascus and Tel Aviv	11 am
Riyadh	12 noon
Perth and Hong Kong	5 pm
Sydney	7 pm
Auckland	9 pm

Time is a commodity that Arabs always seem to have plenty of – something that should take five minutes will invariably take one hour. Trying to speed things up will only lead to frustration – for you. It's better to take it philosophically than try to fight it. A bit of patience goes a long way in Jordan.

ELECTRICITY

Jordan's electricity supply is 220V, 50 AC. Sockets are generally of the European two-pronged variety, although in southern Jordan (particularly in Aqaba) you're more likely to find the British three-pronged ones. Anyone taking electrical appliances and who intends travelling all over Jordan should bring (if necessary) two different types of adaptors. Power is generated by the two large oil-fired generating plants in Zarqa and Aqaba, and supply is usually reliable and uninterrupted.

WEIGHTS & MEASURES

Jordan uses the metric system. There is a standard conversion table at the back of this guidebook.

LAUNDRY

In the bigger cities, ie Amman and Aqaba, and places where tourists flock, ie Wadi Mousa (near Petra), there are plenty of places where washing, dry cleaning and ironing can be done. Look for any place with a sign 'Dry Cleaning', or ask at your hotel.

A pair of trousers or a skirt will cost about 400 fils to wash; a T-shirt, shirt or blouse about 250 fils. It can take as little as 24 hours, but sometimes longer. Ironing costs extra (negotiable) per item. Underwear and socks cost about 150 fils each to wash, but your 'smalls' can be easily washed in your hotel room, where hot water is available and the dry weather ensures quick drying.

TOILETS

Except in mid-range and top end hotels and restaurants, toilets are the hole-in-the-floor variety. They are theoretically more hygienic because only your covered feet come into contact with anything but, in reality, toilets in most communal hotel bathrooms, and all public toilets, are grotty, and the sewerage system always seems inadequate.

It does take a little while to master the squatting technique without losing everything from your pockets. There is always a tap and/or hose at a convenient height if you wish to adopt the local habit of using your left hand and water – whether any water comes out is something else again! Toilet paper is rarely offered, except in the top end hotels and restaurants, but is widely available in shops throughout Jordan. Please remember that the little basket usually provided in the toilet is for toilet paper; trying to flush it will soon clog the system. A few public toilets in the larger cities are indicated on the maps in this guidebook.

HEALTH

Travel health depends on your predeparture preparations, your daily health care while travelling and how you handle any medical problem that does develop. While the potential dangers can seem quite frightening, in reality few travellers experience anything more than an upset stomach.

Predeparture planning

Immunisations Plan ahead for getting your vaccinations: some of them require more than one injection, while some vaccinations should not be given together. Note that some vaccinations should not be given during

Medical Kit Check List

Following is a list of items you should consider including in your medical kit – consult your pharmacist for brands available in your country.

☐ **Aspirin or paracetamol (acetaminophen in the USA)** – for pain or fever
☐ **Antihistamine** – for allergies, eg, hay fever; to ease the itch from insect bites or stings; and to prevent motion sickness
☐ **Cold and flu tablets, throat lozenges and nasal decongestant**
☐ **Multivitamins** – consider for long trips, when dietary vitamin intake may be inadequate
☐ **Antibiotics** – consider including these if you're travelling well off the beaten track; see your doctor, as they must be prescribed, and carry the prescription with you
☐ **Loperamide or diphenoxylate** –'blockers' for diarrhoea
☐ **Prochlorperazine or metaclopramide** – for nausea and vomiting
☐ **Rehydration mixture** – to prevent dehydration, which may occur, for example, during bouts of diarrhoea; particularly important when travelling with children
☐ **Insect repellent, sunscreen, lip balm and eye drops**
☐ **Calamine lotion, sting relief spray or aloe vera** – to ease irritation from sunburn and insect bites or stings
☐ **Antifungal cream or powder** – for fungal skin infections and thrush
☐ **Antiseptic (such as povidone-iodine)** – for cuts and grazes
☐ **Bandages, Band-Aids (plasters) and other wound dressings**
☐ **Water purification tablets or iodine**
☐ **Scissors, tweezers and a thermometer** – note that mercury thermometers are prohibited by airlines
☐ **Syringes and needles** – in case you need injections in a country with medical hygiene problems; ask your doctor for a note explaining why you have them

pregnancy or to people with allergies – discuss this with your doctor.

It's recommended that you seek medical advice at least six weeks before travel. Be aware that there is often a greater risk of disease with children and during pregnancy.

Discuss your requirements with your doctor, but vaccinations you should consider for this trip include the following (for more details about the diseases themselves, see the individual disease entries later in this section). Carry proof of your vaccinations, especially yellow fever, as this is sometimes needed to enter some countries – a condition of entry to Jordan is proof of yellow fever vaccination if you're coming from infected areas (such as sub-Saharan Africa, and parts of South America). Yellow fever, however, is not a risk in Jordan.

Diphtheria & Tetanus Vaccinations for these two diseases are usually combined and are recommended for everyone. After an initial course of three injections (usually given in childhood), boosters are necessary every 10 years.

Polio Everyone should keep up to date with this vaccination, which is normally given in childhood. A booster every 10 years maintains immunity.

Hepatitis A Hepatitis A vaccine (eg Avaxim, Havrix 1440 or VAQTA) provides long-term immunity (possibly for more than 10 years) after an initial injection and a booster at six to 12 months.

Alternatively, an injection of gamma globulin can provide short-term protection against hepatitis A – two to six months, depending on the dose. It's not a vaccine, but is a ready-made antibody collected from blood donations. It's reasonably effective and, unlike the vaccine, it's protective immediately, but because it is a blood product, there are current concerns about its long-term safety.

Hepatitis A vaccine is also available in a combined form, Twinrix, with hepatitis B vaccine. Three injections over a six-month period are required, the first two providing substantial protection against hepatitis A.

Typhoid Vaccination against typhoid is recommended if you're travelling for more than a couple of weeks in Jordan. It's now available either as an injection or as capsules to be taken orally.

Cholera The current injectable vaccine against cholera is very poorly protective and has many side effects, so it's not generally recommended for use by travellers. However, in some situations it may be necessary to have a certificate as travellers are very occasionally asked by immigration officials to present one (but not in Jordan), even though all countries and the World Health Organisation (WHO) have dropped cholera immunisation as a health requirement for entry.

Hepatitis B Travellers who should consider vaccination against hepatitis B include those on a long trip, as well as those visiting countries where there are high levels of hepatitis B infection, where blood transfusions may not be adequately screened or where sexual contact or needle sharing is a possibility. Vaccination generally involves three injections, with a booster available at 12 months. More rapid courses are often available if required.

Rabies Vaccination should be considered by those who will spend a month or longer in a country where rabies is common (rabies is not common in Jordan), especially if they're cycling, handling animals, caving or travelling to remote areas – and for children (who may not report a bite). Pretravel rabies vaccination involves having three injections over 21 to 28 days. If someone who has been vaccinated is bitten or scratched by an animal, they will require two booster injections of vaccine; those not vaccinated require more.

Malaria Malaria is not a problem in Jordan. While anti-malarial tablets are not required for Jordan, they may be a necessary precaution for other countries in the region, depending on where you are travelling. Check with your doctor before leaving home.

Everyday Health

Normal body temperature is up to 37°C (98.6°F); more than 2°C (4°F) higher indicates a high fever. The normal adult pulse rate is 60 to 100 per minute (children 80 to 100, babies 100 to 140). As a general rule the pulse increases about 20 beats per minute for each 1°C (2°F) rise in fever.

Respiration (breathing) rate is also an indicator of illness. Count the number of breaths per minute: between 12 and 20 is normal for adults and older children (up to 30 for younger children, 40 for babies). People with a high fever or serious respiratory illness breathe more quickly than normal. More than 40 shallow breaths a minute may indicate pneumonia.

Health Insurance

Make sure that you have adequate health insurance. See Travel Insurance under Visas & Documents earlier in this chapter for details.

Travel Health Guides

If you're planning to be away or travelling in remote areas for a long period of time, you may like to consider taking a more detailed health guide with you.

CDC's Complete Guide to Healthy Travel, Open Road Publishing, 1997 – the US Centers for Disease Control & Prevention recommendations for international travel.

Staying Healthy in Asia, Africa & Latin America, by Dirk Schroeder, Moon Publications, 1994 – probably the best all-round guide to carry, it's detailed and well organised.

Travellers' Health, Dr Richard Dawood, Oxford University Press, 1995 – comprehensive, easy to read, authoritative and highly recommended, although it is rather large to lug around.

Where There Is No Doctor, by David Werner, Macmillan, 1994 – a very detailed guide intended for someone, such as a Peace Corps worker, going to work in an underdeveloped country.

Travel with Children, by Maureen Wheeler, Lonely Planet Publications, 1995 – includes advice on travel health for younger children.

There are also a number of excellent travel health sites on the Internet. From the Lonely Planet home page at www.lonelyplanet.com there are links to the WHO, and the US Centers for Disease Control & Prevention.

Other Preparations

Make sure you're healthy before you start travelling. If you're going on a long trip make sure your teeth are OK. If you wear glasses take a spare pair and your prescription.

If you require a particular medication take an adequate supply, as it may not be available in Jordan. Take part of the packaging showing the generic name rather than the brand, which will make getting replacements easier. It's a good idea to have a legible prescription or letter from your doctor to show that you legally use the medication to avoid any problems.

Basic Rules

Food There is an old colonial adage which says: 'If you can cook it, boil it or peel it you can eat it ... otherwise forget it.' However, in Jordan, most restaurants are clean and the chances of getting sick from unhygienic food handling and preparation (as opposed to getting sick simply from a change in diet) are slim. Beware of ice cream which is sold in the street or anywhere it might have been melted and refrozen; if there's any doubt (eg a power cut in the last day or two), steer well clear. Shellfish such as mussels, oysters and clams should be avoided as well as undercooked meat, particularly in the form of mince. Steaming does not make shellfish safe for eating.

Generally, if a place looks clean and well run, and the vendor looks clean and healthy, then the food is probably safe. Places that are packed with travellers or locals will be fine, while empty restaurants are questionable. The food in busy restaurants is cooked and eaten quite quickly with little standing around, and is probably not reheated.

Water Generally, the number one rule for travelling in the region is *be careful of the water*, and especially ice. If you don't know

for certain that the water is safe, assume the worst. Reputable brands of bottled water or soft drinks are generally fine, although in some places bottles may be refilled with tap water. Take care with fruit juice, particularly if water may have been added. Milk should be treated with suspicion because it's sometimes unpasteurised, although boiled milk is fine if it's kept hygienically. Tea or coffee should also be OK, because the water should have been boiled.

The tap water is usually OK in Jordan – but *not* in the Jordan Valley where amoebic dysentery is a problem. It always pays to add a water purification tablet or two (see below) to the tap water; this avoids buying

---

Nutrition

If your food is poor or limited in availability, if you're travelling hard and fast and therefore missing meals or if you simply lose your appetite, you can soon start to lose weight and place your health at risk.

Make sure your diet is well balanced. Cooked eggs, tofu, beans, lentils and nuts are all safe ways to get protein. Fruit you can peel (bananas, oranges or mandarins, for example) is usually safe (melons can harbour bacteria in their flesh and are best avoided) and a good source of vitamins. Try to eat plenty of grains (including rice) and bread. Remember that although food is generally safer if it's cooked well, overcooked food loses much of its nutritional value. If your diet isn't well balanced, or if your food intake is insufficient, it's a good idea to take vitamin and iron pills.

In hot climates make sure you drink enough – don't rely on feeling thirsty to indicate when you should drink. Not needing to urinate or small amounts of very dark yellow urine is a danger sign. Always carry a water bottle with you on long trips. Excessive sweating can lead to loss of salt and therefore muscle cramping. Salt tablets are not a good idea as a preventative, but in places where salt is not used much, adding salt to food can help.

masses of expensive non-biodegradable plastic bottles of mineral water.

Water Purification The simplest way of purifying water is to boil it thoroughly. Vigorous boiling should be satisfactory; however, at high altitude water boils at a lower temperature, so germs are less likely to be killed. Boil it for longer in these environments.

Consider purchasing a water filter for a long trip. There are two main kinds of filter. Total filters take out all parasites, bacteria and viruses and make water safe to drink. They're often expensive, but they can be more cost effective than buying bottled water. Simple filters (which can even be a nylon mesh bag) take out dirt and larger foreign bodies from the water so that chemical solutions work much more effectively; if water is dirty, chemical solutions may not work at all. It's very important when buying a filter to read the specifications, so that you know exactly what it removes from the water and what it doesn't. Remember also that to operate effectively a water filter must be regularly maintained; a poorly maintained filter can be a breeding ground for germs.

Simple filtering will not remove all dangerous organisms, so if you cannot boil water it should be treated chemically. Chlorine tablets will kill many pathogens, but not some parasites like giardia and amoebic cysts. Iodine is more effective in purifying water and is available in tablet form. Follow the directions carefully and remember that too much iodine can be harmful.

Medical Problems & Treatment

Self-diagnosis and treatment can be risky, so you should always seek medical help. An embassy, consulate or five-star hotel can usually recommend a local doctor or clinic. Although we do give drug dosages in this section, they are for emergency use only. Correct diagnosis is vital. In this section we have used the generic names for medications – check with a pharmacist for brands available locally.

Note that antibiotics should ideally be administered only under medical supervision. Take only the recommended dose at the prescribed intervals and use the whole course, even if the illness seems to be cured earlier. Stop immediately if there are any reactions and don't use the antibiotic if you're not sure that you have the correct one. Some people are allergic to commonly prescribed antibiotics such as penicillin; carry this information (eg on a bracelet) when travelling.

There are modern, well-equipped public hospitals in the major cities, namely Amman, Irbid, Aqaba and Karak; smaller hospitals in Madaba, Ramtha and Zarqa; and basic health centres in most other towns. Jordan also boasts 52 private hospitals, which cater primarily to patients from neighbouring countries, attracted by the lower medical costs.

Most towns have well-stocked pharmacies, but always check the expiry date of any medicines you buy in Jordan. It's better to bring any unusual or important medical items with you from home, and always bring a copy of a prescription. The telephone numbers for pharmacies (including those open at night) in Amman, and for hospitals in Amman, Zarqa, Irbid and Aqaba, are listed every day (but Friday) in the two English-language daily newspapers. All doctors (and most pharmacists) who have studied in Jordan speak English because medicine is taught in English at Jordanian universities, and many have studied abroad. Dentist surgeries are also fairly modern and well equipped.

If you are really sick or injured, contact your embassy, but bear in mind that they're not sympathetic to anyone who gets themselves into trouble by being stupid (see the boxed text 'Your Own Embassy' earlier in this chapter), and your embassy is *not* an alternative to a reputable travel insurance policy (which you have, don't you?).

Environmental Hazards

Despite the warnings, some visitors get themselves into trouble hiking through the desert in the heat of the day, especially around Wadi Rum. Please read the section below carefully.

Heat Exhaustion Dehydration and salt deficiency can cause heat exhaustion. Take time to acclimatise to high temperatures, drink sufficient liquids and do not do anything too physically demanding. Salt deficiency is characterised by fatigue, lethargy, headaches, giddiness and muscle cramps; salt tablets may help, but adding extra salt to your food is better.

Anhidrotic heat exhaustion is a rare form of heat exhaustion that is caused by an inability to sweat. It tends to affect people who have been in a hot climate for some time, rather than newcomers. It can progress to heatstroke. Treatment involves removal to a cooler climate.

Heatstroke This serious, and occasionally fatal, condition can occur if your body's heat-regulating mechanism breaks down and the body temperature rises to dangerous levels. Long, continuous periods of exposure to high temperatures and insufficient fluids can leave you vulnerable to heatstroke.

The symptoms are feeling unwell, not sweating very much (or at all) and a high body temperature (39° to 41°C or 102° to 106°F). Where sweating has ceased, the skin becomes flushed and red. Severe, throbbing headaches and lack of coordination will also occur, and the sufferer may be confused or aggressive. Eventually the victim will become delirious or convulse. Hospitalisation is essential, but in the interim get victims out of the sun, remove their clothing, cover them with a wet sheet or towel and then fan continually. Give fluids if they are conscious.

Hypothermia Too much cold can be just as dangerous as too much heat. If you're trekking at high altitudes or simply taking a long bus trip over mountains, particularly at night, be prepared. In winter – especially around Amman and northern Jordan, and at night any time of the year in the desert – you should always be prepared for cold, wet or windy conditions, even if you're just out walking or hitching.

Hypothermia occurs when the body loses heat faster than it can produce it and the core temperature of the body falls. It's surprisingly easy to progress from very cold to dangerously cold due to a combination of wind, wet clothing, fatigue and hunger, even if the air temperature is above freezing. It's best to dress in layers; silk, wool and some of the new artificial fibres are all good insulating materials. A hat is important, as a lot of heat is lost through the head. A strong, waterproof outer layer (and a 'space' blanket for emergencies) is essential. Carry basic supplies, including food containing simple sugars to generate heat quickly and fluid to drink.

Symptoms of hypothermia are exhaustion, numb skin (particularly toes and fingers), shivering, slurred speech, irrational or violent behaviour, lethargy, stumbling, dizzy spells, muscle cramps and violent bursts of energy. Irrationality may take the form of sufferers claiming they're warm and trying to take off their clothes.

To treat mild hypothermia, first get the person out of the wind and/or rain, remove their clothing if it's wet and replace it with dry, warm clothing. Give them hot liquids – not alcohol – and some high-kilojoule, easily digestible food. Do not rub victims: instead, allow them to slowly warm themselves. This should be enough to treat the early stages of hypothermia. The early treatment of mild hypothermia is the only way to prevent severe hypothermia, which is a critical condition.

Diving, Snorkelling & Swimming Stonefish have a very nasty habit of lying half-submerged in the sand, so wear something on your feet if you're walking into the sea (as opposed to jumping into the deep water from a jetty or boat). If stung by a stonefish, see a doctor immediately. Other nasty creatures to avoid are lionfish which, like the stonefish, have poisonous spikes, and jellyfish whose sting can be painful. If stung by a jellyfish, douse the rash in vinegar to deactivate any stingers which have not 'fired'. Calamine lotion, antihistamines and analgesics (and urine) may reduce the reaction and relieve the pain. See Cuts & Scratches later for information about coral cuts.

Aqaba has an excellent hospital where cuts, bites and stings can be treated. Most importantly, it has decompression chambers for the 'bends'.

Jet Lag Jet lag is experienced when a person travels by air across more than three time zones (each time zone usually represents a one-hour time difference). It occurs because many of the functions of the human body (such as temperature, pulse rate and emptying of the bladder and bowels) are regulated by internal 24-hour cycles. When we travel long distances rapidly, our bodies take time to adjust to the 'new time' of our destination, and we may experience fatigue, disorientation, insomnia, anxiety, impaired concentration and loss of appetite. These effects will usually be gone within three days of arrival, but to minimise the impact of jet lag:

- Rest for a couple of days prior to departure.
- To select flight schedules that minimise sleep deprivation; arriving late in the day means you can go to sleep soon after you arrive. For very long flights, try to organise a stopover.
- Avoid excessive eating (which bloats the stomach) and alcohol (which causes dehydration) during the flight. Instead, drink plenty of non-carbonated, nonalcoholic drinks such as fruit juice or water.
- Avoid smoking.
- Make yourself comfortable by wearing loose-fitting clothes and perhaps bringing an eye mask and ear plugs to help you sleep.
- Try to sleep at the appropriate time for the time zone you're travelling to.

Motion Sickness Eating lightly before and during a trip will reduce the chances of motion sickness. If you're prone to motion sickness try to find a place that minimises movement – near the wing on aircraft, close to midships on boats or near the centre on buses. Fresh air usually helps; reading and cigarette smoke definitely do not. Commercial motion-sickness preparations, which can cause drowsiness, have to be taken *before* the trip commences. Ginger (available in capsule form) and peppermint (including mint-flavoured sweets) are also natural preventatives.

Prickly Heat Prickly heat is an itchy rash caused by excessive perspiration trapped under the skin. It usually strikes people who have just arrived in a hot climate. Keeping cool, bathing often, drying the skin and

using a mild talcum or prickly heat powder or resorting to air-conditioning may help.

Sunburn In the tropics, desert or at high altitude you can get sunburnt surprisingly quickly, even through cloud. Use a sunscreen, hat, and a barrier cream for your nose and lips. Calamine lotion or a commercial after-sun preparation are good for mild sunburn. Protect your eyes with good quality sunglasses, particularly if you're near water, sand or snow.

Infectious Diseases
Diarrhoea Simple things like a change of water, food or climate can all cause a mild bout of diarrhoea, but a few rushed toilet trips with no other symptoms is not indicative of a major problem.

Dehydration is the main danger with any diarrhoea, particularly in children or the elderly as dehydration can occur quite quickly. Under all circumstances *fluid replacement* (at least equal to the volume being lost) is the most important thing to remember. Weak black tea with a little sugar, soda water, or soft drinks allowed to go flat and diluted 50% with clean water are all good. With severe diarrhoea, a rehydrating solution is preferable to replace minerals and salts lost. Commercially available oral rehydration salts (ORS) are very useful; add them to boiled or bottled water. In an emergency you can make up a solution of six teaspoons of sugar and a half teaspoon of salt to a litre of boiled or bottled water. You need to drink at least the same volume of fluid that you're losing in bowel movements and vomiting. Urine is the best guide to the adequacy of replacement – if you have small amounts of concentrated urine, you need to drink more. Keep drinking small amounts often. Stick to a bland diet as you recover.

Gut-paralysing drugs such as loperamide or diphenoxylate can be used to bring relief from the symptoms, although they do not cure the problem. Only use these drugs if you do not have access to toilets, eg if you *must* travel. Note that these drugs are not recommended for children under 12 years.

In certain situations, antibiotics may be required: diarrhoea with blood or mucus (dysentery), any diarrhoea with fever, profuse watery diarrhoea, persistent diarrhoea not improving after 48 hours and severe diarrhoea. These suggest a more serious cause of diarrhoea and in these situations gut-paralysing drugs should be avoided.

In these situations, a stool test may be necessary to diagnose the cause, so you should seek medical help urgently. Where this is not possible the recommended drugs for bacterial diarrhoea (the most likely cause of severe diarrhoea in travellers) are norfloxacin 400mg twice daily for three days or ciprofloxacin 500mg twice daily for five days. These are not recommended for children or pregnant women. The drug for children is co-trimoxazole, with dosage dependent on weight. A five day course is given. Ampicillin or amoxycillin may be given in pregnancy, but medical care is necessary.

Two other causes of persistent diarrhoea in travellers are giardiasis and amoebic dysentery. **Giardiasis** is caused by a common parasite, *Giardia lamblia*. Symptoms include stomach cramps, nausea, a bloated stomach, watery, foul-smelling diarrhoea and frequent gas. Giardiasis can appear several weeks after you have been exposed to the parasite. The symptoms may disappear for a few days and then return; this can go on for several weeks.

Amoebic dysentery, caused by the protozoan *Entamoeba histolytica*, is characterised by a gradual onset of low-grade diarrhoea, often with blood and mucus. Cramping abdominal pain and vomiting are less likely than in other types of diarrhoea, and fever may not be present. It will persist until treated and can recur and cause other health problems.

You should seek medical advice if you think you have giardiasis or amoebic dysentery, but where this is not possible, tinidazole or metronidazole are the recommended drugs. Treatment is a 2g single dose of tinidazole or 250mg of metronidazole three times daily for five to 10 days.

Fungal Infections Fungal infections occur more commonly in hot weather and are usually found on the scalp, between the toes ('athlete's foot') or fingers, in the groin and on the body (ringworm). Ringworm (which is a fungal infection, not a worm) is caught from infected animals or other people. Moisture encourages these infections.

To prevent fungal infections wear loose, comfortable clothes, avoid artificial fibres, wash frequently and dry yourself carefully. If you do get an infection, wash the infected area at least daily with a disinfectant or medicated soap and water, and rinse and dry well. Apply an antifungal cream or powder like tolnaftate. Try to expose the infected area to air or sunlight as much as possible and wash all towels and underwear in hot water, change them often and let them dry in the sun.

Hepatitis Hepatitis is a general term for inflammation of the liver, and is a common disease worldwide. There are several different viruses that cause hepatitis, and they differ in the way that they're transmitted. The symptoms are similar in all forms of the illness, and include fever, chills, headache, fatigue, feelings of weakness and aches and pains, followed by loss of appetite, nausea, vomiting, abdominal pain, dark urine, light-coloured faeces, jaundiced (yellow) skin and yellowing of the whites of the eyes. People who have had hepatitis should avoid alcohol for some time after the illness, as the liver needs time to recover.

Hepatitis A is transmitted by contaminated food and drinking water. You should seek medical advice, but there's not much you can do apart from resting, drinking lots of fluids, eating lightly and avoiding fatty foods. Hepatitis E is transmitted in the same way as hepatitis A; it can be particularly serious in pregnant women.

There are almost 300 million chronic carriers of **hepatitis B** in the world. It's spread through contact with infected blood, blood products or body fluids, for example through sexual contact, unsterilised needles and blood transfusions, or contact with blood via small breaks in the skin. Other risk situations include having a shave, tattoo or body piercing with contaminated equipment. The symptoms of hepatitis B may be more severe than type A and the disease can lead to long term problems such as chronic liver damage, liver cancer or a long term carrier state. Hepatitis C and D are spread in the same way as hepatitis B and can also lead to long term complications.

There are vaccines against hepatitis A and B, but there are currently no vaccines against the other types of hepatitis. Following the basic rules about food and water (hepatitis A and E) and avoiding risk situations (hepatitis B, C and D) are important preventative measures.

HIV & AIDS Infection with the human immunodeficiency virus (HIV) may lead to acquired immune deficiency syndrome (AIDS), which is a fatal disease. Any exposure to blood, blood products or body fluids may put the individual at risk. The disease is often transmitted through sexual contact or dirty needles – vaccinations, acupuncture, tattooing and body piercing can be potentially as dangerous as intravenous drug use. HIV/AIDS can also be spread through infected blood transfusions. Some developing countries cannot afford to screen blood used for transfusions, but the medical system in Jordan is fairly developed and doctors are well trained.

If you do need an injection, ask to see the syringe unwrapped in front of you, or take a needle and syringe pack with you. Fear of HIV infection should never preclude treatment for serious medical conditions.

Reliable figures aren't available about the number of people in Jordan with HIV or AIDS, but given the strict taboos in Jordanian society about taking drugs, homosexuality and promiscuity, the disease is relatively rare. Contracting HIV through a blood transfusion is about as unlikely as it is in most western countries, and anyone needing serious surgery will probably be sent back home anyway.

Intestinal Worms These parasites are most common in rural, tropical areas and have different ways of infecting people. Some may be ingested on food such as undercooked meat (eg tapeworms) and some enter through your skin (eg hookworms). Infestations may not show up for some time,

and although they are usually not serious, if left untreated some can cause severe health problems later. Consider having a stool test when you return home to check for these and determine the appropriate treatment.

Sexually Transmitted Infections HIV/AIDS and hepatitis B can be transmitted through sexual contact – see the relevant sections earlier for more details. Other STIs include gonorrhoea, herpes and syphilis; sores, blisters or rashes around the genitals and discharges or pain when urinating are common symptoms. In some STIs, such as wart virus or chlamydia, symptoms may be less marked or not observed at all, especially in women. Chlamydia infection can cause infertility in men and women before any symptoms have been noticed. Syphilis symptoms eventually disappear completely but the disease continues and can cause severe problems in later years. While abstinence from sexual contact is the only 100% effective prevention, using condoms is also effective. The treatment of gonorrhoea and syphilis is with antibiotics. The different sexually transmitted diseases each require specific antibiotics.

Typhoid Typhoid fever is a dangerous gut infection caused by contaminated water and food. Medical help must be sought. In its early stages, sufferers may feel they have a bad cold or flu on the way, as early symptoms are a headache, body aches and a fever which rises a little each day until it's around 40°C (104°F) or more. The victim's pulse is often slow relative to the degree of fever present – unlike a normal fever where the pulse increases. There may also be vomiting, abdominal pain, diarrhoea or constipation.

In the second week, the high fever and slow pulse continue and a few pink spots may appear on the body; trembling, delirium, weakness, weight loss and dehydration may occur. Complications such as pneumonia, perforated bowel or meningitis may ensue.

Cuts, Bites & Stings
See the following Less Common Diseases section for details of rabies, which is passed through animal bites.

Cuts & Scratches Wash well and treat with an antiseptic such as povidone-iodine. Where possible avoid bandages and Band-Aids, which can keep wounds wet. Coral cuts are notoriously slow to heal and if they're not adequately cleaned, small pieces of coral can become embedded in the wound.

Bedbugs & Lice Bedbugs live in various places, but particularly in dirty mattresses and bedding, evidenced by spots of blood on bedclothes or on the wall. Bedbugs leave itchy bites in neat rows. Calamine lotion or a sting relief spray may help.

All lice cause itching and discomfort. They make themselves at home in your hair (head lice), your clothing (body lice) or in your pubic hair (crabs). You catch lice through direct contact with infected people or by sharing combs, clothing and the like. Powder or shampoo treatment will kill the lice and infected clothing should then be washed in very hot, soapy water and left in the sun to dry.

Bites & Stings Bee and wasp stings are usually painful rather than dangerous. However, in people who are allergic to them severe breathing difficulties may occur and require urgent medical care. Calamine lotion or a sting relief spray will give relief and ice packs will reduce the pain and swelling. There are some spiders with dangerous bites but antivenins are usually available. Scorpion stings are notoriously painful and in some parts of Asia, the Middle East (including Jordan) and Central America can actually be fatal. Scorpions often shelter in shoes or clothing.

Ticks You should always check all over your body if you have been walking through a potentially tick-infested area as ticks can cause skin infections and other more serious diseases. If a tick is found attached, press down around the tick's head with tweezers, grab the head and gently pull upwards. Avoid pulling the rear of the body as this may squeeze the tick's gut contents through the attached mouth parts into the skin, increasing the risk of infection and disease. Smearing chemicals on the tick will not make it let go, and is not recommended.

Snakes To minimise your chances of being bitten always wear boots, socks and long trousers when walking through undergrowth where snakes may be present. Don't put your hands into holes and crevices, and be careful when collecting firewood.

Snake bites do not cause instantaneous death, and antivenins are usually available. Immediately wrap the bitten limb tightly, as you would for a sprained ankle, and then attach a splint to immobilise it. Keep the victim still and seek medical help. Tourniquets and sucking out the poison are now comprehensively discredited.

Less Common Diseases

The following diseases pose a small risk to travellers, and so are only mentioned in passing. Seek medical advice if you think you may have any of these diseases.

Cholera This is the worst of the watery diarrhoeas and medical help should be sought. Outbreaks of cholera are generally widely reported, so you can avoid such areas. A possible sign of a recent outbreak is the absence of salad served in restaurants. (Cholera can be transmitted via the water that salad greens are washed in.) *Fluid replacement is the most vital treatment* – the risk of dehydration is severe as you may lose up to 20L a day. If there is a delay in getting to hospital, then begin taking tetracycline. The adult dose is 250mg four times daily. It's not recommended for children under nine years or pregnant women. Tetracycline may help shorten the illness, but adequate fluids are required to save lives.

Leishmaniasis This is a group of parasitic diseases transmitted by sandflies, which are found in many parts of the Middle East (but not Jordan), Africa, India, Central and South America and the Mediterranean. Cutaneous leishmaniasis affects the skin tissue causing ulceration and disfigurement, and visceral leishmaniasis affects the internal organs. Seek medical advice, as laboratory testing is required for diagnosis and correct treatment. Avoiding sandfly bites is the best precaution. Bites are usually painless, itchy and yet another reason to cover up and apply repellent.

Rabies This fatal viral infection is found in many countries, but is rare in Jordan. Many animals can be infected (such as dogs, cats, bats and monkeys) and it's their saliva which is infectious. Any bite, scratch or even lick from an animal should be cleaned immediately and thoroughly. Scrub with soap and running water, and then apply alcohol or iodine solution. Medical help should be sought promptly to receive a course of injections to prevent the onset of symptoms and death.

Tetanus This disease is caused by a germ which lives in soil and in the faeces of horses and other animals. It enters the body via breaks in the skin. The first symptom may be discomfort in swallowing, or stiffening of the jaw and neck; this is followed by painful convulsions of the jaw and whole body. The disease can be fatal, but can be prevented by vaccination.

Typhus This disease is spread by ticks, mites or lice. It begins with fever, chills, headache and muscle pains followed a few days later by a rash. There is often a large sore at the site of the bite and nearby lymph nodes are swollen and painful. Typhus can be treated under medical supervision. Seek local advice on areas where ticks pose a danger and always check your skin carefully for ticks after walking in a danger areas. An insect repellent can help, and walkers in tick-infested areas should consider having their boots and trousers impregnated with benzyl benzoate and dibutylphthalate.

Women's Health
Gynaecological Problems The use of antibiotics and synthetic underwear; sweating and contraceptive pills can lead to fungal vaginal infections, especially when travelling in hot climates. Fungal infections are characterised by a rash, itch and discharge and can be treated with a vinegar or lemon-juice douche, or with yoghurt. Nystatin, miconazole or clotrimazole pessaries or vaginal cream are the usual treatment. Maintaining good personal hygiene and wearing loose-fitting clothes and cotton underwear may help prevent these infections.

Sexually transmitted infections are a major cause of vaginal problems. Symptoms include a smelly discharge, painful intercourse and, sometimes, a burning sensation when urinating. Medical attention should be sought and male sexual partners must also be treated. For more details see the section on Sexually Transmitted Infections earlier. Besides abstinence, the best thing is to practise safe sex using condoms.

Pregnancy It is not advisable to travel to some places (but Jordan is OK) while pregnant as vaccinations normally used to prevent serious diseases are not advisable during pregnancy (eg yellow fever). In addition, some diseases are much more serious for the mother (and may increase the risk of a stillborn child) in pregnancy (eg malaria). Jordan is generally OK, but check your travel plans with your doctor.

Most miscarriages occur during the first three months of pregnancy. Miscarriage is not uncommon and can occasionally lead to severe bleeding. The last three months should also be spent within reasonable distance of good medical care. A baby born as early as 24 weeks stands a chance of survival, but only in a good modern hospital. Pregnant women should avoid all unnecessary medication, although vaccinations and malarial prophylactics should still be taken where needed. Additional care should be taken to prevent illness and particular attention should be paid to diet and nutrition. Alcohol and nicotine, for example, should be avoided.

WOMEN TRAVELLERS
As a woman travelling alone around Jordan for three weeks, I have found the people only helpful, hospitable and friendly.

K Millar, UK

Attitudes Towards Women
Attitudes to foreign women in Jordan, and throughout much of the Middle East, can be trying to say the least. The reasons for this are complex and, of course, it would be foolish to lump everyone together into the same category. These largely Muslim societies are, by contemporary western standards,

quite conservative when it comes to sex and women, and most men have little or no contact with either before marriage – you'll soon notice your marital status (whether you're male or female) is a source of considerable interest to pretty much anyone you meet. 'Are you married?' usually figures among the first five standard questions Jordanians put to foreigners.

Western movies and TV give some men in these countries the impression that all western women are promiscuous and will jump into bed at the drop of a hat. The behaviour of some women travelling in these countries doesn't always help either. Flouting local sensitivities about dress not only gets the individuals concerned unwanted attention, it also colours the way locals perceive other travellers.

Safety Precautions

There will probably be times when you have male company that you could well live without. This may go no further than irritating banter or proposals of marriage and even declarations of undying love. Harassment can also take the form of leering, sometimes by being followed and occasionally being touched up.

You cannot make this problem go away and, where possible, you should try to ignore this pubescent idiocy or you'll end up letting a few sad individuals spoil your whole trip. Plenty of women travel through Jordan, often alone, and never encounter serious problems, so please do not become paranoid.

The first rule of thumb is to respect standard Muslim sensibilities about dress – cover the shoulders, upper arms and legs, at least. This is not a magic formula, but it will certainly help. Some women go to the extent of covering their head as well, although this makes little difference, and is not necessary in Jordan. Bear in mind that smaller towns tend to be more conservative than big cities like Amman, and smaller towns are generally more relaxed than tiny villages in the countryside.

Female travellers have reported varying degrees of harassment from local lads on the public beaches in and near Aqaba. Bikinis are permitted on the private beaches run by the hotels and diving centres, but harassment is still common. Elsewhere in Aqaba, and along the Dead Sea (except at the swimming pools at the upmarket hotels), dress conservatively – ie baggy shorts and loose tops, even when swimming. Never go topless.

Avoid eye contact with any man you don't know (wearing dark glasses can help); and try to ignore any rude remarks. Some women also find it's not worth summoning up the energy to acknowledge, for example, being brushed up against. This is not to say that you should simply let everything go unremarked, and some behaviour may well warrant a good public scene. You'll be surprised how quickly bystanders will take matters into hand if they feel one of their own has overstepped the mark.

If you have to say anything to ward off an advance, *imshi* (clear off) should do the trick. A wedding ring will add to your respectability in Arab eyes, but a photo of your children and even husband can clinch it – if you don't have any, borrow a picture of your nephew and/or niece.

Lastly, some advice for single female travellers from single female readers: don't go to any bar unaccompanied; don't sit in the front seat of a chartered private or service taxi; on public transport do sit next to a women if possible; don't venture to remote regions of vast archaeological sites such as Petra – including Al-Beid (little Petra) – and Jerash, where some readers have been harassed and worse; always check for peep holes in rooms and bathrooms (particularly cigarette holes in curtains); and always place a chair against your locked hotel room door in case of 'accidental' (but ostensibly harmless) late night intrusions.

If you suffer any harassment go to a police station, or a tourist police booth, which can be found at most sites visited by tourists.

Restaurants, Bars & Cafes

Some activities, such as sitting in cafes, are usually seen as a male preserve and although it's quite OK for western women to enter, in some places the stares may make you feel uncomfortable.

Quite a few restaurants have a 'family section' where any local and foreign women, unaccompanied by men, can eat in peace. As a rule, mixed foreign groups have no trouble wherever they sit, including in the tea shops and bars. In some of the local bars and cafes there is only one toilet, so try to avoid using these if only for the inevitable smell and lack of hygiene. A few bars and cafes in Amman where women are welcome are listed in the Amman chapter.

Hotels

In theory, the chances of getting harassed are far greater in budget hotels where there are more local male guests; male hangers-on come and go with little or no control; and mostly male staff are rarely hired for their compassion.

Below is a list of the budget hotels in the major towns which have been recommended by single female travellers:

Amman
    Farah Hotel; Cliff Hotel; Merryland Hotel; Palace Hotel.
Aqaba
    Al-Amer Hotel; Al-Naher al-Khaled; Jordan Flower Hotel.
Azraq
    Best avoided because a lot of Saudi and Iraqi truck drivers stop in Azraq town, although the new Azraq Lodge should be OK.
Irbid
    Al-Ameen al-Kabeer Hotel; Omayed Hotel.
Karak
    There are no particularly safe budget places, so try the mid-priced Al-Mujeb Hotel or Karak Rest House.
Madaba
    Black Iris Hotel; Lulu's Pension B&B (both are excellent).
Wadi Mousa (near Petra)
    Cleopatra Hotel; Mussa Spring Hotel; Peace Way Hotel; Qasr al-Bint Hotel; Sunset Hotel.
Wadi Rum
    Camping alone in the desert would be foolhardy, so it's better to stay at the campground at the Government Rest House (staffed by loads of single local men and never entirely safe).

GAY & LESBIAN TRAVELLERS

Homosexuality is prohibited in Jordan, and conviction can result in imprisonment. The public position on homosexuality is that it doesn't really exist. This is not to say that it doesn't, but Jordan is not an ideal place to 'come out'. There is a very underground gay scene in Amman, so if you're keen to explore it make very discreet enquiries. Public displays of affection by heterosexuals are frowned upon, and the same rules apply to gays and lesbians, although two men or two women holding hands is a normal sign of friendship.

DISABLED TRAVELLERS

Jordan is not a great place for disabled travellers. Although Jordanians are happy to help anyone with a disability, the cities are crowded and the traffic is appalling, and visiting tourist attractions, such as the vast archaeological sites of Petra and Jerash, involves lots of walking on uneven ground.

The Jordanian government recently legislated that wheelchair access must be added to all new public buildings, but nothing will ever be done to accommodate wheelchairs elsewhere. The only concession to the incapacitated are horse-drawn carriages (mostly used by weary but able-bodied walkers) which are tolerated as transport for disabled visitors part of the way into Petra.

SENIOR TRAVELLERS

There is no reason why any senior traveller could not travel independently, as long as they can take obvious precautions, eg avoid visiting in the height of summer; don't walk about in the heat of the day; use chartered taxis or rented cars rather than crowded public transport; and stay in decent hotels on the ground floor (budget hotels are often upstairs, and rarely have lifts). Most senior travellers may prefer to join an organised tour from their home country. If you have special needs, be sure to tell the tour operator.

Although the medical system in Jordan is good, bring any medication you need, and prescriptions from home (see the Health section earlier in this chapter for details).

TRAVEL WITH CHILDREN

Taking the kids adds another dimension to a trip in Jordan, and of course it's not all fun and games. Firstly, it's a good idea to avoid coming in the summer because the extreme heat could really make your family journey quite unpleasant. With very young children in particular, you'll find yourself having to moderate the pace. Keeping them happy, well fed and clean is the main challenge.

Always take along a bag of small gadgets and a favourite teddy bear or the like to keep junior amused, especially while on public transport. Luckily, you'll rarely have to embark on really long journeys in Jordan, and chartering a taxi or renting a car is easy, so this should not pose too great a problem.

Fresh and powdered milk is available; otherwise, stick to bottled mineral water. Kids already eating solids shouldn't have many problems. Cooked meat dishes, the various dips (such as *humous*), rice and the occasional more or less western-style burger or pizza, along with fruit (washed and peeled) should all be OK as a nutritional basis. Nuts are also a safe, common and cheap source of protein.

With infants, the next problem is cleanliness. It's impractical to carry more than about a half dozen washable nappies with you, but disposable ones are not so easy to come by. As for accommodation, you're going to want a private bathroom and hot water.

The good news is that children are as loved in Jordan as anywhere else in the Middle East. Few people bring their young ones to this part of the world, so you'll find that your kids are quite a hit. In that way they can help break the ice and open the doors to contact with local people with whom otherwise you might never have exchanged glances.

Some of the more interesting attractions for the kids will be visiting the beaches and snorkelling at Aqaba; exploring castles at Karak, Shobak and Ajlun; riding a camel at Wadi Rum; floating in the Dead Sea; and walking and enjoying picnics in a few of the national reserves. A list of things to see and do with children in and around Amman is included in the Activities section of the Amman chapter.

For more comprehensive advice on the do's and don'ts of travelling with children, pick up a copy of *Travel with Children* by Lonely Planet's very own Maureen Wheeler.

Maureen, and husband Tony, have travelled all around the world with their two children, and have survived to tell the tale.

USEFUL ORGANISATIONS

Below is a list of some organisations that may be useful; others are listed in the relevant sections throughout this book. All are located in Amman (☎ 06).

Amman Chamber of Commerce	☎ 566 6151
Department of Antiquities	☎ 464 4336
	fax 461 5848
General Union of Voluntary	☎ 463 4001
Societies	fax 465 9973
Jordanian Red Crescent	☎ 477 3141
	fax 475 0815
Lions	☎ 569 2231
Ministry of Foreign Affairs	☎ 464 4361
Ministry of Interior	☎ 562 2811
Rotary	☎ 460 3703
Royal Automobile Club of Jordan	☎ 585 0637
UNHCR	☎ 593 0395
	fax 539 8553
UNICEF	☎ 462 9571
	fax 464 0049
WHO	☎ 568 4651
	fax 566 7533

DANGERS & ANNOYANCES

Jordan is very safe to visit and travel around; remarkably so considering the turmoil, restrictions and difficulties in other nearby countries, such as Israel, Lebanon, Iraq and Saudi Arabia. The general advice for all travellers is to take care – but not to be paranoid. The good news is that women who have travelled – or, perhaps, struggled – through places like Turkey will probably find that Jordan is comparatively relaxed and hassle-free – but women who have not visited the region before, and have come straight to Jordan from the west, may be annoyed at the leering and possible harassment from local men. See the Women Travellers section earlier in this chapter for more information.

Traffic

The traffic in Amman (especially in Downtown) is appalling, but probably no worse than any other major city in the region. If renting a car around Jordan, avoid driving anywhere near Amman; if walking around Amman, look both ways several times before crossing any street. For more information about driving around Jordan, refer to the Car & Motorcycle section in the Getting Around chapter.

Public Disorder

During rare political or economic crises (eg an increase in the price of staple goods), occasional impromptu protests and acts of civil disobedience can occur. For some reason, these often take place in Karak, Tafila and Ma'an, and the university areas of Irbid, Mu'tah and northern Amman are sometimes volatile.

Foreigners are never targeted during these protests, but you should avoid becoming involved, and stay away from areas where protests are taking place. The best sources of current information are the English-language daily newspapers published in Amman; the Jordanian embassy/consulate in your home country; or your embassy or consulate in Jordan or elsewhere in the Middle East.

Theft & Crime

Theft is usually no problem for people who take reasonable care. Leaving your bag under the watchful eye of a member of staff in the office of a bus station or hotel for a few hours should be no cause for concern. Shared rooms in hotels are also quite OK as a rule, but don't take unnecessary risks. The only place where there may be some trouble is very late at night outside a nightclub in Amman patronised by intoxicated, vulnerable and comparatively wealthy foreigners.

The military keep a low profile and you would be unlikely to experience anything but friendliness, honesty and hospitality from them. It's generally safe to walk around day or night in Amman and other towns, although women should take a little more caution.

Scams

One reader reported being asked to 'sell' his cornea (part of the eye) to an acquaintance.

The reader initially considered it, before some Jordanian friends warned him that any part of his body could be extracted while under anaesthetic. Needless to say, decline any such request, and keep your body intact.

LEGAL MATTERS

The Jordanian legal system is something of a cross-breed, reflecting the country's history. Civil and commercial law are governed by a series of courts working with a mixture of inherited British-style common law and the French code. Religious and family matters are generally covered by Islamic *Sharia'a* courts, or ecclesiastic equivalents for non-Muslims.

Foreigners would be unlucky to get caught up in the machinations of Jordanian justice. The only things to remember are: penalties for drug use of any kind are stiff and apply to foreigners and locals alike; homosexuality is illegal, and penalties are severe; and criticising the King can land you in gaol for up to three years! Traffic police do generally treat foreign drivers with a degree of good-natured indulgence, so long as there are no major traffic laws broken. However, excessive speeding, drink-driving and not wearing a seat belt will land you in trouble. And if you do get into strife, there is little your embassy can do for you but contact your relatives and recommend local lawyers (see the boxed text 'Your Own Embassy' earlier in this chapter).

BUSINESS HOURS

Government departments, including most tourist offices, are open from about 8 am to 2 pm every day, but Friday – and sometimes they also close on Saturday. Banks are normally open from 8.30 am to 12.30 pm, and sometimes again from about 4 to 6 pm, every day but Friday and Saturday. Moneychangers are open every day from about 9 am to at least 9 pm, but some have restricted hours on Friday. The opening times for post offices vary from one town to another, but tend to be from about 8 am to 6 pm every day, and until about 2 pm on Friday. Some government departments and banks tend to close about 30 minutes earlier in winter.

Museums and art galleries are often closed for one day every week, but their day off varies from one place to another, and often changes from month to month. Almost all major tourist attractions are open every day; normally during daylight hours.

Smaller shops and businesses are open every day from about 9 am to 8 pm, but some close for a couple of hours in the middle of the afternoon, and some do not open on Thursday afternoon and Friday. The *souqs* (markets) and street stalls are open every day and, in fact, Friday is often their busiest day.

During Ramadan (the Muslim month of fasting) business hours are shorter and, because of the restriction on eating or drinking during the day, it can be difficult to find a restaurant that's open in daylight hours, particularly in out-of-the-way places.

PUBLIC HOLIDAYS & SPECIAL EVENTS

As the Islamic Hejira calendar is 11 days shorter than the Gregorian calendar, each year Islamic holidays fall 11 days earlier than the previous year. The precise dates are known only shortly before they fall because they depend upon the sighting of the moon. See the Language chapter at the back of the book for a full listing of the Hejira months.

Ramadan

Ramadan is the ninth month of the Muslim calendar, when Muslims fast during daylight hours to fulfil the fourth pillar of Islam (see the Religion section in the Facts about Jordan chapter for details). During this month, pious Muslims will not allow anything to pass their lips in daylight hours. One is even supposed to avoid swallowing saliva, but ...

Although many Muslims in Jordan do not follow the injunctions to the letter, most conform to some extent. Foreigners are not expected to follow suit, but it's generally impolite to smoke, drink or eat in public during Ramadan.

There are no public holidays during Ramadan, but business hours tend to become more erratic and usually shorter. In out-of-the-way places, it's hard to find a restaurant that opens before sunset, and some places close during all of Ramadan. It's also sometimes difficult dealing with anyone during the day who is hungry, thirsty or craving for a cigarette.

The evening meal during Ramadan, called *iftar* (breaking the fast), is always a bit of a celebration. Go to the bigger restaurants and wait with fasting crowds for sundown, the moment when food is served – it's quite a lively experience.

While Ramadan can be inconvenient at times for visitors, all tourist attractions remain open and all public transport functions normally throughout the day. All restaurants in hotels will be open for guests and the public, so breakfast and dinner are usually easy enough to arrange.

If you're going to be travelling around during the day, remember that the majority of restaurants and cafes will be closed, so the best idea is to buy some food for lunch (grocery shops will normally stay open during the day), and eat it somewhere discreet. Restaurants catering to tourists, eg government rest houses at places like Petra and Jerash, will usually still be open, although these restaurants may look closed if the door is shut, or a curtain is drawn across the front door.

Table of Islamic Holidays

Hejira Year	New Year	Prophet's Birthday	Ramadan Begins	Eid al-Fitr	Eid al-Adha
1421	06.04.00	14.06.00	27.11.00	27.12.00	06.03.01
1422	26.03.01	03.06.01	16.11.01	16.12.01	23.02.02
1423	15.03.02	23.05.02	05.11.02	05.12.02	12.02.03
1424	04.03.03	12.05.03	25.10.03	24.11.03	01.02.04

Public Holidays

Following the death of King Hussein, and the succession of King Abdullah II, the exact number of public holidays, and the dates on which they fall, is likely to change. King Abdullah's Throne Day (9 June) and his birthday (30 January) will probably replace King Hussein's Throne Day (August 11). King Hussein's Birthday (14 November) will remain a public holiday, however, and the death of King Hussein (7 February) will also probably be a holiday.

During the public holidays listed below, all government offices and banks will close. Most shops, moneychangers and restaurants will remain open, and public transport will still function normally on most public holidays, although most shops will close during Eid al-Fitr and Eid al-Adha.

New Year's Day	1 January
Tree Day (Arbor Day)	15 January
Eid al-Fitr	

See Table of Islamic Events. Also known as Eid as-Sagheer (small feast), it starts at the beginning of Shawwal to mark the end of fasting in the preceding month of Ramadan.

Arab League Day	22 March
Eid al-Kabir	

See Table of Islamic Events. This 'big feast' is when Muslims fulfil the fifth pillar of Islam – Haj, or the pilgrimage to Mecca. This period lasts from 10 to 13 Zuul-Hijja.

Eid al-Adha

See Table of Islamic Events. This is the commemoration of Allah sparing Ibrahim (Abraham in the Bible) from sacrificing his son, Isaac, and is the end of the Haj. Every year, about 350,000 sheep are sacrificed throughout the Muslim world at this time.

Good Friday	March/April
Muslim New Year	First Day of Muharram
Labour Day	1 May
Independence Day	25 May
Army Day & Anniversary of the Great Arab Revolt	10 June
Prophet Mohammed's Birthday	

See Table of Islamic Events. Celebrated on 12 Rabi' al-Awal.

King Hussein's Birthday	14 November
Eid al-Isra Wal Mi'raj	

Another feast which celebrates the nocturnal visit of the Prophet Mohammed to heaven.

Christmas Day	25 December

Special Events

The Jordanian tourist authorities are gearing up for what they, perhaps a little optimistically, hope will be a massive influx of up to 1.3 million western tourists to celebrate the Birth of Christ in 2000. The Vatican has designated five places in Jordan as special 'Pilgrimage Sites', and allocated special dates for pilgrimages in 2000 – refer to the special section 'Biblical Jordan' in the Facts about Jordan chapter for details.

Jordan's best known cultural event is the Jerash Festival of Culture & Arts (the boxed text in the Jerash section of the Northern & Western Jordan chapter has the full details). In summer (mainly August), traditional concerts and plays are sometimes held at the Odeon and Roman Theatre in Amman, and in Salt and Fuheis, near the capital.

For further information about special events in Jordan, contact an overseas branch of the Jordan Tourism Board (see the Tourist Offices Abroad section earlier in this chapter); visit the Downtown Visitors Centre in Amman; check out the listings in the two English-language daily newspapers published in Amman; or look out for some of the tourist booklets mentioned under Guidebooks in the Books section earlier.

ACTIVITIES

For more information about activities involving the sea, ie swimming, diving, snorkelling, boat trips and other water sports, refer to Activities in the Aqaba section of the Southern Desert chapter, and the Activities chapter.

Boats & Other Water Sports

In Aqaba, trips on a glass-bottom boat are fun, although the amount of fish and coral that can be seen is sometimes disappointing. The guys who run these boats are savvy, and most have business cards (and mobile telephones), so bargain. These and other boats in Aqaba can be rented out for longer trips.

A couple of hotels in Aqaba are well set up for water sports. Nothing is cheap, of course.

Camel Treks

The camel is no longer a common form of transport for Bedouin: most now prefer the ubiquitous pick-up truck – in fact, it's not unusual to see Bedouin transporting a prized camel in the back of a pick-up! For visitors, however, one truly rewarding experience is a camel trek. Enterprising Bedouin are happy to take big-spending visitors on three to six-night camel treks from Wadi Rum to Aqaba or Petra (see the Wadi Rum section in the Southern Desert chapter for details). Similar trips are possible in a 4WD, but obviously travelling by camel is more charming and cheaper, but more uncomfortable.

Diving & Snorkelling

The coastline between Aqaba and the Saudi border is home to some of the world's better diving spots. Although the diving and snorkelling is generally not as good as places along the Sinai peninsula in Egypt, there's plenty of coral and colourful marine life, and most sites are accessible to snorkellers. Refer to the Diving & Snorkelling section in the Activities chapter for full details.

Hot Springs

Jordan boasts dozens of thermal hot water springs, where the water is usually hot (about 35 to 45°C). The water contains potassium, magnesium and calcium, among other minerals – popular for their apparent health benefits. The most famous and popular is Hammamat Ma'in, near Madaba. Other popular spots around Jordan include the Zarqa (also called Zara) springs, along the Dead Sea Highway; Hammamat Burbita and Hammamat Afra, west of the King's Highway and near Tafila; and the Al-Himma springs in Mukheiba village, very close to the northern border with Israel.

Women are likely to feel more comfortable at Hammamat Ma'in, where there is an area for families and unaccompanied women; and the public baths at Al-Himma which allocates special times solely for the ladies. In other places, local men usually hang around and are likely to leer at any women not conservatively dressed.

Rock Climbing

Wadi Rum offers some challenging and unique rock climbing, equal to just about anything in Europe. The most accessible and popular climbs are well detailed in the excellent books written by Tony Howard and Di Taylor (see Books under Hiking in the Activities chapter). Guides are often necessary, and you will probably need to bring your own climbing gear. The Wadi Rum section in the Southern Desert chapter also has more details.

Swimming

The number of public beaches in Aqaba – Jordan's only town on the sea – is slowly diminishing because they're being commandeered by the growing number of upmarket hotels. The best beaches are now along the coastline south of Aqaba, but most spots have little or no shade, and are not accessible on foot. The beaches run by the upmarket hotels in Aqaba are clean and available to the public for a few dinars.

Most visitors head for the Dead Sea, where swimming is almost impossible because of the incredible buoyancy of the salt water. The Jordanian side of the Dead Sea is not nearly as developed as the western coast in Israel, and public transport along the Dead Sea Highway is limited. Refer to the Dead Sea section of the Northern & Western Jordan chapter for more details.

Turkish Baths

If your muscles ache from traipsing around vast archaeological sites like Petra and Jerash and climbing up and down the *jebels* (hills) of Amman, consider a traditional Turkish bath. In tourist centres, eg Wadi Mousa (near Petra) and Aqaba, a steam bath, massage and 'body conditioning' costs about JD8.

Women are welcome, but should make a reservation so that female attendants can be organised. Public baths can found in Downtown in Amman, but are strictly men-only establishments.

Walking

Jordan is a great place for short hikes, but long-distance and overnight trekking is not really an option. See Hiking in the Activities chapter for more details.

COURSES

For those taken enough by the mystery of the Arab world to want to learn something of the language, there are several possibilities (refer to the relevant chapters for more details about the universities and cultural centres):

British Council
(☎ 06-463 6147, fax 465 6413)
Amman. It offers classes in colloquial Jordanian Arabic and MSA.
Web site www.britcoun.org/jordan

Language Centre of the Centre Culturel Français
(☎ 06-461 2658) Amman. The centre runs intensive courses in MSA (taught in French or English) during the summer. For example, a one-month course for several hours a day, five days a week, costs JD75.

University of Jordan
(☎ 06-584 3555, fax 583 2318, email web master@ju.edu.jo) Northern Amman. It offers summer courses in Modern Standard Arabic (MSA), as well as more leisurely courses throughout the rest of the year.
Web site www.ju.edu.jo

Yarmouk University
(☎ 02-727 1100, email webmaster@yu.edu.jo) Irbid. Yarmouk also runs courses in MSA, but less regularly than the University of Jordan.
Web site www.yu.edu.jo

WORK

Working in Jordan is not really an option for most foreigners passing through, but it is possible for anyone with the necessary qualifications or interests who has done some planning before leaving home. Your employer in Jordan should be able to deal with the bureaucratic requirements of working permits.

Language Teaching

Teaching English is the most obvious avenue. One of the two top schools in Amman is run by the British Council (see Courses earlier). The minimum requirements are the RSA Preparatory Certificate (the Diploma is preferred) or equivalent and two years' experience. For details contact their head office (☎ 020-7930 8466, 10 Spring Gardens, London SW1A 2BN) before coming to Jordan.

The American Language Center (☎ 06-585 9102, fax 585 9101, email info@alc.edu.jo) runs the other top school. Check out their Web site www.alc.edu.jo. Like the British Council, they mainly recruit in their own country. This doesn't mean that someone passing through cannot get work; vacancies can arise at short notice and it is possible to get part-time positions.

German, French and Spanish speakers should contact their respective cultural centres in Amman (see Cultural Centres in that chapter for details) about the possibility of teaching these languages.

Archaeological Digs

If you have any relevant qualifications, you may be able to get work on archaeological digs, but it's usually unpaid. If the Department of Antiquities (☎ 06-464 4336, fax 461 5848) in Amman is no help, try some of the organisations listed in the Digging up the Past section in the Activities chapter.

Diving

If you are a qualified diving instructor, you may be able to get some work at one of the diving centres in Aqaba, particularly during the peak season (about September to March). Refer to Diving & Snorkelling in the Activities chapter for a list of diving centres in Aqaba.

ACCOMMODATION

Jordan does not boast a huge range of accommodation options, and hotels can only be found in the cities and towns of Amman, Irbid, Madaba, Karak, Ma'an, Wadi Mousa (near Petra), Azraq and Aqaba. However, this is not a problem because Jordan is so compact that most attractions can be easily visited in day trips from these places. Other interesting alternatives are the few 'chalets' near some hot springs (eg Al-Himma in Mukheiba); tents in the desert (eg at Wadi Rum); tourist-oriented rest houses (eg Karak); and hotels near major sites (eg near Ajlun castle).

Camping

Rooms in cheap hotels are easy to find, and reasonably comfortable, so bringing a tent just to save money on accommodation makes little sense. Camping is possible just about anywhere in the countryside, but camping on stony ground, with little or no shade or water, is not great fun. Privacy and safety are the prime concerns for campers, and in a densely populated country like Jordan finding a secluded place to pitch a tent is far from easy.

Some great places to discreetly pitch a tent are near Umm Qais, Shaumari Reserve and Ajlun castle. However, the Jordanian authorities prefer that foreigners use designated campsites. The only campsites where pitching your own tent is allowed is at Aqaba (tents catch the sea breezes in summer), Wadi Rum (great fun in the desert) and Dibbeen National Park. Pre-set tents are also available in Wadi Rum, Dana Nature Reserve and the Dead Sea Rest House. Camping is generally not permitted in the national reserves run by the Royal Society for the Conservation of Nature (RSCN), or at Petra.

One popular alternative is to 'camp with the Bedouin', ie share a tent with local Bedouin at Wadi Rum. Facilities are often very basic, but it's a great experience – refer to Places to Stay in the Wadi Rum section of the Southern Desert chapter for more details.

Hotels

A surprising thing about accommodation in Jordan is that there are towns, some of them quite large like Jerash, that have no hotel at all. Other towns, like Ajlun, offer little or nothing in the budget end of the market, and you may find yourself obliged to stay in a mid-range place, or day trip from somewhere with a budget hotel. Pre-booking a hotel room is rarely needed – you'll have little trouble finding a hotel anywhere in your price range if you just turn up, except in Aqaba at peak times (see that section for details). Prices for all accommodation are higher in Amman and Wadi Mousa (near Petra).

Most budget and mid-range places charge an extra JD1 to JD2 for breakfast, which is invariably little more than tea/coffee, bread and jam. It's cheaper to buy this sort of food at a grocery store and make your own breakfast; or enjoy a cooked breakfast at a budget-priced restaurant for about the same price.

For what it's worth, there is a telephone number in Amman for 'hotel complaints' (☎ 06-461 3103).

Budget There are no youth hostels in Jordan. A bed in a shared room (with a shared bathroom) in a cheap hotel will not cost less than JD2 and, generally, will be more like JD3 to JD5. Some places, especially those catering to backpackers, allow guests to sleep on the roof for about JD2 per person – which, in summer, is a good place to be. Private rooms are possible from about JD3/6 for singles/doubles, but anything decent will cost about JD6/10. Prices are negotiable, but often not by more than JD1 per person.

Most budget places have 'triples' (ie rooms with three beds), and often rooms with four beds, so sharing a room with friends, or asking to share a room with another guest, is a way of reducing accommodation costs considerably. Some cheaper places have two choices of accommodation: basic rooms with a shared bathroom, and more expensive ones with a private bathroom, which are also generally quieter, cleaner and nicer.

Especially in Amman, the cheap places can be incredibly noisy because of the traffic and the hubbub of the cafes and shops below, so try to get a room towards the back of the building. Many budget places all over Jordan are located above shops and cafes, which means climbing several flights of stairs to reach your room.

Mid-Range There is a reasonable selection of mid-range hotels, but only in Amman, Wadi Mousa (near Petra) and Aqaba. Rooms in mid-range hotels usually have a colour TV (which does not always feature satellite stations, eg BBC), fridge (sometimes useful) and telephone (rarely needed). A quiet, clean room with reliable hot water and a private bathroom in a mid-range hotel is sometimes worth a splurge, but rarely good value: prices start from about JD15/22 for singles/doubles. Negotiation is always possible, especially when business is quiet or if you're staying for several days – so it is sometimes possible to get a nice room in a decent mid-range hotel for a budget price.

Top End There is no shortage of top end hotels – but only in Amman, Wadi Mousa (near Petra) and Aqaba. They all feature the sort of luxuries you'd expect for the outrageous prices. Most guests at these sort of places are on organised tours; in quieter times negotiation is possible – don't except any bargains. Payment is sometimes required in US dollars, and all major credit cards are accepted. All top end hotels add a 'service charge' of about 10%, and a 'government tax' of about 10%, to their tariffs.

Rental Accommodation In Amman, long-term (monthly) rental is possible: check the two English-language daily newspapers, and the notice boards at the cultural centres. *Your Guide to Amman* (see Guidebooks in the Books section earlier in this chapter) lists real estate agents which deal with rental properties. Expect to pay from JD200 per month for a decent furnished apartment in a reasonable, but not upmarket, area.

In Aqaba, short-term rentals are available to Jordanian and foreign holidaymakers. A furnished two-bedroom apartment with a kitchen costs from JD10 per night in the low season; JD20 in the high season. Most apartments in Aqaba can only be rented for a minimum of one week, however, and must be pre-booked in the peak season. Look for ads in the windows of the travel agents, or ask anywhere you see a sign 'Furnished Flats', or something similar.

FOOD
Food in Jordan ranges from the exotic to the mundane. Unfortunately for the budget traveller, exotic food comes with exotic prices, so it's mostly the mundane you'll be relying on. The food is tasty as a rule, but the lack of variety may have you dreaming about far away meals.

Many restaurants have a 'family' section, basically set aside for families and unaccompanied (local and foreign) women. The entrance may not be entirely obvious, so ask the manager where it is. However, foreign women, especially those with male companions, will rarely have any problem eating wherever they choose.

Most restaurants offer foreigners knives, forks and spoons, but you'll have to use your hands to cope with felafel, shwarma and pastries – even if ordered in a restaurant. If you are offered food from a communal plate in a Jordanian home, and there are no eating implements, always use your right hand.

The new, free *Grumpy Gourmet* restaurant magazine is light-hearted, but is mainly for expatriates and upmarket visitors living/staying in Amman. It is published monthly, but hard to find, so contact them directly for a copy (email grumpy@grumpy gourmet.com) and check out their Web site at www.grumpygourmet.com.

For a comprehensive explanation of the various names and terms of local food, see the boxed text 'Food & Drinks Glossary'.

Restaurants
The most common way for a group to eat in any restaurant is to order *mezze* – a variety of small starters followed by several mains to be shared by all present. Otherwise, simply order one or two starters; bread (which is normally provided free anyway); one course (usually meat); and salad. Some smaller hole-in-the-wall places will specialise in one or two things only, while some just offer chicken or three or four vegetable stews.

Some restaurants close on Friday, usually in the evening, but places frequented by foreigners open every day. (Refer to the Public Holidays & Special Events section earlier in this chapter for information about restaurant opening times during Ramadan.) Only restaurants in upmarket hotels, those set up for the tourist trade and outlets of western fast food chains can usually offer a menu in English. In any other place, it's a matter of asking what's available or pointing to what other patrons are enjoying. Usually someone in the restaurant will know a bit of English, and the words 'kebabs', 'chicken', 'salad' and 'soup' are widely understood by restaurant staff.

Before you start ordering at a restaurant, especially anywhere frequented by foreigners and where there's no menu in English, ask for the prices of each dish. It's very easy to get carried away and order whatever the waiter recommends, and then you're suddenly confronted by six or more huge dishes that you can't possibly finish, and a large bill (not itemised, and in Arabic) which could cost at least JD5 per person. It is also amazing how often a bill comes to a multiple of JD1 (because the waiter rounds it up).

Starters *Humous* is cooked chickpeas ground into a paste and mixed with *tahina* (a sesame-seed paste), garlic and lemon. Available in virtually every restaurant, it's invariably excellent and generally eaten as a starter with bread. It goes very nicely with any of the meat dishes. *Baba ghanoug* is another dip eaten with bread and is made from mashed eggplant and tahina. Fairly similar is *mutabel*; a vaguely hot red dip is *daqqeh*. *Tabouleh* is largely a parsley, cracked wheat and tomato based salad, with a sprinkling of sesame seeds, lemon and garlic. It goes perfectly with the humous in bread.

A couple of more solid and tasty starters include *maqlubbeh*, steamed rice topped with grilled slices of eggplant or meat, grilled tomato and pinenuts; and *fareekeh*, a similar dish with cracked wheat. *Fattoush* is pretty much tabbouleh with little shreds of deep fried bread in it. Turkish-style stuffed vine leaves sometimes go by the name of *yalenjeh*.

Snacks The two most popular local versions of 'fast food' are the shwarma and felafel, both well known to anyone who has travelled elsewhere in the region. They can be eaten in restaurants, but are normally take-away only. For both, spicy sauces are optional, and should be treated with caution.

A shwarma is like the Greek *gyros* or the Turkish *doner*, ie slices of lamb or chicken from a huge revolving spit, and mixed with onions and tomato in bread. The vendor will slice off the meat (usually with a great flourish and much knife sharpening and waving), dip a piece of flat bread in the fat that has dripped off the meat, hold it against the gas flame so it flares, then fill it with the meat and fillings.

Felafel is deep-fried balls of chickpea paste with spices, served in a piece of *khobz* (bread) with varying combinations of pick-led vegetables or *turshi* (not to everyone's taste), tomato, salad and yoghurt.

Bread The Arabic unleavened bread, khobz, is eaten with absolutely everything and is sometimes called *eish* (life) – its common name in Egypt. It's round and flat and makes a good filler if you're preparing your own food. There's a variety of tastes and textures, depending on how it's baked, but the basic principle remains the same. Tastier than plain old khobz is *ka'ik*, round sesame rings of bread, often sold with a boiled egg from stalls over Jordan. A favourite breakfast staple is bread liberally sprinkled with *zata'* (thyme).

Main Dishes Most main dishes are comprised of chicken, meat kebabs, or meat and vegetable stews.

Chicken *(farooj)* is usually roasted on spits in large ovens out the front of the restaurant. The usual serving is half a chicken *(nuss farooj)* and it will come with bread, and a side dish of raw onion, chillies and sometimes olives. Eaten with the optional extras of salad *(salata)* and humous, it's a great meal.

Kebabs are another favourite, and available everywhere. These are spicy minced lamb (or chicken) pieces pressed onto skewers and grilled over charcoal. They are sometimes sold by weight, and are also served with bread and a side plate. *Shish tawouk* is loosely the chicken version of the same thing. Another popular chicken dish is *musakhan*, roast chicken served with onions and pine nuts on khobz. *Kofta* is a delicious and hearty meal of meat, tomatoes and other spices.

Stews are usually meat or vegetable, or both, and make a pleasant change from chicken and kebabs. *Fasooliya* is bean stew; *biseela* is made of peas; *batatas* is mostly potato; and *mulukiyyeh* is a kind of spinach stew with chicken or meat pieces. They are usually served with rice *(ruz)* or, more rarely, macaroni *(makarone)*. A local staple is *fuul*, a cheap, and usually tasty, dish of squashed fava beans mixed with chillis, onions and olive oil.

A Bedouin speciality is *mensaf*, traditionally served on special occasions. It consists of lamb on a bed of rice and pine nuts, topped with the gaping head of the animal. The fat from the cooking is poured into the rice and is considered by some to be the best part. Bedouin men sit on the floor around the big dishes and dig in (with the right hand only), while the women eat elsewhere in the town or camp. Traditionally, the delicacy is the eyes, which are presented to honoured guests (but don't worry if you miss out – there are other choice bits like the tongue!) The meal is eventually followed by endless rounds of coffee and tea, and plenty of lively talk. You can also buy a serve of mensaf in the better restaurants of the larger cities. It's not cheap, but should be tried at least once. A tangy sauce of cooked yoghurt mixed with the fat is served with it.

Fish *(samak)* is not widely available, and always expensive – even in Aqaba. It is often heavily salted and spiced, and tastes like an unappetising anchovy. *Sayadiya* is boiled fish with lemon juice.

Desserts Jordanians love sugar, and their desserts are assembled accordingly; there are pastry shops in every town selling nothing else. Many of the pastry shops are sit-down places, so you can walk in, make a selection and take a seat – or take some away with you. These pastry shops are often good places for solo women travellers to relax.

The basic formula is pastry drenched in honey, syrup and/or rose water. Many of them, however different they look, fall into the general category of *baklava*. Some tasty treats to try include: *kunafeh*, shredded dough with nuts dunked in syrup; *ma'amoul*, like kunafeh but with dates and nuts, and dipped in rose water; *halawat al-jibna*, a soft doughy pastry filled with cream cheese and topped with syrup and ice cream; *isfinjiyya*, a coconut slice; *mahalabiyya*, a very sweet dessert made of ground rice, sugar, milk and rose water; and *mushabbak*, a lace-work shaped pastry drenched in syrup.

Fast Food
All the famous western fast-food chains, eg KFC, McDonald's and Pizza Hut, have restaurants in Jordan, mainly in Amman and Aqaba. There are also outlets of lesser-known chains, such as Chilli House and Chicken Tikka Mankal. While the food at these sort of places may be familiar and quickly prepared, it's never cheap, eg a burger, fries and soft drink at McDonald's cost at least JD2.600, which is about twice as much as the same thing in a local, Jordanian-run shop around the corner. 'Chips', 'burgers' and 'sandwiches' (ie shwarmas) are now part of the local vernacular, and widely understood in most restaurants in Jordan.

Vegetarian
Virtually no restaurants in Jordan specialise in vegetarian food, and there are few specific 'vegetarian' dishes. However, vegetarians will have no problems getting by. Every restaurant offers a number of different salads at reasonable prices, and two salads with bread often makes a decent meal. Vegetable soups are common, although they may be 'contaminated' with small pieces of meat. Starters such as humous, and traditional dishes like fuul, are meat-less and will become staple foods for vegetarians.

Self-Catering
Buying food for breakfast, lunch or dinner, and eating in your hotel room, is very easy to arrange. If you are travelling around during the day, finding a decent restaurant when your stomach starts rumbling is not always easy, so consider taking food with you and enjoying a picnic in the grounds of an ancient castle, or in a park. Just about every town has at least one well-stocked grocery store, and Amman boasts several big western-style supermarkets.

DRINKS
Drinking tea or coffee is a national pastime for locals, and drinking any form of liquid is a preoccupation for most visitors, especially in summer.

Nonalcoholic Drinks
Water Most restaurants offer a jug of free cold water, which is safe to drink; if you don't receive it, ask for the waiter. If you're offered mineral water in a sealed plastic bottle at a restaurant, you'll have to pay for it.

Food & Drinks Glossary

Soup
soup	*shurba*
lentil soup	*shurbat al-'adas*

Vegetables
vegetables	*khadrawat*
cabbage	*kharoum*
carrot	*jazar*
cauliflower	*arnabeet*
cucumber	*khiyaar*
eggplant	*bazinjan*
garlic	*tum*
green bean	*fasooliya*
lentils	*'adas*
lettuce	*khass*
okra	*baamiya*
onion	*basal*
peas	*biseela*
potato	*batata*
salad	*salata*
tomato	*banadura*
turnip	*lift*

Meats
meat	*lahm*
camel	*lahm jamal*
chicken	*farooj*
kidney	*kelaawi*
lamb	*lahm danee*
liver	*kibda*

Fruit
fruit	*fawaka*
apple	*tufah*
apricot	*mish-mish*
banana	*moz*
date	*tamr*
fig	*teen*
grape	*'inab*
lime	*limoon*
orange	*burtuqaal*
pomegranate	*rumman*
watermelon	*batteekh*

Drinks
milk	*haleeb*
mineral water	*maya at-ta'abiyya*
sour milk drink	*ayran*
water	*mayy*

Miscellaneous
bread	*khobz* or *eish*
butter	*zibda*
cheese	*jibna*
egg	*beid*
pepper	*filfil*
salt	*milh*
sugar	*sukar*
yoghurt	*laban*

Small and large bottles of mineral water are easy to buy anywhere in Jordan. (See Water in the Health section earlier in this chapter for more information about how to avoid buying mineral water, and purifying local tap water instead.)

Juices All over Jordan, juice stalls sell freshly squeezed fruit juices *(aseer)*; these stalls are instantly recognisable by the string bags of fruit hanging out the front. Popular juices include lemon, orange, banana, pomegranate and rockmelon, and you can have combinations of any or all of these. Diluting fruit juices with tap water or, worse, a sickly cordial, is a common and irritating practice.

Some stalls put milk in their drinks which you'd be well advised to stay away from, particularly if you have a dodgy stomach. *Sahlab* is a traditional drink, served hot with milk, nuts and cinnamon – delicious, if made properly.

Soft Drinks (Sodas) All the normal international brands are widely available, eg Coke, Pepsi, 7-Up and Fanta. They come in returnable and recycled glass and plastic bottles. Cans are smaller than bottles, and more expensive because you have to pay for the nonrecyclable can – which is why canned drinks are often the only choice in tourist-oriented restaurants.

Alcoholic Drinks

Despite the prohibitions imposed by Islam, alcohol is widely available in bars and from the occasional liquor store in major towns. Before taking alcohol back to your hotel, ask whether the manager (who is probably Muslim) minds. Top end hotels may not like you bringing alcohol into your room because they prefer guests to drink from the expensive minibar.

Amstel beer is brewed in Jordan under licence from the parent European company, and is easily the most widely available (and often the only available) beer. In Amman and Aqaba, beer imported from all over the world – everything from Guinness to Fosters – is available but at prices higher than you'd pay in Ireland or Australia. From a liquor store, a bottle of 650ml Amstel beer costs abut JD1; at least JD1.500 in a dingy bar in Amman and a lot more in a decent pub or nightclub.

Araq is the indigenous firewater, similar to Greek *ouzo* or Turkish *raqi*. Available in shops, bars and restaurants throughout Jordan, it's usually mixed with water and ice and drunk with food – and should be treated with caution. Various other types of hard liquor are available in liquor stores and bars, including all sorts of 'scotch whisky' brewed locally or imported from places like India. Any liquor made by a well-known western company (like Johnny Walker) is outrageously expensive, so pick up a bottle duty free.

Little wine is produced in Jordan, so brands such as Latroun, St Catherine and Cremisan are imported from the West Bank. Wine costs about JD5/10 for a half/full bottle in a restaurant; less from a liquor store.

ENTERTAINMENT

Jordan is not exactly thumping with nightlife. The top end hotels offer the usual expensive and often dull discos and nightclubs, and occasionally present Arab musicians and bellydancing. The wealthier locals in Amman hang around the restaurants and cafes in Shmeisani or Abdoun, which can be quite busy, but most places shut by about 11 pm.

In the evenings, most visitors will probably window shop, stroll around the streets, enjoy a leisurely meal, go to the cinema or watch TV. To find out what is going on, check the listings in the two English-language daily newspapers, and the weekly *Star* newspaper, all published in Amman; ask staff at the local tourist offices; or contact the cultural centres, or the relevant venue.

Pubs/Bars

The bars in the bigger hotels are more comfortable – but certainly more expensive – than the dingy bars, eg those tucked away in the rabbit warren of alleys around Downtown in Amman. The bars in Amman where women will feel more welcome are listed in that chapter. Unaccompanied women will feel far more relaxed at one of the classier bars frequented by foreigners and expats.

Discos/Clubs

Some of the hotels in Amman, Wadi Mousa (near Petra) and Aqaba run nightclubs, but they're nothing to get excited about. Entrance is usually free, drinks expensive, and the lights and music are often grating.

Traditional Music

The various foreign cultural centres in Amman regularly organise musical recitals. Also in Amman, the Royal Cultural Centre occasionally puts on concerts and plays, usually in Arabic; Darat al-Funun art gallery often features recitals of classical and ethnic music; and the Haya Cultural Centre has programs of music and dance for children. Traditional concerts, plays and dances also feature heavily in the Jerash Festival of Culture & Arts, and at special events at places like Salt and Fuheis.

Cinemas

In order to show the films quickly, they cut out some parts. Most of the time they're understandable, except for *Indecent Proposal* with the indecent proposal cut out!

J van den Brink, Netherlands

Many popular western films are eventually given a release in Jordan, although anything considered too risque in the film is deleted by the censors (but all the sickening violence remains untouched).

Only Amman and Irbid have cinemas. Most films at the cheaper cinemas are dubbed into Arabic; the ones at the more expensive places are subtitled in Arabic (and sometimes French), so the original language (usually English) is still audible.

Tickets at the cheaper cinemas cost about JD1.500, and starting times are not standardised, nor are they normally known to even the ticket sellers and ushers. Tickets to the better cinemas (all of which are in Amman) are pricey at about JD4, but the quality of sound and vision, and the comfort of seating, is far superior to the cheap places. Programs for the good cinemas in Amman are advertised regularly in the two English-language daily newspapers.

Cafes

Any traditional cafe is normally drinks only, and that means, coffee, tea and soft drinks. Some may have an unadvertised special section at the back serving as a bar, but it's invariably dingy, and for men only. Very few traditional cafes serve food, except the more modern western-style ones which sometimes offer simple meals and snacks.

Cafes are often great places to watch the world go by, write letters, try the *nargila* (water pipe), meet locals and, maybe, play a hand of cards or backgammon. The cafes in Amman that are generally men-only, and those that welcome women, are listed separately. However, any unaccompanied foreign women, with a bit of courage and very modest attire, are usually welcome at any cafe in Jordan.

SPECTATOR SPORTS

Not surprisingly, the most popular sport in the country is football (soccer). The Premier League Championship plays mostly on Friday during winter (from about September to March), and features teams from Amman and most major towns. The fans take the game so seriously that the League was cancelled in 1998 after a referee was beaten up by fans, and the game was abandoned. The cancellation was not caused by the horror of the injury to the referee, but by the participating teams' vehement disagreement about which team should be the 'winner' of the abandoned game. The British embassy also runs a football competition for the ladies.

Other sports which Jordanians enjoy watching, participating in locally and competing in at overseas events, include: judo; table tennis; kite-flying; volleyball; horse-racing (including long-distance endurance races); golf (at Jordan's only course – see the Amman chapter for details); and, more recently, rugby union.

Major sporting events are often held at the massive Sports City, in northern Amman, and at the Al-Hasan Sports City, in Irbid. During mid-1999, Jordan hosted the 9th Pan Arab Games, with over 4000 athletes from most Arab countries.

The vast deserts and good roads are ideal for car rallies, such as the 700km Jordan International Rally, organised by the Royal Automobile Club of Jordan; and for events such as the Amman-Dead Sea Marathon (about 50km), held every April.

SHOPPING

Jordan does not boast the best range or prices of souvenirs in the Middle East, so if you're travelling elsewhere in the region, you may want to stock up on mementos in Egypt or Syria (where a lot of souvenirs in Jordan are made anyway).

More information about traditional arts and crafts can be found in the Arts section of the Facts about Jordan chapter.

Handicrafts

Salt and Fuheis, both near Amman, have several art galleries and handicraft workshops where visitors can buy ceramics, mosaics, paintings and embroidery. Other places with a good range of souvenirs are Haret Jdoudna, with its 20 arts and crafts shops, in Madaba; Dana village; and the several shops in the visitors centre in Petra which benefit local women's charities.

Several chains of stores around Jordan sell high quality, if pricey, souvenirs made by Jordanians, mostly women. Profits from the sale of all items go to local charities which aim to develop the status of women, or protect the local environment. They are:

Bani Hamida (email bh@go.com.jo) A women's co-operative which started in the remote village of Mukawir; it now also has a store in Amman (see the boxed text 'The Bani Hamida Story' in the King's Highway chapter).

Jordan Design & Trade Centre (email jdtc@ nets.com.jo) Part of the Queen Noor Foundation, it helps to preserve traditional crafts, create jobs for women and raise money for children. It has stores in northern Amman, Petra, Aqaba, Madaba and Jerash.

Web site www.nhf.org.jo

Jordan River Designs Run for the benefit of the Save the Children Fund, it specialises in high quality linen, cushions and rugs, and has a store in Amman.

Wadi Dana Run under the auspices of the RSCN, it sells herbs, fruits, jewellery and pottery to help preserve the welfare of the Dana people, and to protect the wildlife in the Dana Nature Reserve. It has branches in Amman, Madaba and Dana village.

Carpets, Rugs & Kilims

While it's still possible to stumble across an aged handmade 'Persian rug' from Iran, the chances are that it was sewn in an attic above the shop. This is not to say that the carpets are lousy, but it's worth taking a close look at quality. Inspect both sides of the carpet to get an idea of how close and strong the sewing is.

Designs generally tend to consist of geometric patterns, although increasingly the tourist market is being catered to with depictions of monuments, animals and the like – rather kitsch and a poor reflection of Middle Eastern artistic tradition. Rugs and tapestries made by Bedouin and Palestinian women are popular, but you need to look carefully to make sure that they are actually handmade. Madaba is famous for its traditional rugs and you can buy one, and watch others being made, at workshops in the town centre.

Dead Sea Products

'Dead Sea' cosmetic products are a popular souvenir, and available all over Jordan. The lotions, creams, gels – you name it – are made from minerals, such as calcium, magnesium and potassium, and are supposed to be very good for the skin as well as other ailments (see the boxed text 'The Dead Sea'

in the Northern & Western Jordan chapter for more information).

Gold, Silver & Jewellery

Gold shops are scattered all over the bigger cities of Jordan, with the most concentrated in the souqs of Downtown Amman. As a rule, gold is sold by weight, and all pieces should have a hallmark guaranteeing quality. (A hallmark normally indicates where a piece was assayed, and a date.) Verifying all this is difficult, however, so the best advice is to buy items you're happy with even if you find out at home that the gold content is not as high as you were told by that nice salesman.

The same goes for silver, although of course its monetary value is in any case somewhat lower. For that reason, it's the most common material used by Bedouin women to make up their often striking jewellery, eg earrings, necklaces and pendants laden with semiprecious stones.

Depending on your tastes, a plethora of original and reasonably priced items can be bought. Take most of the talk about 'antique jewellery' with a shaker-full of salt, and remember customs regulations about antiques (see Export Restrictions later in this chapter). Silver is not only used in women's jewellery, but to make carry-cases for miniature Qurans and other objects.

Copper & Brassware

From Morocco to Baghdad, you'll find much the same sorts of brass and chased copper objects for sale. The good thing about this stuff is that it's fairly hard to cheat on quality, but check for leaks before buying anything you wish to use (rather than just keep as a useless souvenir). Most common on the souvenir list are the large decorative trays and tabletops, but other items include traditionally styled Arabic coffeepots and even complete coffee sets with small cups. Incense-burners and teapots are among other possible buys.

Instruments

A few stalls in Downtown Amman sell either *ouds* (Arabic lutes) or *darbukkas*, the standard Middle Eastern style drums. The latter can go quite cheaply, and even the ouds are hardly expensive. Such an item's musical value must be considered unlikely to be high – it's the kind of thing you'd buy more to display than to play.

Woodwork

Another popular buy with foreigners are the woodwork items, ranging from simple jewellery boxes to elaborate chess sets and backgammon boards. The better quality stuff tends to be made of walnut and inlaid with mother of pearl. If the mother of pearl gives off a strong rainbow-colour effect, you can be almost sure it's the real McCoy. The actual woodwork on many of these items tends to be a little shoddy, even on the better quality items, so inspect the joints and inlay carefully.

Other Souvenirs

The ubiquitous nargila water pipes are about the most vivid reminder possible of a visit to Jordan. Remember to buy a supply of charcoal to get you going if you intend to use the thing when you return home – a couple of spare tubes would not go astray either. This would have to be about the most awkward souvenir to cart around, however, or post home – and the chances of surviving either are not good.

Another simple idea, and much easier to carry around, is the traditional Arab headcloth, or *kufeyya*, and *'iqal* (the black cord used to keep it on your head), so characteristic of the region. The quality of kufeyyas does vary considerably, and some are very bare strips of white cotton and others densely sewn in red or black patterns – always compare before you buy. The elegant flowing ankle-length *galabeyya* tunic is available at shops all over Jordan.

The small bottles of coloured sand from Petra and Aqaba are a speciality. The sand is poured into bottles to form intricate patterns, and these are sold for as little as 500 fils. Natural, coloured sand was originally used, but these days it's often artificially coloured.

From Aqaba, some interesting souvenirs include: spices, such as cardamom and saffron; cassettes of western music (and dubious legality); and delicious roasted nuts. You may be urged to buy something made from coral but for the sake of the precious marine environment, please don't. In any case, buying anything made of coral is illegal.

Duty Free

There are duty-free shops at the Queen Alia international airport, and next to the Ammon Hotel in Amman; and small ones at the airports at Marka (in Amman) and Aqaba, and at the three border crossings with Israel. The Customs section earlier in this chapter has information about duty-free allowances.

Export Restrictions

Exporting anything more than 100 years old is illegal, so don't buy any souvenir that is deemed by the salesman as 'antique' – if only because it probably isn't. You may be offered 'ancient' coins around some of the archaeological sites. These may be genuine, but buying them – and taking them home – is highly illegal. If you are unsure about what is an 'antique', contact the Customs Department (☎ 06-462 3186) in Amman.

Getting There & Away

Most visitors come to Jordan as part of a jaunt around the Middle East. The national carrier, Royal Jordanian Airlines, and many other international airlines, connect Amman with most cities in the Middle East and Europe, but there are no direct flights on any airline between Amman and Canada, Australia or New Zealand, and very few direct services between Amman and the USA. Schedules for international (and domestic) flights to/from Amman are listed in the two English-language daily newspapers published in the capital.

AIR

Jordan is reasonably well connected by air with Europe and the rest of the Middle East, but cheap tickets are rare, so independent travellers tend to enter the country by land or sea from Syria, Egypt and Israel.

Tourist authorities are hoping up to 1.3 million visitors will come to Jordan in 2000 to celebrate the Birth of Christ. Many will fly into Jordan on organised tours, so try to buy airline tickets early because flights at peak times in 2000 and early 2001 will be heavily booked.

Always remember to reconfirm your onward or return flight at least 72 hours before departure on international flights.

Airports & Airlines

The modern Queen Alia international airport (☎ 06-445 2000), about 35km south of Amman, is the country's main gateway. There are two terminals, only 100m apart and opposite each other: Terminal 1 is used for most Royal Jordanian flights (with the notable exception of flights to/from Amsterdam); and Terminal 2 is used for all other flights on all other airlines. Both terminals have automatic teller machines (ATMs) which take most major credit cards; foreign exchange counters; a post office; and a left luggage counter. Terminal 2 has a tourist information counter (☎ 06-445 3200), but it's of very limited use.

On arrival in Jordan you'll be given an Entry Card to fill out. You must keep this card until you leave the country. At the time of research, the international arrival lounges in both terminals were under renovation and in disarray.

The former military airfield in Marka, north-east of central Amman, is sometimes officially called the Amman Civil Airport. From this airport, there are regular flights to/from Gaza (in the Palestine National Authority) and Tel Aviv in Israel. The only other international (and domestic) airport is at Aqaba. The weekly Royal Jordanian flight between Amman and Paris stops in Aqaba, and there are occasional charter flights between Europe and Aqaba.

The national airline, Royal Jordanian Airlines (Web site www.rja.com.jo), has flights to most major cities in Europe and all over the Middle East. (If you fly with Royal Jordanian, ask them about a free connection to Aqaba.) Royal Wings (Web site www.royalwings.com), a subsidiary of Royal Jordanian, has smaller planes for short flights between Amman and Tel Aviv and Gaza, but uses the same code (RJ) as Royal Jordanian.

Buying Tickets

The plane ticket will probably be the single most expensive item in your budget, and buying it can be an intimidating business. It's worth putting aside a few hours to research the state of the market and check around the many travel agents. The Internet is an increasingly popular way to shop around for tickets, or to at least get some information about Jordan and to communicate with other travellers who have been there recently (see Internet Resources in the Facts for the Visitor chapter).

Start early: some of the cheapest tickets have to be bought months in advance, and some popular flights sell out early. When looking for bargain air fares, it's best to go to a travel agent rather than directly to the

Air Travel Glossary

Baggage Allowance This will be written on your ticket and usually includes one 20kg item to go in the hold, plus one item of hand luggage.

Bucket Shops These are unbonded travel agencies specialising in discounted airline tickets.

Bumped Just because you have a confirmed seat doesn't mean you're going to get on the plane (see Overbooking).

Cancellation Penalties If you have to cancel or change a discounted ticket, there are often heavy penalties involved; insurance can sometimes be taken out against these penalties. Some airlines impose penalties on regular tickets as well, particularly against 'no-show' passengers.

Check-In Airlines ask you to check in a certain time ahead of the flight departure (usually one to two hours on international flights). If you fail to check in on time and the flight is overbooked, the airline can cancel your booking and give your seat to somebody else.

Confirmation Having a ticket written out with the flight and date you want doesn't mean you have a seat until the agent has checked with the airline that your status is 'OK' or confirmed. Meanwhile you could just be 'on request'.

Courier Fares Businesses often need to send urgent documents or freight securely and quickly. Courier companies hire people to accompany the package through customs and, in return, offer a discount ticket which is sometimes a phenomenal bargain. In effect, what the companies do is ship their freight as your luggage on regular commercial flights. This is a legitimate operation, but there are two shortcomings – the short turnaround time of the ticket (usually not longer than a month) and the limitation on your luggage allowance. You may have to surrender all your allowance and take only carry-on luggage.

Full Fares Airlines traditionally offer 1st class (coded F), business class (coded J) and economy class (coded Y) tickets. These days there are so many promotional and discounted fares available that few passengers pay full economy fare.

ITX An ITX, or 'independent inclusive tour excursion', is often available on tickets to popular holiday destinations. Officially it's a package deal combined with hotel accommodation, but many agents will sell you one of these for the flight only and give you phoney hotel vouchers in the unlikely event that you're challenged at the airport.

Lost Tickets If you lose your airline ticket an airline will usually treat it like a travellers cheque and, after inquiries, issue you with another one. Legally, however, an airline is entitled to treat it like cash and if you lose it then it's gone forever. Take good care of your tickets.

MCO An MCO, or 'miscellaneous charge order', is a voucher that looks like an airline ticket but carries no destination or date. It can be exchanged through any International Association of Travel Agents (IATA) airline for a ticket on a specific flight. It's a useful alternative to an onward ticket in those countries that demand one, and is more flexible than an ordinary ticket if you're unsure of your route.

No-Shows No-shows are passengers who fail to show up for their flight. Full-fare passengers who fail to turn up are sometimes entitled to travel on a later flight. The rest are penalised (see Cancellation Penalties).

On Request This is an unconfirmed booking for a flight.

airline. From time to time, airlines do have promotional fares and special offers but generally they only sell fares at the official listed price. The other exception is booking on the Internet. Many airlines, full-service and no-frills, offer some excellent fares to Web surfers. They may sell seats by auction or simply cut prices to reflect the reduced cost of electronic selling.

The days when some travel agents would routinely fleece travellers by running off with their money are, happily, almost over.

Air Travel Glossary

Onward Tickets An entry requirement for many countries is that you have a ticket out of the country. If you're unsure of your next move, the easiest solution is to buy the cheapest onward ticket to a neighbouring country or a ticket from a reliable airline which can later be refunded if you do not use it.

Open Jaw Tickets These are return tickets where you fly out to one place but return from another. If available on your intended route, this can save you backtracking to your arrival point.

Overbooking Airlines hate to fly empty seats and since every flight has some passengers who fail to show up, airlines often book more passengers than they have seats. Usually excess passengers make up for the no-shows, but occasionally somebody gets 'bumped' onto the next available flight. Guess who it is most likely to be? The passengers who check in late.

Point-to-Point Tickets These are discount tickets that can be bought on some routes in return for passengers waiving their rights to a stopover.

Promotional Fares These are officially discounted fares, available from travel agencies or direct from the airline.

Reconfirmation If you don't reconfirm your flight at least 72 hours prior to departure, the airline may delete your name from the passenger list. Ring to find out if your airline requires reconfirmation.

Restrictions Discounted tickets often have various restrictions on them – such as needing to be paid for in advance and incurring a penalty to be altered. Others are restrictions on the minimum and maximum period you must be away, such as a minimum of 14 days or a maximum of one year.

Round-the-World Tickets RTW tickets give you a limited period (usually a year) in which to circumnavigate the globe. You can go anywhere the carrying airlines go, as long as you don't backtrack. The number of stopovers or total number of separate flights is decided before you set off and they usually cost a bit more than a basic return flight.

Stand-by This is a discounted ticket where you only fly if there is a seat free at the last moment. Stand-by fares are usually available only on domestic routes.

Transferred Tickets Airline tickets cannot be transferred from one person to another. Travellers sometimes try to sell the return half of their ticket, but officials can ask you to prove that you are the person named on the ticket. This is less likely to happen on domestic flights, but on an international flight tickets are compared with passports.

Travel Agencies Travel agencies vary widely and you should choose one that suits your needs. Some simply handle tours, while full-service agencies handle everything from tours and tickets to car rental and hotel bookings. If all you want is a ticket at the lowest possible price, then go to an agency specialising in discounted fares.

Travel Periods Ticket prices vary with the time of year. There is a low (off-peak) season and a high (peak) season, and often a low-shoulder season and a high-shoulder season as well. Usually the fare depends on your outward flight – if you depart in the high season and return in the low season, you pay the high-season fare.

Paying by credit card generally offers protection as most card issuers provide refunds if you can prove you didn't get what you paid for. Similar protection can be obtained by buying a ticket from a bonded agent, such as one covered by the Air Transport Operators License (ATOL) scheme in the UK. Agents who only accept cash should hand over the tickets straight away and not tell you to 'come back tomorrow'. After you've made a booking or paid your deposit, call the airline and confirm that the booking was made. It's not advisable to send money (even cheques) through the post unless the agent is very well established – some travellers have reported being ripped off by fly-by-night mail-order ticket agents.

You may decide to pay more than the rock-bottom fare by opting for the safety of a better known travel agent. Firms such as STA Travel, which has offices worldwide, Council Travel in the USA and USIT Campus (formerly Campus Travel) in the UK are not going to disappear overnight and they do offer good prices to most destinations.

Travellers with Special Needs

If you have special needs of any sort – you've broken a leg, you're a vegetarian, travelling in a wheelchair, taking the baby, terrified of flying – you should let the airline know as soon as possible so that arrangements accordingly. You should remind them when you reconfirm your booking (at least 72 hours before departure) and again when you check in at the airport. It may also be worth ringing around the airlines before you make your booking to find out how they can handle your particular needs.

Most international airports will provide escorts from check-in desk to plane where needed, and there should be ramps, lifts, accessible toilets and phones. Aircraft toilets, on the other hand, are likely to present a problem; travellers should discuss this with the airline at an early stage and, if necessary, with their doctor.

Children under two years of age travel for 10% of the standard fare (or free, on some airlines), as long as they don't occupy a seat. They don't get a baggage allowance, however. 'Skycots' should be provided by the airline if requested in advance; these will take a child weighing up to about 10kg. Children between two and 12 can usually occupy a seat for half to two-thirds of the full fare, but do get a baggage allowance. Pushchairs can often be taken as hand luggage.

Departure Tax

The departure tax on all international flights from Amman and Aqaba for foreigners (who are not citizens of a country in the Middle East) is JD10. At Queen Alia airport, the tax must be paid at special counters after you've checked your luggage in, and before you've cleared immigration. If you're in Jordan for less than 72 hours, and depart by air from Queen Alia, you may be exempt from the departure tax, but only if you ask.

The USA

There is very little direct traffic between the USA and Jordan, so it's often worthwhile getting a cheap flight to Europe (normally London, Frankfurt or Amsterdam) first, and looking for a cheap deal from there. Alternatively, get a connection in a country near Jordan on a Middle Eastern airline, eg Saudi Arabian Airlines has flights from New York, via Washington, to Jeddah and Riyadh, and connections to Amman. The cheapest option is probably to fly into Israel, eg El Al airlines to Tel Aviv, and then cross the border into Jordan by bus or service taxi. However, this will mean that your passport will have those disliked Israeli entry stamps – see the 'Travelling To/From Israel' boxed text in the Facts for the Visitor chapter.

The *New York Times*, the *Los Angeles Times,* the *Chicago Tribune* and the *San Francisco Examiner* all produce weekly travel sections in which you will find a number of travel agency ads. Council Travel, America's largest student travel organisation, has around 60 offices in the USA; its head office (☎ 800-226 8624) is at 205 E 42 St, New York, NY 10017. Call for the nearest office or visit its Web site www.ciee.org. STA Travel (☎ 800-777 0112) has offices in Boston, Chicago, Miami, New York, Philadelphia, San Francisco and other major cities. Call the toll-free 800 number for offices or visit its Web site www.statravel.com.

From the USA, low season return fares to Amman start at around US$670 from New York City or US$1000 from Chicago. Royal Jordanian offers direct flights to Amman as well as flights via Europe, generally either via London or Frankfurt.

Discount and rock-bottom options from the USA include charter flights, stand-by and courier flights. Stand-by fares are often sold at 60% of the normal price for one-way tickets. Airhitch (☎ 212-864 2000), Suite 100, 2790 Broadway, New York, NY 10025, specialises in this sort of thing. Check out their Web site www.airhitch.org. You'll need to give a general idea of where and when you need to go, and a few days before your departure you'll be presented with a choice of two or three flights.

Courier flights are where you accompany freight to its destination. There may not be much going to Jordan, but you never know your luck. Generally courier flights require that you return within a specified period (sometimes within one or two weeks, but often up to one month). You'll need to travel light, as luggage is usually restricted to what you can carry onto the plane (the freight you accompany comes out of your luggage allowance).

Travel Unlimited (PO Box 1058, Allston, MA 02134, USA) is a monthly travel newsletter from the USA that publishes many courier flight deals from destinations worldwide. A 12-month subscription to the newsletter costs US$25, or US$35 for residents outside the USA. Another possibility is to join the International Association of Air Travel Couriers (IAATC). The membership fee of US$45 gets members a bimonthly update of air courier offerings, access to a fax-on-demand service with daily updates of last minute specials and the bimonthly newsletter the *Shoestring Traveler.* For more information, contact IAATC (☎ 561-582 8320) or, alternatively, visit its Web site www.courier.org. However, be aware that joining this organisation does not guarantee that you'll get a courier flight.

A good source of information on courier flights is Now Voyager (☎ 212-431 1616), Suite 307, 74 Varrick St, New York, NY 10013. Check out their Web site at www.nowvoyagertravel.com. This company specialises in courier flights, but you must pay an annual membership fee (around US$50), which entitles you to take as many courier flights as you like. Prices drop as the departure date approaches. It's also possible to organise the flights directly through the courier companies. Look in your *Yellow Pages* under Courier Services.

Canada

Air Canada and Royal Jordanian offer flights, via London or Frankfurt, to Amman. Low season return fares from Montreal start at around C$1988 or C$2310 from Toronto.

The *Globe and Mail*, the *Toronto Star*, the *Montreal Gazette* and the *Vancouver Sun* carry travel agents ads and are a good place to look for cheap fares.

Travel CUTS (☎ 800-667 2887) is Canada's national student travel agency and has offices in all major cities. Its Web address is www.travelcuts.com.

For courier flights originating in Canada, contact FB On Board Courier Services (☎ 514-633 0740 in Montreal; or ☎ 604-338 1366 in Vancouver). See The USA section above for more information on courier flights.

Australia

There are no direct flights between Australia and Jordan. One of the cheaper flights to Amman from Melbourne or Sydney is on Qantas or Thai Airways to Bangkok, and a connection on Royal Jordanian. Return low/high season fares start at A$1485/1685. Other airlines flying from Australia include Gulf Air, Emirates and Olympic Airways.

Two well known agents for cheap fares are STA Travel and Flight Centre. STA Travel (☎ 03-9349 2411) has its main office in Melbourne at 224 Faraday St, Carlton, and offices in all major cities and on many university campuses. Call ☎ 131 776 Australia wide for the location of your nearest branch or visit its Web site at www.statravel.com.au. Flight Centre (☎ 131 600 Australia wide) has a central office at 82 Elizabeth St, Sydney, and there are dozens of offices throughout Australia. Its Web address is www.flightcentre.com.au.

New Zealand

Flights to Jordan from New Zealand are generally via Frankfurt or Bangkok. From New Zealand, you can expect to pay around NZ$1620 for a return flight to Amman in the low season. The *New Zealand Herald* has a travel section in which travel agents advertise fares. Flight Centre (☎ 09-309 6171) has a large central office in Auckland at National Bank Towers (corner Queen and Darby Sts) and many branches throughout the country. STA Travel (☎ 09-309 0458) has its main office at 10 High St, Auckland, and has other offices in Auckland as well as in Hamilton, Palmerston North, Wellington, Christchurch and Dunedin. The Web address is www.sta.travel.com.au.

The UK

London and other cities in England are well connected with Amman, although some of the cheapest airlines do not fly there directly and require a lengthy (even overnight) stopover. Some of the airlines mentioned below offer 'open jaw' tickets which, for example, allow you to fly in to Amman, but out of Beirut (Lebanon) or Damascus (Syria).

Some of the cheapest flights from the UK to Amman are on Olympic Airways, via Athens; Turkish Airlines, via Istanbul; and Tarom Romanian Airlines, via Bucharest. Low season return fares start from UK£310.

Royal Jordanian flies between London and Amman every day, once a week via Berlin and once a week via Frankfurt. Expect to pay UK£420 for a return fare.

Discount air travel is big business in London. Advertisements for many travel agents appear in the travel pages of the weekend broadsheets, such as the *Independent* on Saturday and the *Sunday Times*. Look out for the free magazines, such as *TNT*, which are widely available in London – start by looking outside the main railway and underground stations.

For students or travellers under 26, popular travel agencies in the UK include STA Travel (☎ 020-7361 6161), which has an office at 86 Old Brompton Rd, London SW7 3LQ, and other offices in London and Manchester. Visit its Web site at www.sta travel.co.uk. USIT Campus Travel (☎ 020-7730 3402), 52 Grosvenor Gardens, London SW1WOAG, has branches throughout the UK. The Web address is www.usitcampus. com. Both of these agencies sell tickets to all travellers but cater especially to young people and students. Charter flights can work out as a cheaper alternative to scheduled flights,

especially if you do not qualify for the under-26 and student discounts.

Other recommended bucket shops include: Trailfinders (☎ 020-7938 3939), 194 Kensington High St, London W8 7RG; Bridge the World (☎ 020-7734 7447), 4 Regent Place, London W1R 5FB; and also Flightbookers (☎ 020-7757 2000), 177-178 Tottenham Court Rd, London W1P 9LF.

The Globetrotters Club (☎ 020-8674 6229) BCM Roving, London WC1N 3XX, publishes a newsletter called *Globe* that covers obscure destinations and can help in finding travelling companions. Check out their Web site at www.globetrotters.co.uk.

Flying as a courier (see also The USA section earlier) might be a possibility. Contact British Airways Travel Shops (☎ 020-8564 7009) for courier flights with British Airways. If you're coming from Ireland, you're almost guaranteed of getting a better deal by legging it across to London first.

Continental Europe

KLM and Lufthansa offer the most direct flights to Amman, and have excellent connections all around Europe and the UK. Amsterdam and Frankfurt are the two major hubs for air transport in Europe, and home to bucket shops selling discounted fares.

One cheap airline worth considering is Cyprus Airways which flies to Amman, via Larnaca (Cyprus), from: Amsterdam; Berlin; Dresden, Frankfurt and Hamburg; Paris; Milan and Rome; Geneva and Zurich.

From Frankfurt fares start at US$1200 for a return flight. In Frankfurt, you might try SRID Reisen (☎ 069-43 01 91), Bergerstrasse 118. In Munich, a great source of travel information and equipment is the Därr Travel Shop (☎ 089-28 20 32) at Theresienstrasse 66. In addition to producing a very comprehensive travel equipment catalogue, they also run an 'Expedition Service' with available current flight information.

In Berlin, ARTU Reisen (☎ 030-31 04 66), Hardenbergstrasse 9 (near Berlin Zoo), and with five branches around the city, is a good travel agent.

As the base for KLM, and the home of a multitude of bucket shops, Amsterdam is a popular departure point, fares to Amman start at around US$1150. Some of the best fares are offered by the student travel agency NBBS Reiswinkels (☎ 020-620 50 71). They have seven branches throughout Amsterdam, and their fares are comparable to those of London bucket shops. NBBS Reiswinkels also has branches in Brussels (Belgium).

In Italy, the best place to look for cheaper flights is CTS (Centro Turistico Studentesco), which has branches all over Italy, including Rome (☎ 06-46 791), Via Genova 16. Expect to pay US$645 for a return flight to Amman. In Paris, Voyages et Découvertes (☎ 01-42 61 00 01), 21 Rue Cambon, is a good place to start hunting down the best airfares, return fares to Amman start at US$1080.

The Middle East

Jordan is a decent base from which to explore the Middle East, and there are regular flights from Amman (and, to a lesser degree, from Aqaba) all around the region. Flights are not particularly cheap, however, but specials (eg over the Thursday/Friday Islamic 'weekend') are often advertised in the two English-language daily newspapers published in Amman.

From Amman, there are regular nonstop direct flights to:

to	airlines	one way/ return (JD)
Abu Dhabi	Gulf Air/ Royal Jordanian	270/360
Bahrain	Gulf Air/ Royal Jordanian	280/292
Beirut	MEA/Royal Jordanian	76/141
Cairo	Egypt Air/ Royal Jordanian	127/135
Damascus	Royal Jordanian/ Syrian Air	47/95
Dhahran	Saudi Arabian	242/323
Doha	Gulf Air/Qatar Airways/ Royal Jordanian	280/292
Dubai	Royal Jordanian	270/360
Istanbul	Royal Jordanian/ Turkish Airlines	215/253
Jeddah	Royal Jordanian/ Saudi Arabian	200/267
Riyadh	Saudi Arabian	242/323

From Aqaba, there are regular nonstop direct flights available to Gaza (in the Palestine National Authority) on Palestinian Airlines and Royal Wings – both for JD89/ 142 (one way/return); and to Tel Aviv on El Al and Royal Wings for JD54/102.

Asia

Hong Kong is the discount air ticket capital of the region, although Singapore, Penang and Bangkok can also be good places to look for cheap fares. Jordan is a bit off the beaten track, however, and there's not much discounting on these routes. Many travellers tend to use the Hong Kong Student Travel Bureau (☎ 2730 3269), 8th floor, Star House, Tsimshatsui. Khao San Rd in Bangkok is the budget travellers headquarters. Bangkok has a number of excellent travel agents but there are also some suspect ones; ask the advice of other travellers before handing over your cash. STA Travel (☎ 02-236 0262), 33 Surawong Rd, is a good and reliable place to start.

Return fares from Bangkok are around US$1063 or US$1250 from Hong Kong.

LAND

Crossing the border into Jordan from Iraq and Saudi Arabia is nigh impossible, so most travellers come overland from Syria or Israel (or by ferry from Egypt). However, there are three important things to note:

- Any indication of travel to/from Israel will mean that you cannot enter Syria, Lebanon and most other Middle Eastern countries, although Jordan is OK. See the boxed text 'Travelling To/From Israel' in the Facts for the Visitor chapter for details.
- All travellers should obtain a visa for Syria before coming to Jordan – see the boxed text 'Getting Other Visas in Jordan' in the Facts for the Visitor chapter.
- Jordanian visas are not available at the Israel/Jordan border at King Hussein Bridge.

Most travellers arrive in Jordan by bus if travelling overland, however, it's no problem bringing your own car or motorbike. All drivers must have a *carnet de passage en douane* and insurance. It's essential that the carnet is filled out properly at each border crossing, or you could be up for a lot of money. The carnet may also need to list any expensive spares, eg a gearbox, that you're planning to carry with you. At the borders to Jordan (and the ferry terminal in Nuweiba, Egypt) you'll be obliged to take out local insurance of JD32 (valid for one month), plus a nominal 'customs fee' for 'foreign car registration' of JD7.

Obviously, you'll need the vehicle's registration and ownership papers. Strictly speaking you don't need an International Driving Permit (IDP) to drive in Jordan (your national licence is generally sufficient), but bring one with you to avoid any hassles.

Finally, bring a good set of spare parts and some mechanical knowledge, as you will not always be able to get the help you may need. This is especially the case for motorbikes: there are only a few motorbike mechanics in Jordan who are able to deal with anything modern.

Refer to the Car & Motorcycle section in the Getting Around chapter for more information about driving around Jordan.

Syria

If you are in a hurry, you can easily cross the border (by bus, service taxi or hitching) directly between Damascus and Amman, but it makes some sense to stop off at a few places on the way, eg Ezra'a and Bosra ash-Sham from Der'a (Syria) and some of northern Jordan, eg Umm Qais and Al-Himma, from Irbid (Jordan).

If you travel directly between Damascus and Amman, there's little point catching a service taxi to Der'a, organising your own transport across the border, getting another lift to Ramtha, perhaps another to Irbid, and then a connection to Amman. The two border crossings are efficient and relatively painless on both sides, and by the time you juggle all forms of transport (and bargain with drivers), you may end up paying more money and probably using more time than taking a direct bus or service taxi.

Border Crossings There are two borders between Syria and Jordan: Der'a/Ramtha

and Nasib/Jabir. They are both open for 24 hours every day. The Jordanian sides of both borders have a post office and tourist office (both open from about 8 am to 5 pm every day and until about 2 pm on Friday); moneychangers (open most of the time), where Jordanian dinars and Syrian pounds are changed; and places to eat and drink.

Ramtha is the most commonly used border for foreigners travelling on public transport, and best for detours to northern Jordan.

Der'a/Ramtha Refer to the Ramtha section in the Northern & Western Jordan chapter for information about travelling to this border town. From Ramtha, service taxis and minibuses regularly go to the border. If hitching, ask the immigration office on the Jordanian side to flag down a vehicle for a lift to the Syrian border.

Nasib/Jabir Jabir is primarily for trucks travelling between Amman and Damascus, but some public transport is now using this border. If you wish to visit northern Jordan, use the border at Ramtha, but for a detour to eastern Jordan, eg Azraq, the border at Jabir is useful for connections to Zarqa or Mafraq.

Bus Several air-conditioned buses travel every day between Amman and Damascus. JETT bus company has services from its international office (just up from the Abdali bus station in Amman); Afana has buses from its office (at the Abdali bus station); and the Syrian government bus company, Karnak, has buses from Abdali bus station. All services from Amman stop at the Karnak bus station in Damascus.

Tickets cost JD4.500 from Amman, and US$5 from Damascus – and can only be bought in these currencies. The trip takes about four hours – plus border formalities – and is the easiest way to make the crossing, but book as soon as you can.

Train The famous Hejaz Railway between Amman and Damascus leaves Amman on Monday and Thursday at 8 am and Friday at 1 pm; the trains leave Damascus at the same time. Tickets cost JD2.500.

The Hejaz Railway

The Hejaz Railway was built between 1900 and 1908 to transport pilgrims from Damascus to the holy city of Medina, reducing the journey by camel and foot from about two months to as little as three days. For Jordan, and Amman in particular, this meant an increased boom in trade. The 1462km line was completely funded by donations from Muslims – but lasted less than 10 years.

The trains and railway line were partially destroyed during the Arab Revolt of 1917, co-led by TE Lawrence, and during WWI. The line was rebuilt as far south as Ma'an, but is now only used for cargo. The line between Damascus and Amman is still used for passenger services in both directions, and anyone with enough money can charter a carriage between Amman and a nearby town.

The train may be quaint, but quick it ain't. The trip officially takes eight hours – plus stops at both sides of the border (allow at least an extra three hours). The ticket office (☎ 06-489 5413) at the charming old station in Amman (see Train in the Getting There & Away section of the Amman chapter) is open every day except Friday from 7 am to 3 pm.

Car & Motorcycle If you intend to drive between Jordan and Syria, the better border to cross is at Der'a/Ramtha.

Service Taxi The service taxis – or *servees* – are slightly faster than the buses and run at all hours, although it's harder to find one in the evening. Service taxis take less time to cross the border than trains and buses because there are fewer passengers to process, and the driver is experienced in helping passengers with immigration and customs formalities. These taxis are huge, yellow (but sometimes white) and American-made.

From Amman, service taxis leave from along the main roads on both sides of the Abdali bus station; from Damascus, they leave from next to the Karnak bus station.

The trip costs JD5.500 from Amman, and S£385 from Damascus. Service taxis also travel between Damascus and Irbid (South bus station) in northern Jordan for JD4 or S£300.

Service taxis often smuggle cigarettes across the border. Drivers are keen to take foreigners so the taxi looks like it has been chartered, and the fare is far less – or sometimes free. However, smuggling is illegal (albeit undertaken with the apparent connivance of border officials on both sides).

Iraq

Iraq is obviously not on the itinerary of most travellers, and getting an Iraqi visa is virtually impossible. From offices outside the Abdali bus station in Amman, buses (JD8, 13 hours) and service taxis (JD15) leave every day to Baghdad. JETT and Hijazi have services to Baghdad (JD12) several times a week.

A steady stream of trucks travel between Amman and Baghdad, so hitching is fairly easy, although some drivers may be reluctant to be seen with foreigners. The best spot to wait for a lift is anywhere along the highways from Zarqa and Amman towards Azraq, or the more direct route east of Mafraq. The only border is at Al-Karama.

Saudi Arabia

As with Iraq, getting a visa to Saudi Arabia is nigh impossible. The only visas currently dished out to tourists seem to be transit visas, which sometimes allow you to travel along the Tapline (Trans Arabia Pipeline) in three days, but sometimes only lets you fly in and out, and spend a day, in Riyadh.

The main land route for public transport into Saudi Arabia is Al-Umari, along the highway south of Azraq. The other two crossing points are Ad-Durra, south of Aqaba, and further east at Al-Mudawwara.

Bus Comfortable JETT buses go every day (from its international office in Amman) to Jeddah, Riyadh and Dammam. Tickets to any of the three cities cost JD31. The Hijazi bus company has services (from its office in the Abdali bus station) to the same three cities (all for JD25) on Monday and Thursday. Cheaper and less comfortable buses leave from outside the Abdali bus station in Amman for Riyadh (JD25, 20 hours) most days of the week.

Service Taxi From outside the Abdali bus station in Amman, huge yellow service taxis also go to Riyadh (about JD20). They do not leave regularly, so book as soon as possible.

Elsewhere in the Middle East

Plenty of other bus and service taxis go elsewhere around the Middle East from inside or near the Abdali bus station in Amman, but are only useful if you have the time, patience – and most importantly – the necessary visas. These trips are long, so you're better off flying.

Service taxis go to Kuwait (JD30) and Beirut (JD15); and Hijazi has buses to Dubai (JD25) on Monday and Friday, and to Kuwait (JD25) on the same days.

From outside its international bus office in Amman, JETT has services to most cities in the Middle East. (* the fare to Cairo – US$54 – must be paid for in US dollars, and includes the Aqaba-Nuweiba ferry ticket.)

to	day(s)	one-way (JD)	hours
Abu Dhabi	Mon & Fri	62	36
Bahrain	Mon & Fri	38	24
Beirut	Thu & Sun	15	6
Cairo	Tue & Sat	(see * above)	24
Dubai	Mon & Fri	62	36
Kuwait	Fri	30	18
Doha	Mon & Fri	49	30

Israel & the West Bank

Peace with Israel, and the setting up of the partially autonomous Palestine National Authority (PNA), means there are now three border crossings: King Hussein Bridge, Sheikh Hussein Bridge and Wadi Araba. Despite what some maps may indicate, there is no border crossing at King Abdullah Bridge (at the western end of the road from Amman to the Dead Sea); and the Prince Mohammed Bridge, near Deir Alla, is for trucks only.

Border Crossings Before crossing into Jordan from Israel, there are a few things to remember:

- Only change as much money as you need because the commission charged by money-changers is often ridiculously high.
- Ignore claims by taxi drivers that 'buses have finished'. If you cross during normal working hours, some form of public transport will be available.
- Jordanian visas cannot be obtained on arrival at the King Hussein Bridge.
- Private vehicles cannot drive across the King Hussein Bridge, but they can be taken across the Sheikh Hussein Bridge and Wadi Araba borders.
- Refer to the boxed text 'Travelling To/From Israel' in the Facts for the Visitor chapter for information about how deal with the Israeli passport-stamp issue.

On both sides of all three borders, there are foreign exchange facilities, places to eat and drink and duty-free shops. On the Jordanian side of all three borders, there is a post office and tourist information counter (both open every day from about 8 am to 2 pm, closed on Friday).

Wadi Araba/Arava This crossing – known as Wadi Araba to the Jordanians and Wadi Arava to the Israelis – is in southern Jordan, and links Aqaba (Jordan) with Eilat (Israel). The border is open from 7 am to 9 pm, Sunday to Thursday; and 7 am to 7 pm, Friday and Saturday. Get there early (before opening time, if possible) to beat the vehicles which start rolling up at 7 am. Don't forget the Israeli departure tax of 48.50NIS.

The border is only about 2km from central Eilat, so you can simply walk in from the Israeli side, or catch bus No 16 (4NIS), which leaves about every 20 minutes between 7 am and 4 pm, Monday to Thursday. A taxi will cost about 25NIS. If coming down from Jerusalem on No 392 or 444 bus, and you want to skip Eilat, ask the driver to let you out at the turn-off for the border, a short walk away. Refer to Getting There & Away in the Aqaba section of the Southern Desert chapter for details about travelling between Aqaba and the border.

King Hussein Bridge/Allenby Bridge For a long time the only crossing between Jordan and the Palestine National Authority (PNA) or West Bank – and hence, tacitly, Israel – this crossing over the Jordan River remains somewhat of an anomaly. Although known as the Allenby Bridge to the Israelis, the bridge is the Jisr al-Malek al-Hussein (King Hussein Bridge) to the Jordanians and Palestinians.

The historic oddity of this crossing has remained enshrined in the fact that, on leaving Jordan, you're not really considered to be leaving Jordan. Prior to 1988, Jordan still laid claim to the West Bank as its own territory, and somehow this idea has remained in the approach to visas. If you wish to return to Jordan from the PNA on your present Jordanian visa, you need only keep the stamped exit slip and present it on returning by the same crossing (it won't work at the other crossings). For this reason there is no Jordanian exit tax either. Going the other way, however, the Israeli exit tax is a hefty 140NIS (and rising all the time), supposedly because you're paying to leave Israel *and* the PNA.

The King Hussein Bridge is the most convenient border because it's only about 30km to Jerusalem, and about 40km to Amman. It's a common way to exit, but not enter, Jordan, because Jordanian visas are not issued at this border – so get a Jordanian visa at an embassy/consulate beforehand, or use another border crossing.

The Israeli passport control process can be a little wearying, with plenty of waiting and bag checking. Note: if you're entering Jordan this way and intend to return to Israel, you must keep the entrance form given to you by the Jordanians – they could well insist on you prolonging your stay in Jordan if you cannot present it.

The border is currently open from 8 am to 10.30 pm, Sunday to Thursday; and from 8 am to 1 pm, Friday and Saturday. These times are subject to frequent change, so it's advisable to check with the tourist offices in Jerusalem or Amman. Crossing the border can take up to three hours; avoid 11 am to 3 pm when delays are more common.

From Amman, JETT buses go to the border, but only one way – ie there are no services from the border to Amman. The bus leaves at 6.30 am from outside the JETT domestic office in Amman, and tickets cost JD6, which includes the short ride over the bridge to the Israeli side. This bus is more convenient, but certainly more expensive, than taking the minibus (JD1.500) or service taxi (JD2) from Abdali bus station in Amman to the Jordanian side of the border – but you'll then have to pay for a ride to the Israeli side. Service taxis also go to this border from Irbid.

It's not possible to walk, hitch or take a private car between the two borders, so a ride in a (white) service taxi costs about JD2, or up to JD10 in a chartered (yellow) taxi.

The last bus from the Israeli side to Damascus Gate in Jerusalem (45 minutes) leaves by about 7 pm. Alternatively, take a *sherut* (direct share taxi) for about 30NIS per person from the garage opposite the Damascus Gate in Jerusalem.

Sheikh Hussein Bridge Sheikh Hussein Bridge – known to the Israelis as simply 'Jordan Bridge' – is the least convenient, because it's not particularly close to anywhere in Israel or Jordan. But it is handy if you wish to visit northern Jordan before/after crossing the border, and it's the closest crossing to Jerusalem and Amman which will issue Jordanian visas on arrival. The border is open from 8 am to 8 pm, Sunday to Thursday; and Friday and Saturday, 8 am to 5 pm. The Israeli departure tax is 50NIS.

If coming from Israel, get a bus to Tiberias, and change at Beit She'an (6km from the border). From Beit She'an, take another bus to the Israeli border for 8.40NIS, but allow enough time because there are only a handful of buses per day. After passport formalities, a compulsory bus (3NIS) takes you to the Jordanian side.

From the Jordanian side, either wait for a minibus or shared taxi to Irbid, from where there are regular connections to Amman; go to Shuneh ash-Shamaliyyeh (North Shuna) by private or service taxi, or walk (3km) to the main road and flag down a minibus or service taxi to the town, and then get a connection to Amman or the Dead Sea; or hitch a ride in any direction you wish.

Bus Several cities in Jordan are now regularly linked to cities in Israel. Travelling by bus directly between Amman and Tel Aviv, for example, will save you the hassle of getting to/from the Jordanian and Israeli borders, and getting transport between the borders, but it is more expensive than crossing independently, and you'll have to wait for all bus passengers to clear customs and immigration. Most buses to/from Amman go via Irbid, and most tend to use the Sheikh Hussein Bridge.

From Amman, Trust International Transport has buses (from its office at 7th Circle) to: Tel Aviv (JD14), everyday but Saturday; and also to Haifa (JD10.500) and Nazareth (JD10.500) every day. Trust also offers services most days to Haifa and Nazareth from Irbid and Aqaba.

Car & Motorcycle If driving from Israel, use the border crossings at Sheikh Hussein Bridge or Wadi Araba/Arava (it is not possible to drive over the King Hussein Bridge).

Departure Tax

All foreign tourists leaving Jordan by land must pay a departure tax of JD4. The only exception is across to the PNA (West Bank), via the King Hussein Bridge – but the Israelis will slug you with a hefty departure tax of 140NIS if you continue from the PNA in to Israel.

SEA

To avoid the expensive ferry between Nuweiba (Egypt) and Aqaba (Jordan), it is possible – and probably cheaper – to cross from Taba (Egypt) to Eilat (Israel) and then to Aqaba. However, you'll be hit for the high Israeli departure tax, and you'll receive stamps in your passport indicating travel to/from Israel – which precludes travel to most other Middle Eastern countries.

Two types of boats ply the Gulf of Aqaba between Nuweiba and Aqaba. The 'fast boat' is a turbo-catamaran, and on a good day takes just one hour. It leaves Aqaba every day at midday, and from Nuweiba every day at 3 pm. From Aqaba, tickets cost US$28 one-way, excluding the Jordanian departure tax (JD6); from Nuweiba, tickets are more expensive at US$43, which includes the Egyptian departure tax.

The 'slow boat' is a car-ferry, which is meant to take three hours but can often take much longer. It leaves from both Aqaba and Nuweiba at 3 pm. From Aqaba, tickets cost US$21 one-way (excluding Jordanian departure tax); from Nuweiba, US$33 (including Egyptian departure tax). A car in either direction costs an extra US$103.

Occasionally, a southerly wind blows up so that both types of boats have to wait until it subsides, but the biggest delays are usually caused by the chaos at one or both ports.

Tickets in either direction must be paid for in US dollars (which can be bought from the Cairo-Amman Bank inside the ferry office in Aqaba). It is not possible to buy return tickets – if you want to return the same way, you must buy two one-way tickets. Beware of buying ferry tickets in Amman because you may be charged for nonexistent 1st class seats – buy the tickets in Aqaba. Refer to Getting There & Away in the Aqaba section of the Southern Desert chapter for details about buying tickets in Aqaba, and getting to the passenger terminal south of Aqaba.

The Egyptian consulate in Aqaba issues visas with relatively little fuss, often on the same day – which is a lot easier than doing battle at the crowded embassy in Amman. Most nationalities can obtain tourist visas on arrival at Nuweiba, but it's best to check this with the Egyptian consulate in Amman or Aqaba; travellers from some countries (notably, Eastern Europe) have been refused entry on to the ferry at Aqaba because they had no Egyptian visa. It is imperative to note that if you wish to travel further than Sharm el-Sheikh you need a visa for Egypt, rather than a visa just for the Sinai peninsula. (See the boxed text, 'Getting Other Visas in Jordan' in the Facts for the Visitor chapter.)

The worst time for travelling is just after the Haj, when Aqaba fills up with Hajis (pilgrims) returning home from Mecca to Egypt.

At the peak, they sometimes put on two extra boats, and although foot passengers should have little problem getting a ticket, the delays and confusion are a rude introduction to the bureaucratic frustrations that await in Egypt.

There are money exchange facilities at the terminals at Nuweiba and Aqaba, primarily for buying visas on arrival. Only change enough cash (avoid travellers cheques which attract hefty commissions) to last until you reach a decent bank or moneychanger.

Nuweiba is not the most attractive of Sinai's beach resorts. In the north, in an area called Tarabin, there are several places where a mattress in a bamboo or concrete hut costs about E£5. City Beach Village, halfway between Tarabin and Nuweiba city, is one of the best options. You can pitch a tent for E£5; camp out in their reed huts for E£10 or enjoy a comfortable single/double for E£35/55, including breakfast. From Nuweiba city and the ferry terminal, buses regularly go to Taba, Sharm el-Sheikh, Dahab, Suez and Cairo.

Departure Tax
The departure tax on the ferry from Aqaba to Nuweiba is JD6.

ORGANISED TOURS
Organised tours take all the hassle out of travelling on your own, but limit your independence and are more expensive. Don't forget that travelling around Jordan on public transport is easy, renting a private car and chartering a taxi is not difficult, and you can get by using English almost all the time. Refer to the Organised Tours section in the Getting Around chapter for details of companies within Jordan that organise tours.

Overland Buses & Trucks
Overland companies offer long-distance, budget-priced trips around Jordan or include Jordan in their trips around the Middle East. Two UK-based companies are: Dragoman (☎ 01728-861 133, fax 861 127, email brox@ dragoman.co.uk) Web site www.dragoman .co.uk; and Exodus (☎ 020-8675 5550) Web site www.exodustravels.co.uk.

Tour Groups
Australia
Adventure World
(☎ 02-9956 7766) 73 Walker St, North Sydney, NSW 2060
Ya'lla Tours
(☎ 03-9523 1988, fax 9523 1934, email yal lamel@yallatours.com.au) 661-5 Glenhuntly Rd, Caulfield, Vic 3162

UK
Exodus
(☎ 020-8675 5550, fax 8673 0779, email sales@exodustravels.co.uk) 9 Weir Road, London SW12 OLT
Web site www.exodustravels.co.uk
Imaginative Traveller
(☎ 020-8742 8612 fax 8742 3045, email info@imaginative-traveller.com, email sales@ kumuka.co.uk) 14 Barley Mow Passage, Chiswick, London W4 4PH
Web site www.imaginative-traveller.com

USA
Journeys Unlimited
(☎ 212-366 6678) 150 West 28th St, New York
Web site www.journeys-intl.com

Warning

The information in this chapter is particularly vulnerable to change: prices for international travel are volatile, routes are introduced and then cancelled, schedules change, special deals come and go, and rules and visa requirements are amended. Airlines and governments seem to take a perverse pleasure in making price structures and regulations as complicated as possible. Check directly with the airline or a travel agent to make sure you understand how a fare (and ticket you may buy) works. In addition, the travel industry is highly competitive and there are many lurks and perks.

The upshot of this is that you should get opinions, quotes and advice from as many airlines and travel agents as possible before you part with your hard-earned cash. The details given in this chapter should be regarded as pointers and are not a substitute for your own careful, up-to-date research.

Getting Around

Jordan is so small that it's possible to drive from the Syrian border in the north to the Saudi border in the south in little more than five hours. There is only one domestic flight (Amman-Aqaba), and no internal public train service, so the main forms of public transport are public buses and minibuses, private buses, service taxis and private taxis.

Where public transport is limited or nonexistent, hitching is a common way of getting around. Hiring a car is a popular alternative, but while it offers flexibility and independence, it is expensive and driving can be an unpleasant experience (see the Car & Motorcycle section later in this chapter). Chartering a service taxi (white), or private taxi (yellow), is probably cheaper than hiring a car (depending on your bargaining skills and the distance), and the driver (who may speak English, and should know the area) will take the hassle out of driving.

AIR
Domestic Air Services
Since only 430km separates Ramtha in the north from Aqaba in the south, Jordan has a dearth of internal flights. In fact, the only domestic flight is operated by Royal Wings, a subsidiary of Royal Jordanian Airlines, between Amman and Aqaba. Refer to Getting There & Away in the Aqaba section of the Southern Desert chapter for details. Schedules for this domestic flight (and other international flights) are listed in the two English-language daily newspapers, the *Jordan Times* and the *Arab Daily*, published in Amman.

There is no departure tax on domestic flights within Jordan.

BUS & MINIBUS
Public buses and, to a larger extent, public minibuses are the normal form of transport for locals and visitors. These normally leave from obvious bus/minibus stations, although sometimes minibuses leave from other specific spots (as indicated on the maps). Public and private buses, and public minibuses, can be hailed down from anywhere along the route (although you may have to stand). Private buses leave from outside their booking offices.

While private buses are normally labelled in English, virtually no public bus or minibus in Jordan is labelled in English – although they sometimes have 'English' numbers. Public buses and minibuses also do not stand under any destination signs in English. Bus/minibus stations are normally fairly chaotic, so you'll invariably have to ask directions to the correct bus or minibus. Jordanians are happy to help, and simply asking 'Amman?' or 'Karak?' is all that is usually necessary – but always double-check with other passengers when embarking.

Tickets for public buses and minibuses are normally bought on the bus; a ticket seller usually comes around to collect fares some time during the journey, or sometimes you pay the driver when you get off. For private buses, tickets are normally bought from an office or booth at the departure point. Tickets for private buses can be – and should be in peak times – bought several days in advance; on public buses and minibuses it's every man, woman, child and goat for themselves. Private buses are also quicker than public buses/minibuses because they travel directly from one destination to another along the quickest route, and don't stop constantly to pick up passengers or take detours.

There are no set ground rules about men and women sitting next to each other. Unaccompanied men and women can sit next to each other, but some seat-shuffling often takes place to ensure that an unaccompanied foreign man or woman does not sit next to a member of the opposite sex that he/she does not know.

If you have any complaints about public transport anywhere in Jordan, contact the Public Transport Complaints line in Amman (☎ 06-464 2311).

DISTANCE CHART (KM)

	Ajlun	Amman	Aqaba	Azraq	Irbid	Jerash	Karak	King Hussein Bridge	Ma'an	Madaba	Ramtha	Tafila	Wadi Mousa (Petra)
Ajlun	---												
Amman	73	---											
Aqaba	396	328	---										
Azraq	155	103	415	---									
Irbid	32	89	408	143	---								
Jerash	22	51	370	132	38	---							
Karak	182	118	252	205	202	164	---						
King Hussein Bridge	78	56	367	152	109	89	151	---					
Ma'an	279	212	116	289	294	255	154	252	---				
Madaba	95	32	325	119	115	77	86	64	210	---			
Ramtha	57	94	410	141	28	40	205	130	296	118	---		
Tafila	242	179	189	266	267	229	63	215	90	151	296	---	
Wadi Mousa (Petra)	297	230	97	317	313	275	142	268	45	228	316	81	---

Private Bus

It is often worth paying extra for a comfortable and air-conditioned private bus, especially between Amman and Aqaba.

Hijazi runs a very regular service between Amman and Irbid, and other private buses travel between Amman and Jerash, and Amman and Aqaba. The best two private companies are Jordan Express Travel & Tourism (known simply as JETT), and Trust International Transport (which, wisely, does not use an acronym!). Both offer pretty much the same standard of bus, and have identical prices. JETT has several services a day between Amman and Aqaba, Petra, Hammamat Ma'in and the King Hussein Bridge (for the border to Israel). Trust has several services a day between Amman and Aqaba. Refer to the relevant Getting There & Away sections later in this book for details about costs and departure times.

Public Bus & Minibus

Large public buses are not common, and normally only travel between Amman and Irbid, Karak and Jerash. For longer distances, public minibuses are the normal form of transport.

The correct fares for both are nearly always posted in Arabic somewhere inside the front of the bus/minibus. Ask the other passengers what to pay. Unfortunately, sometimes you will have to pay the full fare even if you're not going to the end of the route, or if you have picked up the ride along the way.

Public buses and minibuses normally only leave when full, so waiting is often required – except where passengers are likely to be picked up along the way. Standing is not normally allowed on public buses or minibuses (there's little room anyway) before departure, but they will sometimes pick up extra passengers along the way.

TRAIN

There is no internal passenger train service in Jordan. The Hejaz Railway is an international passenger service between Amman (Jordan) and Damascus (Syria), and does not stop anywhere inside Jordan – refer to Syria in the Land section of the Getting There & Away chapter for details. The railway line south of Amman to Aqaba, via Ma'an, is for phosphate and other cargo, and not for passengers.

TAXI

Jordan has thousands and thousands of service taxis (white) and private taxis (yellow). The service taxi – known sometimes as a *servee* – is a common form of transport which runs along set routes within many towns, and between most towns, as well as between Jordan and the neighbouring countries of Iraq, Syria and Saudi Arabia (see the Getting There & Away chapter).

Service taxis and private taxis (which, unlike service taxis, go wherever you want them to go) can be chartered: hiring a service taxi for a day is usually cheaper than renting a car (especially considering the charges and conditions associated with car rental), but a long-distance trip (eg Amman to Petra) in a private taxi will probably cost more than renting a car.

If the taxi driver does not speak English, use the Arabic script in this guidebook or ask a local who does speak English to write down the destination(s) in Arabic. A pocket calculator will help with negotiating charter costs and determining normal fares.

Service Taxi

This is the most popular mode of transport around Jordan. Service taxis are usually battered Peugeot 504 or 505 station wagons with seven seats, or battered Mercedes sedans with five seats. They are always white, and usually have writing and numbers indicating their route – but normally only in Arabic.

Because of the limited number of seats, it usually doesn't take long for one to fill up. They cost up to twice as much as a minibus, and about 50% more than a public bus, but are quicker because they stop less often along the way to pick up or drop off passengers. However, they are not always as comfortable as a bus or minibus, especially if you have to share the front passenger seat with someone you don't know.

The seven-seaters normally have one passenger in the front (obviously the prized seat and the one lone women travellers should wait for), and two rows of three passengers behind the driver – try to avoid the airless and bumpy seats right at the back.

The five-seaters normally squeeze two passengers in the front, and three in the back. To avoid waiting for passengers, or to give yourself extra room, you can always pay for an extra seat, eg both front seats of a five-seater. To avoid sitting next to a local man in the back seat, women should always do this. However, if chartering a taxi, single females should always sit in the back.

Chartering a service taxi along a set route (eg Aqaba to Ma'an) will always be cheaper than chartering a private taxi (yellow), but drivers of private taxis are often more amenable to chartering for long distances and more indirect routes. To find out the cost of chartering a service taxi from one destination to another (eg Aqaba to Ma'an), one person (the other passengers should hide) should ask the driver the cost *per person* of a fare in the shared service taxi, and simply multiply this fare by five or seven, depending on the taxi size. For longer distances, detours and stopovers, the price is far more negotiable.

Private Taxi

Private yellow taxis can be chartered for any long-distance trip, but are normally more expensive than a service taxi. For indirect routes, longer trips and stopovers, drivers of private taxis are more amenable than service taxis, and all fares are very negotiable. See under Local Transport later in this chapter for more about private taxis.

CAR & MOTORCYCLE

You need courage to drive in Jordan. The people are exceptionally friendly, welcoming, hospitable and courteous, but their driving is quite appalling, selfish and takes no account of any other driver.

MJ & EM Bissett, UK

Visitors from any country where road rules are obeyed may be shocked with the traffic in Jordan, especially in Amman. But anyone who has driven elsewhere in the Middle East may find the traffic comparatively sedate.

There are three main highways south of Amman:

Desert Highway A boring dual-carriageway which detours all major tourist attractions (see the Desert Highway section of the Southern Desert chapter for more information).

Dead Sea Highway Hot and uninspiring, this is the quickest way to travel between Amman and Aqaba (see the Dead Sea Highway section in the Northern & Western Jordan chapter).

King's Highway By far the most interesting – but most difficult and time-consuming – is the ancient King's Highway, which goes through most major attractions in Jordan (see the King's Highway chapter).

Trips

It makes very little sense to hire a car to travel to places like Petra and Jerash, which need a day or more to explore properly, and can only be visited on foot; or to Wadi Rum, where a 4WD is needed. Three days is often the minimum period of rental allowed by rental companies, and is just enough to see most sites in Jordan (see the Suggested Itineraries section in the Facts for the Visitor chapter for more information).

Road Rules

Vehicles drive on the right-hand side of the road in Jordan – or so the theory goes. Rules are not given great attention by locals, scant regard is paid to lane divisions and use of the indicator seems to be an optional extra. Horn-honking, on the other hand, seems to be a national pastime.

Wearing a seat belt is now compulsory, which is fairly pointless because most vehicles don't have them – including passenger seats in service taxis and private taxis. Traffic police are positioned at intervals along the highways, but are normally found lazing about waiting for someone to speed past at 200 km/h. Police tend to be fairly indulgent towards foreigners so long as they do nothing serious – but don't tempt fate by doing something highly illegal, or really stupid, like drink-driving.

The general speed limit inside built-up areas is 50km/h, 70km/h on multi-lane highways in Amman, and 90 to 110km/h on the highways. Roads are generally pretty good, and anywhere with a bad road is somewhere you probably shouldn't be going, eg the middle of the desert or a very remote area near a border.

Checkpoints

All major roads, especially near the borders, have occasional checkpoints manned by the police. There is no need to worry: King Abdullah II has ordered a reduction in the number of military checkpoints along the main highways, as well as the major borders and the Queen Alia international airport, in an effort to make Jordan more accessible for, and friendly towards, foreign tourists.

Checkpoints are mainly for Jordanian drivers of private vehicles, and for trucks. Buses, minibuses, service taxis and private taxis rarely need to stop; if they do, drivers just quickly show their papers to the police. Sometimes the police come into a bus (there's rarely room in a minibus) to check the identification papers of passengers (usually young men). Foreigners are rarely bothered, and if you are asked to show your passport (more common anywhere near a border) it's probably more out of curiosity than anything else.

If you have chartered a private taxi, the driver is often waved through the checkpoint when the policeman sees smiling foreigners in the taxi, obviously out for a day trip. If you're driving a rented or private vehicle, slow down when approaching the checkpoint area, especially if flagged down. Again, there is a very good chance you'll be waved on unless the policeman is friendly or bored. You are only likely to be asked serious questions if you seem to be going near the border with Iraq.

Accidents

Despite the small population, and relatively good roads, accidents are alarmingly frequent. In 1998, over 43,000 accidents were reported – resulting in 612 deaths and 17,177 injuries. These figures have recently prompted the Jordanian government to force the traffic police to become more vigilant.

The roads where accidents are more common are those frequented by long-distance trucks, eg the short stretch of Highway 65 (south of Aqaba to the Saudi border) and Highways 10 and 40 east of Amman.

In case of an accident in a rental car, do not move the vehicle, get a policeman from the local station to attend the scene immediately, obtain a police report (Arabic is OK) and contact the car rental company – not obtaining a police report will normally invalidate your insurance. If there is any serious injury to you or someone else, also contact your travel insurance company at home and your embassy/consulate in Amman.

If your own private car is involved in an accident, your driving licence and passport will be held by the police until the case has been finalised in a local court – which may drag on for weeks. One unfortunate reader recommended that anyone driving their own vehicle and involved in an accident should do a 'deal' with the other parties involved on the spot (which will eventually save a lot of time and money), and leave quickly before the police become involved. However, if there are serious injuries, contact the police and ring your embassy/consulate.

Telephone numbers for local police stations are mentioned throughout the book, but two emergency numbers (☎ 191 and 192) are valid for police emergencies anywhere in Jordan, and should be answered by English-speaking staff. In Amman, there are separate numbers for the Highway Police (☎ 06-534 3401) and Traffic Police (☎ 06-489 6390) – the exact difference between the two, however, is unclear.

Driving Tips

If you're driving around Jordan, carefully read the following:

- Many road signs are in English, but are sometimes badly transliterated (eg 'Om Qeis' for Umm Qais). Brown signs are for tourist attractions; blue signs for road names; and green signs for anything Islamic, eg a mosque.
- Take care when it's raining: water and sand and, sometimes, oil make a lethal combination on the roads.
- Before and after most small towns and villages, there are nice brown signs with lots of Arabic writing, and the words 'welcome' or 'goodbye' in English – but these signs never indicate in English the *name* of the town or village.
- One-way streets and speed humps are often not signposted.
- Always watch out for obstacles: eg pedestrians who walk along the road; cars darting out of side roads; and herds of goats and camels, even on the major highways.
- Roundabouts are often large, and all drivers (local and foreign) find them totally confusing.
- Petrol stations are not that common, so fill up as often as you can.
- Parking in major towns is a problem, especially Amman and Karak; but is easy to find (and normally free) at major attractions like Jerash, Petra and Madaba.
- Most roads (and even the highways) are dangerous at night, because white lines are not common and catseyes are nonexistent; obstacles (eg herds of camels) are still roaming about; and some cars have no headlights, or put them permanently on high beam.

Rental

Many things in Jordan are expensive and renting a car is no exception, but if you can split the costs between others, it's a great way of seeing a lot of the country quickly and easily. There is nowhere in Jordan to rent a motorbike.

There are many rental agencies in Amman, a few in Aqaba and one or two at Terminal 2 in the Queen Alia international airport, but elsewhere they are rare. Any car rental agency in a small town, or even a city like Irbid, is usually just an office with one guy, one desk, one telephone and one car for hire (usually his!). There are all sorts of ways of getting ripped off, and there's usually no fall-back in case of an accident. Avoid these smaller agencies unless a local friend can do the negotiation and driving. It's best to stick with the big international crowds like Hertz and Avis, or some of the larger local agencies.

Expect to pay about JD25 for the smallest, cheapest sedan in Aqaba or Amman – plus 10% sales tax, insurance and petrol. This price usually includes free unlimited kilometres. If you plan to drive more than 100km per day (which most people will) rent a car with free unlimited kilometres rather than accept a cheaper set rate with a charge per kilometre.

Discounts of about 5% are available for weekly rentals; anything longer than one week should come with a substantial discount. Cars can be booked, collected and paid for in Amman or Aqaba and dropped off in the other city, but the rental companies charge about JD35 for this service – and it's only possible with major companies which have offices in both cities. Companies need a credit card for a deposit, but payment can be also made with cash; most major credit cards are accepted.

Some readers have booked their car over the Internet. This is fine if you absolutely must have a car immediately on arrival in Aqaba or Amman (or elsewhere with an exorbitant extra fee), but it will be much cheaper to wait until you get to Aqaba or Amman, and then shop around and negotiate.

Most rental cars have air-conditioning which is a godsend in summer, and vital along dusty tracks. Smaller companies have cheaper cars without air-conditioning. Cars with automatic transmission are more expensive, but anyone not used to driving on the right-hand side of the road should consider renting an automatic rather than a manual. Always carry a decent road map – not provided by rental agencies. Child-restraining seats are available for an extra fee.

Some agencies are closed on Friday and public holidays. If so, prearrange collection and delivery to avoid longer rental periods. Always check the car with a staff member for bumps, scratches and obvious defects, and check brakes, tyres etc before driving off.

Finally, there are a myriad of complicated conditions and charges to remember and consider:

- Most agencies only rent to drivers over 21 years old; some stipulate that drivers must be at least 26 years.
- Some offer free delivery and collection within the same city, but only during working hours.
- Most international agencies, eg Hertz, Avis and Europcar, accept your licence from your home country, but only if you've been driving for more than one year. Smaller companies may only accept an International Driving Permit. It's worth bringing along both anyway. The agency will also need to see your passport for extra identification.
- Rental is often for a minimum of three days, sometimes two and barely ever for one day. Very rarely will any agency give a refund if you return the car earlier.
- Rented cars cannot be driven outside of Jordan.

Insurance

All rental companies offer insurance for an extra JD7 to JD8 per day for a normal sedan. In case of an accident, you'll then have to pay an excess of about JD200 to JD300. To avoid this, major rental agencies (but not the smaller ones) offer a Collision Damage Waiver (CDW) fee of about JD7 per day for normal cars, which will absolve you of all accident costs – definitely worth considering.

Other options offered by the major companies include Personal Accident Insurance and Theft Protection, which are both fairly unnecessary, add considerably to your total bill and may be covered by your travel insurance policy from home anyway.

If driving into Jordan in a private vehicle, compulsory third-party insurance must be purchased at the border for about JD32 (valid for one month), plus a nominal customs fee for 'foreign car registration' of JD7.

4WDs

Four-wheel drives are only necessary if you're going to out-of-the-way places in the deserts, such as Burqu or Wadi Rum. However, 4WDs should only be hired – and driven – by someone who is experienced: driving in the desert where there are no signs, and getting bogged in sand in 45°C heat, is no fun.

Four-wheel drive vehicles can be rented from reputable agencies in Aqaba and Amman, but are far, far more expensive than normal sedans: at least JD65 per day. Insurance is higher (about JD12 per day), and most companies do not offer a CDW fee, so you're liable for an excess in case of accident of about JD300. Also, companies only offer 100 to 200 free kilometres; you then pay extra for each kilometre.

To get around Wadi Rum, it's better to charter a 4WD jeep with a local driver – see Getting Around in the Wadi Rum section of the Southern Desert chapter for details.

Petrol & Repairs

Benzin 'adi (regular) petrol costs 221 fils per litre, and the less frequently available *mumtaz, khas* (super) costs 301 fils. Most rental cars take regular, so there's no need to buy super. *Khal min ar-rasas* (unleaded petrol) costs about 250 fils per litre, but is only reliably available in Amman – look for the 'unleaded petrol' signs in English at stations in the more upmarket suburbs, eg around 6th, 7th and 8th Circles. Any other stations in Jordan which claim to sell 'unleaded petrol' are probably just giving you leaded petrol at the 'unleaded price'. Diesel is available at about 110 fils per litre.

Petrol stations are obvious, but the only sign in English is 'Jordan Petroleum Refinery Co Ltd' (the state-run monopoly). Stations can be found in the outskirts of major towns, and at some junctions. Along the Desert Highway, there are plenty of stations; less so along the King's Highway; and very infrequently along the Dead Sea Highway.

Garages with reputable mechanics can be found in the outskirts of most towns. They can handle most repairs, at negotiable prices.

BICYCLE

Cycling is a popular option, but not necessarily always a fun one. March to May and September to November are the best times to get on your bike.

The disadvantages are: the stifling heat in summer; the few places to stop along the highways; the terrible traffic, with drivers not being used to cyclists; the steep streets in some cities, such as Amman and Karak; and the paucity of spare parts because so few locals ride bikes. We have also heard reports of mischievous children throwing stones at unwary cyclists. The good news, however, is the road system is satisfactory and the roads are smooth, while the cities and tourist attractions are well signposted in English.

With some preparation, and an occasional lift in a bus, cyclists can have a great time. Most major sights are conveniently placed less than a day's ride apart heading south from the Syrian border – ie Irbid-Amman-Madaba-Karak-Tafila-Wadi Mousa (near Petra)-Ma'an – but the final bit from Ma'an to Aqaba, via Wadi Rum, is tough. All these places have hotels and restaurants, so there's no need to carry tents, sleeping bags and cooking equipment. Other attractions can be easily visited on day trips, by bike or public

transport, from places such as Amman, Irbid, Madaba, Karak and Ma'an. The King's Highway is the most scenic route, but also the most difficult. The Desert Highway is boring and the traffic is heavy; and the Dead Sea Highway has extremely few stops, and is always hot. Two stretches along the King's Highway where you may want to take public transport are across the extremely wide and steep Wadi Mujib valley between Madaba and Karak, and between the turn-off to Wadi Rum and Aqaba, which is very steep, has appalling traffic and plenty of treacherous turns.

If you are carrying a tent and want to camp, the quickest route between Amman and Aqaba is:

Day 1 Amman to Ariha – 91km (seven hours).
Day 2 Ariha to Wadi Hasa – 66km (five hours).
Day 3 Wadi Hasa to Dana Nature Reserve – 65km (six hours).
Day 4 Dana Nature Reserve to Wadi Mousa – 48km (four hours).
Day 5 Wadi Mousa to 20km south of the turn-off to Wadi Rum – 106km (seven hours).
Day 6 20km after the Wadi Rum turn-off to Aqaba – 50km (three hours).

What to Bring

Bicycles can travel by air. You can take them to pieces and put them in a bike bag or box, but it's much easier simply to wheel your bike to the check-in desk where it should be treated as a piece of baggage. You may have to remove the pedals and turn the handlebars sideways so that it takes up less space in the aircraft's hold. Check with the airline well in advance, preferably before you pay for your ticket.

Spare parts are not common in Jordan, so carry a spare tire, extra chain links, spokes, two inner tubes, repair kit and tool kit with spanner set. Also bring a low gear set for the hills, a couple of water containers and confine your panniers to a maximum of 15kg.

HITCHING
Getting a Ride

Hitching is never entirely safe in any country in the world, and we don't recommend it. Travellers who hitch should understand that they are taking a small, but potentially serious, risk. People who choose to hitch will be safer if they travel in pairs and let someone know where they are planning to go.

Despite this general advice, hitching is definitely feasible in Jordan. The traffic varies a lot from place to place, but you generally don't have to wait long for a lift on main routes. There is no need to hitch around Jordan to save money, because public transport to most places is frequent, and always cheap, but hitching is often necessary to avoid backtracking, detouring and chartering expensive taxis where public transport is limited or nonexistent, eg southern sections of the King's Highway and to the desert castles east of Amman. Avoid hitching too close to the borders with Israel and Iraq, and always carry your passport.

Always start hitching early, and avoid 1 to 4 pm when it's often too hot, and traffic is reduced while many locals enjoy a siesta. Also, don't start hitching after about 4 pm unless it's a short trip on a road with frequent traffic, because hitching after dark increases the risk. The best places to look for lifts are junctions, checkpoints, tourist attractions (eg lookouts) or shops where cars often stop. Police stationed at major junctions and checkpoints are often happy to wave down drivers and cajole them into giving you a lift.

To indicate that you're looking for a lift, simply raise your index finger in the direction you're heading. If you hail down a bus, minibus, private taxi, service taxi or pick-up (with other passengers and/or cargo) you'll obviously have to pay for the fare. On a large truck, you may be asked for a fare; in a private vehicle, you probably won't need to pay anything. However, to avoid a possibly unpleasant situation, ask beforehand if payment is expected and, if so, establish how much they want. Otherwise, simply offer a small amount when you get out – it will often be refused.

Finally, a few general tips: don't look too scruffy; don't hitch in groups of more than two; women should be very careful, and look for lifts with families, or in a car with another local or foreign female; trucks on some steep and windy roads (eg between the Wadi Rum turn-off and Aqaba) can be painfully slow; and make sure you carry a hat and lots of water.

Picking up Hitchhikers

If you have chartered a service taxi or private taxi you are under no obligation to pick up any hitchhikers, but if you're driving a private or rented car, the pressure to pick up people along the way can be intense. You can, of course, simply drive past the locals alongside the road waving their arms frantically, but if you stop at a checkpoint, petrol station, lookout or shop you may often be approached for a lift (single female drivers should not pick up male hitchhikers). If you don't want an extra passenger, make excuses about lengthy detours, long stopovers and late arrivals – this may not always work, however, because the passenger(s) may also like to visit a few remote castles on the way.

On major highways, such as the Desert Highway (where there's plenty of public transport), the obligation to pick up passengers is far less because they're normally just looking for a free ride. However, on remote stretches where public transport is limited or nonexistent, eg across the Wadi Mujib valley, you should try to pick up a few passengers.

One advantage about picking up a hitchhiker is the chance to meet a local, and readers have often been invited into a home in return for a lift. Although you may be charged, you should never charge a local for a lift. They will assume that any foreign hitchhiker can afford to pay for public transport, and that any foreigner driving a private or rental car doesn't need the extra money.

LOCAL TRANSPORT
Bus

The two largest cities, Amman and Irbid, have efficient and cheap public bus networks, but they're unlikely to be of any use to visitors. These buses cater to locals travelling to/from their homes in the suburbs, so they rarely go anywhere useful. Also, none of the buses have destination signs in English (although some have 'English' numbers), no schedules or timetables are available and local bus stations are often chaotic. Service taxis are more common throughout Jordan, and private taxis are still cheap by western standards, so most visitors never need to worry about the local bus system.

Service Taxi

Major cities, such as Amman and Irbid, are well served by service taxis which run along set routes within each city, and often go to places of interest to visitors. As with intercity service taxis, the route is listed in Arabic on the driver's door and drivers wait until they are full before departing.

Private Taxi

The other common mode of transport for visitors is the yellow private taxi. Some travellers avoid using private taxis on principle, but after climbing up and down the *jebels* (hills) of Amman, or staggering around in the infernal summer heat of Aqaba, you'll be glad to fork out the dinar equivalent of less than US$1 for a comfortable, air-conditioned ride across town. Some drivers can speak a fair amount of English, especially in Amman.

Yellow private taxis are very common in major towns like Amman, Irbid, Jerash, Ma'an, Madaba, Wadi Mousa (Petra) and Aqaba, and important transport junctions like Shuneh al-Janubiyyeh (South Shuna) and Tafila. Not all taxis are metered, and there is no standard method of payment in the country: in Amman, all taxis are metered, but foreigners sometimes need to persuade the driver to use it; in Wadi Mousa, taxis are unmetered and the standard fare anywhere local is JD1; and elsewhere, taxis are unmetered and fares are negotiable, especially in Aqaba where most drivers are unscrupulous.

ORGANISED TOURS

Many visitors to Jordan come on organised tours, prearranged from their own country. (The Organised Tours section in the Getting There & Away chapter has more information about foreign companies which offer tours to and around Jordan.)

Most travel agencies in Jordan simply sell airline tickets and/or serve as ground opera-

tors for major foreign tour companies. They do not offer organised tours on a regular basis, but will if you provide the itinerary and find the passengers – in which case it's cheaper to arrange everything yourself.

If you're travelling independently, and on a tight budget, jumping on an irregular and budget-priced organised tour to remote places like Wadi Rum, and the desert castles of eastern Jordan, is far easier, and often cheaper, than doing it yourself.

The local agencies listed below offer something a little different, and have been recommended by some readers:

Atlas Travel & Tourist Agency
(☎ 06-465 4046, fax 461 0198, email info@atlastours.net) PO Box 7131, Amman 11118. Also offers water sports, and side trips to Israel, Syria and Lebanon.
Web site www.atlastours.net
Discovery
(☎ 06-569 7998, fax 569 8183, email discovery@nets.com.jo) PO Box 3371, Amman 11118.
Golden Crown Tours
(☎ 06-551 1200, fax 551 1202) PO Box 183522, Amman 11118. Also specialises in archaeological, religious and adventure tours.
International Traders
(☎ 06-560 7014, fax 566 9905, email sahar@traders.com.jo) PO Box 408, Amman 11118. Also the representative for American Express in Amman and Aqaba.
Petra Moon Tourism Services
(☎ 03-215 6665, fax 215 6666, email petram@go.com.jo) PO Box 129, Wadi Mousa (Petra) 71811. Also offers an interesting range of treks in remote areas, such as Petra and Dana Nature Reserve.
Web site www.petramoon.com
Royal Tours
(☎ 06-585 7154, fax 585 6845, email rtours@rja.com.jo) PO Box 815433, Amman 11180. Part of the Royal Jordanian Airlines group, and is good for stopover packages if flying with Royal Jordanian.
Universal General Tourist Services
(☎ 03-203 1078, fax 203 1079, email rock@firstnet.com.jo) PO Box 2262, Aqaba 226. Can organise German-speaking guides, and specialises in southern Jordan.
Zaman Tours & Travel
(☎ 03-215 7723, fax 215 7722, email zamantours@joinnet.com.jo) PO Box 158, Wadi Mousa (Petra) 71811. Arranges adventure tours, camping, camel treks and hiking.

Amman

عمان

☎ 06 • pop 1.7 million

Amman will certainly never win any prizes for being the most interesting city in the world – the town centre, known as Downtown, is a busy, chaotic jumble of traffic, and just crossing the street is an achievement. A small village of about 2000 at the beginning of the 20th century, Amman has grown incredibly in recent years and now sprawls over a large area. Surveying the scene from one of the hills or *jebels* the city is built on, it's easy to get the impression that Amman is nothing more than an interminable spread of thousands upon thousands of concrete blocks.

On closer inspection, however, the situation is not quite so dire. There are some leafy, agreeable areas in the city and, while there is no feeling of being in one of the ancient metropolises of the Orient, Downtown has a good deal of atmosphere: it teems with locals hunting through the *souqs* (markets) and its old cafes hum with men playing cards and backgammon, sipping tea or coffee and smoking a *nargila* (water pipe). And there are just enough leftovers from the city's distant Roman past – particularly the Roman Theatre – to keep most visitors occupied for a day or two.

As many sights in Jordan are close to Amman, the capital also makes an obvious base for day trips to places like Jerash, Umm Qais and Madaba; and there are numerous other attractions near Amman (see the Around Amman section later in this chapter).

HISTORY

Excavations in and around Amman have turned up finds from as early as 3500 BC, with most earlier inhabitants living on Jebel al-Qala'a – now referred to as the Citadel. Occupation of the town, called Rabbath Ammon or 'Great City of the Ammonites' in the Old Testament, has been continuous, and objects dating back to the Bronze Age show that the town was involved in trade with Greece, Syria, Cyprus and Mesopotamia.

HIGHLIGHTS

- **Citadel** – walk around the ruins of ancient Amman, with its National Archaeological Museum, and admire the views of the modern city (see page 119)

- **Roman Theatre** – sit and watch Jordanians come and go, and visit the nearby Odeon and Forum, and the two museums inside the theatre (see page 120)

- **Darat al-Funun** – this renovated former Byzantine church features contemporary art, enchanting gardens and one of the nicest cafes in Jordan (see page 125)

- **Salt** – this charming town near Amman boasts fine Ottoman architecture, and several workshops with arts and crafts (see page 140)

- **Wadi as-Seer** – from this town near Amman, it's a pleasant walk to some caves and the impressive Iraq al-Amir castle (see page 142)

Biblical references are numerous, and indicate that by 1200 BC Rabbath Ammon was the capital of the Ammonites. During David's reign, he sent Joab at the head of Israelite

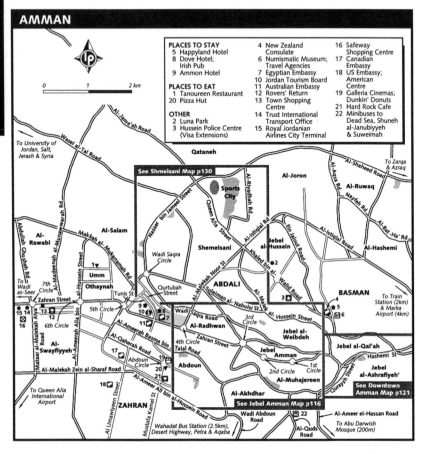

AMMAN

PLACES TO STAY
5   Happyland Hotel
8   Dove Hotel;
    Irish Pub
9   Ammon Hotel

PLACES TO EAT
1   Tanoureen Restaurant
20 Pizza Hut

OTHER
2   Luna Park
3   Hussein Police Centre
    (Visa Extensions)

4   New Zealand
    Consulate
6   Numismatic Museum;
    Travel Agencies
7   Egyptian Embassy
10 Jordan Tourism Board
11 Australian Embassy
12 Rovers' Return
13 Town Shopping
    Centre
14 Trust International
    Transport Office
15 Royal Jordanian
    Airlines City Terminal

16 Safeway
    Shopping Centre
17 Canadian
    Embassy
18 US Embassy;
    American
    Centre
19 Galleria Cinemas;
    Dunkin' Donuts
21 Hard Rock Cafe
22 Minibuses to
    Dead Sea, Shuneh
    al-Janubiyyeh
    & Suweimah

armies to besiege Rabbath, after being insulted by the Ammonite king Nahash. After taking the town, David burnt the inhabitants alive in a brick kiln. Amman continued to flourish and supplied David with weapons in his ongoing wars. His successor, Solomon, erected a shrine in Jerusalem to the Ammonite god, Molech. From here on, the only Biblical references to Rabbath are prophecies of its destruction at the hands of the Babylonians, who did in fact take over but did not destroy the town.

The history of Amman between then (circa 585 BC), and the time of the Ptolemies of Egypt, is unclear. Ptolemy Philadelphus (283-246 BC) rebuilt the city during his reign, and it was named Philadelphia after him. The Ptolemy dynasty was succeeded by the Seleucids and, briefly, by the Nabataeans, before Amman was taken by Herod around 30 BC, and fell under the sway of Rome. The city, which even before Herod's arrival had felt Rome's influence as a member of the Decapolis (see the boxed text), was totally replanned in typically grand Roman style, and the city became an important centre along the trade route between the Red Sea and Syria.

The Decapolis

The Roman commercial cities of what is now modern-day Jordan, Syria and Israel first became known as the Decapolis in the 1st century AD. Despite the etymology of the word, it seems that the Decapolis consisted of more than 10 cities, and possibly up to 18. No-one knows for certain the reason behind such a grouping. In all likelihood the association of the cities served a double function: to unite the Roman possessions and to enhance commerce. In Jordan, the main Decapolis cities were Philadelphia (now called Amman), Gadara (Umm Qais), Gerasa (Jerash) and Pella, and possibly Abila.

The cities were linked by paved roads that allowed wagons to circulate rapidly; at Umm Qais and Jerash, the ruts carved by these wagons can still be seen in the stones of the city streets. The cities flourished during the period of Roman dominance in the east, but fell into decline with the dawn of the Umayyad dynasty, which was based in Damascus. Afterwards, the choice of Baghdad as the centre of the Muslim world dealt the Decapolis a final blow.

Philadelphia was the seat of Christian bishops in the early Byzantine period, but the city declined and fell to the Sassanians (from Persia) in about 614 AD. At the time of the Muslim invasion in about 636 AD, the town – by then named Amman – was still alive and kicking because it was located on the caravan trade. From about the 10th century, however, the city declined, and it was apparently reduced to a prison town for exiled princes and other notables.

Amman was nothing more than a sad little village when a colony of Circassians resettled there in 1878. It boomed temporarily in the early 20th century when it became a stopover on the new Hejaz Railway between Damascus (Syria) and Medina (Saudi Arabia); and, in 1921, it became the centre of Transjordan when Emir Abdullah made it his headquarters. In 1948, many Palestinians

settled in and around Amman and, two years later, it was officially declared the capital of the Hashemite kingdom.

ORIENTATION

Like Rome, Amman was born on seven major *jebels* (hills), but today it spreads across 19 – many of which are over 800m above sea level (so the winters can be cold and snow is not uncommon). Amman can be confusing, but it's easy to remember that Downtown – known locally as *il-balad* – is the area immediately around the King Hussein Mosque, and is literally the lowest level of the city.

The only way to make any sense of Amman in a short time is to pick out the major landmarks on the jebels. The main hill is Jebel Amman, where many embassies and some of the flash hotels, shops and restaurants are located. The traffic roundabouts on Jebel Amman are numbered west of Downtown; ie from 1st Circle to 8th Circle. (Just to confuse matters, the 'circles' west of 4th Circle are just regular junctions with traffic lights.) The main landmark on Jebel Amman is the Jordan Tower Centre about 150m east of 3rd Circle – it's the high, circular white tower topped by a 'crown'.

Jebel al-Hussein, north-west of Downtown, has the Housing Bank Centre which sticks out a mile – it's the tall, terraced building with creepers hanging down the sides. Closer to Downtown is the big, blue dome of the huge King Abdullah Mosque; and on top of Jebel al-Ashrafiyeh' to the south is the distinctive black and white striped Abu Darwish Mosque.

The smartest areas are along Al-Kulliyah al-Islamiyah St in Jebel Amman (which turns into Zahran St), where some embassies are located; Shmeisani, home to upmarket shops, top end hotels and modern shopping centres; and the newer and trendier Abdoun, with its coffee shops, western fast food venues and classy restaurants.

Books & Maps

Your Guide to Amman is a free monthly booklet which includes embassies, airlines, travel agencies, car rental companies and

Streets & Circles

With its endless one-way streets, narrow lanes and jebels, Amman is confusing enough to get around anyway, but the ambiguous names for the streets and circles will make most visitors a little crazy. We have used the more common names on the maps and in the text, but if the street signs, directions given by locals and queries from taxi drivers are driving you really batty, refer to the list below.

Don't forget that Al-Malek means King, so King Faisal St is sometimes labelled Al-Malek Faisal St. Similarly, Al-Malekah is Queen and Al-Emir (Al-Amir) is Prince. And don't be too surprised that some 'circles' are now called 'squares'.

Streets

Al-Kulliyah al-Islamiyah St – sometimes known as Zahran St
Mango St – Omar bin al-Khattab St
Quraysh St – Saqf Sayl St
Rainbow St – Abu Bakr as-Siddiq St

Circles

2nd Circle – Wasfi at-Tall Square
3rd Circle – King Talal Square
4th Circle – Abdullah bin Hussein Square
5th Circle – Emir (Prince) Faisal Square
6th Circle – Princess Tharwat Square
Ministry of the Interior Circle – Gamal Abdul Nasser Square

other helpful information in English and Arabic. It's not particularly easy to find: so either ring the publisher (☎ 465 6593), or try to pick up a copy at an airline office or travel agent.

The Amman brochure printed by the Jordan Tourism Board is not very useful and the map on the back is fairly hopeless. Other useful booklets include the pocket guide printed by Al-Kutba, which details numerous, but fairly uninteresting, archaeological sites in the region; and the colourful guide published by Arabesque. Both cost about JD3, and are available at some bookshops in Amman.

Most maps of Jordan include a basic map of Amman, but none are detailed enough; the maps in this guidebook should be sufficient for most visitors. If you intend to stay for some time, visit places in the remote suburbs or do lots of walking, it's a good idea to pick up a quality map. Easily the best map of Amman is *Today's Amman* (1:20,000), published by the Royal Jordanian Geographic Centre, although it (and all other maps of Amman) lacks detail of Downtown. The map costs JD2, and is usually available in some bookshops around the city.

INFORMATION
Tourist Offices

The Downtown visitors centre (☎ 464 6264, email t.i.c@n2.com) is the name of the tourist office close to the Roman Theatre. It's run by friendly staff who speak good English, and reasonable French. Although helpful, they do not always provide reliable information; but the centre does offer most of the interesting free brochures published by the Jordan Tourism Board (see Tourist Offices in the Facts for the Visitor chapter). The centre is open from 8.30 am to 6 pm every day.

Less convenient and helpful is the Public Relations office (☎ 464 2311, fax 464 8465) on the ground floor of the Ministry of Tourism & Antiquities on Al-Mutanabbi St, near 3rd Circle, but it can offer a wider range of brochures than the Downtown visitors centre. It's open from 8 am to 2 pm every day except Friday.

Visa Extensions

Most visas, whether issued by a Jordanian embassy/consulate or at the airport or border, are valid for 14 days. Anyone wishing to stay longer must apply for an extension (see the Visas & Documents section in the Facts for the Visitor chapter). Which police station in Amman you need to visit for an extension depends on where you're staying, although you won't always be asked your hotel name when applying. If staying in Downtown, the closest police stations are Hussein Police Centre or Muhajireen Police Station; if staying elsewhere, ask your hotel where to go.

The visa section at the Hussein Police Centre is at the back of the complex, and is open from 8 am to 2 pm every day except Friday. It's located on Khalid ibn al-Walid St (see Amman map). Take the unnumbered service taxi from Raghadan station to Jebel Al-Hussein, although it's probably easier to charter a taxi. Another place for visa extensions is the Muhajireen Police Station, on Al-Ameerah Basma Bint Talal Rd (see the Jebel Amman map). It's open from 10 am to 1 pm every day except Friday. Take service taxi No 35 from along Quraysh St.

If you want another extension, or wish to reside in Jordan, or there is something unusual about your visa or passport (eg a curious number of Israeli stamps), you may be sent to the Directorate of Residence, Borders & Foreigners, on Suleiman an-Nabulsi St (see the Jebel Amman map), for further checking and paperwork. Take service taxi Nos 6 or 7 from Downtown.

Money

Changing money is very easy, and Downtown is full of banks and moneychangers. (See Money in the Facts for the Visitor chapter for more information.) The American Express representative is International Traders (☎ 566 1014), virtually opposite the Ambassador Hotel on Al-Shareef Abdulla Hameed Sharaf St (see the Shmeisani map).

Most branches of the Arab Bank have ATMs for Visa and MasterCard; there are branches along Al-Malek Faisal St and almost opposite Hashemite Square. Other banks offering quick and easy service are: ANZ Grindlays Bank on Al-Malek al-Hussein St in Downtown, and on 1st Circle; Jordan National Bank, between 2nd and 3rd Circles; and Bank of Jordan on Al-Malek Faisal St and 1st Circle. There are also ATMs for most major international credit cards at the Safeway Shopping Centre in Shmeisani, many upmarket hotels around the city and at the Queen Alia international airport.

Many moneychangers are located along Al-Malek Faisal St in Downtown – one that is especially good for travellers cheques is Sahloul Exchange Co, on the ground floor of the same building as the Aicco Internet Cafe.

Post

The Central Post Office (☎ 462 4120) is along Al-Amir Mohammed St in Downtown; it's signposted ambiguously in English as 'Postal Savings Bank'. The poste restante mail is kept in a box behind a counter at the main entrance. Nothing inside the office is signed in English, but most staff speak a little. It's open from 8 am to 7 pm every day except Friday when it closes at 1.30 pm.

There are also smaller post offices in the Jordan InterContinental Hotel complex between 2nd and 3rd Circles; and in the Housing Bank Centre in Shmeisani.

Parcels The Parcel Post Office is along Omar al-Khayyam St in Downtown. It looks more like a shop than a post office, so look for the tell-tale weighing machine on the counter in the shop opposite the rear entrance to the Central Post Office. To send a large parcel anywhere, first go to the Parcel Post Office, where it's weighed. Then take it *unwrapped* to the Customs Office virtually opposite (look for the sign with the word 'Customs' in English on the crest), where a customs declaration must be completed. Finally, take the parcel back to the Parcel Post Office for packing and paying. The Parcel Post Office and Customs Office are both open from 8 am to 2 pm daily except Friday.

Telephone

There is now no central telephone office in Amman: the Jordan Telecommunications Company (JTC) building, on Omar al-Khayyam St in Downtown, is used by locals to pay their telephone accounts. To make a telephone call, use a telephone in your hotel, or one of the numerous payphones operated by JPP and Alo. (See Post & Communications in the Facts for the Visitor chapter for more information.) These can be found outside the JTC building; near the Downtown visitors centre; and at many tourist spots and on street corners. Telephone cards for either company are available at shops near the telephone booths, at the JTC building and grocery stores around the capital. Long-distance calls can also be made at obvious private telephone agencies

AMMAN

JEBEL AMMAN

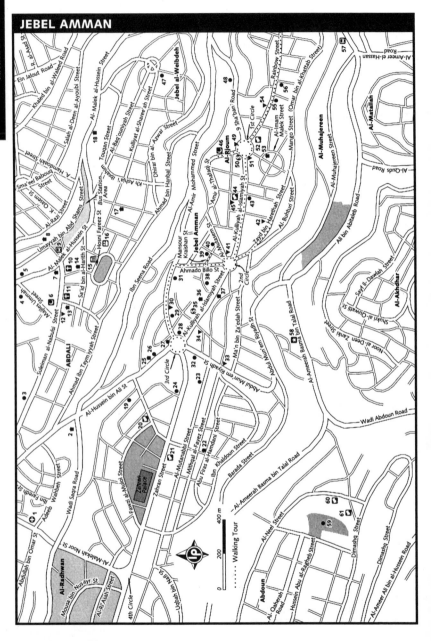

JEBEL AMMAN

PLACES TO STAY
2 Radisson SAS Hotel;
   Royal Club Restaurant
7 Mirage Hotel;
   Oasis Coffee Shop
8 Al-Monzer Hotel;
   Cleopatra Hotel
13 Caravan Hotel
14 Remal Hotel
17 Canary Hotel
18 Merryland Hotel
22 Hisham Hotel;
   Forest Inn Restaurant
25 Grand Hyatt Jordan;
   Grand Café; L'incontro
   Restaurant; JJ Mahoney's
   Nightclub
36 Jordan InterContinental
   Hotel; Pasha Nightclub;
   Post Office; Royal
   Jordanian Airlines Office;
   Dutch Embassy;
   Jordan Gifts Store
37 Carlton Hotel
53 Granada Hotel;
   After Eight Bar

PLACES TO EAT
12 Snack Box
30 Chicken Tikka Inn
33 Taiwan Tourismo

34 Bonita Inn
41 Kawkab Al-Sharq
42 Pizza Hut
45 Fakhr ed-Din
49 Diplomat Restaurant
51 Terrace Cafeteria Petra;
   ANZ Grindlays Bank
54 Adam's Apple Cafe,
   Bar & Restaurant

OTHER
1 Jordan Hospital
   & Medical Centre
3 Directorate of Residence,
   Borders & Foreigners
4 Parliament
5 Royal Jordanian Airlines
   Office
6 King Abdullah Mosque
   & Islamic Museum
9 Abdali Bus Station
10 Greek Orthodox Church
11 Coptic Orthodox Church
15 Jordan National Gallery
   of Fine Arts
16 Ammoun Cinema
19 Goethe Institut
20 Syrian Embassy
21 French Embassy
23 Ministry of Tourism
   & Antiquities

24 Ministry of Foreign Affairs
26 Library (Ministry of Culture)
27 Oriental Souvenirs Store
28 Jacob's Pharmacy
29 Amman Bookshop
31 Jordan Tower Centre;
   Philadelphia Cinemas
32 American Language Center
35 Jordan National Bank; Uncle
   Sam's Restaurant & Bar
38 Al-Alaydi Jordan
   Craft Centre
39 Artisana
40 Instituto Cervantes
43 Islamic College
44 Iraqi Embassy;
   Museum of Political
   History
46 Mosque
47 Centre Culturel Français
48 Nator Car Rental
50 Bank of Jordan; Firas Car
   Rental
52 Saudi Arabian Consulate
55 British Council
56 Amusement Centre
57 Minibuses to Wadi as-Seer
58 Muhajireen Police Station
59 Orthodox Club
60 Lebanese Embassy
61 UK Embassy

around Downtown – a few are located along Omar al-Khayyam St, not far from the JTC building.

All telephone numbers in Amman now have seven digits. In general, add 5 to the start of all old six-digit numbers starting with 60, 66, 67, 68 and 69; or add 4 to any old number starting with 61, 62, 63, 64 and 65.

Fax

Most of the private telephone agencies around Downtown also offer fax services, as does the Central Post Office.

Email & Internet Access

The cheapest places to access the Internet are opposite the University of Jordan in northern Amman, but this is too far from Downtown for most visitors. The following places are all in the Downtown area, except Safeway which is in Shmeisani, and open from about 10 am to about 11 pm daily.

Aicco Internet Cafe
   (aicco@go.com.jo) Upstairs in the Arab International Centre, Al-Malek Faisal St: JD1.500 per hour.
Al-Saha Internet Centre
   (ashrafa@index.com.jo) Located on Hashemi St: JD1.500 per hour.
Books@cafe
   (contact@books-cafe.com) Mango St: JD2 per hour, but doubles that to JD4 per hour on Wednesday, Thursday and Friday. Anyone who eats there (see Places to Eat) receives a discount on Internet use. (Refer to Bookshops).
Farah Hotel
   (farahhotel@hotmail.com) Cinema al-Hussein St (see Places to Stay later in this chapter): JD2 per hour.
Safeway
   (cybertunnel@safeways.com.jo) Nasser bin Jamil St, Shmeisani: JD2.500 per hour.

Travel Agencies

There is a plethora of travel agencies dotted around the city – a crowd of them is strung along Al-Malek al-Hussein St, north of Downtown and near the flyover. Although some claim to organise tours within Jordan, the bulk are little more than general sales agents for international airlines.

Bookshops

Amman has a reasonable number of bookshops, but for the best selection, or to find anything a little unusual, you'll have to visit several. Most of the souvenir shops in the mid-range and top end hotels, and all of those along the northern end of Hashemite Square, have very good selections of books and maps.

Al-Aulama Bookshop
(☎ 463 6192) Al-Amir Mohammed St, Downtown. Good for hard-to-find locally produced guidebooks, maps and postcards.
Amman Bookshop
(☎ 464 4013) Just down from 3rd Circle, has the best range of books and novels in Amman.
Books@cafe
(☎ 465 0457, email contact@books-cafe.com) Mango St, Downtown. The sort of place where you can forget you're in Jordan – or even the Middle East. It has a huge collection of books in English (but little about Jordan); a small book exchange; a useful notice board; and an Internet centre (see Email & Internet Access). It has an expensive indoor and outdoor cafe with wonderful views and hosts film nights.
Gibraltar Bookshop
Next to the entrance for Hashem Restaurant in Downtown. Most convenient for foreign newspapers and magazines.
Jordan Gifts Store
(☎ 464 1463) In the Jordan InterContinental Hotel, between 2nd and 3rd Circles. Has a wide range.
Regency Palace Bookshop
In the Regency Palace Hotel, Queen Alia St, Shmeisani. Very good for all sorts of hard-to-find titles about Jordan; and has a range of Lonely Planet titles.

Libraries

The Amman Central Library (☎ 462 7718) is in the same building as the Downtown visitors centre, near the Roman Theatre. About half of the 1st floor is given to titles in English, and there are some current magazines in English and French on the top floor. The library is open from 9 am to 5 pm every day except Friday.

The Ministry of Culture has a small library (open from 8 am to 2 pm daily except Friday), next to the Grand Hyatt Jordan hotel on Al-Hussein bin Ali St (see Jebel Amman map), but there are few English titles.

The Darat al-Funun art gallery (see Art Galleries later in this chapter) has terrific art books. The main library at the University of Jordan is your best option for research. There are also libraries in the American, French, British, Spanish and German cultural centres.

Universities

One of the biggest universities in Jordan is the University of Jordan (Web site www.ju.edu.jo), a few kilometres north-west of Downtown. It boasts several museums (see Museums later in this chapter) and a huge library. It also offers language courses (see Courses in the Facts for the Visitor chapter), and is a great place to meet locals. Numerous Internet centres and western fast-food outlets are dotted at various points along the main road, just opposite the university. Take any minibus or service taxi to Salt from either Raghadan or Abdali bus stations – the university is quite easy to spot from the main road.

Cultural Centres

All of the following cultural centres regularly organise film nights and lectures (generally in their own language); exhibitions (usually in English); and concerts (in their own language or Arabic). Tourists are normally welcome at these events, but it is always a good idea to ring the centre first to double-check on the information. You will also find details of functions at the various cultural centres listed in the two English-language newspapers published in Amman.

American Center
(☎ 585 9102) US Embassy, Abdoun. Has a library with US newspapers and magazines. Open from 8 am to 7 pm, Sunday to Thursday.
British Council
(☎ 463 6147, fax 465 6413) Rainbow St, south-east of 1st Circle. Has a library with cur-

rent English newspapers. Open from 10 am to 6 pm, Sunday to Thursday.
Web site www.britcoun.org/jordan

Centre Culturel Français
(☎ 463 7009) By the roundabout at the top of Jebel al-Weibdeh. Has a useful library. Open from 9 am to 1 pm, and 4 to 7 pm, every day except Friday.

Goethe Institut
(☎ 464 1993) Just off Al-Hussein bin Ali St, north-west of 3rd Circle. This is primarily for German-speakers and is open from 9 am to 12.30 pm, Saturday to Wednesday, and from 5.45 to 6.45 pm on Saturday.

Haya Cultural Centre
(☎ 566 5195) Ilya Abu Madhi St, Shmeisani. Has a library, playground and museum (see Museums later in this chapter), and regularly organises activities for children. Open from 9 am to 2 pm, and 4 to 6 pm, every day.

Instituto Cervantes
(☎ 461 0858, fax 462 4049, email icamman@ go.com.jo) Al-Mutasem St, north-east of 2nd Circle. Primarily for Spanish-speakers; it has a library. Open from 9 am to 1 pm, and 4 to 7 pm, Sunday to Thursday.

Royal Culture Centre
(☎ 566 1026) Queen Alia St, Shmeisani. This large, modern complex often holds concerts and exhibitions. Functions are sometimes advertised at the Downtown visitors centre.

Laundry
Several tiny laundries and dry-cleaning services are dotted around Downtown, particularly along Basman and Al-Malek Faisal streets, and in the laneways between both.

Toilets
Most public toilets are grotty, eg the one at the top end of Cinema al-Hussein St, but the toilets near the Downtown visitors centre are clean enough. Entry to either costs 50 fils. It's better to use a toilet in a restaurant, or at a museum; or ask nicely at any hotel.

Medical Services
Amman has more than 20 hospitals. Among the better ones are:

Islamic Hospital
(☎ 568 0127) Just off Al-Malekah Noor St, Jebel al-Hussein. See Shmeisani map.

Italian Hospital
(☎ 477 7101) Just off Italian St, southern Downtown. See Downtown Amman map.

Jordan Hospital & Medical Centre
(☎ 560 7550) Al-Malekah Noor St. See Jebel Amman map.

Palestine Hospital
(☎ 560 7071) Queen Alia St, Shmeisani. See Shmeisani map.

University Hospital
(☎ 535 3444) University of Jordan complex, northern Amman.

Your Guide to Amman, and the two English-language daily newspapers, list the current telephone numbers of these and other hospitals; and of doctors on night duty throughout the capital. The two newspapers also publish a list of pharmacies open after hours. The most convenient for many is Jacob's Pharmacy (☎ 464 4940), right on 3rd Circle.

Emergency
We hope you won't need to contact any of the following numbers (staff answering these numbers should be able to speak English):

Ambulance	☎ 193
Fire Department	☎ 199
Police	☎ 192
Traffic Police/Accidents	☎ 489 6390

The main police station (☎ 465 7788) in Downtown, upstairs along Al-Malek Faisal St and opposite the Arab Bank, is hard to find. There are also small tourist police booths near the Roman Theatre, and at the Citadel. The two police stations in the suburbs, where complaints can be made and visas extended, are detailed in the Visa Extensions section earlier in this chapter.

Dangers & Annoyances
The only problem you're likely to encounter is the traffic. If driving, avoid Downtown; if walking, always look both ways several times before crossing any street. Nightclubs frequented by foreigners are more likely to attract pickpockets and bag snatchers, but crime in Amman is extremely rare.

ANCIENT AMMAN
Citadel
The first inhabitants of the area lived at the highest point of Amman, Jebel al-Qala'a

(about 850m above sea level), and artefacts dating from the Bronze Age show that the hill served as a fortress and/or agora for thousands of years. The complex is surrounded by 1700m-long **walls**, which were built and rebuilt many times during the Bronze and Iron ages, and the Roman, Byzantine and Umayyad periods.

The Citadel's most impressive building is the **Umayyad Palace**, which stands behind (north of) the National Archaeological Museum (detailed in Museums later in this chapter). Originally believed to be the work of the Umayyad Arabs, dating from about 720 AD, no-one now seems certain about its exact function, but one theory is that the building was once the residence of the governor of Amman.

At the entrance (to the south) of the palace is the **audience hall**, shaped like a cross because it was built over a Byzantine church. A **courtyard** immediately north of the hall leads to a **colonnaded street**, which was 10m wide, lined with numerous arches and columns, and flanked by residential and administrative buildings. Further inside (to the north) was probably the **governor's residence**.

Not far from the entrance to the palace is the **Umayyad Cistern**, an enormous (about 5m by 16m) water cistern partially made from remains of other nearby buildings.

Closer to the museum is the small **Byzantine Basilica**, or church. Little remains as most of it was destroyed by earthquakes (rather than invaders and looters). Probably dating back to the 6th or 7th century AD, it contains **mosaics** which have been covered for their own protection.

About 100m south of the basilica is the **Temple of Hercules**, similar to the Temple of Artemis at Jerash. It was once connected to the Forum by an extraordinary set of stairs and dates from the reign of the emperor Marcus Aurelius (161-80 AD). The only obvious remains are parts of the podium, and the columns which can be seen from many places in Amman. Close by is a **lookout** with great views of Amman, although various places within the Citadel also provide views.

Most of the ruins in the Citadel are not labelled in English which makes the whole complex a bit haphazard and frustrating, but guides can be hired – ask at the museum or tourist police booth. Excavations will continue for many years, and more of the ruins are likely to be accessible in the future. Entrance to the grounds is free, but there is some talk about fencing off the area and charging visitors. The complex is also home to the fine National Archaeological Museum.

Although it looks close to Downtown, the only way into the Citadel is along the access road off Al-Malek Ali bin al-Hussein St. However, from the Citadel, it's possible to walk past the tourist police booth, and along a marked path and then jump (about 1m) from a wall on to Sa'id Khair St (but it's not possible to get in this way because the wall is too high).

Roman Theatre

The restored Roman Theatre is the most obvious and impressive remnant of Roman Philadelphia and, for many, the highlight of Amman. It is cut into the northern side of a hill that once served as a necropolis, and has a seating capacity of 6000. It was built on three tiers: the rulers, of course, sat closest to the action; the military had the middle section; and the ordinary folks sat way at the top.

The theatre was probably built in the 2nd century AD during the reign of Antoninus Pius, who ruled from 138 to 161. These theatres often had religious significance, and the small structure built into the rock above the top row of seats is believed to have housed a statue of the goddess Athena, who was prominent in the religious life of the city.

Full restoration began in 1957, unfortunately using nonoriginal materials so the reconstruction is partially inaccurate. In recent years, the theatre has again become a place of entertainment, and productions take place irregularly (more often in July and August) – check at the Downtown visitors centre for details. The theatre also houses two museums (see Museums later in this chapter).

Entrance to the theatre is free, but you may be accosted by a 'guide' trying to rope you into a tour (for about JD2 per person), which can be useful if you have an interest in the theatre. Probably the best time for

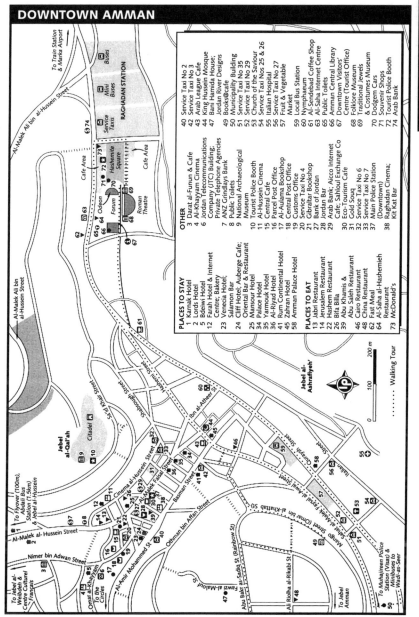

DOWNTOWN AMMAN

PLACES TO STAY
1 Karnak Hotel
2 Lords Hotel
5 Bdeiwi Hotel
12 Farah Hotel & Internet Centre; Bakery
23 Venecia Hotel; Salamon Bar
24 Cliff Hotel; Auberge Cafe; Oriental Bar & Restaurant
25 Mansour Hotel
34 Palace Hotel
35 Yarmouk Hotel
36 Al-Riyad Hotel
41 Rum Continental Hotel
45 Zahran Hotel
58 Amman Palace Hotel

PLACES TO EAT
13 Jabri Restaurant
14 Jerusalem Restaurant
22 Hashem Restaurant
26 Bifa Billa
39 Abu Khamis & Abu Saleh Restaurant
46 Cairo Restaurant
48 China Restaurant
62 Fast Meal
64 Al-Saha al-Hashemieh Restaurant
73 McDonald's

OTHER
3 Darat al-Funun & Cafe
4 Al-Khayyam Cinema
6 Jordan Telecommunications Company (JTC) Building; Private Telephone Agencies
7 ANZ Grindlays Bank
8 Public Toilets
9 National Archaeological Museum
10 Tourist Police Booth
11 Al-Hussein Cinema
15 Central Cafe
16 Parcel Post Office
17 Al-Aulama Bookshop
18 Central Post Office
19 Customs Office
20 Service Taxi No 4
21 Gibraltar Bookshop
28 Bank of Jordan
29 Jordan Bar
30 Arab Bank; Aicco Internet Cafe; Sahloul Exchange Co
31 Eco-Tourism Cafe
32 Gold Souq
33 Service Taxi No 6
37 Service Taxi No 7
38 Main Police Station (Downtown); Raghadan Cinema; Kit Kat Bar

40 Service Taxi No 2
42 Service Taxi No 3
43 Arab League Cafe
44 King Hussein Mosque
47 Bani Hamida House; Jordan River Designs
49 Books@cafe
50 Municipality Building
51 Service Taxi No 35
52 Service Taxi No 29
53 Church of the Saviour
54 Service Taxi Nos 25 & 26
55 Italian Hospital
56 Service Taxi No 27
57 Fruit & Vegetable Market
59 Local Bus Station
60 Nymphaeum
61 Al-Sendebad Coffee Shop
63 Al-Saha Internet Centre
65 Public Toilets
66 Amman Central Library
67 Downtown Visitors' Centre (Tourist Office)
68 Folklore Museum
69 Traditional Jewels & Costumes Museum
70 Dodgem Cars
71 Souvenir Shops
72 Tourist Police Booth
74 Arab Bank

0   100   200 m

········ Walking Tour

Ambling Around Amman

Some places, like the Citadel, are best reached by taxi, but there are a few sights, as well as excellent souvenir shops, cafes, art galleries and bookshops, that can be visited as part of a walking tour around Amman. Start at 3rd Circle and walk down to the city centre. Allow at least three hours. More details about most sights are mentioned in the relevant text.

From the trendy **3rd Circle** (see the Jebel Amman map) follow the sign to 'City Centre' down Al-Amir Mohammed St, past the impressive **Oriental Souvenirs Store** on the left (north), and the large **Amman Bookshop** on the right (south). Just past the Philadelphia Cinemas, turn up Ahmado Billo St (the only uphill stretch on the tour). For more shopping or browsing, head south-east along Mansour Kraishan St to the **Artisana** arts and craft shop.

Continue up Ahmado Billo to 2nd Circle, just south of which there are several decent places to eat. From 2nd Circle, walk east along Al-Kulliyah al-Islamiyah St, named after the **Islamic College** on the right (south). It is opposite the new, and grandly named, **Museum of the Political History of HM Late King Abdullah bin al-Hussein**. You may wish to stop for a drink at a **cafe** around the relatively unimpressive **1st Circle**. There are excellent **views** of Amman from the sandstone **mosque** along Amir al-Thaqafi St, just north of 1st Circle.

From 1st Circle, head down Rainbow St – to the right as you face the Cairo-Amman Bank – to Downtown. The **British Council** and **Amusement Centre** are on the right (south). Further down, look for signs to the left (north) up Fawzi al-Malouf St to **Bani Hamida House**, which boasts several classy souvenir shops. Detour down Mango St to **Books@cafe**, an expensive western-style Internet centre-cum-cafe-cum-bookshop.

Here comes the tricky bit. Don't worry if you get disoriented – just keep heading down to Downtown. From the end of the steps which start on Mango St, walk 200m to the left (north) to a junction with more great **views** of the city and the Citadel. Turn immediately right and then immediately left (along Rafat al-Dajani St); then down more steps about 50m to the right which lead to the Odaha Hotel.

You should end up near the **King Hussein Mosque** (a good place to finish the tour). Head south-west along Sahat al-Malek Faysal al-Awal St, where there are plenty of **souvenir shops**. Finish at the semi-circular building, part of the new **Municipality Building**, where there's some welcome shade and public toilets.

Head back into Downtown along Quraysh St, past a strange variety of **shops**. On the right (south-east) is the orthodox **Church of the Saviour** and, on the left (north-west), is the hidden **fruit & vegetable market**. Continue past the unimpressive **Nymphaeum**, and along Quraysh until you see the sign along a path to the Roman Theatre. In this area is the **Forum**, **Odeon**, **Folklore Museum** and **Traditional Jewels & Costumes Museum**. Continue west along the raised steps and wander around **Hashemite Square**.

Avoid the chaos of the Raghadan bus/minibus/service taxi station and head back (west) along Hashemi St, past McDonald's. Stop off at the friendly **Downtown visitors centre** and finish up at the **King Hussein Mosque**. Finally, enjoy a well-earned hot or cold drink at the **Arab League Cafe** opposite the mosque.

---

good photographs is in the morning, but most shots are spoilt by the ugly scaffolding around some of the columns. The theatre is open every day during daylight hours.

Forum

The row of columns immediately in front (north) of the Roman Theatre is all that is left of the Forum, once one of the largest public squares (about 100m by 50m) in the Roman Empire. Built in 190 AD, the square was flanked on three sides by columns, and on the fourth side by the Seil Amman stream, almost everything (including the stream which still runs) is underneath the modern streets.

Today, the Forum has a few vendors selling nothing particularly interesting, but for most it's just a walkway between Downtown and the Raghadan bus/minibus/service taxi station.

Odeon

On the eastern end of what was the Forum stands the 500-seat Odeon. Built in the 2nd century AD, it served mainly as a venue for musical performances. The amphitheatre was probably enclosed with a wooden or temporary tent roof to shield performers and the audience from the elements. It has been nicely restored and, although not as spectacular as the Roman Theatre, it's certainly worth a look.

The Odeon is not signposted, and some visitors walk straight past it. The building is to the left (north), just before the start of the steps which pass Hashemite Square, and is behind a large wooden door. The **views** of the city, and the busy square, are worth the short climb to the top of the amphitheatre.

Entrance is free. There are occasional performances at the Odeon held in July and August: check with the Downtown visitors centre, and see what is advertised in the two local English-language daily newspapers.

Nymphaeum

Built in 191 AD, the Nymphaeum was once a large, two-storey complex with fountains, mosaics, stone carvings and, possibly, a 600 sq-metre swimming pool – all dedicated to the Nymphs (young girls who apparently lived in and around the rivers). Excavations started in earnest in 1993, and restoration will continue for many years. Except for a column and an archway, there is very little to see.

The site is easy to find along Quraysh St, not far from the King Hussein Mosque. Entrance is free.

HASHEMITE SQUARE

The main meeting places for locals (mostly men) is the large Hashemite Square, between the Roman Theatre and the Raghadan station, and flanked by the incongruous golden arches of a nearby McDonald's. The square is a thriving spot every evening, especially Friday, and has many cafes and souvenir shops, and even some dodgem cars for the kids.

MUSEUMS

Amman boasts several good museums, but the best is the National Archaeological Museum in the Citadel. The others are for those with more time and specific interests.

National Archaeological Museum

This museum (☎ 463 8795) is just northwest of the Temple of Hercules, in the grounds of the Citadel. It houses a small, cluttered but nevertheless interesting collection of ancient bric-a-brac, ranging from 6000-year-old skulls from Jericho to artwork from the Umayyad period. It also boasts some examples of the Dead Sea Scrolls found in 1952; a copy of the Mesha Stele (see the boxed text in the King's Highway chapter for details); and some bits and pieces from the ruins at Jerash and Petra.

Everything is very well captioned in English. Entrance costs JD2, and it's open every day in summer (April to September) from 9 am to 5 pm, and in winter (October to March) from 9 am to 4 pm. The **views** across the modern city near the entrance are worth admiring and photographing.

Folklore Museum

This museum (☎ 465 1742) is immediately to the right (west) as you enter the Roman Theatre. It houses a modest collection of items displaying the traditional lifestyles of Jordan- ians, eg a Bedouin goat-hair tent complete with tools; musical instruments, such as the single-string *rababah*, a classic Bedouin instrument; woven rugs; some weapons; and various costumes.

Captions are in English. Opening hours are from 9 am to 5 pm, Saturday to Thursday (closed Tuesday); and from 10 am to 4 pm, Friday and public holidays. Entrance is JD1.

Traditional Jewels & Costumes Museum

Also known as the Jordan Museum of Popular Traditions, this museum (☎ 465 1760) is immediately to the left as you enter the Roman Theatre. It features well-presented displays of traditional costumes, jewellery, face masks and utensils. The best is the mosaic collection, mostly from churches in Madaba and dating back to the 6th century. The museum is open from 9 am to 5 pm Saturday to Thursday (closed Tuesday); and from 10 am to 4 pm Friday and public holidays. Entrance is JD1 (which is marginally better value than the Folklore Museum).

Museum of Archaeology & Anthropology

If you have a special interest in archaeology and/or anthropology, or happen to be out at the University of Jordan, check out this small museum (☎ 535 5000). It contains artefacts from all around Jordan dating back to the Bronze and Iron ages, as well as the Roman, Greek and Umayyad periods.

Entrance is free, and it's normally open from 8 am to 5 pm, Saturday to Wednesday. Take any minibus or service taxi heading towards Salt from Abdali or Raghadan bus stations, get off at the entrance to the university and ask directions to the museum.

Martyr's Memorial & Military Museum

The simple and solemn Martyr's Memorial to Jordan's fallen, houses the small and mildly interesting Military Museum (☎ 566 4240). The museum chronicles Jordan's recent military history, from the Arab Revolt in 1916 (scrupulously avoiding all mention of 'Lawrence of Arabia' and the British involvement) and continues through to the Arab-Israeli wars.

Entrance is free. The museum is normally open from 9 am to 4 pm every day except Saturday, and is located on the road to Zarqa, about 1km east of Sports City Junction (see the Shmeisani map). Take any minibus or service taxi towards Zarqa, but check first because these sometimes bypass the museum. It's probably best to charter a taxi.

Other Museums

If you have the time and interest there are other museums to check out. The Numis-matic Museum (☎ 463 0301), in the Central Bank of Jordan (CBJ) building along Al-Malek al-Hussein St (see the Amman map), will appeal to coin collectors. Entrance is free, and it's officially open from 9 am to 2 pm every day except Tuesday and Friday – but in reality it's rarely open, so inquire first inside the CBJ.

Museum of the Political History of HM Late King Abdullah bin al-Hussein (☎ 462 1151), between 1st and 2nd Circles, may not have a particularly memorable title, but it does promise to be reasonably interesting. It was not yet opened at the time of research, but will be soon.

Inside the King Abdullah Mosque, the small Islamic Museum (☎ 567 2155) (see the Jebel Amman map) contains a few bits of pottery and photographs of King Abdullah (the first). Opening hours are erratic, but it's generally open every day during daylight hours, except at morning prayers on Friday. Entrance is free, but donations are welcome.

The Haya Cultural Centre, Shmeisani (see Cultural Centres earlier in this chapter) has the Children's Heritage & Science Museum (☎ 566 5196). It is open from about 9 am to 6 pm every day except Friday, and entrance is free.

ART GALLERIES

Jordan has a tradition of art, both old and new, which can be appreciated by visiting one or two of the galleries around Amman.

Jordan National Gallery of Fine Arts

This small gallery (☎ 463 0128) claims in its brochure to be 'probably the best of its kind in the Middle East'. Although not quite as grandiose, the gallery is worth a look if you're interested in contemporary art, sculpture and pottery from Jordan and the region. Inside, there's a gift shop and a small cafe. See the Jebel Amman map.

The gallery is on Hosni Fareez St and is signposted from Suleiman an-Nabulsi St, opposite the King Abdullah Mosque. It is open from 9 am to 5 pm every day except Tuesday; and entry costs JD1.

Darat al-Funun

Darat al-Funun (☎ 464 3251, fax 464 3252, email daratf@arabbank.com.jo) means 'Little House of the Arts', and is a renovated former Byzantine church where TE Lawrence partially wrote *The Seven Pillars of Wisdom*. Check out the Web site at www.daratalfunun.org.

The complex features a small **art gallery** with works by contemporary artists from Jordan, and elsewhere in the region. It's worth visiting for the enchanting **gardens**; the small outdoor cafe, which serves hot and cold drinks, but no food; and some of the best **views** of Amman. It also features regular lectures about art and evenings of classical and traditional music; and has an **art library**. A schedule of upcoming exhibitions is available at the counter inside the main gallery.

Entrance is free, and opening hours are from 10 am to 7 pm, Saturday to Wednesday, and from 10 am to 8 pm on Thursday. It's not easy to find, and there are no signs in any language outside. It's Downtown on Nimer bin Adwan St, but access is easiest on foot. From near the southern end of Al-Malek al-Hussein St, head up the stairs under the sign 'Riviera Hotel'. At the top of the stairs, turn immediately right and walk uphill for 100m. At the end of the street turn left and look for one of the unsigned gates on the corner.

MOSQUES

Amman doesn't boast any truly spectacular mosques. Non-Muslims will feel most comfortable at King Abdullah's; King Hussein's is probably the most interesting, because of the number of people in the vicinity; and Abu Darwish has some great views.

King Hussein Mosque

Built by King Abdullah (the first) in 1924, and restored in 1987, King Hussein Mosque stands in Downtown on the site of a mosque built in 640 AD by 'Umar, the second caliph of Islam. This is a working mosque so there's nothing much to see inside, and nonbelievers, while generally welcome at any time (except during prayers), may feel intrusive.

Perhaps more interesting is the area in front of the mosque: a hive of activity (except during the heat of the sun) with locals chatting, selling, buying and walking. The best place to watch all this is the Arab League Cafe, directly opposite (see Cafes in the Entertainment section later in this chapter).

King Abdullah Mosque

Completed in 1989 as a memorial by the late King Hussein to his grandfather, the unmistakable blue-domed mosque on Suleiman Al-Nabulsi St can house up to 7000 worshippers inside, and another 3000 in the courtyard area (see the Jebel Amman map). This is the only mosque which openly welcomes non-Muslim visitors, and inside is the small **Islamic Museum**.

Women are required to wear something (which can often be borrowed at the mosque) to cover their hair; and, of course, everyone must remove their shoes before entering the main mosque. Baksheesh of up to JD1 may be expected too for a 'guided tour'.

Abu Darwish Mosque

On top of Jebel al-Ashrafiyeh' is the curious Abu Darwish Mosque. It was built in 1961, and is unmistakable from its alternating layers of black and white stone. The mosque itself is rarely open, and non-Muslims are not that welcome inside, but the **views** on the way up are worth the trip. There is also a wonderful view of the Abu Darwish Mosque overlooking the King Hussein Mosque from the Arab League Cafe.

To get to the Abu Darwish mosque, take a No 25 or 26 service taxi from Italian St in Downtown, or charter a taxi. Don't attempt to walk, because the streets are very steep.

ACTIVITIES
Swimming

The top end hotels charge at least JD5 for nonguests to use their swimming pools. The cheapest is Manar Hotel (see Places to Stay later in this chapter), which charges nonguests JD4. Sports City (☎ 566 7181) in northern Amman (see the Shmeisani map) has an Olympic-sized pool, but nonmembers are charged JD6, including the use of a locker. Swimming is mixed and women may feel uncomfortable. If you know a member, or you're able to obtain a guest pass, try the Orthodox Club (☎ 592 0491) in Abdoun, which has other sports facilities.

Other Activities

The Bisharat Golf Course has a nine hole course, putting 'greens' (well, 'browns') and even a golf pro. It costs JD15 for as much golf as you would like in one day, plus JD10 club hire. The course is about 25 minutes drive south of Downtown, and signposted from the Desert Highway on the way to Queen Ali international airport (see the Around Amman map).

For something completely different, gliding is possible at the Gliding Club (☎ 487 4587) at the Marka airport, east of Amman. The Royal Racing Club (☎ 585 0630) holds races – for horses and camels – in spring and summer, and offers horse riding classes. Details are available from the club, located off the Desert Highway and on the way to Queen Alia international airport.

For the Kids

Children, and the young at heart, can enjoy dodgem cars at Hashemite Square, Downtown (only in the evening), and video games at a parlour near the souvenir shops in front (north) of the square. The Amusement Centre, next to the British Council on Rainbow St (see the Jebel Amman map), has roller-skating, dodgem cars, video games and bowling alleys. It is instantly recognisable by the caged 'Panda' suspended above the footpath. Luna Park has a cable car and other attractions for the kids. It's open from about 10 am to 10 pm every day, and located on Khalid ibn al-Walid St in Jebel al-Hussein (see the Amman map).

The Haya Cultural Centre in Shmeisani (see Cultural Centres earlier in this chapter) is predominantly for children, and has a small playground and museum (see Museums earlier in this chapter). It also organises regular concerts and performances for the youngsters. There are very few parks in Amman, and nothing within walking distance of Downtown. For some space, tranquillity and greenery head to Amman National Park, just off the Desert Highway;

or go further out to somewhere like Dibbeen National Park (detailed in the Northern & Western Jordan chapter).

ORGANISED TOURS

Amman is an ideal place to base yourself while exploring anywhere north, east and west of Amman, and as south far as Karak. It's easy enough to day trip to these places using public transport – which is just as well because very few travel agencies in Amman bother offering any organised tours (other than long and expensive bus tours to Wadi Rum and Petra).

Four budget hotels which cater to independent travellers – ie the Venecia, Bdeiwi, Cliff and Farah – offer day trips from Amman. These cost about JD10 per person, depending on the number of passengers (or about JD40 per vehicle), and visit: Madaba, Mt Nebo and the Dead Sea; Jerash, Ajlun and Umm Qais; or the 'desert castles' to the east.

A very hurried trip including Karak, Shobak castle and Petra is possible, but costs about JD20 per person (or about JD80 for the vehicle). It is usually up to you to find other passengers to share the costs, so ask around these hotels and put up notices on their notice boards.

SPECIAL EVENTS

Concerts, plays and various performances are occasionally held at the Odeon and Roman Theatres, usually in the summertime (mainly July and August). The Downtown visitors centre is the best source of detailed information, but also check out the two daily English-language newspapers published in Amman. The Special Events section in the Facts for the Visitor chapter has more details about events in and near Amman, such as the Jerash Festival.

PLACES TO STAY

Most cheap hotels are in Downtown, but there are a few around Abdali bus station. Many mid-range places are around Abdali and between 1st and 5th Circles, while most top end places are located further out in Shmeisani.

PLACES TO STAY – BUDGET

The cheapest places are around the King Hussein Mosque, but these are only for the frugal and deaf. Many have shops on the ground floor, a tea shop on the 2nd and rooms on the 3rd and 4th floors, so getting to and from your room often involves a lot of climbing – as if walking around Amman didn't involve enough strenuous climbing already. All budget places mentioned below come with shared bathroom facilities unless stated otherwise.

Downtown

Zahran Hotel (☎ 462 5473, *Sahat al-Malek Faysal al-Awal St)* is about the best of a bad lot near the King Hussein Mosque. It has singles/doubles for JD1.500/3, plus an extra 500 fils for a shower – but don't expect much privacy or sleep.

Yarmouk Hotel (☎ 462 4241, *Al-Malek Faisal St)* is great value for doubles, but not for single travellers, and is quieter than others in the vicinity. Each room has a ceiling fan, and costs JD5/6.

Al-Riyad Hotel (☎ 462 4260, *Al-Malek Faisal St)* is another place with varied spellings (such as 'Reyad Hotel'). It's not as good as places like the Cliff, but it is cheap at JD3/6 and each room has a ceiling fan.

Cliff Hotel (☎ 462 4273, *fax 463 8978, Al-Amir Mohammed St)* is very popular, and the best place to meet other backpackers. The rooms are OK, but the beds do sag a bit and the stairs are very dirty. Sleeping on the roof (a good idea in the heat of summer, especially as some rooms don't have fans) costs JD2; and rooms, JD5/8. A hot shower costs 500 fils extra. Guests can use the kitchen, and staff are friendly and helpful.

Mansour Hotel (☎ 462 1575, *Al-Malek Faisal St)* is central, and quieter than most places because it's a little back from the busy main road. Simple, but satisfactory, rooms cost JD4.400/6.600.

Venecia Hotel (☎ 463 8895, *email venecia@hotmail.com, Al-Amir Mohammed St)* also has signs with alternative spellings (such as 'Venice Hotel'). It is quite OK, and becoming an increasingly popular rival to the Cliff, although the rooms are a bit grubby. Singles/doubles/triples cost JD5/8/11, and hot showers are an extra 500 fils.

Bdeiwi Hotel (☎ 464 3394, *fax 464 7878, Omar al-Khayyam St)* is an alternative to the Cliff and Venecia. The rooms are small, but clean and comfortable, and cost JD8 per double – no single rates are available. Readers have complained about cold rooms in winter, but this is offset by warm quilts. Shared rooms cost JD4. Hot showers are free, and the helpful staff speak good English.

Farah Hotel (☎ 465 1443, *fax 465 1437, email farahhotel@hotmail.com, Cinema al-Hussein St)* has young and friendly staff, and is worth paying a little more for. Good, clean rooms cost JD7/9; dorm beds are available for JD4; and sleeping on the roof costs JD2.500. There is an Internet centre (see Email & Internet Access section earlier), and an outdoor tent where guests can enjoy hot and cold drinks.

Palace Hotel (☎ 462 4326, *fax 465 0603, Al-Malek Faisal St)* is also worth a little splurge. The rooms are clean and large (some are quiet too), have private bathrooms with hot water and cost JD8.800/15.400. The manager speaks very good English. It's located just off the main road; look for the signs to 'Mango Market St'.

Al-Malek al-Hussein St

If you head north up Al-Malek al-Hussein towards Abdali bus station there are several more budget places, but this road is extremely noisy and it's a bit of a walk up from Downtown.

Lords Hotel (☎ 465 4167) is cavernous and a bit gloomy. The rooms, which vary in size, cleanliness and quietness (so check out a few), cost JD5/10 with a shared bathroom, or a reasonable JD8/12/15 for singles/doubles/triples with a private bathroom.

Happyland Hotel (☎ 463 9832, *fax 462 8550)* has been recommended by readers. Some rooms are reasonably quiet, and all have a small bathroom. For JD5.500/11, it's top value. (See Amman map.)

Karnak Hotel (☎/fax 463 7361) is neat and comfortable. The rooms have bathrooms and some have balconies (overlooking the noisy road) for a negotiable JD10/14.

Abdali

Four reasonable places are all within a short walk of the Abdali bus station (see the Jebel Amman map). They are especially useful for late night or early morning departures or arrivals, but they're all overpriced: better value can be found in Downtown.

Al-Monzer Hotel (☎ 463 9469, fax 465 7328, email mfj@nol.com.jo, Umayyah bin Abd Shams St) has acceptable rooms with private bathrooms for a negotiable JD10/12. *Cleopatra Hotel (☎ 463 6959)* is in the same building as the Al-Monzer, but is not as good. The official price is JD14/18 and while the rooms, with private bathrooms, are OK, this is too much. Check out both places, and negotiate.

Remal Hotel (☎ 463 0670, fax 465 5751, email safwat@index.com.jo, Sa'id bin al-Harith St) is tucked away in a side street, so it's far quieter than the others. The large, comfortable rooms have private bathrooms, and cost a negotiable JD15.400/19.800. The hotel gets mixed reviews, however: one reader wrote that 'they are still struggling to rid ourselves of fleas'; another stayed one week and was 'very content with the place'.

Merryland Hotel (☎/fax 463 0370, Al-Malek al-Hussein St) is worth the short walk from the bus station, and is the best budget place in the area. Large, clean rooms, with private bathrooms, cost from JD12/15 to JD18/22, and staff are capable and friendly.

PLACES TO STAY – MID-RANGE

Most of the places listed below have air-conditioning, satellite TV and a fridge in the rooms, and all have private bathrooms with hot water. All prices listed below include taxes. Very few places are located in Downtown, but around Abdali and between 1st and 5th Circles.

Downtown

Amman Palace Hotel (☎ 464 6172, fax 465 6989, Quraysh St) is one of the few mid-range places in Downtown. The large, spotless rooms cost JD18/24, with breakfast, and prices are negotiable.

Rum Continental Hotel (☎ 462 3162, fax 461 1961, Basman St) has clean, although rather small, rooms for JD17.600 per double (no single rates), including breakfast. It's convenient, reasonably quiet and good value.

Around Abdali

Canary Hotel (☎ 463 8353, fax 465 4353, email canary-h@hotmail.com, Jebel al-Weibdeh) is in a leafy part of town. The rooms are quiet, large and comfortable and cost from JD16/24, including breakfast. The hotel gets its name from the resident birds in the forecourt.

Caravan Hotel (☎ 566 1195, fax 566 1196, email caravan@go.com.jo, Al-Mamouin St) is not far from the King Abdullah Mosque. Some rooms are musty but it's only JD22/26.400, including breakfast.

Mirage Hotel (☎ 568 2000, fax 568 8890, email mirageh@go.com.jo), located on the corner of Al-Malek al-Hussein and Suleiman an-Nabulsi streets, is a charming place. Although directly opposite the Abdali bus station, it's reasonably quiet and the views of the chaos at the station from some of the rooms, and the restaurant (see Places to Eat), are fascinating. Large, comfortable rooms cost JD30/36.

Western Amman

Carlton Hotel (☎ 465 4200, fax 465 5833, St, Al-Kulliyah al-Islamiyah St), between 2nd and 3rd Circles, is a top end place with a mid-range price. Comfortable rooms cost from JD54/66. (See the Jebel Amman map.)

Ammon Hotel (☎ 568 0090, fax 560 5688, email achte@go.com.jo, Tunis St) is tucked away in a quiet spot between 4th and 5th Circles. It is a classy place with top end facilities, such as a swimming pool, but a more reasonable mid-range price of JD54/60. (See Amman map.)

Hisham Hotel (☎ 464 2720, fax 464 7540, email hisham@nets.com.jo, Mithqal al-Fayez St) is a couple of blocks south of the French embassy. It's a very pleasant place, in a leafy part of town, and is popular with visiting journalists and diplomats. Rooms cost JD44/55/66 for singles/doubles/triples. (See the Jebel Amman map.)

Granada Hotel (☎ 463 8031, fax 462 2617, Al-Imam Malek St) has small rooms

Top Left: The remains of the colonnade of the Forum in Amman serves as a modern thoroughfare.
Top Right: Abu Darwish Mosque, Amman, is an interesting example of modern Islamic architecture.
Bottom: View of Amman from the Citadel with the Roman Theatre prominent in the foreground.

SIMON BRACKEN

SIMON BRACKEN

EDDIE GERALD

Fresh produce, tailored clothes and hand-woven rugs are all available in the souqs of Amman.

for JD19/25. It's in a pleasant, quiet part of town and very close to 1st Circle, and staff are friendly. (See the Jebel Amman map.)

Dove Hotel (☎ 569 7601, fax 567 4676, *Qurtubah St*), off Zahran St and between 4th and 5th Circles, is one of the best in this price range. Nice rooms with all necessities cost JD24/31.200. One added attraction is the Irish Pub downstairs (see Entertainment), although some guests complain of the noise. (See the Amman map.)

Shmeisani
Manar Hotel (☎ 566 2186, fax 568 4329, *Al-Shareef Abdulla Hameed Sharaf St*) is the best value in the Shmeisani area, and one of the cheapest places in Amman with a swimming pool. The staff are efficient, and the rooms are worth a splurge for JD24.200/33.800, including breakfast. It continues to get good reviews from all who stay.

Ambassador Hotel (☎ 560 5161, fax 568 1101, *Al-Shareef Abdulla Hameed Sharaf St*) has good rooms from JD48/66, but the management is willing to negotiate down to as little as JD22/30 – which is top value.

PLACES TO STAY – TOP END
Amman has its share of four and five star international hotels. Most are in the inconvenient Shmeisani district, and not easily accessible by service taxi. Prices include all the mod-cons you would expect for these prices, and the rates listed below include taxes and other charges of up to 20%.

Jordan InterContinental Hotel (☎ 464 1361, fax 464 5217, *Al-Kulliyah al-Islamiyah St*), midway between 2nd and 3rd Circles, has singles/doubles for JD163/174, and suites. (See the Jebel Amman map.)

Grand Hyatt Jordan (☎ 465 1234, fax 465 1634, email hyatt@go.com.jo, *Al-Hussein bin Ali St*) is quite good value for JD93.500/104.500, but the rates do vary according to the season. (See the Jebel Amman map.)

Amman Marriott (☎ 560 7607, fax 567 0100, email jomarriott@go.com.jo, *Islam al-Ajlouni St*) has rooms from JD114. (See the Shmeisani map.)

Le Meridien (☎ 569 6511, fax 567 4261, email meridien@go.com.jo, *Islam al-Aljouni*

St), formerly the Forte Grand, charges from JD168/180, but is willing to negotiate discounts from these outrageous 'official' rates. (See the Shmeisani map.)

Regency Palace Hotel (☎ 560 7000, fax 566 0013, email regency@nets.com.jo, *Queen Alia St*) is just as good as the rest, and has rooms for JD132/150. (See the Shmeisani map.)

Radisson SAS Hotel (☎ 560 7100, fax 566 5160, *Al-Hussein bin Ali St*) has all of the luxuries expected from this international chain. Check out their Web site at www.radisson.com/ammanjo. Rooms start from JD120/144. (See the Jebel Amman map.)

PLACES TO STAY – RENTALS
The two English-language daily newspapers, and the notice boards at the cultural centres (see Cultural Centres earlier in this chapter) and at Books@cafe (see Bookshops earlier in this chapter), are the best places to check for any apartments and houses to rent. *Your Guide to Amman* (see Tourist Offices earlier in this chapter) lists real estate agents which deal with rental properties, but these are mainly for long-term rentals. Alternatively, wander around the nicer areas, eg just off the main road between 1st and 5th Circles, and look for signs on residences which are available for rent, and notices in the windows of nearby shops.

Expect to pay from JD200 per month for a furnished apartment in a reasonable area; a little less for something not furnished. A furnished apartment or small house in a working-class suburb is possible for as little as JD100 per month, but little in this range is advertised (so ask around). Anything this cheap will probably be unfurnished, nor will everything necessarily be in working order.

PLACES TO EAT
Amman offers a range of food options, eg cheap eateries for *shwarmas* and other Arab delights in Downtown; expensive restaurants serving French, Italian and Chinese food (among other cuisines) in places not far from the main road between 1st and 5th Circles; and western fast food outlets in the nicer suburbs, such as Shmeisani and Abdoun.

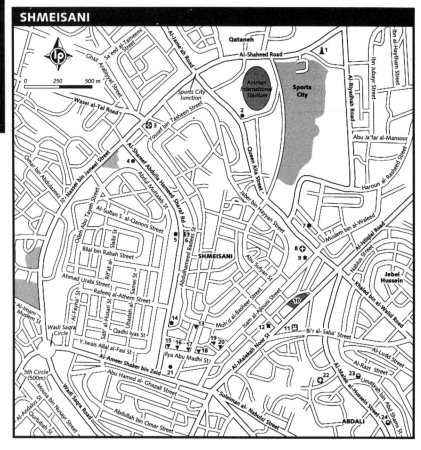

SHMEISANI

Don't leave it too late to head out for your evening meal – many places start shutting their kitchens as early as 9 pm.

If you prefer self-catering, the small but busy fruit and vegetable market is tucked away between Sahat al-Malek Faysal al-Awal and Quraysh streets; the main entrance is from Quraysh. There are very few grocery stores in Downtown; the closest to Downtown are located along Rainbow St, just down from 1st Circle. The western-style supermarkets are in the newer and more remote suburbs (see Supermarkets in the Shopping section later in this chapter).

PLACES TO EAT – BUDGET

If money's scarce, your mainstay in Amman will be felafel and shwarma, but there are some budget restaurants. Unless specified, all places listed below are in Downtown.

Hashem Restaurant (Al-Amir Mohammed St) is a legendary place with a small shady courtyard. It's incredibly popular with locals for felafel, *humous* and *fuul*, and is open 24 hours. A filling meal with bread and tea costs less than JD1. As one reader noted: 'nothing but bread, humous, fuul and felafel, but everything is fresh and dirt cheap. I love this place!'.

SHMEISANI

PLACES TO STAY		16	New York, New York	8	Palestine Hospital
5	Ambassador Hotel	17	La Terrasse	10	Housing Bank Centre;
7	Regency Palace Hotel;	18	La Coquette		Post Office; Royal
	Regency Palace Bookshop;	19	Chilli House		Jordanian Airlines
	Europcar Car Rental	20	Pizza Hut		Head Office
9	Amman Marriott; Champions			11	Concord Cinema
	Nightclub; Europcar Car	**OTHER**		21	Haya Cultural Centre;
	Rental	1	Martyr's Memorial		Tarwea Restaurant;
12	Le Meridien; 1001 Nights		& Military Museum		Children's Heritage
	Restaurant; Israeli Embassy	2	Royal Cultural Centre		& Science Museum
14	Manar Hotel	3	Safeway Shopping Centre;	22	Islamic Hospital
			KFC; Internet Centre; ATMs	23	JETT Bus Office
PLACES TO EAT		4	Budget Car Rental		(International)
13	Baskin Robbins; Dunki Donuts	6	International Traders	24	JETT Bus Office
15	KFC		(American Express)		(Domestic)

Abu Khamis & Abu Saleh Restaurant *(☎ 462 2782)* is a huge, breezy place between two laneways off Al-Malek Faisal St. There is no menu in English, but the staff are happy to show what is available, eg chicken, chips and a variety of meat and vegetable stews, soups, salads and starters. A filling meal costs about JD2, but check the prices before ordering.

Jerusalem Restaurant *(☎ 463 0168, Al-Malek al-Hussein St)* specialises in sweets and pastries, but has a large restaurant at the back. The menu is in Arabic, but one of the staff can order for you. The service is good, but waiters often annoyingly hang around looking for generous tips from foreigners. The *mensaf* is recommended, and it's one of the few places open early for breakfast (from about 7.30 am).

Jabri Restaurant *(Al-Malek al-Hussein St)* has a distinctive yellow awning, and is signposted in small English letters. It serves mainly sweets and pastries, but the restaurant upstairs is large, modern and has good views. It's open from about 9 am for breakfast (eg about J1.500 for an omelette), and serves morning and afternoon teas (a plate of delicious mixed sweet pastries is JD1) and lunch (most meals about JD2.200). Sadly, it is not open in the evening.

Cairo Restaurant, just off Sahat al-Malek Faysal al-Awal St, has a pleasant, clean eating area inside, and staff speak some English. A meal of chicken, rice, salad and a soft drink costs about JD1.500, but

it's also a good place to try some tempting local cuisine. There are several similar little restaurants on the same street.

Two cheap cafes serve food in adjacent buildings in the same laneway as the Cliff Hotel, but a few metres further south. ***Oriental Bar & Restaurant***, also known as 'Al-Shark', specialises in eastern, rather than Middle Eastern, cuisine and is clean and cheap (eg vegetable dishes start from 600 fils). The service, however, can be excruciatingly slow. ***Auberge Cafe*** also has a popular dining area, but it's often filled with local men enjoying alcoholic beverages, and is not conducive to a leisurely, peaceful meal.

One of the best places in Amman (if not the Middle East) for delicious pastries is the small ***bakery*** right next to the laneway leading to the Farah Hotel, along Cinema al-Hussein St. For less than JD1, it's easy to fill up with a plateful of tasty tidbits, all made in the wood oven.

Bifa Billa, just south of Cinema al-Hussein St, is one of the better places in Downtown for hamburgers and shwarmas. A shwarma on a plate with salad and chips, and a large drink, costs a modest JD1.500.

Fast Meal *(Hashemi St)* – well, that's the name in English outside – is clean and close to the Roman Theatre. A tasty burger, chips and a milkshake costs as little as JD1.250. There is a special area upstairs for families and unaccompanied women; men (ie without female dining partners) can eat at a table on the ground floor.

Books@cafe has an interesting and tasty menu which changes monthly, but prices are high, eg salads are JD3, sandwiches JD4.800 and tea an exorbitant JD1.920.

Pizza Hut has several restaurants all over Amman, including just south of Abdoun Circle; just down from 2nd Circle; and in central Shmeisani. *KFC* is also well represented, with outlets at Safeway Shopping Centre in Shmeisani; and another in central Shmeisani. *McDonald's* has restaurants incongruously next to Hashemite Square in Downtown, and another strategically placed opposite the University of Jordan.

In central Shmeisani, some other popular places include: *Chilli House* for American hot dogs and tasty burgers; *Baskin Robbins* for ice cream; and *Dunkin' Donuts* for donuts and drinks.

Snack Box (☎ 566 2402, Suleiman an-Nabulsi St), opposite the King Abdullah Mosque, is take-away only, but comes highly recommended: a burger and chips will cost you JD1.750; Chinese food, about JD2.250; and pasta dishes, about JD2.500. It's closed on Friday.

PLACES TO EAT – MID-RANGE

Most of the mid-priced restaurants cater to wealthier locals and western expats, and many of these are close to the main road between 1st and 3rd Circles on the Jebel Amman map.

Chicken Tikka Inn (☎ 464 2437, Al-Amir Mohammed St) is just down from 3rd Circle, and one of the surprisingly few Indian restaurants in town. Good curries cost from JD2.500. It's signposted with the words 'Indian Restaurant' in English.

Diplomat Restaurant, right on 1st Circle, has a good range of dishes from about JD1.500, including reasonable pizza. It's open early for breakfast; and is one of the few outdoor places where patrons can enjoy an alcoholic beverage, eg a large beer (JD1.800) or a bottle of local wine (JD7).

Kawkab Al-Sharq (☎ 464 2690), only metres down from 2nd Circle, has a good range of local dishes, as well as pizza. It is recognisable by the picture of Umm Kolthum on the sign.

For terrific Lebanese food, for about JD10 per person, try *Fakhr ed-Din (☎ 465 2399)*, behind the Iraqi Embassy; or the *Tannoureen Restaurant (☎ 551 5987, Shat al-Arab St)*, just up from 6th Circle (see Amman map). The Haya Cultural Centre, Shmeisani, also has *Tarwea Restaurant (☎ 566 5195)*, where large serves of Lebanese food cost from JD2.

For authentic Chinese food, for about JD5 per person, head for *Taiwan Tourismo (☎ 464 1093)*, just off Abdul Mun'em Riyadh St and near 3rd Circle (see Jebel Amman map); or *China Restaurant (☎ 463 8968)*, between Rainbow and Mango streets, where the atmosphere is cosy and the staff are affable (see Downtown map).

Al-Saha al-Hashemieh Restaurant (Hashemi St) is signposted all around the Roman Theatre area as 'Tourist Restaurant & Coffee Shop'. The menu is in English (well, sort of), and prices are generally high, but it is possible to get away with a soup, shwarma and salad for about JD2.200 – if you order wisely.

Of the hotels (see Places to Stay), two places are recommended, both on the Jebel Amman map: *Forest Inn Restaurant*, at the Hisham Hotel, has meals from JD5 in a pleasant outdoor setting; and the *Oasis Coffee Shop*, in the Mirage Hotel, has good views of the chaotic Abdali bus station, reasonable prices and daily specials from JD3.

Other places to try for good, but pricey, western food include: the small and cosy *Uncle Sam's Restaurant & Bar (☎ 465 1122)*, about 100m west of the Jordan Inter-Continental Hotel and between 2nd and 3rd Circles; *Adam's Apple Cafe, Bar & Restaurant (☎ 463 0150, Rainbow St)*, a quaint, family-oriented place, with meals from JD1 to JD4.950 for three-course daily specials; and *Hard Rock Cafe (☎ 593 4901)*, south of Abdoun Circle (see the Amman map).

PLACES TO EAT – TOP END

The classy and expensive places are often in remote suburbs, eg Shmeisani, and in upmarket hotels. Reaching these (especially at night) isn't easy by public transport, so factor in taxi fares to the total bill for the evening.

Bonita Inn (☎ 461 5060), just down from 3rd Circle (see the Jebel Amman map) does a Jordanian version of paella and tapas, but much of the menu includes quite an odd mix of iternational dishes.

Popular, swish places in Shmeisani include *La Terrasse (☎ 566 2831)*, which often features Arab music in the evening; *La Coquette (☎ 568 0094)*, for genuine French cuisine; and *New York, New York (☎ 560 5307)*.

The big hotel restaurants are expensive, and generally lack ambience. The Grand Hyatt Jordan has the *Grand Cafe*, and *L'incontro* for Italian food. *Royal Club Restaurant*, in the Radisson SAS, often features international cuisines (see Jebel Amman map for both); and *1001 Nights*, in the Le Meridien, Shmeisani, has good Arabic food.

ENTERTAINMENT

There is not much to do in the evenings but window shop, stroll around the Roman Theatre complex and Hashemite Square, have a leisurely meal or, perhaps, go to the cinema. To find out what's going on, check out the listings in the two English-language newspapers; also, ask the Downtown visitors centre about upcoming attractions.

Pub/Bars

Several bars in Downtown, mainly visited by men, are tucked away in the rabbit warren of alleys around the Cliff and Venecia hotels. Women will probably feel more comfortable at some of the more upmarket bars located between 1st and 3rd Circles (Jebel Amman map) and in the mid-range and top end hotels. There are several liquor stores around the traps if you want to drink in your hotel (but ask the management first).

Mainly Men *Kit Kat Bar (Basman St)* is about as sleazy and dingy as it gets – strictly for those more interested in cheap alcohol than ambience. In the laneway leading to the Cliff Hotel, *Auberge Cafe* and *Oriental Bar & Restaurant* (also known as 'Al-Shark') have separate bar areas, popular with local men. *Jordan Bar* is OK, although it's a bit dark. *Salamon Bar*, next to the entrance to Venecia Hotel, is more modern than the others, and has beer on tap, but it's tiny and full of smoke.

Women Welcome Of the mid-range hotels, *Hisham Hotel (Mithqal al-Fayez St)* has an 'English pub' where a pint of draught lager costs about JD2.500; and the bar downstairs at the *Rum Continental Hotel (Basman St)* is probably the best in Downtown. (See the Jebel Amman map.)

Rovers' Return (Ali Nasouh al-Taher St), is popular with trendy locals and expats, and has a fun atmosphere – but drinks are not cheap. (See the Amman map.)

The thumping *Irish Pub*, in the Dove Hotel *(Qurtubah St)*, between 4th and 5th Circles stays open until about 1.30 am. Beers cost JD1.800 (about JD1.200 during happy hours), and a scotch with a mixer, about JD2. It's popular with expats and embassy staff. (See the Amman map.)

After Eight, in the Granada Hotel *(Al-Imam Malek St)*, just south of 1st Circle (J is a popular place to relax. The beer is reasonable, and the bar snacks and meals are tasty. (See the Jebel Amman map.)

Discos/Clubs

Some of the larger hotels run modest nightclubs. The Grand Hyatt Jordan has *JJ Mahoney's*, which features live music and video entertainment; *Champions* at the Amman Marriott, Shmeisani, has live sports on TV screens; and *Pasha Nightclub* is in the Jordan InterContinental Hotel.

Cinemas

Three cinema complexes usually offer recent releases in a not-too-censored form: Philadelphia (☎ 463 4144), in the basement of the Jordan Tower Centre, just down from 3rd Circle; Galleria (☎ 593 4793), on Abdoun Circle (see the Amman map); and Concord (☎ 567 7420), just off Al-Malekah Noor St in Shmeisani. Tickets cost about JD4, which is not cheap, but the quality of sound, vision and chairs are superior to the other cinemas. Programs for all three cinema complexes are advertised in the two English-language daily newspapers.

A few other cinemas show western films, but these may be subtitled or dubbed into English and anything risque (but not violent) will be censored. Seats cost about JD1.500, but nothing is advertised in the English-language newspapers. In Downtown, the better ones are the Al-Hussein Cinema, Cinema al-Hussein St; the Al-Khayyam, on Omar Al-Khayyam St; and the Raghadan, on Basman St. Slightly better is the Ammoun Cinema, just south of Abdali bus station.

Darat al-Funun art gallery, Downtown, (see Art Galleries earlier in this chapter) shows films most Thursday evenings – details and schedules are available at the gallery. Also in Downtown, Books@cafe (see Bookshops earlier in this chapter) has a 'Film Club Night' every Tuesday evening with newish films (without subtitles) for JD2, which includes food. The British, American, French, German and Spanish cultural centres (see Cultural Centres earlier in this chapter) show films regularly. Some western and Arabic films are also shown at the University of Jordan.

Exhibitions & Music

The various foreign cultural centres regularly organise lectures, exhibitions and musical recitals. The Royal Cultural Centre also occasionally puts on concerts and plays, usually in Arabic. Darat al-Funun frequently features recitals of classical and traditional music – check with the gallery for a schedule of upcoming events. The Haya Cultural Centre often has programs for children, but usually in Arabic. See the Cultural Centres section earlier in this chapter for more details.

Cafes

Some of the cafes in Downtown are great places to watch the world go by, write letters, smoke a nargila, meet locals and play a hand of cards or backgammon. The ones which are generally men-only are listed separately below, although foreign women with some gumption, very modest attire and, especially, accompanied by a male, will be welcome.

Mainly Men *Arab League Cafe* (enter from Al-Malek Faisal St), Downtown, is a popular, male-dominated place with breezes and great views, especially of King Hussein Mosque. It's not signposted in English, but is recognisable by the long Pepsi sign and lack of windows.

Central Cafe, also Downtown, just up (north) of the corner of Al-Malek al-Hussein and Al-Amir Mohammed Sts, has lost some of its charm since the outdoor terrace was ripped away, and the balconies are small.

Auberge Cafe, one floor below the Cliff Hotel, is very popular. The tiny balcony is usually crowded, and great for people-watching.

Women Welcome *Eco-Tourism Cafe (Al-Malek Faisal St)*, Downtown, is a foreign version of an Arab cafe, and the best place for the uninitiated to try the nargila. Mostly patronised by westerners and trendy locals, it's not hard to miss – look for the numerous flags. It has the best views of Al-Malek Faisal St, and is a great spot for staring at the chaos below.

Other places to try are: *Al-Sendebad Coffee Shop*, along the path leading to the Roman Theatre, which has great views, but not of the theatre; *Jabri Restaurant (Al-Malek al-Hussein St)* for pastries, but it's fairly charmless and not open in the evening; and *Terrace Cafeteria Petra* and *Diplomat Restaurant*, both great places to relax and watch the chaotic traffic around 1st Circle.

A dozen or more *cafes* are lined up along Hashemi St, and along the unnamed street between Hashemite Square and Raghadan station. They all serve shwarmas (for about 500 fils), and other unremarkable meals, as well as milkshakes and soft drinks. The main attraction is watching people walk along the busy footpath.

SPECTATOR SPORTS

Football (soccer) is followed by most locals. The capital's two main teams are Wahadat (supported by Palestinians) and Faisaly (supported by other Jordanians). Games are played mostly on Friday at the Amman International Stadium near Sports City,

Shmeisani. Because it can be hard to find a seat, and easy to get caught up in the throng, it's a good idea to go with a local friend.

SHOPPING

Amman is one of the better places to shop for souvenirs in Jordan, and to stock up on some of life's necessities before going to remote places like Wadi Rum.

Souvenirs

Al-Ayadi Jordan Craft Centre (☎/fax 464 4555), just up from 2nd Circle, is a quaint house, with handmade rugs, glassware, jewellery and ceramics. Prices are high, but this is quality stuff, mostly made by Palestinian refugees. Oriental Souvenirs Store (☎ 464 7998), only metres from 3rd Circle, has a good selection, and friendly staff. Artisana (☎ 464 7858, Mansour Kraishan St) is a new place with a good range at reasonable prices, and knowledgable staff.

Along Fawzi al-Malouf St (look for the signs off Rainbow St, Downtown) are showrooms where authentic goods are for sale, with profits going to charity (see Shopping in the Facts for the Visitor chapter). Nothing is cheap, however. Bani Hamida House (☎ 465 8696) sells items such as pottery, baskets and jewellery made by villagers in and around Mukawir (see the boxed text in the King's Highway chapter for details), and Dana village (near the Dana Nature Reserve). In the same complex, Jordan River Designs (☎ 461 3081) specialises in quilts, pillows and linen.

Around the southern end of Al-Malek Faisal St, Downtown, is the gold souq, where over 50 shops sell almost nothing but gold and silver, and jewellery. Very little is good enough, or cheap enough, to spend a lot of time looking around, unless you know what you're doing. The souvenir shops on a lower level beneath the cafes in front (north) of Hashemite Square have a better range than those at the southern end of the square.

Shopping Centres

Most of the upmarket shops and large, modern shopping centres are in the remote suburbs. On Nasser bin Jamil St, Shmeisani,

the enormous and modern Safeway Shopping Centre (☎ 568 5311) has both a supermarket and department store, both open 24 hours. It also boasts an Internet centre (see Email & Internet Access earlier); a KFC and other fast food outlets; an ATM for most credit cards; and a bank with foreign exchange facilities. Around 7th Circle is another, but less convenient, Safeway (☎ 581 5558) and the popular C-Town Shopping Centre (☎ 581 4129).

GETTING THERE & AWAY

For more information about travelling to and from Amman from outside of Jordan, refer to the Getting There & Away chapter earlier in the book.

Air

Amman is the main arrival and departure point for international flights (although some touch down in Aqaba, too).

Royal Jordanian Airlines' head office (☎ 560 7300, fax 567 2527) is inconveniently located in the Housing Bank Centre in Shmeisani. There are more convenient offices in the Jordan InterContinental Hotel complex (☎ 464 4266, fax 464 2152); and another (☎/fax 566 3525) along Al-Malek al-Hussein St, up from the Abdali bus station; as well as smaller offices at the University of Jordan (☎ 534 6868) and Queen Alia international airport (☎ 585 6835).

Anyone travelling on Royal Jordanian can check in their bags, pay the departure tax (JD10) and get a free lift to Queen Alia by bus (between 10 am and 10 pm) from the Royal Jordanian Airlines city terminal (☎ 585 6855, fax 585 6808), located near 7th Circle.

The Royal Jordanian subsidiary, Royal Wings, has an office (☎ 487 5201, fax 487 5656) at the Marka airport, but it's easier to book and confirm tickets at any of the Royal Jordanian offices.

The following major international airlines have offices in Amman (to avoid cluttering they are not listed on the maps).

Air France
(☎ 566 6055) 50 Al-Shareef Abdulla Hameed Sharaf St, Shmeisani

Alitalia
  (☎ 462 5203, fax 465 7341, email testco@ go.com.jo) Y. Iwais Allal St, Shmeisani
American Airlines
  (☎ 566 9068) Behind the Haya Culture Centre, Shmeisani
British Airways
  (☎ 582 8801) Hashweh Corporation Building, Kalha St, Swayfiyyeh
Egypt Air
  (☎ 463 6011) Zaatarah & Co, Al-Malek al-Hussein St, Downtown, near flyover
El Al
  (☎ 462 2526) Al-Malek al-Hussein St, Downtown, near flyover
Gulf Air
  (☎ 465 3613, fax 464 6190) Al-Malek al-Hussein St, Abdali, down from Abdali bus station
KLM
  (☎ 465 5267) Al-Malek al-Hussein St, Downtown, near flyover
Lufthansa
  (☎ 560 1744) Ilya Abu Madhi St (near KFC), Shmeisani
Middle East Airlines
  (☎ 463 6104, fax 461 9105) Al-Malek al-Hussein St, Downtown, near flyover
Saudi Arabian Airlines
  (☎ 463 9333) Al-Malek al-Hussein St, Abdali, just down from Abdali bus station
Syrian Airways
  (☎ 462 2147) Al-Amir Mohammed St, north of 2nd Circle
Turkish Airlines
  (☎ 465 9102) Al-Hussein bin Ali St, near 3rd Circle

Private Bus

All private buses leave from outside their offices; all public buses leave from the bus stations mentioned below. Tickets for private buses should be booked at least one day in advance.

Domestic The office (☎ 566 4146, fax 560 5005) for all domestic services with JETT is on Al-Malek al-Hussein St, about 800m up from the Abdali bus station. It offers at least five buses every day to Aqaba (JD4 one way); one to Hammamat Ma'in (JD4 return, plus entrance fee); and day trips to Petra (JD11 return, plus entrance fee) three times a week – refer to the relevant sections for more details. JETT also has a daily bus to the King Hussein Bridge for JD6 one way

(but not in the other direction) – refer to Israel in the Land section of the Getting There & Away chapter for details.

Trust International Transport has regular services to Aqaba. All buses leave from their office (☎ 581 3428) inconveniently located at 7th circle, near the Safeway shopping centre – it is best to charter a taxi to/from Downtown. Trust also has a booking office (☎ 464 4627) at the Abdali bus station.

International Refer to the relevant sections in the Getting There & Away chapter for details about buses between Amman and Israel, Syria and other countries in the region.

JETT has a separate office (☎ 569 6152) for international services, about 800m farther up from its domestic office, and just off Al-Malek al-Hussein St. Service taxis No 6 and 7 link the office with Downtown.

Trust International Transport has services from its office (see address above) at 7th Circle to Nazareth, Tel Aviv and Haifa, all in Israel.

Public Bus & Minibus

The three main bus stations in Amman are: Abdali bus station for transport to the north and west; Wahadat for transport to the south; and Raghadan for Amman, and nearby towns. There are also less well-defined bus stops for other destinations.

Abdali Station Abdali station is on Al-Malek al-Hussein St, about 20 minutes' walk (uphill) from Downtown. A No 6 or 7 service taxi from Cinema al-Hussein St goes right by. From Abdali, minibuses leave (when full) to Jerash (250 fils, 1¼ hours); Ajlun (500 fils, 1½ hours); Irbid (650 fils, about two hours); Fuheis (150 fils, 45 minutes); Salt (200 fils, 45 minutes); Deir Alla (400 fils, one hour), for Pella; and Ramtha (500 fils, two hours), near the Syrian border. There are also frequent minibuses to the transport junctions of Shuneh ash-Shamaliyyeh (North Shuna), Zarqa and Mafraq. For some reason, minibuses also leave here for Ma'in (JD1.250, 1¼ hours), although it's south of Amman.

From the bottom (eastern) end of the station, minibuses leave (far more frequently in the morning) for King Hussein Bridge (JD1.500, 45 minutes).

From further up (north-west) in the station, buses go every 20 or so minutes to Jerash (250 fils); and Irbid (500 fils). More comfortable, air-con Hijazi buses leave every 15 to 20 minutes to Jerash (350 fils) and Irbid (850 fils); tickets are available from the obvious office (☎ 465 1341) in the centre of the station. From the bottom (eastern) end of the station, Afana (☎ 461 4611) has buses (JD3.300, five hours) every hour between about 7 am and 10 pm to Aqaba – and Abdali is a more convenient departure and arrival point than Wahadat.

Wahadat Station All buses and service taxis heading south (except one to Ma'in and another to Aqaba, which also leave from Abdali) leave from Wahadat station. It's way out in the southern suburbs by Middle East Circle (Duwaar Sharq al-Awsat), and connected to Abdali by an unnumbered service taxi, by No 27 service taxi from Downtown (near the fruit and vegetable market), and by a local bus from along Quraysh St. If you have luggage, charter a taxi for less than JD1.

From Wahadat, minibuses depart regularly for Karak (750 fils, two hours); Aqaba (JD3, five hours); Ma'an (JD1.050, three hours); and Tafila (JD1, 2½ hours). They go less often to Wadi Mousa (JD1.650, three hours), for Petra, via Shobak (JD1.500, 2½ hours); Hammamat Ma'in (JD1.500, 1½ hours); and to Qadsiyya (JD1.250, about three hours), for Dana Nature Reserve.

Buses to Karak (750 fils) and Aqaba (about JD3) leave at least every hour until early afternoon. Buses (250 fils) and minibuses (200 fils) also run to Madaba (one hour), but it's more convenient to get one from Raghadan.

Raghadan Station The chaotic Raghadan station is a few minutes walk east of the Roman Theatre. It is divided into three sections: the first (when coming from the theatre) is a mass of service taxis going to nearby villages and suburbs of little interest to travellers. A few hundred metres further

east, there are minibuses to Madaba (250 fils), Salt (200 fils), Wadi as-Seer (200 fils, 30 minutes) and Zarqa. Further east is a confusing mass of local buses which is thankfully of no use to visitors.

Other Stations Minibuses for Wadi as-Seer (200 fils) also depart from a station on Ali bin Abi Taleb St, a 15 minute walk south of 1st Circle (or take a private taxi).

Minibuses for Shuneh al-Janubiyyeh (South Shuna; 400 fils, one hour), and occasionally directly to the Dead Sea Rest House at Suweimeh (500 fils, 1¼ hours) leave from Al-Quds St. (The area is also commonly known as Ras al-'Ain.) From there, minibuses also go to Madaba (250 fils) and Wadi as-Seer (200 fils). To the Al-Quds St station, take a No 29 service taxi from Quraysh St, and get off as it veers right from Al-Quds St; or take a private taxi.

Train

Refer to Syria in the Land section of the Getting There & Away chapter for information about the train service between Amman and Damascus.

The quaint old station – marked in English 'Amman Station: Hedjaz Jordan Railway' – is along Al-Malek Abdullah St, about 15 minutes by taxi east of Downtown. Catch the unnumbered service taxi from Raghadan station or, a lot easier, take a private taxi (about 800 fils).

Service Taxi

The service taxis are a much faster and more convenient way of getting to/from Amman than the buses and minibuses, but are more expensive – although only by a few hundred fils. Service taxis use the same stations as the buses (eg Abdali, Wahadat and Raghadan), and departures are considerably more frequent in the morning. Most service taxis are not labelled in English (except a few going to Ramtha and Irbid from Abdali), so ask for the correct vehicle.

From Abdali station, they run to Irbid (850 fils, 1½ hours), Jerash (500 fils, one hour), Ajlun (650 fils, one hour), Salt (400 fils, 45 minutes), King Hussein Bridge

(JD2, 45 minutes) and Ramtha (500 fils, two hours). Some go all the way to Damascus (JD5.500) in Syria – refer to the Getting There & Away chapter for more details.

From Wahadat station, there are departures to Karak (JD1.250, two hours); Wadi Mousa (JD2.500, three hours), for Petra, via Shobak (JD2, 2½ hours); Ma'an (JD2, 2½ hours); and, also but infrequently, to Aqaba (JD3.250, five hours).

The only service taxi of interest from Raghadan station is the one which goes past the Hejaz railway station (about 800 fils), and the turn-off to the tiny Marka airport (about 800 fils).

Car & Motorcycle

Amman and Aqaba are the only two cities where visitors can normally rent a car. Remember that the traffic and confusing roads make driving a nightmare in the capital, so perhaps consider renting a car in Aqaba, hiring a car with a driver in Amman, or renting a car from an agency in the outskirts of Amman (so you don't have to drive to/from central Amman).

Listed below are a few agencies which have been recommended by travellers. Charges, conditions and insurance costs (and waiver fees in case of accident) vary considerably, so shop around. Most places only rent cars for a minimum of two or three days.

Avis
  (☎ 445 1888) Terminal 2 of Queen Alia international airport. A small sedan costs from JD25 per day, with unlimited kilometres; Collision Damage Waiver (CDW) fee is JD5 per day.
Budget
  (☎ 569 8131, fax 567 3312, email budget@ go .com.jo) 125 Al-Shareef Abdulla Hameed Sharaf St, Shmeisani. Charges from JD32 per day, with unlimited kilometres; CDW is JD5 per day. They may even deliver the car to your hotel.
Europcar
  (☎ 560 7607) Amman Marriott; Regency Palace (☎ 560 1360). Charges from JD36.300 per day, including 200 free kilometres (80 fils per kilometre thereafter); CDW is JD5 per day.
Firas Rent a Car
  (☎ 461 2927, fax 461 6874, email frc@nets .com.jo) 1st Circle. Charges from JD22 per

day, plus 200 free kilometres (100 fils per kilometre thereafter); CDW is JD8 per day.
Nator
  (☎/fax 462 7455, email mnator@go.com .jo) 9th Sha'ban St. Charges start from JD22 per day, with unlimited kilometres; no CDW is available.

Hitching

To hitch down the King's Highway, catch a minibus to Madaba. For the Desert Highway, take a bus to Queen Alia international airport, and disembark at the turn-off to the airport. For the Dead Sea Highway, think again: this is a long, boring road with little traffic. But if keen, take a minibus to Shuneh al-Janubiyyeh (South Shuna) and try from there. For anywhere north and east, take a minibus from Abdali bus station to the obvious roundabout in Suweileh, from where several roads branch out to Jerash, Azraq, Irbid and Salt.

GETTING AROUND
To/From the Airports

The Queen Alia international airport is about 35km south of the city. The Airport Express bus (☎ 585 8874) leaves every day from the upper end of Abdali bus station for Terminals 1 and 2 every 30 minutes between 6 am and 10 pm, and at 12 pm, 2 am and 4 am. It departs for Abdali from outside the arrival area of Terminal 2 every 30 minutes between 6 am and 11 pm, and at 1 am and 3 am. The bus stops outside Shmeisani's Housing Bank Centre, but doesn't go via Downtown. Tickets cost JD1, plus 250 fils per large piece of luggage. (An airport service between Hashemite Square and Raghadan station no longer runs.)

Taxis travel between the airport and anywhere in Amman (or anywhere else in Jordan for that matter). Drivers use the meter, and the trip costs at least JD12. The bus is cheaper, and almost as convenient, as a taxi.

To the small Marka airport in north-eastern Amman, take the unnumbered service taxi (about 800 fils) from Raghadan station. It drops you at a roundabout, with a small plane in the middle, with signs pointing down (about 400m) Al-Mataar St to the airport terminal. Alternatively, a chartered private taxi from Downtown costs about JD1.

Bus
The local bus system is almost impossible to figure out for visitors because nothing is labelled in English (but they are numbered in 'English'), and most go to remote suburbs. Two services which are worth using to get back to Downtown are Nos 26 and 43. Tickets cost about 50 fils.

Service Taxi
Most fares on service taxis cost about 100 fils, and you pay the full amount regardless of where you get off. An exception is the Abdali-Wahadat service taxi, which costs 150 fils. After 8 pm the price for all service taxis goes up by 25%.

The cars queue up, and sometimes so do you. Often the queue starts at the bottom of a hill – you get into the last car and then the whole line rolls back a car space and so on. The boxed text 'Service Taxi Routes' indicates which service taxis go where, but always double-check whether the taxi is going to your destination before climbing in. If in doubt, remember that any service taxi going downhill, eg past Abdali station, is going to somewhere reasonably convenient in Downtown.

Private Taxi
Most drivers of private taxis use the meter, but gently remind them when they don't. Beware of unscrupulous drivers who hang around the stop for the Airport Express bus at Abdali bus station, and at the train station, looking for naive, just-arrived-in-Jordan folk. The drivers make all sorts of excuses about 'broken meters', so insist that they use the meter or wait another two seconds for another taxi to come along that will use the meter.

The flagfall is 150 fils. Fares are cheap and worth considering to avoid aching leg muscles, eg between Abdali and Downtown the fare is about 450 fils, and between Shmeisani and Downtown about 800 fils.

Car & Driver
Most hotels – especially the Bdeiwi, Farah, Rum Continental, Cliff and Venecia – can organise a private car and driver for day trips

Service Taxi Routes
All departure points are listed on the Downtown map.

No 2 From Basman St for 1st and 2nd Circles
No 3 From Basman St for 3rd and 4th Circles
No 4 From the side street near the central post office for Jebel al-Weibdeh
No 6 From Cinema al-Hussein St for the Ministry of the Interior Circle, past the Abdali bus station and the JETT domestic and international offices
No 7 From Cinema al-Hussein St, up Al-Malek al-Hussein St, past Abdali bus station and King Abdullah Mosque, and along Suleiman an-Nabulsi St
Nos 25 & 26 From behind the Church of the Saviour, Downtown, continues to the top of Jebel al-Ashrafiyeh' and near Abu Darwish Mosque
No 27 From opposite the fruit and vegetable souq, and continues to Middle East Circle for Wahadat station
No 29 From near the front of the Church of the Saviour for Al-Quds St station
No 35 From near the front of the Church of the Saviour, passing close to the Muhajireen Police Station

in and around Amman. These range from about JD25 to JD40 per day per vehicle depending on distance, time and, most importantly, your negotiation skills – and are often cheaper, and far less hassle, than renting a car. Refer to the Organised Tours section earlier in this chapter for more information.

Around Amman

Just about anywhere in Jordan can be visited on a day trip from Amman: even Aqaba is only 3½ hours away by car. Any place to the north, west and east of Amman, and anywhere south as far as Karak, can easily be visited on a day trip from Amman. While Petra, Wadi Rum and Aqaba can be done,

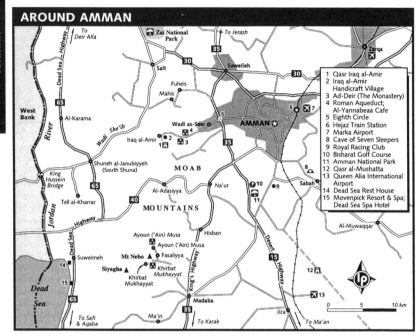

AROUND AMMAN

1 Qasr Iraq al-Amir
2 Iraq al-Amir Handicraft Village
3 Ad-Deir (The Monastery)
4 Roman Aqueduct; Al-Yannabeaa Cafe
5 Eighth Circle
6 Hejaz Train Station
7 Marka Airport
8 Cave of Seven Sleepers
9 Royal Racing Club
10 Bisharat Golf Course
11 Amman National Park
12 Qasr al-Mushatta
13 Queen Alia International Airport
14 Dead Sea Rest House
15 Movenpick Resort & Spa; Dead Sea Spa Hotel

they are really too far away for a day trip, and need more time to explore.

By public transport, it's easy to visit in one day: Madaba and Mt Nebo; Karak; Jerash and Ajlun; the Dead Sea and Pella; Irbid and Umm Qais; or Wadi as-Seer, Salt and Fuheis.

By private car or chartered taxi, the following places can be visited, albeit briefly, in one day:

• Madaba, Mt Nebo, Machaerus, Hammamat Ma'in and Karak
• 'desert castles' in eastern Jordan
• Salt, Fuheis, Wadi as-Seer, the Dead Sea, Deir Alla, Pella and Umm Qais
• Jerash, Dibbeen National Park, Ajlun, Umm Qais, Pella and the Dead Sea.

CAVE OF SEVEN SLEEPERS (AHL AL-KAHF) أهل الكهف

The legend of the 'seven sleepers' is mentioned in the Quran and the Bible. It involves several Christian boys who were persecuted,

then escaped to a cave and slept there for up to 300 years. Inside the main cave – also known as Ahl al-Kahf (Cave of the People) – are eight smaller tombs which are sealed, but one can be explored a little with a torch (flashlight) or candle. About 500m to the west of the cave is a large **Byzantine cemetery**.

Entrance is free, and the site is open daily from 8 am to 6 pm. The cave is next to the main mosque in the village of Rajib, just off the road to Sabah. A bus from Quraysh St goes to a spot about 1km west of the cave, from where you'll have to walk. The best way there is by chartered taxi (about JD3).

SALT السلط
☎ 05

In Salt, we were invited into two houses … At one house, we had singing in Arabic from the eldest son, and then we had to demonstrate disco-dancing to a cassette of 'Saturday Night Fever', while the whole extended family stood around clapping. It was most embarrassing!

Mark Hilton, UK

The friendly town of Salt, about 30km north-west of Downtown in Amman, was the area's administrative centre under Ottoman rule, but was passed over as the new capital of Transjordan in favour of Amman. Consequently, Salt has retained much of its charm. Salt was apparently named from the Greek word *saltus* meaning 'forests' (although most forests in the area are long gone); or from the word *sultana* for the grapes which were once abundant in the region.

Salt is easy to walk around; the bus station is on the main road and the centre of town is the market. The Archaeological & Folklore Museum is the tourist office. The Arab Bank has an ATM for Visa and MasterCard.

Things to See & Do

Around town there are fine examples of **Ottoman architecture**, particularly along the western end of Hammam St. None of the old houses are signposted, but it's nice to wander around and admire **Muasher House** and **Abu Jaber House**. The **views** from Jebel al-Qala'a are worth the short hike up the steep streets.

The **Archaeological & Folklore Museum** (☎ 355 5651) is mildly interesting, and worth a look if you're walking by. Downstairs, there are some pots and other artefacts from the region, all labelled in English; and, upstairs, some tacky dummies indicating 'traditional activities', with nothing explained in any language. The museum is open from 8 am to 6 pm every day except Friday when it is open until 1 pm. Entrance is free.

The **Salt Culture Centre** is set up by the Salt Development Corporation for the benefit of locals, rather than tourists, but visitors are welcome to wander around. Performances are sometimes held (ask at the centre, or museum). Visitors can watch weaving, pottery and other handicrafts being made and, of course, buy something here or at the **Salt Handicraft Training Centre** (☎ 551 781).

The road from the bus station leads into **Wadi She'ib**, a refreshing valley with some **hiking** opportunities and interesting **caves**.

Places to Stay & Eat

There is no official accommodation, but some readers have been able to stay at the

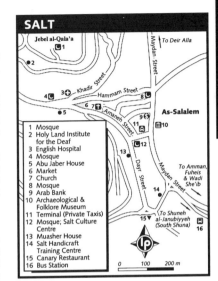

SALT

1 Mosque
2 Holy Land Institute for the Deaf
3 English Hospital
4 Mosque
5 Abu Jaber House
6 Market
7 Church
8 Mosque
9 Arab Bank
10 Archaeological & Folklore Museum
11 Terminal (Private Taxis)
12 Mosque; Salt Culture Centre
13 Muasher House
14 Salt Handicraft Training Centre
15 Canary Restaurant
16 Bus Station

Holy Land Institute for the Deaf, which offers a few rooms, with breakfast and lunch or dinner, for about JD20 per person. It's about 150m up from the English Hospital.

The northern end of Maydan St is lined with traditional *cafes*, full of local men doing little but drinking tea, smoking nargilas and staring out of the window. A few basic *restaurants* along the same street serve kebabs. *Canary Restaurant*, obvious from the bridge, is probably the best of a limited number of eateries.

Getting There & Away

From Amman, minibuses (200 fils, 45 minutes) regularly leave for the bus station in Salt from the Abdali and Raghadan stations, but demand often exceeds supply so the queues are long. Service taxis (400 fils) from Abdali are less regular and harder to find. From Salt, minibuses head down into the Jordan Valley to Shuneh al-Janubiyyeh (South Shuna), and to Wadi as-Seer and Fuheis – so Salt can be part of a day trip with Fuheis and Wadi as-Seer from Amman.

Taxis can be chartered from the terminal indicated on the Salt map for nearby trips, and back to Amman.

AMMAN

ZAI NATIONAL PARK
حديقة الزي الوطنية

This small piece of greenery is popular with Jordanians for picnics, but there is little reason to make a special visit. Dibbeen National park (mentioned in the Northern & Western Jordan chapter) is better for hiking, accommodation and food.

If driving to Zai, go to Suweileh, follow the road towards Salt, then bypass Salt and head towards Deir Alla and look for signs to the park. There is no public transport in the area, so charter a taxi from Salt.

FUHEIS
فحيص

☎ 05

This pleasant village, located a cool 1050m above sea level, is famous in Jordan for producing fruit and cement. But Fuheis, which was first built in about 2000 BC, is of interest to visitors for its restaurants, churches and arts and craft shops.

Fuheis has several **galleries** and **workshops** which produce ceramics, mosaics, paintings and embroidery, but these are often badly signposted. A green board near the Al-Hosh Restaurant explains in English the locations of galleries, shops and workshops, but is still not entirely clear. The best idea is to have a walk around and look, or ask a local. The largest and most modern gallery in the village is **Riwak al-Balkaa for the Arts** (☎ 472 0677).

Fuheis is overwhelmingly a Christian village and has several **churches**; three are less than 200m down from the bus stop. **Hiking** in the area is good: just head down the valley from the bus stop. Ask around the village, or at the tourist office in Amman, about any concerts and exhibits in Fuheis; they are sometimes held in summer (usually July and August), but are not well advertised.

From the bus stop, a sign points to the *Al-Hosh Restaurant* (☎ 472 9152). Classier, and worth a trip from Amman for its shady setting and fabulous food, is *Al-Zuwwadeh* (☎ 795 3241), less than 100m down from the pink monument at the bus stop. The restaurant is not signposted in English, but the menu is in English and features a vast range of pricey, but delicious, meals from

about JD3, as well as a good selection of cheaper teas and pastries.

Getting There & Away

Fuheis is easy to reach by minibus (but less often by service taxi) from Abdali bus station in Amman (150 fils, 45 minutes). Fuheis is also regularly connected by minibus to Wadi as-Seer and Salt (each 250 fils), so you can visit all three places in one day. Taxis can also be chartered to Fuheis from Salt.

The bus stop in the older (and lower) part of town known as *il-balad* is at a roundabout where the 'Stop & Go' shop (signed in English) is located.

WADI AS-SEER & IRAQ AL-AMIR
وادي عسير / عراق الأمير

The valley was green and restful; the traffic was far away, only the sound of goat bells on a nearby hill, birdsong and the occasional distant cries of children.

Annie Caulfield
Kingdom of the Film Stars

The narrow fertile valley of Wadi as-Seer is a real contrast to the bare, treeless plateau around Amman to the east. Spring (particularly April and May) is the best time to visit, when black iris and other colourful flowers are plentiful.

Wadi as-Seer is a largely Circassian village, and now virtually part of western Amman. About 10km down the gorgeous valley are the Iraq al-Amir castle and caves. Along the way (about 4km from Wadi as-Seer), and next to the charming *Al-Yannabeaa cafe*, is an ancient **Roman aqueduct** on the right. Shortly after, on the left, is a facade cut into the rock, known as **ad-deir** ('the monastery'), although it was probably a medie val dovecot (a place to house pigeons).

Iraq al-Amir (Caves of the Prince) are on the right of the road about 5km farther past the Al-Yannabeaa cafe from Wadi as-Seer. The caves are arranged in two tiers – the upper one forms a long gallery along the cliff face. The eleven caves were apparently used as cavalry stables, but local villagers now use them to house their goats and store chaff, so they're not that interesting.

A short and well signposted walk from the caves is the **Iraq al-Amir Handicraft Village**.

Qasr Iraq al-Amir

About 700m farther down the road, and visible from the caves, stands the ruins of an impressive castle, also known as Qasr al-Abad ('Palace of the Slave'). Mystery surrounds the reason for its construction, and even its precise age, but Hyrcanus, of the powerful Jewish Tobiad family, probably started building it in the 2nd century BC – for unknown reasons it was never fully completed. Today, reconstruction of the palace is complete.

The place is unique because it was built out of some of the biggest blocks of any ancient structure in the Middle East – the largest measures 7m by 3m. The blocks were, however, only 20cm or so thick, making the whole edifice quite flimsy, and a perfect victim for the earthquake that flattened it in 362 AD.

The castle is open every day during daylight hours, and entrance to the grounds is free. The inside of the castle itself is locked, so you'll have to find the gatekeeper (he'll probably find you first) and slip him about 500 fils to open it up. Inside the castle, there's a useful explanation on a notice board. The room at the back of the complex is only used to show videos for the occasional tour group.

Getting There & Away

Minibuses leave regularly from the station on Ali bin Abi Taleb St in Amman for Wadi as-Seer village (200 fils, 30 minutes); they also leave less frequently from Raghadan and Al-Quds St stations. From Wadi as-Seer, take another minibus (100 fils) – or walk about 10km – to the mosque in Iraq al-Amir village, virtually opposite the entrance to the caves. From the caves, it's an easy stroll down (but a little steep back up) to the castle.

If driving, look for the signs to Wadi as-Seer from 8th Circle, but you may still need to ask some directions because signs to Wadi as-Seer are conspicuous by their absence.

Northern & Western Jordan

The area to the north of Amman is the most densely populated in Jordan, with the major centres of Irbid and Jerash, as well as dozens of small towns dotted in amongst the rugged and relatively fertile hills. In this area also lie the ruins of the ancient Decapolis cities of Jerash (Gerasa) and Umm Qais (Gadara), and the magnificent castle at Ajlun.

North-east of Irbid, the country flattens out to plains that stretch away into Syria. To the west lies the Jordan Valley, one of the most fertile patches of land in the Middle East. To the south-west is the moribund but popular Dead Sea.

JERASH
جرش

☎ 02

The ruins at Jerash are one of Jordan's major attractions (only Petra is more spectacular), and have the advantage of being very accessible and compact. Jerash is also one of the best examples in the Middle East of a Roman provincial city, and is remarkably well preserved.

In its heyday, Jerash (known in Roman times as Gerasa) had a population of around 15,000 and, although it wasn't on any of the main trade routes, its citizens prospered from the good corn-growing land that surrounds it. The ancient city preserved today was the administrative, civic and commercial centre of Jerash. The bulk of the inhabitants lived on the eastern side of Wadi Jerash (now the modern town of Jerash).

History

Although there have been finds to indicate that the site was inhabited in Neolithic times, the city rose to prominence from the time of Alexander the Great (333 BC).

In the wake of the Roman general Pompey's conquest of the region in 64 BC, Gerasa became part of the Roman province of Syria and, soon after, a city of the Decapolis (see the boxed text in the Amman chapter). Over the next two centuries trade with the Nabataeans flourished and the city

HIGHLIGHTS

- **Jerash** – this is one of the best examples in the Middle East of a Roman provincial city and it is remarkably well preserved (see page 144)

- **Ajlun** – this cool, shady region is great for hiking, and boasts the wonderful Qala't ar-Rabad (see page 151)

- **Museum of Jordanian Heritage** – arguably Jordan's best museum is in the vibrant Yarmouk University of Irbid (see page 154)

- **Umm Qais** – these remote and fascinating ruins offer awesome views over the Jordan Valley, Israel and across to Syria (see page 156)

- **The Dead Sea** – try going for a swim in the incredibly salty water and finish with a mud pack to help improve your skin (see page 163)

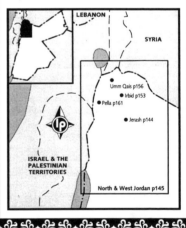

grew extremely wealthy. Local agriculture and iron-ore mining in the Ajlun area contributed to the city's wellbeing. A completely new plan was drawn up in the 1st century AD, centred on the typical feature

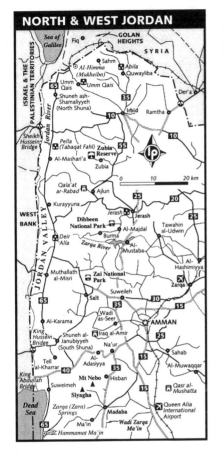

NORTH & WEST JORDAN

with the rank of Colony; but with disturbances such as the destruction of Palmyra in 273 AD, the demise of the overland caravans and development of sea trade, it slipped into a slow decline. The only respite came during the reign of Diocletian (circa 300 AD), which saw a minor building boom.

By the middle of the 5th century, Christianity was the major religion and the construction of churches proceeded quickly. Under Justinian (527-65 AD) seven churches were built, mostly out of stones filched from the earlier pagan temples and shrines, but no more churches were built after 611.

With the invasion of the Sassanians from Persia (now Iran) in 614, the Muslim conquest in 636 and the devastating earthquake in 747, Gerasa was really on the skids and its population shrank to about one-quarter of its former size.

Apart from a brief occupation by a Crusader garrison in the 12th century, the city was completely deserted until the arrival of the Circassians (from Russia) in 1878, when the site's archaeological importance was realised and excavations began.

Orientation & Information

Entrance The best place to start (and/or finish) your visit is Hadrian's Arch. From here, you can walk past (and visit) the Hippodrome before paying the entrance fee to the main site at the South Gate. The visitors centre (☎ 635 1272) was being redeveloped at the time of research, but promises to be informative and worth visiting before entering the main site. Allow at least three hours to see everything in Jerash.

The site is open from 8 am until 7 pm daily. Tickets cost JD5. If travelling to Jerash independently, it's a good idea to come before 10 am or after 4 pm because it's cooler, there will be less glare in your photos and less people shattering the ambience. Some of the buildings really glow in the late afternoon, and on the right day you could enjoy dinner before returning for the sound-and-light show. However, public transport back to Amman is very limited after about 5 pm.

The only toilets at the site are in the Government Rest House.

of a colonnaded main street intersected by two side streets.

When Emperor Trajan annexed the Nabataean kingdom (around 106 AD) more wealth found its way to Gerasa. Many of these buildings were torn down to be replaced by more imposing structures. The town administration went into top gear again when Emperor Hadrian visited in 129 AD. To mark a visit of such importance, the Triumphal Arch (now known as Hadrian's Arch) at the southern end of the city was constructed.

Gerasa reached its peak in the beginning of the 3rd century, when it was bestowed

NORTHERN & WESTERN JORDAN

JERASH

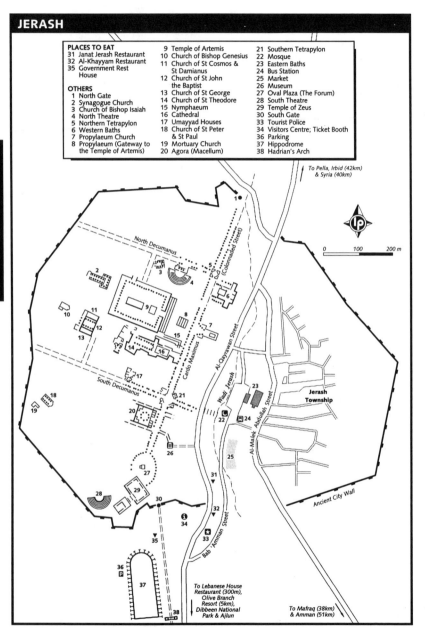

PLACES TO EAT
31 Janat Jerash Restaurant
32 Al-Khayyam Restaurant
35 Government Rest
   House

OTHERS
1 North Gate
2 Synagogue Church
3 Church of Bishop Isaiah
4 North Theatre
5 Northern Tetrapylon
6 Western Baths
7 Propylaeum Church
8 Propylaeum (Gateway to
   the Temple of Artemis)

9 Temple of Artemis
10 Church of Bishop Genesius
11 Church of St Cosmos &
   St Damianus
12 Church of St John
   the Baptist
13 Church of St George
14 Church of St Theodore
15 Nymphaeum
16 Cathedral
17 Umayyad Houses
18 Church of St Peter
   & St Paul
19 Mortuary Church
20 Agora (Macellum)

21 Southern Tetrapylon
22 Mosque
23 Eastern Baths
24 Bus Station
25 Market
26 Museum
27 Oval Plaza (The Forum)
28 South Theatre
29 Temple of Zeus
30 South Gate
33 Tourist Police
34 Visitors Centre; Ticket Booth
36 Parking
37 Hippodrome
38 Hadrian's Arch

To Pella, Irbid (42km)
& Syria (40km)

0   100   200 m

North Decumanus

(Colonnaded Street)

Cardo Maximus

Al-Qayrawan Street

South Decumanus

Wadi Jerash

Jerash
Township

Al-Malek Abdullah Street

Ancient City Wall

Bab 'Amman Street

To Lebanese House
Restaurant (300m),
Olive Branch
Resort (5km),
Dibbeen National
Park & Ajlun

To Mafraq (38km)
& Amman (51km)

Guides Anyone with a deep interest in the history of Jerash may wish to hire a guide. Guides are available at the ticket office at the South Gate for JD5 per group (maximum of ten), for as long as the tour takes. They can speak English, German, Spanish, French, Italian and Greek.

Dangers & Annoyances A few foreign women have reported unwanted attention and mild harassment from local men, particularly in the more remote regions of this vast site. If this happens, report it immediately to the tourist police, which has an office outside the site opposite the visitors centre.

Books & Maps The free Jerash brochure published by the Jordan Tourism Board includes a map, some photos and a recommended walking tour. The brochure is available in English, French and German (and, sometimes, Italian and Spanish), and available at the visitors centre in Jerash, and the Downtown visitors centre in Amman.

Anyone with a deep interest in the history of Jerash should pick up one of three decent pocket-sized guides: *Jerash: The Roman City*, published by Arabesque; *Jerash: A Unique Example of a Roman City*; or, the most comprehensive and readable, *Jerash*, published by Al-Kutba. All three are available at bookshops in Amman for about JD3 each. *Jerash* by Iain Browning is a more detailed and expensive guidebook and is highly praised.

The souvenir stalls and the Government Rest House at Jerash, and the bookshops and souvenirs shops around Amman, sell several souvenir coffee-table books with lots of photos, but little useful information. The books are printed in English, French, Spanish, Italian and German.

The Ruins

At the most southern entrance is the striking **Hadrian's Arch**, sometimes known as the **Triumphal Arch**. Although its present height is still daunting, it was twice as high when first built in 129 AD, in honour of the visiting Emperor Hadrian. There are actu-

Jerash Festival

Since 1981, the ancient city of Jerash has hosted the annual Jerash Festival of Culture & Arts. Events are held in the South Theatre, North Theatre and Oval Plaza (also known as the Forum) in Jerash, as well as the Royal Cultural Centre in Amman, and other places like Umm Qais and Mt Nebo. Special programs for children are also held at the Haya Cultural Centre in Amman.

The festival is held over 17 days from about mid-July to mid-August. It features an eclectic array talent from around the world. More information is available from the organisers in Amman (☎ 06-567 5199, fax 568 6198, email jerashfs@go.com.jo), and the informative Web site (www.jerashfestival.com.jo). Events are listed in English in the official souvenir book; the *Jerash Daily*, printed in English every day of the festival; and the English-language newspapers published in Amman.

Tickets cost at least JD5 for events in Jerash, and about JD20 for more formal events in Amman and elsewhere. They are available from the Royal and Haya cultural centres, and the office (for domestic services) in Abdali (Amman) of the JETT bus company. JETT also offers one-way and return transport to Jerash during the festival (especially useful when public transport stops at night).

ally three arches; the highest is 13m, and all three once had huge wooden doors. One unusual feature of the construction is the wreaths of carved acanthus leaves above the bases of the pillars. The arch was originally constructed as a new southern entrance, but the area between the arch and the South Gate was never completed.

Behind the arch is the partially restored **hippodrome**, built sometime between the 1st and 3rd centuries AD. This old sports field (244m by 50m), once surrounded by seating for up to 15,000 spectators, hosted mainly athletics competitions and horse races. Recent excavations have unearthed remains of stables, pottery workshops and indications that it was also used for polo by invading Sassanians from Persia during the early 7th century.

The obvious entrance to the main site, and the ticket office, are near the Government Rest House (see Places to Eat) and the **South Gate**. The South Gate, originally one of four along the city wall (little of which remains), also bears the acanthus leaf decoration of Hadrian's Arch. The gate was built in 130 AD, and a new city quarter was possibly planned between the two gates.

Once inside the main site, the **Temple of Zeus** is on the left. It was built in about 162 AD over the remains of an earlier Roman temple, which in turn was probably built over the ruins of a Byzantine church. The Temple of Zeus once had a flight of stairs leading up to it from a lower sacred enclosure, itself supported by a vaulted corridor built to compensate for the unhelpful local geography. The corridor was probably used as stables, barracks or as a warehouse. The lower level *temenos* (sacred courtyard) had an altar and served as a holy place of sacrifice. Little remains of the main temple except the outer walls.

The **South Theatre**, behind the Temple of Zeus, was built in the 1st century, and could hold 5000 spectators. (It currently seats about 3000 along the 32 rows.) The back of the stage was originally two storeys high, and has now been rebuilt to the first level. From the top of the theatre, there are excellent **views** of the ancient and modern towns of Jerash. The theatre was built in a similar style to the Roman Theatre in Amman, and boasts astounding acoustics which amaze anyone lucky enough to go to the Jerash Festival (see the boxed text earlier in this chapter).

The **Oval Plaza** – sometimes known as the **forum** – is unusual because of its oval shape and huge size (90m long and 80m at its widest point). Some scholars attribute this to the desire to gracefully link the main north-south axis (the cardo maximus) with the Temple of Zeus, or its predecessor. The Oval Plaza was probably a market or meeting place, although some historians believe the site may have been a place of sacrifice linked to the temple because of the two altars in the middle. The 56 reconstructed Ionic columns surrounding the plaza are very impressive, and the centre is paved with limestone and other softer blocks.

Heading north-east, the **cardo maximus** (main street), known as the **colonnaded street**, stretches for 800m from the Oval Plaza to the North Gate. The street was originally built in the 1st century AD, and rebuilt and redesigned several times since. It is still paved with the original stones, and the ruts worn by thousands of chariots over the years can be clearly seen. Some of the 500 columns that once lined the street were deliberately built of an uneven height to complement the facades of the buildings that once stood behind them.

ANN JEFFREE

Hadrian's Arch was erected in 129 AD to commemorate the visit of Emperor Hadrian. Its Corinthian columns are set high on pedestals, and the structure still bears the emperor's name.

Just prior to the intersection with the **south decumanus**, and where the columns are taller, is the entrance to the **agora** (which is sometimes referred to as the **macellum**) where the market was held and people gathered for meetings.

Where the cardo maximus joined the south decumanus and north decumanus, ornamental *tetrapylon* (arches with four sides) were built. The **southern tetrapylon** consisted of four bases, each supporting four pillars topped by a statue. Only the bases have been rebuilt; the south-eastern one is the most complete. This intersection was made into a circular plaza at the end of the 3rd century.

To the east of the intersection of cardo maximus and south decumanus, a footbridge leads towards former residential areas, now buried beneath the **mosque**, bus station and the modern town of Jerash. To the west of the intersection are the ruins of some more **Umayyad houses** supporting the theory that the newly arrived Muslims lived in reasonable harmony with the city's earlier, largely Christian inhabitants.

About 100m north of the intersection are steps belonging to the 4th century **cathedral** (probably little more than a modest Byzantine church, despite the name). The gate and steps actually cover the remains of an earlier temple to the Nabataean god, Dhushara.

Next along the main street is the elegant **nymphaeum**, the main ornamental fountain of the city and a temple dedicated to the nymphs. Built in about 191 AD, the two storey construction was elaborately decorated, faced with marble slabs on the lower level and plastered on the upper level. Water used to cascade over the facade into a large pool at the front and the overflow went out through seven carved lions' heads to drains in the street below.

Further up on the left (west) is the **propylaeum**, the gateway to the Temple of Artemis. A stairway, flanked by shops, originally started in the eastern city (now under modern Jerash) and crossed over the cardo maximus before finishing here.

Behind the propylaeum, and on top of a small hill, is the well-preserved **Temple of Artemis** dedicated to the goddess of hunting and fertility and of Gerasa city. The temple was built between about 150 and 170 AD, and had 12 columns (11 are still standing), but the marble floors and statues have disappeared. Large vaults had to be built to the north and south of the temple to make the courtyard level. The temple was fortified by the Arabs in the 12th century, but was substantially destroyed later by the Crusaders.

South and west of the Temple of Artemis lie the ruins of several **churches**. In all, 15 churches have been uncovered and more are likely to be found. Behind (west of) the cathedral, the **Church of St Theodore**, built in 496 AD, has some limited remains of mosaics. The **Church of St Cosmos & St Damianus** was dedicated to twin brothers, both doctors. It once had some marvellous mosaic tiles, but most are now in the Traditional Jewels & Costumes Museum in Amman. The **Church of St John the Baptist** was built in about 531 AD, but is badly damaged. The **Church of St George**, built in about 530 AD, is also badly destroyed.

Little remains of the other churches, ie the **Mortuary Church** and **Church of St Peter & St Paul** in the far south-western corner of the ruins; the **Synagogue Church** and **Church of Bishop Genesius**, behind the Temple of Artemis; the **propylaeum church**, opposite the propylaeum itself; and, near the north theatre, the **Church of Bishop Isaiah**, built in 611 but virtually destroyed by the earthquake of 747.

Back on cardo maximus, on the right (east) heading towards the North Gate, is the **Umayyad Mosque**, built in about 8th century from the stone and bricks of nearby buildings.

At the intersection of cardo maximus and the north decumanus is the **Northern Tetrapylon**, dedicated to the Syrian wife of the emperor Septimus Severus. It was probably built as a gateway to the north theatre; this tetrapylon differs to the southern one because it consisted of four arches surmounted by a dome.

Just downhill (to the south-east) are the huge **western baths**, measuring about 70m by 50m. Dating from the 2nd century AD, they represent one of the earliest examples of a dome atop a square room. Once an impressive complex of hot and cold water baths, they were badly destroyed by various earthquakes. Lost in the chaos of modern Jerash are the decrepit ruins of the **eastern baths**.

The **north theatre** is smaller than the south theatre, and differs considerably in shape and design. It was built in about 165 AD for government meetings rather than general artistic performances, and in 235 it was doubled in size. It has been magnificently restored and still holds about 2000 people. There are great **views** of parts of the ancient city from the very top.

The cardo maximus ends at the comparatively unimpressive **North Gate**. Built in about 115 AD, it has one arch and an odd shape – probably because it had to be aligned with the cardo maximus and the main road outside which linked Gerasa with Pella.

Surrounding the ancient city for about 4.5km are **city walls**, which are between 2m and 3.5m wide and once featured 24 towers. The walls were built in the 1st century AD.

The Government Rest House sells unashamedly expensive souvenirs. The souvenir stands outside the South Gate and Hadrian's Arch, and over the main road to the east, are growing visibly fat on the passing trade, and prices for souvenirs and guidebooks are a few dinars up on the Amman average. A popular local souvenir is coloured sand in bottles.

Sound-and-Light Show A sound-and-light show is held in the ruins every night, except Friday, from 8 to 9 pm, between about 1 May and the end of September. It features commentary and historical re-enactments in English (on Saturday and Sunday), Arabic (Monday and Tuesday), German (Wednesday) and French (Thursday).

The good news is that admission to the show and to Jerash (for the length of the show only) is free; the bad news is that there is no reliable public transport between Jerash and Amman in the evening. You may be able to leave Amman at about 6 pm by bus or minibus, but you'll probably have to rely on chartered taxis, or hitching a ride, back to the

capital. For further information about the sound-and-light show, call ☎ 02-635 1053.

Museum

Before you finish exploring the ancient city, make sure you visit the small **museum** (☎ 632 267), just to the east of (and up from) the Oval Plaza. It houses a selection of artefacts from the site, such as pottery, jewellery, glass and gold jewellery, as well as coins found in a tomb near Hadrian's Arch. Everything is well labelled in English. The **views** of the Oval Plaza and cardo maximus from the front of the museum are worth the short climb. It's open every day from 8.30 am to 6 pm (in summer), and closes at 5 pm in winter. Entrance is free.

Places to Stay

Surprisingly, there is still no hotel in Jerash, although there are a couple of decent places to stay in Ajlun (see below). With an early start, you can cover Jerash and Ajlun in a day trip from Amman.

Olive Branch Resort (☎ *079-523 546, fax 06-582 6034, email olivekh@go.com.jo*), about 5km from Jerash and along the road to Ajlun, has modern, luxurious and spacious rooms. The resort also has great views, a welcome (heated) swimming pool (available to the public for JD2 per person) and a *restaurant*. Singles/doubles cost JD28/36, including breakfast. Camping with your own tent costs JD4 per person; or in a preset four-person tent, JD5 per person. Take the Jerash to Ajlun minibus or charter a taxi from Jerash.

Places to Eat

Government Rest House (☎ *635 1437*) has an expensive restaurant, but it costs nothing to sit in the air-conditioned entrance area. It unashamedly caters to tour groups, although the public are welcome. The menu is limited and pricey: most meals are about JD6, salads about JD3 and soft drinks at least JD1. Beer is at least double the price it is in Amman.

You will find better value outside the site. *Al-Khayyam Restaurant,* just over the road from the visitors centre, offers nice views and some shade, and has main meals from about JD3. Next door, *Janat Jerash Restaurant* is about the same price, setting and standard.

Lebanese House Restaurant (☎ 635 1301) is good if you have your own transport, or any energy left for a short walk: it's about 300m south-west of the turn-off to Ajlun which starts just south of Hadrian's Arch. A few more tourist-oriented *restaurants* are dotted along the road in to Jerash from Amman or Irbid, but they're too far to walk to from Jerash, and mainly cater to tour groups and visitors with their own transport.

A few boys sell a limited range of expensive cold drinks around the site, but you should always take plenty of water with you: it's hot in summer, there's almost no shade and the site is large. The bus station in Jerash hosts a collection of unexciting *cafes* selling the usual felafel and shwarma, as well as cold drinks.

Getting There & Away

Jerash is 51km north of Amman, and the roads are well signed from the capital. The ancient city is adjacent to the modern town, and unmissable from the main road in to Jerash. If coming from Amman or Irbid, get off (or park) when you first see the ruins. This is Hadrian's Arch, the best place to start your exploration.

The station for buses, minibuses and service taxis is a short walk from the visitors centre – over the obvious footpath and past the mosque. From Abdali bus station in Amman, public minibuses and buses (both about 250 fils, 1¼ hours) and air-conditioned Hijazi private buses (350 fils) leave every 20 minutes. Or catch anything between Amman and Irbid, disembark at the turn-off to Jerash, and walk (about 5km) along the pleasant, shady road. (It is, however, best to save your energy for walking around the site.)

From Abdali, service taxis (500 fils, one hour) are irregular because the buses and minibuses are so frequent. A one-way chartered taxi ride to or from Amman (which may be necessary after about 5 pm) will cost a negotiable JD7 or more.

From Jerash, plenty of minibuses travel regularly to Irbid (300 fils, 45 minutes) and

Ajlun (250 fils, 30 minutes), as well as to Mafraq and Zarqa.

If you're still in Jerash after about 5 pm, be prepared to hitch back to Amman because most buses and minibuses stop running soon after that. Service taxis are sometimes available until about 8 pm; possibly later during the Jerash Festival and the sound-and-light show. The staff at the tourist police office are usually happy to cajole a passing motorist into offering a free ride back to Amman.

AJLUN   عجلون
☎ 02

Ajlun is another popular and easy day trip from Amman, and can be combined with a trip to Jerash. The only thing of interest in Ajlun town is the **mosque**, just south-west of the main roundabout, which has a minaret dating back some 600 years. The highlight of the trip, however, is unquestionably the wonderful Qala'at ar-Rabad, near Ajlun.

The area is also popular with locals and the surrounding hills are a few degrees cooler than the rest of Jordan.

Orientation & Information

The castle is about 2.5km west of the town centre of Ajlun. In the Bonita Ajloun Restaurant, the tourist office (☎ 642 0115) hands out uninformative brochures and is open from 8 am to 2 pm every day except Friday. The Housing Bank, just south of the main roundabout in Ajlun, changes money.

Qala'at ar-Rabad   قلعة الربد

Ar-Rabad Castle, built on top of Mt 'Auf (about 1250m), is a fine example of Islamic military architecture. The castle was built by one of Salah ad-Din's generals and nephews, 'Izz ad-Din Urama bin Munqidh, in 1184-85, and was enlarged in 1214 with the addition of a new gate in the south-eastern corner. It once boasted seven towers, and was surrounded by a dry moat over 10m deep.

The castle commands views of not only the Jordan Valley but three wadis leading to it – the Kufranjah, Rajeb and Al-Yabes – making it an important strategic link in the defensive chain against the Crusaders, and a counter to the Crusader Belvoir Fort on the Sea of Galilee (Lake Tiberias) in Israel. With its hill-top position, ar-Rabad castle was one in a chain of beacons and pigeon posts that allowed messages to be transmitted from Baghdad to Cairo in one day.

After the Crusader threat subsided, the castle was largely destroyed by Mongol invaders in 1260, only to be almost immediately rebuilt by the Mamluks. In the 17th century an Ottoman garrison was stationed there, after which it fell into disuse and was used by local villagers. The castle was 'discovered' by the well-travelled JL Burckhardt, who also stumbled across Petra (see the boxed text in the Petra chapter). Earthquakes in 1837 and 1927 damaged the castle badly, but its restoration is continuing.

The castle is open every day from 8 am to 7 pm (in summer); until 5 pm in winter. Entrance fee is JD1. There is a useful explanation in English just past the entrance, but nothing is signposted or labelled inside. It's easy to get lost and disoriented while exploring the castle, so allow plenty of time.

The castle is a tough uphill walk (2.5km) from the town centre, but minibuses occasionally go to the top for about 100 fils. Alternatively, take a taxi from Ajlun for about JD1 one way, or hitch a ride. A return trip by taxi from Ajlun, with about 20 minutes to look around, will cost about JD3.

Places to Stay & Eat

The only reason to stay in Ajlun is to enjoy the magnificent sunset from the castle. There are two hotels, and neither have, nor need, air-conditioning. With their high prices, and proximity to Amman, it's not surprising that both places are empty most of the time – so prices are negotiable.

Al-Rabad Castle Hotel (☎ 642 0202, fax 463 0414), about 500m before the castle, has large and comfortable rooms with TV, private bathrooms and commanding views of the valley and town. Prices are correspondingly high, however – JD26.200/35.200 for singles/doubles – but the manager is willing to come down a few dinars. It also boasts an elegant outdoor *restaurant* with great views.

Ajlun Hotel (☎/fax 642 0542) is about 100m further towards the castle from Al-Rabad Castle Hotel. Rooms, with a private bathroom and balcony, also officially go for JD26.200/35.200, but are offered for as little as JD10/15 without a/c – if so, this is very good value. One reader did complain, however, about a smelly bathroom without hot water.

Bonita Ajloun Restaurant (☎ 642 0981), less than 100m down from the castle, is the only place to eat nearby. The views are superb, but the prices are not surprisingly high: from JD3.500 for main courses to JD6 for the usual tourist buffet; and a large beer is JD2.500.

Green Mountain Restaurant, by the main roundabout in the town centre, has – surprise, surprise – roast chicken, humous, salad and bread. There are also a couple of *shwarma joints* around the town centre. It's best to join the locals for a *picnic*; bring some food from Amman or Jerash, or buy some goodies at the shops in Ajlun. There are *drink stands* at the entrance to the castle.

Getting There & Away

Ajlun is 73km north-west of Amman, and 15km north-west of Jerash. While the castle can clearly be seen from most places in the region, there are few signs from the town centre. If driving or walking, take the main road (Al Qal'a St) heading west at the main roundabout in the centre of Ajlun.

From the centre of Ajlun, minibuses regularly travel to Jerash (250 fils, 30 minutes) along a very scenic road, and Irbid (270 fils, 45 minutes). Direct minibuses (500 fils, 1½ hours) from Abdali bus station in Amman are not that regular, so it's probably best to go to Jerash first, see the ruins there, take a minibus to Ajlun – ask the minibus driver to drop you off in the middle of Ajlun – and catch something back to Amman from Ajlun before 5 pm.

ZUBIA RESERVE

حديقة زوبيا الوطنية

Lost among the beautiful forests surrounding Ajlun is the fairly unimpressive Zubia Reserve (12 sq km), established by the

Royal Society for the Conservation of Nature (RSCN) in 1988 to protect native fauna, including the roe deer.

This reserve is not nearly as well set up for tourists, nor as accessible, as the other RSCN reserves. There is very little to do, although some **hiking trails** of 3km to 5km are being developed. Staff at the ranger station are fairly uninterested in tourists, and speak little English. Visitors can pitch their own *tents* near the ranger station, and use the basic toilets and showers for free.

Getting there is an adventure in itself, and no public transport goes anywhere close. Minibuses from Irbid (South bus station) and Jerash go to Zubia village, but this is still about 5km from the ranger station. It's best to charter a taxi from Jerash or Ajlun. If driving, ask lots of directions because the roads are windy, confusing and unsigned.

DIBBEEN NATIONAL PARK
حديقة دبين الوطنية

This large, semi-protected area of forest is great for **hiking** and **picnics**, and is a lovely drive from Amman. The area has great **views** of the valleys, and is about the coolest place in northern Jordan during the summer.

Places to Stay & Eat
In the middle of the park is a tourist complex, with a children's playground, places to eat and the *Debbeen Rest House* (☎ *02-633 9710)*. The comfortable 'chalets' (which sleep three) have a basic kitchen, large bathroom with hot water, TV and fan. They cost JD25/32 for doubles/triples (no single rates), but the manager readily admits that no-one is silly enough to pay this, so discounts are readily accepted. Visitors can pitch their own *tent* in the grounds for JD2.500 per person, and have access to toilets and hot showers.

The tourist complex is not quite as tacky as it sounds, and from Sunday to Wednesday you may have the whole complex, and the entire park, to yourself. On Thursday and Friday, however, it's jam-packed with happy picnicking locals. Entrance to the park and tourist complex is free; and both are permanently open.

Getting There & Away
Public transport is very limited. From Jerash, the minibus to the villages of Burma or Al-Majdal goes through the park and can drop you off within 1km of the entrance to the tourist complex – a detour to the complex can be arranged with the minibus driver for an inducement of about JD1. Chartering a private taxi from Jerash is the best idea, and will cost about JD4 one way. If driving from Jerash or Ajlun, follow the initial signs from along the Jerash-Ajlun road, and then ask directions to the Rest House – nothing much is signposted and the roads are confusing.

IRBID
إربد
☎ 02

Although artefacts and graves in the area show Irbid has been inhabited since the Bronze Age, the city has little to offer the visitor. However, it's the best place in northern Jordan for accommodation, restaurants and transport, and makes a handy base for day trips to Umm Qais, Al-Himma springs at Mukheiba, Ajlun and Jerash; it is also a good staging post while travelling to or from the Syrian border, via Ramtha.

With a population of about 500,000, Irbid is Jordan's second-largest city and boasts a large university campus, with fast-food restaurants, Internet centres and cafes nearby.

Information
Irbid has plenty of banks for changing money, eg ANZ Grindlays Bank, near the post office; Cairo-Amman Bank, opposite the Abu Baker Hotel; Bank of Jordan, on the 1st floor of the same building as the Abu Baker Hotel; and Arab Bank, across the road from Hotel al-Wahadat al-Arabiyya. Better are the moneychangers clustered around Hotel al-Wahadat al-Arabiyya, although some will not change travellers cheques.

The post office, on King Hussein St, is open from 7 am to 5 pm every day except Friday when it's open until 1.30 pm. The police station is above the market area, and offers great **views** of the city. The Royal Jordanian Airlines office (☎ 724 2333) is on the corner of King Hussein and Al-Jaish

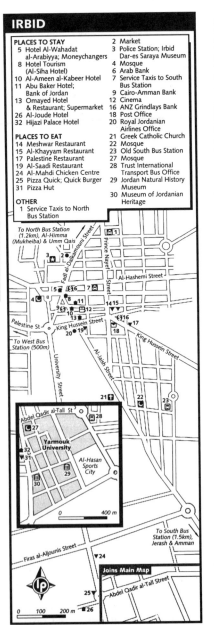

IRBID

PLACES TO STAY
5 Hotel Al-Wahadat
   al-Arabiyya; Moneychangers
8 Hotel Tourism
   (Al-Siha Hotel)
10 Al-Ameen al-Kabeer Hotel
11 Abu Baker Hotel;
   Bank of Jordan
13 Omayed Hotel
   & Restaurant; Supermarket
26 Al-Joude Hotel
32 Hijazi Palace Hotel

PLACES TO EAT
14 Meshwar Restaurant
15 Al-Khayyam Restaurant
17 Palestine Restaurant
19 Al-Saadi Restaurant
24 Al-Mahdi Chicken Centre
25 Pizza Quick; Quick Burger
31 Pizza Hut

OTHER
1 Service Taxis to North
   Bus Station

2 Market
3 Police Station; Irbid
   Dar-es Saraya Museum
4 Mosque
6 Arab Bank
7 Service Taxis to South
   Bus Station
9 Cairo-Amman Bank
12 Cinema
16 ANZ Grindlays Bank
18 Post Office
20 Royal Jordanian
   Airlines Office
21 Greek Catholic Church
22 Mosque
23 Old South Bus Station
27 Mosque
28 Trust International
   Transport Bus Office
29 Jordan Natural History
   Museum
30 Museum of Jordanian
   Heritage

To North Bus Station
(1.2km), Al-Himma
(Mukheiba) & Umm Qais

Fadil al-Dakamseh Street

Prince Nayef Street

Al-Hashemi Street

Palestine St

King Hussein Street

King Hussein Street

To West Bus
Station (500m)

University Street

Al-Jaish Street

Abdel Qadir al-Tall St

Yarmouk
University

Al-Hasan
Sports
City

0   400 m

To South Bus
Station (1.5km),
Jerash & Amman

Firas al-Aljounis Street

Joins Main Map

Abdel Qadir al-Tall Street

0 100 200 m

streets. Dozens of Internet centres are dotted along the southern end of University St. Internet access at any of these places costs about JD1 per hour, and less after about 9 pm.

Things to See & Do

There are two good museums in the grounds of the vast **Yarmouk University**. Foreigners are welcome to wander around the university, which also runs Arabic language courses (see Courses in the Facts for the Visitor chapter.)

Museum of Jordanian Heritage (☎ 727 1100) features exhibits of ancient stone implements, coins, pottery and other handicrafts, and a reconstructed courtyard typical of northern Jordan. The explanations are in English, and the displays are generally superior to those in the National Archaeological Museum in Amman. It is open from 10 am to 5 pm every day except Tuesday, and entrance is free.

Jordan Natural History Museum (☎ 727 1100) contains a range of mildly interesting stuffed animals, birds and insects, as well as rocks from the region, but very little is explained in English. The museum is in a huge green hangar, and is open from 10 am to 5 pm every day except Tuesday, and entrance is free.

Next to the police station, the **Irbid Dar-es Saraya Museum** is currently being developed, and should be open soon. The public are welcome at the **Al-Hasan Sports City**, adjacent to the university. It has a swimming pool (JD1 entrance), and squash courts and pool tables are available for hire.

Places to Stay – Budget

There are a few basic hotels in the busy downtown area, all along the far north-western end of Al-Jaish St. The best are the four listed below. They are all pretty much the same standard and mostly the same set price: JD5/8/10.500 for singles/doubles/triples with a shared bathroom (a hot shower costs an extra 500 fils). All will reduce the rate by about JD1/2/3 per night with a little friendly persuasion.

Hotel al-Wahadat al-Arabiyya (☎ 724 2083) is friendly and has large, clean and simple rooms (some with huge old lounge chairs). Inside the foyer, there's a tiny indoor tent for sipping tea – a bit silly really, but the idea is nice.

Hotel Tourism (☎ 724 2633) – also known as *Al-Siha Hotel* – is pretty much the same as the others, but the rooms are noisier.

Al-Ameen al-Kabeer Hotel (☎ 724 2384) is slightly better than the other two mentioned above. It has clean and bright doubles/triples (no singles) for JD8/10.500. The staff are friendly, and speak good English.

Abu Baker Hotel (☎ 724 2695), upstairs in the Bank of Jordan building, has rooms with sweeping views of central Irbid. It also offers dorm-style beds for only JD2.

Omayed Hotel (☎ 724 5955, King Hussein St) is on the 2nd floor of the Jordan Arab Investment Bank building. It's the best of the budget range and worth the splurge. The rooms are sunny and clean, have a private bathroom and fan, and cost a negotiable JD15.400/20 for singles/doubles. It was described by one reader as having the 'friendliest staff in Jordan'.

Places to Stay – Mid-Range

Al-Joude Hotel (☎ 727 5515, fax 727 5517), about 100m down a lane off University St, offers very nice singles/doubles with private bathroom, satellite TV and air-con, for a negotiable JD30/42. It's in a nice quiet area, and has an attached *cafe* and **craft shop**.

Hijazi Palace Hotel (☎ 727 9500, fax 727 9520, University St), opposite the University, offers overpriced but well-appointed rooms for JD40/50, including breakfast.

Places to Eat

There is a huddle of *felafel and shwarma stands* around the centre of town, and an excellent *supermarket* in the basement of the same building as the Omayed Hotel.

A few of the cheap eateries include: *Meshwar Restaurant*, near the post office, which does all sorts of tasty sandwiches; *Palestine Restaurant (King Hussein St)*, which offers fairly standard fare and doubles as a tearoom serving alcohol; *Al-Saadi Restaurant (King Hussein St)*; and *Al-Khayyam Restaurant*, near the Meshwar,

which is more of a bar than anything else, but does serve reasonable meals.

Omayed Restaurant, in the hotel of the same name, is the classiest place in town. It has a menu in English, the best views of Irbid (although this is nothing to get too excited about) and excellent service. A tasty main course, plus soup and salad, costs about JD2.

Along the southern end of University Street is a plethora of western-style fast food joints: *Pizza Quick* and *Quick Burger* offer pizzas for about JD2 and hamburgers from 500 fils; *Pizza Hut* is trendy and popular; and *Al-Mahdi Chicken Centre* is more reasonably priced, with chicken meals for about JD1.200.

Getting There & Away

Irbid is 85km north of Amman, and easy to reach from just about anywhere in Jordan. It has three main bus/minibus stations (most visitors can safely ignore the Old South bus station which serves local villages).

From the North bus station, minibuses go to Umm Qais (200 fils, 45 minutes); Mukheiba (300 fils, one hour), for Al-Himma springs; and Quwayliba (150 fils, 25 minutes), for the ruins of Abila.

From the large South bus station – or New Amman bus station *(mujama Amman al-jadeed)* – air-conditioned Hijazi buses (850 fils, 90 minutes) leave every 15 to 20 minutes until about 6.30 pm for Amman (Abdali bus station). To Amman (Abdali), there are other less comfortable buses and minibuses (both 650 fils, about two hours) and plenty of service taxis (850 fils). From the South station in Irbid, minibuses also go to Ajlun (270 fils, 45 minutes) and Jerash (300 fils, 45 minutes), as well as to Zubia, Zarqa and Mafraq.

From the West bus station, just off Palestine St, minibuses go to Al-Mashari'a (300 fils, 45 minutes) for the ruins at Pella; and other places in the Jordan Valley, such as Shuneh ash-Shamaliyyeh (North Shuna).

Syria From the South bus station, service taxis go to Damascus; the trip takes three to four hours (depending on border formalities) and costs JD4. From the same station, service taxis, and less frequent minibuses, go to Ramtha village, from where plenty of other service taxis and minibuses go to the Syrian border. Refer to Syria in the Land section of the Getting There & Away chapter for more information about crossing the border to Syria.

Israel Regular service taxis leave the West bus station for the border at Sheikh Hussein Bridge. The trip takes about 50 minutes, and costs about 500 fils per person. Alternatively, charter a taxi from Irbid to the border for about JD3, or catch anything to Shuneh ash-Shamaliyyeh (North Shuna) or Al-Mashari'a, and then something else to the border. Most travellers find it easier, however, to use the King Hussein Bridge further south.

From the Trust International Transport office (☎ 725 1878), near the Al-Hasan Sports City, buses leave every morning for Haifa (Israel), via Nazareth, for JD8.500.

Refer to Israel in the Land section of the Getting There & Away chapter for more information about crossing the border to Israel.

Getting Around
Irbid is a transit point for most places in northern Jordan, and it's possible to travel to Irbid, and get from one bus station to the other, without getting caught up in the town. For about 100 fils, service taxis and mini-buses run between all the stations and the middle of town. Service taxis leave from along Prince Nayef St to the North bus station, or it's a 20-minute walk from the town centre. From anywhere along Al-Jaish and Al-Hashemi streets, service taxis go to the South (New Amman) bus station, and Yarmouk University, for about 80 fils.

Few of the private yellow taxis use meters; the standard price for anyone, including locals, for most trips around town is 500 fils.

ABILA (QUWAYLIBA)
أبيلا(قويلبا)

Possibly one of the Decapolis cities (see the boxed text in the Amman chapter), the ancient city of Abila was built some time in the Early Bronze Age (about 3000 BC) between two small hills, Tell Abila and Tell Umm-al-Amad.

There is little to see, however, because what was left after the earthquake in 747 AD remains largely unexcavated. Nothing is labelled or set up for visitors, but there are enough **tombs** and eerie **caves** dotted around the fields to interest archaeology buffs. The **theatre** is fairly obviously carved out of the hill, and there are also some **columns** from markets, temples and baths lying around the place.

Entrance is free, and it's open every day during daylight hours. The site is close to the village of Quwayliba, about 15km north of Irbid. Buses leave from the North bus station in Irbid (150 fils, 25 minutes) for Quwayliba; ask the driver to drop you off at the ruins.

RAMTHA
الرمثا

One of the main businesses in this dreary town close to the Syrian border is smuggling (eg cigarettes and alcohol from Syria). There is no need to linger, except to catch onward transport, and there's nowhere to stay, so keep going.

It's best to get direct transport between the border and Irbid or Amman, without stopping in Ramtha. Minibuses and service taxis (both 500 fils, two hours) leave Abdali bus station in Amman for Ramtha, and often go as far as the border, but start early from Amman because most transport has left by 10 am. Plenty of minibuses and service taxis travel between the border and Ramtha.

Refer to Syria in the Land section of the Getting There & Away chapter for more information regarding crossing the border to or from Syria.

UMM QAIS
أم قيس
☎ 02

In the far north-west corner of Jordan are the ruins of another ancient town, Gadara (now called Umm Qais). The ruins are interesting and remote enough to make the effort, and the site offers awesome (but often hazy) views over the Golan Heights in Syria and the Sea of Galilee (Lake Tiberias) in Israel to the north, and the Jordan Valley to the south.

The ancient town of Gadara was captured from the Ptolemies by the Seleucids in 198 BC, and then the Jews under Hyrcanus cap-

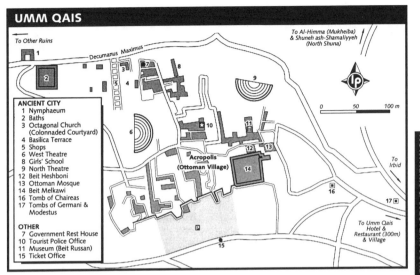

UMM QAIS

To Other Ruins

Decumanus Maximus

To Al-Himma (Mukheiba)
& Shuneh ash-Shamaliyyeh
(North Shuna)

0   50   100 m

To
Irbid

ANCIENT CITY
1 Nymphaeum
2 Baths
3 Octagonal Church
   (Colonnaded Courtyard)
4 Basilica Terrace
5 Shops
6 West Theatre
8 Girls' School
9 North Theatre
12 Beit Heshboni
13 Ottoman Mosque
14 Beit Melkawi
16 Tomb of Chaireas
17 Tombs of Germani &
    Modestus

OTHER
7 Government Rest House
10 Tourist Police Office
11 Museum (Beit Russan)
15 Ticket Office

Acropolis
(Ottoman Village)

To Umm Qais
Hotel &
Restaurant (300m)
& Village

tured it from them in 100 BC. When the Romans (led by Pompey) conquered the east and the Decapolis was formed, the fortunes of Gadara, taken from the Jews in 63 BC, increased rapidly and building was undertaken on a typically large scale.

The Nabataeans controlled the trade routes as far north as Damascus. This interference with Rome's interests led Mark Antony to send Herod the Great to conquer them. He failed to do this completely, but did wrest a sizable chunk of territory from them in 31 BC. Herod was given Gadara following a naval victory and he ruled over it until his death in 4 BC – much to the disgust of the locals who had tried everything, in vain, to put him out of favour with Rome. On his death, the city reverted to semi-autonomy as part of the Roman province of Syria.

With the downfall of the Nabataean kingdom in 106 AD, Gadara continued to flourish, and was the seat of a bishopric until the 7th century. By the time of the Muslim conquest, however, it was little more than a small village. In 1806, Gadara was 'discovered' by western explorers, but excavations did not commence until 1982 when locals were finally repatriated to Umm Qais village.

Information

Some visitors enter the site from the western end of the car park, but if you start from the eastern side you will walk past most things in chronological order (more or less), ie from the more recent ruins of the Acropolis (Ottoman village) going further back in time as you head west.

Nothing much is signposted in any language, so you'll have to use the map in this book to make any sense of the place. The brochure about Umm Qais published by the Jordan Tourism Board is also useful, and contains photos; it should be available in the museum. *Umm Qais: Gadara of the Decapolis*, published by Al-Kutba (JD3), is ideal for anyone who wants further information.

There are some toilets in the Government Rest House, and a tourist police office along a laneway to the museum.

The Ruins

Around the eastern entrance from the main road are several pretty, but empty, tombs, ie the **Tomb of Germani**, and, nearby, the

NORTHERN & WESTERN JORDAN

Tomb of Modestus. About 100m further west, the **Tomb of Chaireas** clearly dates to 154 AD.

The first thing to see (if coming from the east) is the **acropolis**, the ruins of an Ottoman village dating from the 18th and 19th centuries. Inside are two houses, **Beit Melkawi** (now used as an office for archaeological groups), and the nearby **Beit Heshboni**. In the south-east corner is the **Ottoman mosque**, and in the far north the remains of the **girls' school**.

Also in the Acropolis, but accessible from the Government Rest House if you follow the signs, is **Beit Russan** house, a former residence of an Ottoman governor, and now the **museum** (☎ 721 7211). The museum is open from 9 am to 5 pm every day except Tuesday, and is set around a quaint and shady courtyard. One of the mosaics on display, a 4th century example found in a mausoleum, is among the most interesting exhibits, overshadowed perhaps by the headless, white marble statue of a goddess that was found sitting in the front row of the West Theatre. Please note: photos are not allowed inside the rooms.

North-east of the Acropolis is the **north theatre**, but little remains because the black basalt rocks were used for other buildings by villagers. From there, head west along the **decumanus maximus**, the main road which once linked Umm Qais with other nearby ancient cities, such as Abila and Pella, and eventually reached the Mediterranean coast.

West of the Government Rest House is the **basilica terrace** complex, about 95m by 30m. The western section housed a row of **shops**, but the most interesting remains are of the 16th-century **octagonal church**, also known as the **colonnaded courtyard**, recognisable by its unusual eight-sided base.

To the south is the well-restored **west theatre**, which once provided seating for about 3000 people. Like the north theatre, it was also made from black basalt and now provides incredible **views** out over the Sea of Galilee. West along the decumanus maximus, are the overgrown **baths**. Built in the 4th century, there was an impressive complex of fountains and baths, but little re-

mains after the various earthquakes. Virtually opposite, the decrepit **nymphaeum** was probably adorned with statues and fountains, but some scholars believe it may have had some different (but unknown) function.

The decumanus maximus continues west for another 1km or so, leading to some very limited ruins of **baths**, **mausoleums** and **gates**. Most are beyond repair or not excavated, and probably not worth too much effort to reach and explore.

The site is open every day from 8 am to late in the evening (depending on the number of customers dining in the Government Rest House); and the entrance fee is JD1. The glow over the site, and the views from it, are wonderful in the late afternoon, so try to time your visit accordingly if you have your own transport, or stay overnight.

Places to Stay & Eat
Umm Qais Hotel (☎ 750 0080, fax 242 313) is a comfortable place, and easy to find in the village. It has clean, quiet and sunny singles/doubles for JD6/8 with shared bathroom facilities; and JD8/16 with a private bathroom (but unreliable hot water). It also has a small *restaurant*.

A few basic *eateries* are scattered around the village; otherwise, buy food in one of the shops and enjoy a *picnic* among the ruins.

Government Rest House (☎ 750 0555), inside the ruins, is a pleasant place to rest weary bones, but it caters mainly to packaged tours, and the menu is limited and expensive, eg roast chicken is JD3.600, and a mixed grill, JD6. Still, it is worth visiting for the outstanding views.

Getting There & Away
Umm Qais village, and the ruins a few hundred metres to the west, are about 25km north-west of Irbid, and about 110km north of Amman. (The site is often signposted along the roads as 'Om Qeis'.) No public transport directly links Umm Qais with Amman, but minibuses regularly leave the North bus station in Irbid (200 fils, 45 minutes) for Umm Qais. Keep your passport handy for possible military checkpoints along the way.

AL-HIMMA (MUKHEIBA)

☎ 02　　　　　(الحمى) مخيبا

The Al-Himma hot springs in the village of Mukheiba are literally a stone's throw from the border with Israel. The area is generally lush, in stark contrast to the bare, steeply rising plateau of the Israeli-occupied Golan to the north, although very hot in the summer. The springs, which reach about 33°C, were famous in Roman times for their health-giving properties, and are still used today.

Mukheiba is a pleasant village, and the springs are worth a day trip from Irbid; better still, stay overnight. Some readers have told of annoying kids begging in the village, and giant wasps in the area, so beware.

Hot Springs

In Mukheiba village, there are a few private baths with mixed swimming and bathing. The entrance fee to these private places is usually negotiable.

The public baths complex run by the Jordanian Hot Springs Company (☎ 750 0505) has separate bathing times for men and women. The complex is open from 2 to 8 pm every day – and until later if there's enough demand. However, avoid Friday when this place is crowded with visitors from Irbid and Amman. Entrance to the public baths costs JD1.100, and it's easy to find in the village.

Places to Stay & Eat

The *chalets* (☎ 750 0505) overlooking the public baths cost JD8.800 per person, and are good value, although a little noisy when the baths are busy. *Apartments*, suitable for three people or a small family, cost JD27 per night.

Sah al-Noum Hotel (☎ 750 0510) has clean, simple and bright singles/doubles, with a private bathroom and fan, for JD10/12, including breakfast. A large, shady *restaurant* at the back is open for guests and the public, and the manager has access to a superb private bathing area nearby. The hotel is well signposted from the entrance to the village.

Jordan Himeh Restaurant (☎ 750 0512), also overlooking the public baths, offers welcoming cold drinks (eg a large beer for JD1.500) and meals from JD2.500.

Getting There & Away

Mukheiba (also spelt Mukhaybeh) is about 10km north of Umm Qais, and down the hill towards the Golan. Public transport between Umm Qais and Mukheiba is not regular, but there is usually something – ask at the hotels in either place. Alternatively, hitch a ride, or go back to Irbid (North bus station) and get a direct minibus (300 fils, one hour) from there to Mukheiba.

The village is well signposted along the roads north of Jordan; follow the signs to 'Al-Himma', which means 'the springs' in Arabic. On the northern edge of Umm Qais, along the road to Mukheiba, there's a military checkpoint (a good place to hitch a ride), so keep your passport ready. There is another checkpoint at the entrance to Mukheiba, where there is an entrance fee of 300 fils per person (demanded by the villagers).

SHUNEH ASH-SHAMALIYYEH (NORTH SHUNA)　شونه الشمالية

This junction town (also known as North Shuna) has little to offer, and there's nowhere to stay, but it does boast another **hot springs** complex. These springs aren't nearly as nice as the ones at Mukheiba, but they are often more popular with locals because it's cheaper (500 fils) to enter.

There are simple *chalets* (☎ 02-658 7189) in the complex for JD4 per person, and a shady *restaurant*, but the sulphur smell makes this far less pleasant for staying and eating than Mukheiba. The complex is open from 8 am to 9 pm every day and signposted as 'Touristic Spa Hot Springs'.

Shuneh ash-Shamaliyyeh is accessible by minibus from Amman (Abdali bus station) and Irbid (West bus station), and has connections to anywhere along the Jordan Valley road (Highway 65), eg Al-Mashari'a (for Pella) and Deir Alla.

PELLA (TABAQAT FAHL)　بيلا

In the midst of the Jordan Valley are the ruins of the ancient city of Pella (known locally as Tabaqat Fahl), one of the ten cities of the Decapolis (see the boxed text in the Amman chapter). Although not as spectacular as Jerash, Pella is far more important to

NORTHERN & WESTERN JORDAN

archaeologists because it has revealed evidence of life from the Stone Age through to medieval Islamic times.

The ruins are interesting enough, but they are a little hard to reach without private transport, and the buildings are fairly decrepit and spread out, so some walking and imagination are needed. But the setting is pretty, and there are places to stay and eat close by.

History

Although the site was inhabited from as early as 5000 BC, and Egyptian texts make several references to it in the 2nd millennium BC, Pella really only flourished in the Greek and Roman periods. Pella followed the fate of many other cities in the region, coming successively under the rule of the Ptolemies, Seleucids and Jews.

The city reached its peak during the Byzantine era, and by 451 AD Pella had its own bishop. The population at this time may have been as high as 25,000. The defeat of the Byzantines by the invading Islamic armies near Pella in 635 was quickly followed by the knockout blow at the Battle of Yarmouk the next year.

Until the massive earthquake that shook the whole region in 747, Pella continued to prosper under the Umayyads. Archaeological finds show that even after the earthquake the city remained inhabited on a modest scale. The Mamluks occupied it in the 13th and 14th centuries, but afterwards Pella was virtually abandoned. The ruins were 'discovered' by western explorers in 1852, but excavations did not start in earnest until 1967.

Anyone with any specific interest should buy *Pella*, published by Al-Kutba (JD3), and available in major bookshops in Jordan.

The Ruins

The Byzantine **west church**, recognisable by the three standing columns, was built in the 6th century. The **main mound** comprises the ruins of many residences, shops, storehouses and the like, built and used mainly during the Umayyad period. Also, on top of the hill are the remains of a 14th century **Mamluk mosque**.

The main structure remaining is the Byzantine **civic complex church**, built in the 5th century, and modified several times in the subsequent two centuries. Adjacent, is the small, 1st century **odeon** (theatre). It once held about 400 spectators, and is now the best preserved building in Pella. Just east of the civic complex church are the

Part of the marble screen which separated the chancel from the nave and the trancepts in a church at Pella

CHRIS BARTON

PATRICK SYDER

DAMIEN SIMONIS

PAUL GREENWAY

The ancient city of Jerash was mainly buried under sand until its excavation in the 1920s which accounts for the good condition of many of its buildings, notably the Oval Forum and Cardo Maximus (top & middle), the Temple of Artemis (bottom left) and the Nymphaeum (bottom right).

PATRICK SYDER

OLIVIER CIRENDINI

OLIVIER CIRENDINI

DAMIEN SIMONIS

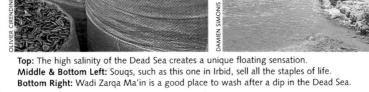

Top: The high salinity of the Dead Sea creates a unique floating sensation.
Middle & Bottom Left: Souqs, such as this one in Irbid, sell all the staples of life.
Bottom Right: Wadi Zarqa Ma'in is a good place to wash after a dip in the Dead Sea.

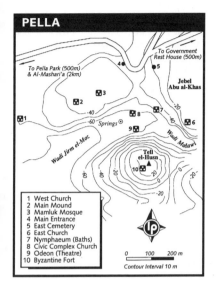

PELLA

To Government
Rest House (500m)

To Pella Park (500m)
& Al-Mashari'a (2km)

Jebel
Abu al-Khas

Springs

Wadi Jirm el-Moz

Wadi Malawi

Tell
el-Husn

1 West Church
2 Main Mound
3 Mamluk Mosque
4 Main Entrance
5 East Cemetery
6 East Church
7 Nymphaeum (Baths)
8 Civic Complex Church
9 Odeon (Theatre)
10 Byzantine Fort

0   100   200 m

Contour Interval 10 m

MARGARET JUNG

**Corinthian column capital from the civic
complex church at Pella**

remains of the Roman **nymphaeum** (baths);
and farther east again, perched up on a rise,
is the 5th-century **east church**, which still
has four columns standing. To the south is
Tell al-Husn, on the top of which are the
now completely unrecognisable ruins of a
Byzantine fort.

The small entrance is about 700m below
the Government Rest House, and accessible
from it or from the main road by foot; the
entrance and site are well signposted in
English. Entrance is free, but visitors are
often accosted by local girls and boys hoping to sell some tacky souvenirs.

Places to Stay & Eat
Government Rest House (☎ 06-464 4227)
is the huge building (recognisable by the
three arches) about 700m up the hill from
the entrance. It caters mainly to tour groups,
but independent travellers are welcome.
Meals cost about JD5 and the views of Pella
are superb.

Pella Park, about 100m off the road to
Pella and about 500m from the entrance to
the ruins, has two small, but adequate,
rooms which cost JD10/15 for singles/
doubles, including breakfast. Cold and hot

drinks, and simple meals, are also available
in the small *restaurant*. The best thing
about this place is the swimming pool,
which is open to the public for JD1.

There is nowhere to stay in Al-Mashari'a,
the nearest village to Pella, but it has plenty
of shops and cheap *restaurants*, and the
Housing Bank can change money.

Getting There & Away
From Irbid (West bus station), catch a
minibus to Al-Mashari'a (300 fils, 45 minutes), the nearest village to Pella along the
Jordan Valley road (Highway 65). From
Amman, there is nothing direct, so get a
connection at Irbid. Minibuses also go up
and down the Jordan Valley road between
Shuneh ash-Shamaliyyeh (North Shuna)
and Shuneh al-Janubiyyeh (South Shuna),
and stop at Al-Mashari'a.

The turn-off to Pella is about 1.5km north
of Al-Mashari'a, and easy to spot from the
main road. Pella is a steep 2km walk up
from the turn-off, which can be punishing in
summer, so charter a taxi in Al-Mashari'a or
Shuneh ash-Shamaliyyeh.

DEIR ALLA   دير علا
Deir Alla was first settled in the 3rd century
BC, but later abandoned. After the Islamic
invasion in the 7th century AD, it served as
a cemetery for nearby villages.

Deir Alla is of some minor historical and
religious importance to scholars, but other
than a small **museum** (☎ 05-573 136), there
is little else to see. The site can be combined
with Pella in a day trip from Irbid or Ajlun,

but most visitors would be satisfied enough with the more interesting ruins at Pella. A notice board at the base of the ruins has some limited explanations.

Deir Alla is 35km north of Shuneh al-Janubiyyeh (South Shuna), and to the left (west) of the main road heading north. Getting there from Amman is not easy; it's best to charter a taxi from Jerash or Ajlun, or go by minibus via Shuneh ash-Shamaliyyeh.

TELL AL-KHARRAR   تل الخرار

Tell al-Kharrar (also known as Wadi Kharrar) is an important Christian site (see the special section 'Biblical Jordan' in the Facts about Jordan chapter). It was hitherto off-limits because of its proximity to the Jordan/Israel border, and the number of landmines in the area. However, authorities are busy building a visitors centre, a series of walkways around the site and a new road in time for the pilgrimages in 2000.

Things to See

Over 20 important Christian sites have been uncovered in the area, including the Byzantine **Bathabara Monastery**, built in about the 6th century AD to commemorate St John. The monastery once contained a complex system of mills which channelled water, presumably for the multitude of baptisms taking place. Artefacts from the region indicate that the monastery dates back to at least the early Roman period (circa 1st century AD).

The countryside surrounding the site may soon become part of the Jordan River Reserve (see the National Parks section in the Facts about Jordan chapter for details).

The Jordan Valley

Forming part of the Great Rift Valley of Africa, the fertile valley of the Jordan River was of considerable significance in Biblical times and is now the food bowl of Jordan.

The river rises from several sources, mainly the Anti-Lebanon Range in Syria, and flows down into the Sea of Galilee (Lake Tiberias), 212m below sea level, before draining into the Dead Sea which is the lowest point on earth. The actual length of the river is 360km, but as the crow flies the distance between its source and the Dead Sea is only 200km.

In this valley some 10,000 years ago, people first started to plant crops and abandon their nomadic lifestyle for permanent settlements. Villages were built, primitive irrigation schemes were undertaken and by 3000 BC produce from the valley was being exported to neighbouring regions. The river itself is also highly revered by Christians because Christ was baptised by St John in its waters.

Since 1948, the Jordan River has marked the boundary between Israel and Jordan from the Sea of Galilee to the Yarbis River. From there to the Dead Sea, the river marked the 1967 cease-fire line between the two countries (but since the two sides signed a peace agreement in 1994 it instead marks the continuation of the official frontier).

During the 1967 war with Israel, Jordan lost the land it had annexed in 1950, the area known as the West Bank, now partly under Israeli control and partial administration of the Palestine National Authority. The population on the east bank of the valley dwindled from 60,000 before the war to 5000 by 1971. During the 1970s, new roads and fully serviced villages were built and the population has now soared to over 100,000. There are no cities along the river course, although the ancient city of Pella (Tabaqat Fahl) used to occupy a commanding position on the eastern bank.

The hot dry summers and short mild winters make for ideal growing conditions, and (subject to water restrictions) two or three crops a year are grown. Thousands of tonnes of fruit and vegetables are produced annually, with the main crops being tomatoes, cucumbers, melons and citrus fruits. The introduction of portable plastic greenhouses saw a sevenfold increase in productivity and this has meant that Jordan can now afford to export large amounts of its produce to surrounding countries.

Getting There & Away

Tell al-Kharrar is about halfway between the road from Amman to King Hussein Bridge and the road from Amman to Suweimeh. There will be little or no public transport directly to the site, so hitch a ride at the turn-off to the site from along the Amman-King Hussein Bridge road or charter a taxi from Shuneh al-Janubiyyeh (South Shuna).

SHUNEH AL-JANUBIYYEH (SOUTH SHUNA) شونا الجنوبية

This nondescript town is simply a junction for public transport to the Dead Sea, Tell al-Kharrar and Deir Alla. The town is well connected by minibus with Al-Quds St station in Amman (400 fils, one hour), as well as with Madaba and Salt.

There are a few cheap *restaurants* in town, and places to buy food for a picnic. Because of the limited public transport in the area, chartering a taxi from Shuneh al-Janubiyyeh to visit several sites in a few hours is a good idea, and cheaper than chartering transport from Amman.

THE DEAD SEA البحر الميت
☎ 05

I visited the Dead Sea twice: once I stayed in the Dead Sea Rest House; and once I stayed outside it. My advice is to go to the Rest House. Without showers and clean water, it's the same as hell.
Leo Bouwman, Netherlands

Part of the border between Jordan and Israel goes through the Dead Sea, a lake with such high salinity that your body floats – drowning or sinking is a tricky feat. Swimming is also just about impossible because you're too high in the water to stroke properly, but of course you can always float on your back while reading the newspaper and have your picture taken. While paddling about you'll probably discover cuts you never knew you had, and if any water gets into your eyes, be prepared for a few minutes of agony.

The Jordanian authorities are developing the Dead Sea as a tourist attraction, but facilities are very limited. If you're going to Israel, the resorts on the western side at Ein Feshka (West Bank) and Ein Gedi (Israel) are better, so you may wish to save your time, money and energy and visit the Dead Sea from the western side.

Information

Try to avoid Friday and public holidays when the Dead Sea Rest House complex is in chaos and public transport is crowded; on any other day you may be floating around alone. Always take lots of water as the humidity and heat (over 40°C in summer) can be dehydrating, and there is little or no shade.

After a dip in the Dead Sea, you're left with a mighty uncomfortable, itchy coating of salt on your skin that you can't get off quickly enough. A shower (and shampoo!) afterwards is vital.

Most visitors (foreign and Jordanian) head for the Dead Sea Rest House complex on the north-eastern edge of the lake. The entrance fee of JD2.500 provides visitors with access to the lake, a partially shaded beach and – essentially – showers. The beach and showers are available from 6 am to sunset every day, but no swimming is allowed after dark.

A free **public beach** is located about 200m north of the Rest House, but this area is fairly dirty, the showers are unreliable and visitors are often hassled by locals. The alternative places to swim (float) in the lake, and wash afterwards, are the two hotels further south, and anywhere near the Zarqa springs. Elsewhere along the Dead Sea there is little privacy, transport is very limited, access is often difficult from the main road and factories producing potash and other nasty things pollute the water.

The facilities at the Dead Sea Spa Hotel are also open to the public, but cost JD7.500 per day. For this, visitors have access to a cleaner and quieter private beach, showers, changing rooms and the superb swimming pool.

An all-body Dead Sea 'mud pack' is supposed to do wonders for your skin. This costs about JD2 at the Rest House, but 'Mud Therapy' costs a lot more at the Dead Sea Spa Hotel. Women are advised to apply their own mud (or get the help of a close friend) rather than rely on male staff at the Rest House or hotels.

The Dead Sea

The Dead Sea – known locally as Al-Bahr al-Mayit or Bahr Lut (Sea of Lot) – is about 65km long and from 6 to 18km wide. Its main source is the Jordan River, but it has no outlet.

The name is apt because the incredibly high salt content (30%) is up to seven times saltier than the ocean, so plant and animal life is impossible – eleven species of bacteria survive, but no fish at all. The concentration of salt has nothing to do with the Dead Sea being below sea level; rather, it comes about because of the high evaporation rate which has, over the years, led to the build-up of salts.

The level of the Dead Sea has been falling by about 500cm every year for the past 20 years or more, mainly because there is no longer any regular inflow from the stagnant Jordan River, water is diverted from the sea for irrigation and evaporation is so high. The level has shrunk from 392 to 409m below sea level, and about 30% (approximately 300 sq km) of the original area has vanished. Some experts believe the lake may even dry up completely in 50 years. One way out of this mess is the mooted construction of a canal from the Red Sea down to the Dead Sea in order to raise the level of the Sea, and to create enough hydroelectricity along the way to power desalination plants in Israel and Jordan.

At the southern end of the lake, Jordanians are exploiting the high potash content of the mineral-rich water. Each day more than one million tonnes of water are pumped into vast evaporation ponds covering some 10,000 hectares. The concentrated potash salts are then refined at processing plants south of Safi. The project is now producing about four million tonnes of potash annually, making Jordan one of the world's largest producers.

The Dead Sea also contains various other minerals. Some are apparently excellent for health and skin, eg calcium and magnesium are good for allergies and bronchial infections; the pungent bromine helps with relaxation; iodine has a beneficial effect on certain glandular ailments; and bitumen improves the skin (and is good for making roads). Most souvenir shops in Jordan stock various 'Dead Sea' creams, lotions, gels and soaps, all of which contain extractions from the lake, thereby exacerbating the environmental damage.

Zarqa (Zara) Springs

ينابيع الزرقاء (زارا) الساخنة

The Zarqa (also called Zara) springs are where Wadi Zarqa Ma'in (the source of Hammamat Ma'in, near Madaba) joins the Dead Sea Highway.

This is probably the best free place for a float in the lake, because you can wash yourself afterwards at the springs. There is little or no privacy at these springs or the nearby Dead Sea, however, and women particularly should dress conservatively. Anyone with enough energy left may want to hike (about 10km) between Hammamat Ma'in and Zarqa springs (see Hiking in the Activities chapter).

Zarqa is about 15km south of the Dead Sea Rest House. Public transport along this part of the Dead Sea Highway is limited, so hitching is the only way of getting around if you don't have your own transport.

Places to Stay & Eat

The choice of hotels is limited, but this doesn't worry most visitors who day trip from Amman. The only reason to stay is to admire the sunset over the Dead Sea.

Anyone with a tent can *camp* for free at the public beach, about 200m north of the Dead Sea Rest House, but there is little privacy or safety. It's better to camp at the Rest House, which charges JD5 per person (plus JD2.500 entrance fee). If you don't have a tent, you can sleep in the open-air 'Bedouin-style' *tent* on a concrete floor for the same price.

Dead Sea Rest House (☎ 572 900, fax 546 112) is the resort at Suweimeh village, and where most visitors go for day trips. (See Around Amman map in the Amman chapter.) It offers comfortable, but unexciting, individual air-con family-style bungalows with a sitting room, TV and fridge (but no views) for JD30/35 for singles/doubles with breakfast; JD35/50 including breakfast and dinner. Set meals at the *restaurant* cost JD5 for guests and JD6 for the public; and buffets (about JD5) are usually available on Friday and public holidays.

About 5km south of the Rest House are two upmarket hotels. *Mövenpick Resort & Spa* (☎ 325 2030, fax 325 2020, email *dseamp@globalone.com.jo*) is the newest and grandest place on the Jordanian side of the lake. (See the Around Amman map in the Amman chapter.) The outside (but certainly not the inside) of the rooms resemble a 'typical' Bedouin village home. The rooms cost from JD120/145 in the low season to a whopping JD142/210 in the high season (about October to March). Prices include breakfast.

Dead Sea Spa Hotel (☎ 325 2002, fax 568 8100, email dssh@nets.com.jo), about 200m further south, charges JD100/120, including breakfast.

Getting There & Away

Buses & Minibuses About three minibuses (500 fils, 1¼ hours) a day link the Dead Sea Rest House complex with Amman (Al-Quds St station). It's probably easier to get a more frequent minibus (400 fils, one hour) from Amman (Al-Quds St), or from Madaba or Salt, to Shuneh al-Janubiyyeh (South Shuna), from where minibuses leave about every 30 minutes to the Dead Sea Rest House. (The last one leaves Shuneh al-Janubiyyeh for Amman at about 6 pm.) Alternatively, charter a taxi from Shuneh al-Janubiyyeh to the Rest House, or the other two hotels further south.

To the less interesting and developed southern areas of the Dead Sea, irregular minibuses go to Safi village from Karak and from Aqaba, along the Dead Sea Highway.

Hitching Hitching back to Amman from the Rest House is relatively easy; Friday and Sunday are the best days, although many cars are full. The military checkpoint at the junction of the Dead Sea Highway (Highway 65) and the road to the King Abdullah Bridge (Highway 40), just north of Suweimeh, is the best place to hail something down.

Chartered Taxi Taxis can be rented for about JD40 per day from Amman, and for far less from Shuneh al-Janubiyyeh. Chartering a taxi for the day is a bit pointless if you're only interested in a long and leisurely bathe at the Rest House, but chartering does allow you to swim (float) at secluded, free (but showerless) spots, explore more of the coastline, look for salt crystals, and tie in a trip to other places like Pella and the Zarqa Springs.

DEAD SEA HIGHWAY

The Dead Sea Highway (Highway 65) is the least used of the three main highways in southern Jordan, but it is a more interesting, and quicker, alternative to the Desert Highway if you're driving between Amman and Aqaba. There is little to see except the Dead Sea, however, and the road goes through desolate areas where camels seem to outnumber Bedouin shepherds. If you're driving, be aware that petrol stations, and places to eat, are few and far between.

From Amman, the road to the highway starts at Al-Quds St, heads through Na'ur and past the Dead Sea Rest House at Suweimeh. From Aqaba, the highway is easy to find if you follow the signs to the King's Highway Aqaba airport. The map in the chapter includes the places listed below.

Lot's Cave   كهف لوط

One of the few places to visit along the south-western side of Jordan is Lot's Cave, where Lot and his daughters took refuge (see the special section 'Biblical Jordan' in the Facts about Jordan chapter for more details). The cave is on top of a hill offering views of the Dead Sea, and nearby there's a small **Byzantine church** and what is purported to be the 'pillar of salt' referred to in the Bible.

The site is signposted from the highway, and private or chartered vehicles can drive almost to the cave. If relying on public transport, or hitching, be prepared for a long (3km), steep and hot walk up the hill to the cave from the highway. Check in with the building at the start of the road up the hill (1km east of the highway), because staff may be able to find you a chartered vehicle to the top. It's also possible to day trip from Karak; take a minibus to Safi from Karak, and look for the obvious turn-off.

South to Aqaba

Visible between the miserable towns of Umm Mathla and Ar-Risha is the small white **shrine** on top of Jebel Haroun (see Hiking in the Getting Around section of the Petra chapter for details). Note: there is no access by road or on foot between the Dead Sea Highway and Petra.

The last turn-off before Aqaba is to **Gharandal**, obvious by the bizarre **Chinese pagoda** which is now a military checkpoint. The highway continues to Aqaba, and past the airport and the turn-off to the border with Israel.

Eastern Jordan

الأردن الشرقي

To the east of Amman, the stony desert rolls on to Iraq and Saudi Arabia. The region is cut by the Trans Arabia Pipeline and the highway to Iraq, and if not for these, eastern Jordan would probably be left alone to the Bedouin.

Apart from the transport junction towns of Azraq, Mafraq, Zarqa and Safawi, there are no towns to speak of. The main attractions for visitors are the castles and forts collectively known as the desert castles, which dot the inhospitable land, and the Azraq and Shaumari wildlife reserves. Public transport is limited in eastern Jordan, so travelling around in a chartered taxi or rented car is a popular, and often necessary, alternative.

ZARQA
الزرقاء

The third largest city (after Amman and Irbid) in Jordan is Zarqa, now virtually part of the ugly urban sprawl of northern Amman. There is nothing to see or do, or anywhere to stay in the city, but anyone travelling around eastern and northern Jordan may end up in Zarqa waiting for onward transport.

There are two terminals for buses, minibuses and service taxis. All forms of transport from Raghadan and Abdali bus stations in Amman (about 200 fils, 30 minutes), and places near Amman such as Salt and Madaba, use the New (Amman) station. From the Old station in Zarqa, there is public transport to smaller villages in the region, eg Hallabat (for Qasra al-Hallabat and Hammam Sarah nearby), Mafraq and Azraq. Minibuses travel between the two terminals in Zarqa every few minutes.

MAFRAQ
المفرق

Despite appearances on some maps, Mafraq is much smaller than Zarqa. There is nothing to see and nowhere to stay, but travellers heading to eastern Jordan may need to go there for onward transport.

Like Zarqa, Mafraq has two terminals for buses, minibuses and service taxis: the larger Bedouin station has minibuses and service

HIGHLIGHTS

- **Umm al-Jimal** – more eerie than spectacular, these ruins are worth exploring for their remote setting (see page 168)

- **Qasr al-Azraq** – the most accessible, and one of the more interesting, desert castles has a fascinating link to the enigmatic TE Lawrence (see page 176)

- **Qusayr Amra** – one of the best preserved desert castles is plastered with wonderful – and risque – frescoes (see page 176)

- **Qasr Kharana** – seemingly lost in the middle of the desert, this mighty two storey fort has been well restored (see page 178)

EASTERN JORDAN

taxis to most places, eg Abdali and Raghadan bus stations in Amman (250 fils, one hour), Salt, Zarqa, Madaba, Umm al-Jimal, Deir al-Kahf (for Qasr Deir al-Kahf) and Ruwayshid (for Burqu). From the Fellahin station, buses, minibuses and service taxis go to places in northern Jordan, eg Jerash and Irbid, and Ramtha and Jabir on the border with Syria.

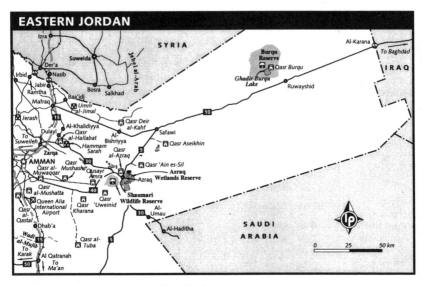

UMM AL-JIMAL أم الجمال

Umm al-Jimal ('Mother of Camels') has been more aptly described as 'eerie' rather than spectacular – eg there are no grand temples or theatres like in Jerash. Much of what remains at this large site (800m by 500m) is unpretentious urban architecture: over 150 simple buildings, including 128 houses and 15 churches, have been identified and named.

Comparatively little is known about the strange, black city of Umm al-Jimal, but it does provide a fascinating insight into rural life during the Roman, Byzantine and early Islamic periods.

It was prosperous for a long time because of its sophisticated method of storing water. Although mostly in ruins, many of the buildings are still discernible because, compared to others at the time, the city was rarely looted or vandalised, and superior materials were used in its construction – Umm al-Jimal is notable for the 'cobelling' method of constructing roofs from large bricks of black basalt.

History

Umm al-Jimal was probably founded in the 1st century BC by the Nabataeans, but was quickly taken over by the Romans, who used it as part of their defensive line. Roads lead north to Bosra (in present-day Syria) and south-west to Philadelphia (modern Amman), and because it served as an important trading station for Bedouins and passing caravans, Umm al-Jimal prospered. The city grew during the Byzantine period, and churches were constructed and some Roman buildings were demilitarised.

The boom time was in the early Islamic period when this thriving agricultural city boasted about 3000 inhabitants. However, Umm al-Jimal declined soon after following the invasion by the Sassanians from Persia in the early 7th century AD; the city never recovered from an earthquake in 747. The ruins were occupied by Druze refugees fleeing persecution in Syria early in the 20th century, and as an outpost by French soldiers during WWI.

Information

It's a good idea to allow several hours to explore the ruins. Visit early in the morning, or late in the afternoon, when the light shines dramatically on the black basalt and it's not too hot (there is precious little shade).

For more details about the site, pick up the booklet *Umm el-Jimal* (JD3), published by Al-Kutba, and available at most major bookshops in the larger cities of Jordan. The site is open every day during daylight hours. Currently, there is no entrance fee, but this will probably change when the visitors centre and museum are built (no further details were available at the time of research).

Things to See

The large structure just past the southern entrance is the **barracks**, built by the Romans. The two towers were added about 100 years later and, like the castle at Azraq, the door is made of basalt and still functions. The **barracks chapel** was added to the east of the Barracks during the Byzantine period (around the 5th century). About 150m to the left (west) of the Barracks is what some archaeologists believe is a **Nabataean temple** because of the altar in the middle.

About 100m north of the barracks is the **numerianos church**, one of several very decrepit ruins of Byzantine churches. Another 100m to the north-east is the **double church**, a really wonderful structure which has been renovated and extended several times over the centuries. About 80m to the right (east) is **house XVII**, with elaborate gates and an arch leading to a courtyard, presumably once built by a wealthy man. A few metres to the south is the **sheikh's house**, which is notable for its expansive courtyard, stables and stairways.

Heading north, and about 150m north of the Double Church, is the **main reservoir**, one of several oval-shaped water storage facilities around the city. Less than 100m to the left (south-west) is **house XIII**, originally a stable for domestic goats and sheep, and later renovated and used as a residence by Druze settlers.

To the west (about 100m) is the **cathedral**, built in about 556 AD, but mostly in ruins. The **praetorium** (military headquarters) is less than 100m to the south-west. Built in the late 2nd century AD by the Romans, it was extended by the Byzantines, and features a triple doorway.

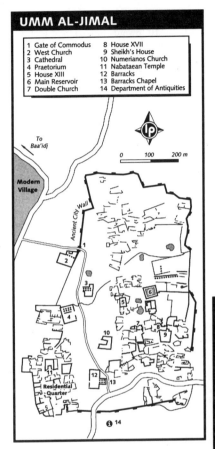

UMM AL-JIMAL

1 Gate of Commodus	8 House XVII
2 West Church	9 Sheikh's House
3 Cathedral	10 Numerianos Church
4 Praetorium	11 Nabataean Temple
5 House XIII	12 Barracks
6 Main Reservoir	13 Barracks Chapel
7 Double Church	14 Department of Antiquities

About 200m to the north is the **west church**, easily identifiable with its four arches and Byzantine crosses.

Getting There & Away

Umm al-Jimal is only about 10km from the Syrian border, and about 20km east of Mafraq. With an early start, it is possible to day trip from Amman by public transport. From the Abdali or Raghadan bus stations in Amman, catch a bus or minibus to Bedouin station in Mafraq (possibly with a connection in Zarqa), and from Mafraq another minibus to Umm al-Jimal (200 fils, 30 minutes).

EASTERN JORDAN

If driving, head east of Mafraq along Highway 10 towards Safawi, and look for the turn-off heading north to Umm al-Jimal. If you have chartered a taxi from Amman for a day trip around the desert castles, it is possible to include Umm al-Jimal on the itinerary for a little extra (maybe JD5) – but start early to fit it all in.

BURQU

Similar in design and purpose to some of the other desert castles (see later in this chapter) is **Qasr Burqu**. It was originally built in the 3rd century AD by the Romans, became a monastery during the Byzantine period, and restored by the Umayyads in about 700 AD.

The castle is not worth visiting as such, and is certainly too difficult to reach to be a part of a day trip around the desert castles. It is the remote location of the castle on the edge of the **Ghadir Burqu** lake, and the apparent incongruity of the lake in the harsh desert, which makes this place so special.

The lake is home to a number of bird species (such as finch, stork and pelican) which come to roost because the water level rarely changes, even in summer. The lake also hosts wildflowers and animals such as gazelle, fox and hyena.

The place is so unique and precious that the Jordan-based Royal Society for the Conservation of Nature (RSCN) hopes to establish Burqu as a protected reserve. Contact the RSCN in Amman before heading to Burqu as permission may be required. (See the National Parks section in the Facts about Jordan chapter for details about Burqu Reserve.)

Getting There & Away

The good news for the flora and fauna, and the bad news for visitors, is that Burqu is only accessible by 4WD – and with a guide. The lake and castle are about 25km northwest of Ruwayshid, which is on the road from Mafraq to the Iraqi border. Although public transport is available between Mafraq and Ruwayshid, there is no chance of even hitching north of the highway to Burqu, and the access road to Burqu is strictly for 4WDs.

AZRAQ   الأزرق
☎ 05

The oasis town of Azraq (which means 'blue' in Arabic) lies 103km east of Amman. It forms a junction of roads heading northeast to Safawi and Iraq, and south-east to Saudi Arabia. Azraq was one of the very few sources of water in the region and the area is archaeologically very important, but there is nothing of historical significance in Azraq, except the Qasr al-Azraq.

These days, Azraq is a stop for vehicles travelling to/from Iraq and Saudi. The town is not particularly interesting, but as it is the only place in eastern Jordan with accommodation it's the obvious local base for exploring the desert castles and the Azraq and Shaumari reserves.

Orientation & Information

Azraq is divided into two, and is located either side of the T-junction of Highway 5 and the highway from Amman: Azraq al-Janubi is about 1km south of the junction, while Azraq ash-Shomali (where Qasr al-Azraq is located) is about 5km north.

Azraq al-Janubi is basically a truckies' paradise of restaurants, cafes and mechanics. Although far less appealing than Azraq ash-Shomali, the southern end has the only budget hotel, cheap restaurants, money-changers and private telephone agencies. The post office is in Azraq ash-Shomali.

Places to Stay

Zoubi Hotel (☎ 383 5012) is the only budget accommodation available. It offers comfortable rooms, with charming old-fashioned furniture, a private bathroom and fan for JD10 per person. It's located behind the Refa'i Restaurant in Azraq al-Janubi, about 800m south of the T-junction.

Al-Sayad Hotel (☎ 644 9800) – also known as *The Hunter* – looks quite flash with a permanently empty pool and well-manicured gardens, but the rooms are fairly disappointing. They are overpriced at (a negotiable) JD24/32 for singles/doubles and don't have private bathrooms. It's about 500m south of Qasr al-Azraq, and about 5km north of the T-junction.

Azrak Resthouse (☎ *681042, mobile* ☎ *079-61544, fax 681028)* is a little sterile but is comfortable and has the attraction of a full swimming pool. Nice rooms with air-con, fridge and TV – all overlooking the inviting pool – cost JD19.200/24, including breakfast. It is, however, a pain to reach: the turn-off for the access road (1.5km) is about 2km north of the T-junction.

Azraq Lodge (☎ *383 5017, email azraq@ rscn.org.jo)* was being developed at the time of research by the RSCN and looks promising. The five rooms inside the renovated 1940s British Hospital will cost about JD10 per person. The ten new bungalows outside are better value for the same price. Meals can be pre-arranged; alternatively, guests can use the kitchen or walk to Azraq al-Janubi. *Camping* may be allowed at some time in the future. The Lodge is just south of the main road to Amman, about 300m before (west of) the T-junction.

Places to Eat

A bunch of small eateries lines a 1km stretch of the road south of the T-junction. The best are arguably *Turkey Restaurant* and *Refa'i Restaurant* (in front of the Zoubi Hotel).

Azrak Resthouse has an elegant restaurant, but mainly caters to tour groups and visiting Saudis and Iraqis keen to sample the array of alcoholic beverages. Main courses cost from JD4 to JD5.

Al-Montazah Falls Restaurant (☎ *647 610, mobile* ☎ *079-62061)* is along the main road in northern Azraq, not far from the castle. It's shady (ie lots of trees) and offers main courses from JD4.500, and buffets for about JD6.

Getting There & Away

Minibuses (500 fils, 1½ hours) travel between the post office (north of the castle in Azraq ash-Shomali), and the Old station in Zarqa, which is well connected to Amman and Irbid. Minibuses run up and down the road along northern and southern Azraq in search of passengers before hitting the highway to Zarqa. Use this minibus to travel between both parts of Azraq, or hitch a ride.

AZRAQ WETLANDS RESERVE
حديقة الأزرق المبللة

The Azraq Basin lies mostly in Jordan, and comprises huge areas of mud flats, pools and marshlands. Before some of this was declared an 'internationally important wetland' in 1977 (because of the number of species of migratory birds which roosted there) the wetlands suffered appalling ecological damage (see the boxed text 'What happened to the Wetlands?').

The RSCN has now taken control of the Azraq wetlands and, at the time of research, was busy establishing a small (12 sq km) reserve. Until more water is pumped into the wetlands to attract the birds, there will be little to see, but it is easy to reach and can be combined with a trip to the desert castles and Shaumari Reserve.

The entrance fee will probably be JD3, and the reserve will be open every day from about 8 am to 4 pm. To see more birds, enthusiasts can pre-arrange (by telephone) an earlier opening time or later closing time. Don't bother visiting in the height of summer (July and August), when the water level recedes and wildlife is far too sensible to be walking about in the heat of the day.

Wildlife

The RSCN estimates that about 300 species of resident and migratory birds still use the wetlands, including raptor, lark, eagle, plover and duck. A few buffalo enjoy the marshy environs, and there are some semi-wild horses about, and jackal and jerbil at night. The best time to see bird life is winter (December to February) and early spring (March and April), although the raptor arrives in May.

The authorities plan to establish a short (30 minute) walking trail around the wetlands, ideal for **bird watching** and the exploration of some small **ruins** of Umayyad buildings. An observation tower will also be built soon.

Places to Stay & Eat

There is nowhere to stay in the reserve. Most of the hotels listed under Places to Stay in the Azraq section above are nearby, and camping is permitted at Shaumari Reserve.

EASTERN JORDAN

What Happened to the Wetlands?

The Azraq Basin was originally about 12,710 sq km (an area larger than Lebanon), and excavations in the region clearly indicate that it was a popular place to live thousands of years ago. As recently as the 1960s, about 350,000 birds each year were attracted to the Azraq wetlands, a freshwater oasis in the midst of the desert. But the wetlands are now an ecological disaster.

Extraction of water from the wetlands to the developing cities of Amman and Irbid started in the late 1960s. Some of the water was 'fossil water' – perhaps about 10,000 years old – and was being replaced less than half as quickly as it was being pumped out. Experts believe that 3000 cubic metres of water filled the wetlands every year about 40 years ago. The figure plummeted to a catastrophic 10 cubic metres per year in 1980, and by the mid-1990s, the wetlands had dried up completely. A generation ago, there was surface water, but by the mid-1990s the water level dropped to over 10m below the ground. At this time, salt water seeped into the wetlands, making the water unpalatable for wildlife, and hopeless for drinking and irrigation.

The Azraq wetlands were declared a national reserve in 1965, but it never eventuated because of bureaucratic bungling, lack of funds and political instability. In 1977, the Azraq Wetlands Reserve was finally established by the RSCN.

Since 1994, some serious funding and commitment from the United Nations Development Program (UNDP), Jordanian government and RSCN has successfully halted the pumping of water from the wetlands to urban centres. Enough fresh water is now being pumped back into the reserve each year enabling about 10% of the original wetlands to be restored. This should also decrease salinity and attract wildlife and birdlife once again.

Getting There & Away

The access road to the reserve is in the middle of Azraq al-Janubi (southern Azraq), and starts opposite the petrol station. The new visitors centre (☎/fax 05-383 5225, email azraq@rscn.org.jo) is about 200m along the access road.

SHAUMARI RESERVE

حديقة شومـاري

The Shaumari Reserve was established in 1975 and was the first of its kind in Jordan to reintroduce wildlife which had long since disappeared from the region. For example, the Arabian oryx, which became extinct in Jordan in the 1920s, was reintroduced in 1978 when eight US-born oryx, and three wild animals from Qatar, were successfully transported to Shaumari. Five years later, the herd numbered 30 and was let loose into the reserve.

Despite poaching and natural predators, there are currently about 280 of the beasts in Shaumari Reserve. About 20 or 30 of these will be released into the desert when the Wadi Rum National Reserve is up and running. (Arabian oryx have been known to live 22 months without water, and some recently walked more than 150km to find precious supplies.)

The small (22 sq km) Shaumari Reserve is more like a children's zoo than a wildlife reserve, but the staff seem to be trying hard. Unfortunately, visitors see little apart from onager (wild ass), gazelle, oryx and ostrich (reportedly now being farmed for meat and feathers) – all in captivity.

Information

From the high observation tower, many of the animals can be seen, although a 'safari' of sorts is also available. The Nature Centre features most impressive exhibits of flora and fauna, especially the oryx, and very wisely caters to impressionable young children with hands-on displays.

Entrance costs JD3. It is open every day from 8 am to 5.30 pm, but bird watching is available with prior arrangement from 6 am. There is no telephone in the reserve, but it is in contact with the visitors centre at Azraq Wetland Reserve by radio telephone.

EASTERN JORDAN

ANN JEFFREE

Oryx (large antelope) were once common in the Jordanian desert. Today they can be seen in the Shaumari Reserve.

Wildlife

As well as Arabian oryx, Shaumari is home to blue-necked and red-necked ostrich; Subgutu Rosa and Darcas gazelles; and Persian onager. Nearly 250 species of bird have been identified, including raptor, golden eagle and Egyptian vulture. The best time of year to see birds and wildlife is spring (March to May) and early winter (December).

Places to Stay & Eat

No camping is allowed inside the reserve, but with permission (easy to obtain) from staff, you can pitch your *tent* opposite the entrance and use the toilets and drinking water for free. (There are no showers.) The nearest hotels and restaurants are in Azraq – see the relevant section for details.

Getting There & Away

Shaumari is well signposted, and 15km south of the T-junction between northern and southern Azraq. The road into the reserve is paved until the final 1km, but is accessible by normal (non-4WD) vehicles. It should be easy to charter a taxi to the reserve from Azraq, but from the reserve arrange for the taxi driver to either pick you up later or to wait a while.

Getting Around

There are a few very short walks around the grounds, but no hiking is allowed in the reserve: the danger from jackal and hyena is real. To see a little more of the wildlife than from the observation tower, take the 'Oryx Safari' (45 minutes) in a glorified truck (holding 10 people) – but you may have to wait hours for enough visitors to come to share the cost, which is JD20 per truck.

Desert Castles

A string of buildings and ruins – known collectively (if a little erroneously) as the desert castles – lie in the desert of eastern Jordan. Most of them were built, or taken over and adapted, by the Damascus-based Umayyad rulers in the late 7th and early 8th centuries. Two of the castles, Azraq and Al-Hallabat, date from Roman times and excavations of some others indicate Nabataean occupation.

There are various theories about their use. The early Arab rulers were still Bedouin at heart and their love of the desert probably led them to build (or take over) these pleasure palaces, which appear to have been surrounded by artificial oases teeming with wild game and orchards. They pursued their pastimes of hawking, hunting and horse-racing for a few weeks each year. The evenings were apparently spent in excessive festivities with plenty of wine, women, poetry and song.

Some historians believe that only here did the caliphs (Islamic rulers) feel comfortable about flouting the Quran. Others have suggested that they came to avoid epidemics in the big cities or even to maintain links with, and power over, their fellow Bedouin, the bedrock of their support in the conquered lands.

Information

Some of the castles are locked, so you may have to find the caretaker. If he opens any

EASTERN JORDAN

door especially for you (or provides a commentary), a tip (about 500 fils) is obligatory, but not just for signing a 'guest book'.

The five main castles listed below (except Qasr al-Mushatta) have useful explanations inside their entrances. All of the castles are open every day during daylight hours, and entrance to all of them is currently free. However, a small fee may be charged at Qusayr Amra after the opening of the visitors centre there.

Before setting off, make sure you pick up a free copy of the excellent *Desert Castles* brochure, published by the Jordan Tourism Board and available at the Downtown visitors centre in Amman. If you wish for more information about the castles than we can provide in this guidebook, pick up the small and affordable (JD3) *The Desert Castles*, published by Al-Kutba and available from the larger bookshops around Jordan.

Organised Tours

Jumping on an organised tour of the desert castles from Amman make s a lot of sense, and is one of the few times when independent travellers on a tight budget will probably have to bite the bullet and pay for a tour.

Tours can be arranged at the Cliff, Venecia, Bdeiwi and Farah hotels in Amman. These hotels charge about JD40 per vehicle (holding four or five passengers) per day, or about JD10 per person if you can find other passengers to share the cost. You're unlikely to get a better deal by negotiating directly with the driver of a service taxi or private taxi in Amman, and regular taxi drivers may not speak English or know the way.

Getting Around

The five castles which most visitors see are: Qasr al-Hallabat (with nearby Hammam Sarah), Qasr al-Azraq, Qusayr Amra, Qasr Kharana and Qasr al-Mushatta. Most people on day trips in rented or chartered vehicles from Amman visit the castles in this order (ie clockwise from Amman) but they can, of course, be visited in the reverse order.

These five castles can be visited quickly in half a day, but it's best to allow a full day for a leisurely drive, a visit to Azraq Wet-

lands and/or Shaumari reserves and lunch in Azraq. If you start really early (and pay more for a chartered taxi), it is possible to fit in Umm al-Jimal also.

If you have rented a car for a few days to tour around southern Jordan, consider renting it for an extra day for a jaunt around the castles and reserves. If driving from Amman, head east of Raghadan bus station towards Zarqa, and follow the signs to Azraq or the individual castles. If you can't afford to rent a car or charter a taxi for the day, or you want to spend more time looking around, base yourself in Azraq town, and use public transport, hitch or charter a vehicle from there.

Of the other castles around eastern Jordan (see the Other Castles section later in this chapter), Qasr Deir al-Kahf, Qasr Mushash and Qasr 'Uweinid are mostly in ruins and mainly of interest to archaeologists; and the latter two castles plus Qasr al-Tuba and Qasr Aseikhin are only accessible by 4WD.

Public Transport & Hitching With the exception of Qasr al-Mushatta, it is feasible to visit the other four main castles in one day using a combination of public transport and hitching. However, it is very important to note that only the castles at Hallabat and Azraq are accessible by public transport.

QASR AL-HALLABAT

قصر الحلابات

This first stop for many visitors on a day trip from Amman is not necessarily the most interesting, so this could be missed if you're pushed for time.

The caretaker lives in a tent at the entrance, and will open it up (for a small tip, of course). The castle is a good place to watch the sun set, so if you have your own transport, and don't mind driving back to Amman in the dark, try to finish at Qasr al-Hallabat late in the afternoon.

History

Qasr al-Hallabat was originally a Roman fort during the reign of Caracalla (198-217 AD) as a defence against raiding desert tribes, although there's evidence that Trajan

The Umayyads

Princes of conquest rather than princes of religion, lords of the desert not disciples of prayer, the Umayyad caliphs intrigue historians. And for a good reason: they occupy an important place in history as the first dynasty of Islamic rulers.

The main aspects of Umayyad history are well known: their headquarters were in Damascus, their authority lasted from 661 to 750, and history records the names of four famous rulers: Mu'awiya, 'Abd al-Malik, Walid I and Walid II. However, their culture is clouded in mystery and their most extensive legacies are to be found in the desert castles in eastern Jordan.

These castles are more like organised residences or palaces comprising baths, irrigation systems, and hunting and agricultural shelters. They were located away from the religious demands of the holy cities, where the caliphs could indulge in the fruits of their victories. The unexpected presence – notably inside Qusayr Amra – of numerous representations of naked women seems to agree with the identification of these palaces as centres of pleasure and indulgence. However, some historians believe that the women are depicted in domestic rather than erotic scenes.

Others see in the choice of a semidesert zone the sign of obvious nostalgia. Although the success of their conquests led to a more sedentary lifestyle, the Umayyad caliphs found in their desert castles a return to the ambience of their earlier nomadic existence.

Whatever, the success of the Umayyad regime was short-lived. The Umayyad form of government was proven to be 'insufficiently Muslim' in the eyes of the fervent. They were soon pursued, massacred and replaced by the Abbasids (see the History section in the Facts about Jordan chapter).

at the time of the Sassanid invasion from Persia during the early 7th century. About a hundred years later, the Umayyads further strengthened the fort, and the hedonistic caliph Walid II converted it into a pleasure palace. It once featured baths, with frescoes and mosaics, mosques, forts and reservoirs.

Things to See

Today, the ruins are a jumble of crumbling walls and fallen stones, with only two buildings of much interest.

The square **Umayyad fort** was built of black basalt (possibly from near Umm al-Jimal) and a lighter shade of limestone. The fort once contained four large towers, and was three storeys high. In the north-west corner are the ruins of the smaller original **Roman fort** on which the Umayyad fort was apparently built.

Just east of the fort is the rectangular **mosque**, built in the 8th century. Three walls are still standing, and there's a restored and discernible *mihrab* (niche facing Mecca) in the south wall. Part of the same complex is the separate baths of Hammam Sarah.

Getting There & Away

Qasr al-Hallabat is in the village of Hallabat, and one of the few castles that can be easily visited by public transport. Hallabat has a few basic shops selling food and cold drinks, but nowhere to stay or eat.

From Amman (Abdali or Raghadan bus stations), take a minibus to the New (Amman) station in Zarqa, another local minibus to the Old station in Zarqa, and another to Hallabat village (250 fils, 45 minutes). The minibus drives past Hammam Sarah, and can drop you off (if you ask the driver) at the turn-off, about 300m from Qasr al-Hallabat.

HAMMAM SARAH حمّام الصرح

Hammam Sarah ('Desert Baths') is a tiny bathhouse and hunting lodge built by the Umayyads, and officially part of (but separate to) the complex at Qasr al-Hallabat. Built from limestone, the building has been well restored over the years, and you can see the channels that were once used for the

before him had established a post on the site of a Nabataean emplacement. During the 6th century, it was renovated and became a Byzantine monastery, and was abandoned hot water and steam. Outside the main building is a **well**, nearly 20m deep, and the remains of a **mosque** nearby.

The gate is permanently open, so there's no need for a caretaker. It is located along the main road to Hallabat village, about 4km east of Qasr al-Hallabat.

QASR AL-AZRAQ قصر الأزرق

Azraq castle is the most accessible, and one of the more interesting, desert castles. Although it's also one of the most visited castles in eastern Jordan, comparatively little is known about its history and relatively little excavation and renovation has been carried out. For most visitors, the attraction is the historical link to TE Lawrence.

History

Greek and Latin inscriptions date earlier constructions on the site to around 300 AD – about the time of the reign of the Romans. The building was renovated in the Byzantine period, and the Umayyad caliph Walid II used it for hunting, and as a military base. It was again substantially rebuilt in 1237 by the Ayyubids, and the Ottoman Turks stationed a garrison there in the 16th century.

It is most famous because TE Lawrence and Sherif Hussein bin Ali based themselves there in the winter of 1917, during the Arab Revolt against the Turks. Lawrence set up his quarters in the room above the southern entrance, while his men used other areas of the fort and covered the gaping holes in the roof with palm branches and clay. They were holed up here for months in crowded conditions with little shelter from the intense cold. Much of the building collapsed in an earthquake in 1927.

Information

The fort is open every day during daylight hours. Entrance is free, but if the place is crawling with tour buses the caretaker may be trawling for a healthy 'donation' (500 fils is enough).

Things to See

This large building was initially constructed out of black basalt stone, and originally three storeys high. The main **entrance** (to the south) is a single massive slab of basalt. Lawrence describes in his book *The Seven Pillars of Wisdom* how it 'went shut with a clang and crash that made tremble the west wall of the castle'. Some of the **paving stones** inside the door have small indentations, carved by former gatekeepers who played an old board game using pebbles to pass the time.

Above the entrance is **Lawrence's Room**. Opposite the entrance, and just to the left, are the remains of a small **altar**, built in the 3rd century AD by the Romans. In the middle of the expansive **courtyard** is a small **mosque**, facing Mecca. It dates to the Ayyubid period (early 13th century), but was built on the ruins of a Byzantine church. In the north-east corner of the courtyard, a hole with stairs leads down to a **well**, full of water until about 20 years ago. In the north-west corner are the ruins of the **prison**.

The northern sections are residential areas with barely discernible ruins of a **kitchen** and **dining room**, and nearby **store rooms** and **stables**. The **tower** in the western wall is the most spectacular, and features another huge **door** made of basalt.

Getting There & Away

Qasr al-Azraq is the most accessible of the castles, and is easy to reach from Amman by public transport. The castle is situated in Azraq ash-Shomali (northern Azraq), about 5km north of the T-junction at the end of the highway from Amman. Refer to the Azraq section earlier in this chapter for details about travelling to and around Azraq, and for information about places to stay and eat.

QUSAYR AMRA قصر عمرا

Heading back towards Amman along Highway 40 (if travelling in a clockwise loop) is Qusayr ('little castle') Amra. It is one the best preserved of the desert castles, although the attractions are the rooms plastered with fascinating frescoes – some 350 sq m all up. The building was part of a greater complex that served as a caravanserai, with baths and a hunting lodge, possibly in existence before the arrival of the Umayyads.

ANN JEFFREE

Qusayr Amra, the most intact of the desert castles, is characterised by its barrel vaults, domes and frescoes, testifying to the influence of earlier Roman architecture of the region.

History

Although historians are undecided, the general consensus is that the building was constructed during the reign of Umayyad caliph Walid I (705-15 AD), who also built the Umayyad Mosque in Damascus. A Spanish team of archaeologists began excavations in the mid-1970s: the frescoes have been restored with the assistance of governments and private institutions from Austria, France and Spain. The building is now a UNESCO World Heritage site.

Information

If the main building with the frescoes is closed, ask someone at the souvenir stall in the car park to find the caretaker. Entrance to the grounds is currently free, but the caretaker will want a tip to open the main building. At the time of research, a visitors centre was being built outside the entrance. The centre should provide some useful information about the frescoes, and an entrance fee (about JD1) may be charged in the future.

Things to See

The entrance opens immediately to the **audience hall**, which contains most of the **frescoes**. On the right (western) wall, there is a depiction of a nude woman bathing. What makes such a fresco remarkable is that under Islam any kind of illustration of living beings, let alone nudes, is prohibited – yet the more your eyes roam the walls within, the more this particular theme becomes apparent.

To her left stand six great rulers, of whom four have been identified – Caesar, a Byzantine emperor; the Visigoth king, Roderick; the Persian emperor, Chosroes; and the Negus of Abyssinia. The fresco either implies that the present Umayyad ruler was their equal or better, or is simply a pictorial list of Islam's enemies.

A small doorway leads to the left through three small rooms, all part of the baths: the **apodyterium** (changing room) features further lurid frescoes; the **tepidarium**, where medium hot water was offered; and the **caldarium**, which had hot water. The **dome** in the caldarium is of special interest because it features a map of the heavens on it, although it's not particularly accurate because it was probably painted from another drawing, map or globe, and not from peering into the sky.

The floors of the two rooms at the back of the main hall bear a modest layer of **mosaics**, but these are hard to see without a torch (flashlight).

Outside, a few metres north of the main building, is a partially restored 40m-deep stone **well**. It was built to supply water for the baths, and for passing caravans.

Getting There & Away

Qusayr Amra is along the main road and hard to miss, but it is also impossible to reach by public transport. It is located on the right (northern) side of the road, 25km south-west of the junctions of Highways 30 and 40. From Azraq, get a minibus towards Zarqa as

EASTERN JORDAN

far as the junction, and then hitch a ride. Alternatively, charter a taxi from Azraq and combine it with a visit to Qasr Kharana.

QASR KHARANA   قصر الكرانه

Stuck in the middle of a treeless plain, this mighty two-storey edifice clearly looks like a fortress, but historians are divided: the narrow windows were probably made for air and light rather than for shooting arrows; and it probably wasn't a caravanserai, because it was not located on any popular trade route, nor close to any water source. The most recent supposition is that it was a meeting room for Umayyad rulers and local Bedouin.

Although small (35 sq m), the castle is remarkably well preserved, and has been wonderfully restored, and is worth visiting despite its comparative inaccessibility.

History
A painted inscription above one of the doors on the upper floor mentions the date 710 AD, which is when it was probably renovated extensively by the Umayyads. The presence of stones with Greek inscriptions in the main entrance suggests it was built on the site of a Roman or Byzantine building, possibly as a private residence.

Information
If the building is closed, find someone from the tent in the grounds, or the souvenir stall, to open it up.

Things to See
About 60 rooms surround the **courtyard** inside the castle. The long rooms either side of the arched **entrance** were used as **stables**, and in the centre of the courtyard was a **basin** for collecting rainwater.

Make sure you climb to the top levels along one of the elegant **stairways**. Most of the rooms in the upper levels are decorated with well-restored **carved plaster medallions**, set around the top of the walls. Stairs in the south-east and south-west corners lead to the 2nd floor and the roof, from which there are great **views** of the stark landscape – although the nearby highway and power station spoil the ambience somewhat.

Getting There & Away
This castle is 16km further west along Highway 40 from Qusayr Amra. It is impossible to miss from the highway, but is also impossible to reach by public transport. Either hitch from Azraq or Amman, or charter a vehicle from Azraq and combine it with a visit to Qusayr Amra.

QASR AL-MUSHATTA   قصر المشتى

Of the five major desert castles, Qasr al-Mushatta ('Winter Palace') is the most difficult and time-consuming to reach. After a day visiting the other four (if on a day trip travelling in a clockwise loop from Amman), some visitors choose to miss this one.

However, the ruins are extensive and fun to wander around. Many pieces have disappeared over the years, ending up in museums around the word, eg the elaborate carving on the facade was shipped off to Berlin (now in the Pergamum Museum), after the palace was 'given' to Kaiser Wilhelm in 1903 by Sultan Abd al-Hamid of Turkey.

History
Qasr al-Mushatta was planned as the biggest and most lavish of all the Umayyad castles, but it was never finished. It was probably started in about 743 AD, under caliph Walid II (who intended to establish a city in the area). He was later assassinated by angry labourers, many of whom had died during the construction of Qasr al-Mushatta because of a lack of water in the area, so building was never completed.

Information
The site is open every day during daylight hours. Entrance is free, and although a caretaker hangs around, there's nothing to open or close, so no tip is required. Because the castle is located near sensitive areas – primarily the airport – make sure you have your passport ready to show the guards along the way.

Things to See
There isn't a lot to see because the castle was never finished. It was also later looted,

and partially destroyed by earthquakes, so only the walls of incomplete buildings can be seen, and most of the columns and towers have fallen down.

To the right from the entrance are the ruins of a **mosque**, with its obvious mihrab. In the northern sections are the remains of an **audience hall** and **residences**; the existing pieces provide some idea of how it must have once looked. One unusual feature of the site is that the vaults were made from burnt bricks (an uncommon material in buildings of this style) rather than black basalt.

Getting There & Away

Qasr al-Mushatta is impossible to reach by public transport or hitching. It's also not well signposted, and involves going through at least two military checkpoints. If driving from Amman, head towards the Queen Alia international airport, turn left (east) off the Desert Highway to the airport, and then turn right at the roundabout by the Alia Gateway Hotel. Follow the road for about 12km around the perimeter of the airport, and then turn right just before the third, and largest, checkpoint.

One alternative is to charter a taxi from the airport – so if you have some time to kill while waiting for a flight, and a few dinars left over, why not have a quick look?

OTHER CASTLES

The five castles above are the most accessible, interesting and well restored. There are numerous other castles in eastern Jordan, and just south of Amman, but they are mostly in ruins and of interest only to archaeologists; often impossible to reach by public transport and sometimes only accessible by 4WD; or boring, and simply not worth the effort.

Qasr 'Ain es-Sil   قصر عين السيل

This is not really a castle or palace but a farmhouse built by the Umayyads, possibly over the fortifications of a Roman building. It is small (17 sq m), and was built from basalt brick. There are some ruins of a **courtyard**, flanked by seven rooms; **equipment** for making bread and olive oil; and some **baths**.

It is located just off the main road through Azraq ash-Shomali (northern Azraq), and only about 2km from Qasr al-Azraq.

Qasr Aseikhin   قصر الشيخين

This small Roman fort was built from basalt in the 3rd century over the ruins of a 1st-century Nabataean building. It has great **views** from the hilltop, but nothing else to justify a detour. It's about 22km north-east of Azraq ash-Shomali, and only accessible by 4WD. Go along the road north of Qasr al-Azraq for about 15km, and follow the signs to the fort.

Qasr Deir al-Kahf

Deir al-Kahf ('Monastery of Caves') is another Roman fort, built in the 4th century, also from black basalt. The ruins are more extensive than some others (which makes it more interesting), but it is still very difficult to reach. There is an access road north of Highway 10, or look for the signs along the back roads east of Umm al-Jimal.

Qasr Mushash

This large (2 sq km) Umayyad settlement is mostly in ruins. The highlights are the remains of the **palace**; large **courtyard**, surrounded by a dozen rooms; the **baths** and **cisterns**; and **walls** built to protect against possible flooding. It is only accessible by 4WD. Look for the sign along Highway 40.

Qasr al-Muwaqqar

This former caravanserai was built in the Umayyad period, but the ruins are so decrepit that it's not worth bothering to find. There are some remains of **reservoirs**, **Kufic inscriptions** and **columns**, but little else to see; and the most interesting item, a 10m stone tower with Kufic inscriptions, is now in the National Archaeological Museum in Amman. The **views** are wonderful, however.

It is located about 2km north of Highway 40, but is only accessible by private car, chartered taxi or hitching.

Qasr al-Qastal   قصر القسطل

This ruined Umayyad settlement was ornately renovated by the Mamluks in the 13th century AD, but very little remains. The main building still standing is the 68 sq m **palace**, but there are ruins of an **Islamic cemetery** and **baths** nearby. It is located just to the west of the Desert Highway, before the turn-off to the airport, but is poorly signposted.

Qasr al-Tuba   قصر التوبة

This is one of the most impressive of the lesser-known castles, but is also the most difficult to reach. It was conceived by the Umayyad caliph Walid II in about 743 AD, but (like Qasr al-Mushatta) it was never finished after he was assassinated. The castle was probably going to be a caravanserai, and is unusual because it's made out of bricks.

The castle is only accessible by 4WD along a poorly signed dirt track (35km) west of the Desert Highway, or an unsigned dirt track south (50km) of Highway 40. Because the roads are so difficult to find and follow, a knowledgable guide is recommended.

Qasr 'Uweinid   قصر عوينيد

This Roman military fort was built in the 3rd century AD to protect the source of Wadi as-Sarhan (now in Saudi Arabia), but was abandoned less than 100 years later. It is only accessible by 4WD, and is located about 15km south-west of Azraq al-Janubi (southern Azraq) – look for the turn-off along the road towards Shaumari Reserve.

King's Highway

The King's Highway – known in Arabic as At-Tariq as-Sultani (Sultan's Rd) – is of great historical and religious significance: it has been used by the Israelites; Nabataeans travelling to and from Petra; Christian pilgrims going to Moses' memorial at Mt Nebo; and, finally, Muslims heading to or from Mecca.

Of the three main highways between Amman and Aqaba, the King's Highway is easily the most interesting, and it goes through, or near, the popular tourist attractions of Madaba, Karak, Dana Nature Reserve, Shobak and Petra. The highway traverses the majestic Wadi Mujib valley, another major attraction but also the main reason why public transport along the highway is limited and all traffic is slow.

Getting Around

Public transport along the King's Highway is not frequent. In some parts, hitching is often the quickest way to get around, but be prepared for waits of an hour or two on deserted stretches.

Rented Car & Private Taxi Renting a car to travel between Amman and Aqaba (the only two cities where vehicles can be rented), via the King's Highway, is well worth considering. Alternatively, charter a private (yellow) taxi, or service (white) taxi, in Amman, Madaba, Wadi Mousa (near Petra) or Aqaba. With an early start, it's possible to travel between Madaba and Wadi Mousa in one day, with brief visits to Mt Nebo, Wadi Mujib, Umm ar-Rasas, Ar-Rabba, Karak, Dana Nature Reserve and Shobak castle. If chartering a taxi, it's worth staying overnight in Karak, and getting onward transport from there.

If driving, take care along the stretch between Mu'tah and Tafila, because the roads are confusing, and many signposts are either missing or vandalised. Never make any assumptions, and always ask for directions from locals if you're even remotely unsure.

HIGHLIGHTS

- **Madaba** – this easy-going town is renowned for its extensive mosaics, and is an alternative base to Amman (see page 182)

- **Hammamat Ma'in** – many visitors love splashing around in the hot springs and baths, and the cold swimming pool (see page 190)

- **Wadi Mujib Valley** – a portion of this incredibly vast and beautiful valley is in a protected reserve (see page 194)

- **Karak** – this charming old Crusader city is dominated by a magnificent castle (see page 195)

- **Dana Nature Reserve** – this huge reserve is an impressive attempt at ecotourism, with hiking options and the ancient Dana village to explore (see page 202)

- **Shobak** – this Crusader castle offers wonderful views of a desolate landscape, and attracts far fewer tour groups than any of the other castles (see page 204)

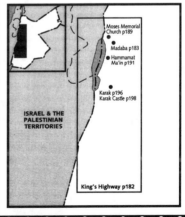

KING'S HIGHWAY

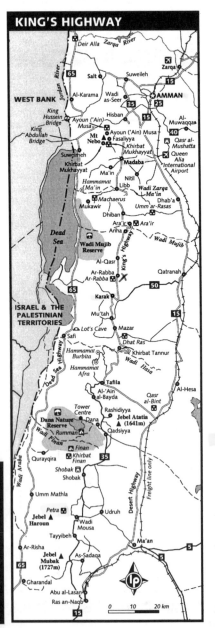

KING'S HIGHWAY

Public Transport & Hitching Travelling all the way along the King's Highway from Amman to Wadi Mousa (near Petra) is a heady mixture of minibuses, hitching and, possibly, chartered service taxis. A summary of the main options is below; more information is included in the relevant Getting There & Away sections throughout the chapter.

Amman to Madaba Take the regular minibus.

Madaba to Karak Try the daily university bus. To fully appreciate Wadi Mujib valley, catch a regular minibus from Madaba to Dhiban, charter a taxi to Ariha, and then get the minibus to Karak. (The authorities in Madaba and Dhiban swear that when the extensive road works along the highway through Wadi Mujib are completed –certainly not before late 2000 – minibuses will travel infrequently between Dhiban and Ariha.)

Karak to Dana Nature Reserve, Shobak or Wadi Mousa (near Petra) Take an irregular minibus to Tafila, and another to Qadsiyya (for Dana) or Shobak village. If you don't fancy stopping off to see Shobak castle or Dana reserve, catch a minibus or service taxi from Karak to Ma'an (mostly along the Desert Highway), and another to Wadi Mousa.

Shobak or Dana Nature Reserve to Wadi Mousa (near Petra) Public transport south of Qadsiyya (near Dana) and Shobak village is infrequent, because most public and private transport heads to Aqaba along the Desert Highway, via Ma'an. Hitching is therefore often necessary, but allow plenty of time. Alternatively, charter a taxi in Qadsiyya or Shobak. If you find a lift or minibus to Ma'an, take it and get a minibus or service taxi from there to Wadi Mousa.

MADABA
مأدبا
☎ 05

This easy-going town is best known for its Byzantine-era mosaics. As ongoing excavations continue to reveal more of these priceless treasures, greater attention is being focused on Madaba's past, raising its profile as a major stop on the tourist trail. Madaba is the most important Christian centre in Jordan, and has long been an example of religious tolerance; it's one of the few places in the Middle East where the call to prayer from the mosques often competes with melodious church bells.

Madaba is worth considering as an alternative place to stay to Amman: Madaba is far

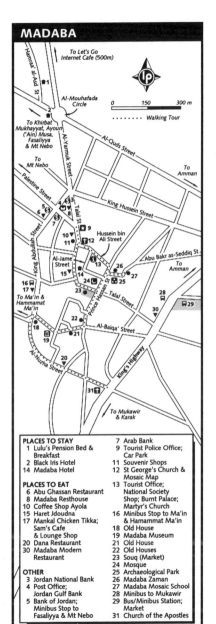

MADABA

To Let's Go
Internet Cafe (500m)

Hamraa al-Asd St.

Al-Mouhafada
Circle

0   150   300 m

········· Walking Tour

To Khirbat
Mukhayyat, Ayoun
('Ain) Musa,
Fasaliyya
& Mt Nebo

To
Mt Nebo

Al-Quds Street

Al-Yarmouk Street

Palestine Street

To
Amman

King Hussein Street

Talal St.

Hussein bin
Ali Street

King Abdullah Street

Al-Jame
Street

Abu Bakr as-Seddiq St.

To
Amman

Prince Hassan Talal Street

Al-Baiqa' Street

Al-Nuzha Street

King's Highway

To Ma'in &
Hammamat
Ma'in

To Mukawir
& Karak

PLACES TO STAY
1 Lulu's Pension Bed &
  Breakfast
2 Black Iris Hotel
14 Madaba Hotel

PLACES TO EAT
6 Abu Ghassan Restaurant
8 Madaba Resthouse
10 Coffee Shop Ayola
15 Haret Jdoudna
17 Mankal Chicken Tikka;
  Sam's Cafe
  & Lounge Shop
20 Dana Restaurant
30 Madaba Modern
  Restaurant

OTHER
3 Jordan National Bank
4 Post Office;
  Jordan Gulf Bank
5 Bank of Jordan;
  Minibus Stop to
  Fasaliyya & Mt Nebo

7 Arab Bank
9 Tourist Police Office;
  Car Park
11 Souvenir Shops
12 St George's Church &
  Mosaic Map
13 Tourist Office;
  National Society
  Shop; Burnt Palace;
  Martyr's Church
16 Minibus Stop to Ma'in
  & Hamammat Ma'in
18 Old House
19 Madaba Museum
21 Old House
22 Old Houses
23 Souq (Market)
24 Mosque
25 Archaeological Park
26 Madaba Zaman
27 Madaba Mosaic School
28 Minibus to Mukawir
29 Bus/Minibus Station;
  Market
31 Church of the Apostles

more compact, has a few good hotels and restaurants, and is less than an hour by regular public transport from the capital. In any case, there are enough things to see and do in and around Madaba to justify a stopover for a couple of days.

History
The Biblical Moabite town of Medeba was one of the towns divided among the 12 tribes of Israel. It's also mentioned on the famous Mesha Stele (Moabite Stone) raised in about 850 BC by the Moab king Mesha (refer to the boxed text 'A Stele at Twice the Price' later in this chapter).

By 165 BC the Ammonites were back in control of Madaba; about 45 years later it was taken by Hycranus 1 of Israel, and then promised to the Nabataeans by Hyrcanus II in return for helping him recover Jerusalem. Under the Romans from 106 AD, Madaba became a prosperous provincial town with the usual colonnaded streets and impressive public buildings. That prosperity continued during the Byzantine period up until the Sassanid invasion from Persia in 614 AD, and most of the mosaics in Madaba date from this period.

A devastating earthquake in 747, lead to the town's eventual abandonment for about 1100 years. In the late 19th century, 2000 Christians from Karak migrated to Madaba, and found the mosaics when they started digging foundations for houses. News that a huge mosaic map of the Holy Land had been found in St George's Church in Madaba reached Europe in 1897, leading to a flurry of exploratory activity in the region – which continues to this day.

Orientation
The central, older and most interesting part of Madaba is easy to get around, and there is no reason to venture further into the suburbs. The centre of town is St George's Church, and many facilities are located in the area between the church and Al-Mouhafada Circle. All streets are clearly labelled in English, and most major intersections have brown signs pointing to the major attractions.

The map in this book will be sufficient for most visitors. If you wish to explore the town

KING'S HIGHWAY

Meandering Around Madaba

Madaba is compact, so all the main attractions (and more) can easily be visited on foot. More details about the major sites are mentioned in the text. Allow about two hours; longer if you want to spend more time admiring the mosaics.

The obvious place to start is **St George's Church**, with its **Mosaic Map**, and the **cafes** and **souvenir shops** opposite. From there, head south along Talal St and visit the souvenir shops in **Haret Jdoudna** – maybe stop for lunch. Continue farther south along Talal to the fairly uninteresting **souq**, which may be supplanted by a shopping centre currently under construction.

Then head north up Prince Hassan St, past the **mosque**, and visit the **Archaeological Park**. Next door is the **Madaba Mosaic School**. Then back to Hussein bin Ali St to the **tourist office**, **Burnt Palace** and **Martyr's Church**, all in the same complex. Backtrack down Prince Hassan St and look for some interesting **old houses** to the right (west). Continuing west along Al-Baiqa' St is another **old house** to the left (south); some old men are probably playing cards directly opposite.

Down an alley left (south) of Al-Baiqa' is the entrance to the **Madaba Museum**. Currently, there is no access from the museum to An-Nuzha St, so head further west along Al-Baiqa', and at the corner with An-Nuzha look for some more **old houses**, which have been converted into shops. Finally, head further down An-Nuzha to the **Church of the Apostles**.

in depth, the *Tourist Map of Madaba* (JD2), published by the Royal Jordanian Geographic Centre, lists all sites and street names in English, and also includes handy maps of Dhiban, Ma'in and Hammamat Ma'in. It's available in a few bookshops in Amman. The *Madaba* map (JD3), published by the American Centre of Oriental Research, shows some of the mildly interesting old homes, churches and mosques in town, and is available at the souvenir shops opposite St George's Church.

The brochure *Madaba and Mount Nebo*, published by the Jordan Tourism Board (JTB), provides a brief, but satisfactory, explanation of the attractions in Madaba, although the map of Madaba is poor. The brochure is printed in English, French, German and Italian, and is available at the tourist office and, probably, your hotel in Madaba. The JTB also publishes several smaller brochures: *Madaba Archaeological Park*, although most of this information is included in *Madaba and Mount Nebo*; *Madaba Mosaic Map*, which has slightly more detailed explanations about the mosaics in St George's Church; and the excellent *Mount Nebo* (see the Around Madaba section later).

If you crave more information about the mosaics in Madaba, pick up the definitive but weighty *Madaba: Cultural Heritage* (JD22), published by the American Centre of Oriental Research. Much cheaper and more portable is *Mosaic Map of Madaba*, by Herbert Donner. The best is the pocket-sized and affordable *Madaba, Mt Nebo*, published by Al-Kutba (JD3). Most books and maps relevant to Madaba are available at the souvenir shops opposite St George's Church.

Information

Tourist Office The tourist office (☎ 543376) is in front of the Burnt Palace, along Hussein bin Ali St. It can provide useful brochures about Madaba, Mt Nebo and other major attractions throughout Jordan in several languages. The office is open from 8 am to 2 pm every day except Friday, but there is someone around until 4 pm on working days.

The National Society for the Preservation of the Heritage of Madaba and its Suburbs (quite a mouthful!) is in the same spot as the tourist office. The friendly guy who runs it speaks good English, and is usually more than happy to help with local information if the tourist office is closed. (See Shopping later in this chapter for more information about the Society and its shop.)

Entrance to the main attraction, St George's Church, is free but donations are welcome. However, a combined ticket to visit one or all of the three other sites – ie the Archaeological Park, Madaba Museum and

Church of the Apostles will cost you JD3. Photographs are allowed at sites in Madaba.

Money Several banks can change cash and travellers cheques, including the Bank of Jordan on the corner of Palestine and King Abdullah streets; Jordan Gulf Bank, near the post office; and the Jordan National Bank, on the corner of King Abdullah and Talal streets. The Arab Bank on Palestine St also has an automatic teller machine (ATM) for Visa and MasterCard.

Post & Communications The post office on Palestine St is small but reliable, and is open from 8 am to 5 pm daily. Long-distance telephone calls can be made from inside.

Some business cards and brochures still list the local area code for Madaba as 08. However, all telephones and faxes in and around Madaba now have an area code of 05.

About 500m up (follow the obvious signs) from Al-Mouhafada Circle is the Let's Go Internet Cafe (☎ 325 0620, email altwal@hotmail.com), which charges a reasonable JD2 per hour.

Emergency There is a tourist police office (☎ 191) along Talal St, just north of St George's Church.

St George's Church & Mosaic Map

This 19th century Greek Orthodox Church was built over a Byzantine church, apparently to hide an old floor which contained what is now known as the Mosaic Map.

Unearthed in 1884, the mosaic is a clear map with 157 captions (in Greek) of all major Biblical sites from Lebanon to Egypt, and down to the Mediterranean – including obvious references to the Nile River, Dead Sea and, in the middle, Jerusalem and the Church of the Holy Sepulchre. The mosaic was constructed in 560 AD, and was originally about 25m long (some experts claim it was 15m) and 6m wide. It once contained more than two million pieces, but only one-third of the original mosaic has survived.

The mosaic is inside the church, which is open to visitors from 7 am to 6 pm every

Making Mosaics

Mosaics are traditionally made from tiny squares called *tesserae*, chipped from larger rocks. The tessera are naturally coloured, and carefully laid on a thick coating of wet lime. Unlike the mosaics found in some other countries (eg Italy), mosaics found in and around Madaba were made for the floor, and were hardy enough to withstand anything – except massive earthquakes.

The larger mosaics found in and around Madaba required much painstaking effort, and took a long time to complete, so they were only created for wealthier citizens who could afford them, and for important buildings (in particular, churches). For some reason, very few of the artists signed their names on the mosaics, possibly because so many people were involved over many years, although other names are often listed, eg people who helped to pay for the mosaics, and clergy in the church.

Designs were fairly standard in and around Madaba, and featured things from everyday life such as animals, fish, plants and people; activities, such as hunting; and various religious events or mythological gods and goddesses. Most were enhanced with intricate edges.

day, but is closed during Mass from 7.30 to 9 am on Friday and 7.30 to 10.30 am on Sunday. During these times, the church is not open to tourists, but anyone is welcome to join the Mass. There is no entrance fee, but donations to help maintain the church and mosaic are always welcome.

Archaeological Park

Careful excavation and restoration in the early 1990s led to the creation of this 'park' (☎ 546681) – so called probably because a 'museum' already exists in Madaba. Its core takes in the sites of the 6th century churches of the Virgin Mary and of the Prophet Elias, along with parts of an earlier structure now known as the Hippolytus Hall. Between the two churches lies the well-preserved remains of the **Roman Road**, which ran east to

KING'S HIGHWAY

west between the then Roman city's gates. Several mosaics have been uncovered, and ramps have been built to allow visitors to examine them.

Hippolytus Hall was built in the mid-5th century, and contains the most impressive mosaic. The corners of the floor have decorations depicting the four seasons, and elsewhere there are pictures of flowers and birds; scenes from the classic Oedipal tragedy of Phaedre and Hippolytus; and portraits of the goddess Aphrodite, clearly unhappy with Adonis.

Church of the Virgin Mary was built sometime in the 6th century AD, and uncovered in 1887. Inside, the mosaic (mostly created in about 767) is a masterpiece of geometrical design. **Church of the Prophet Elias** dates back to 608 AD, but the surviving mosaics are not as eye-catching.

The displays are well labelled in English, and a clear map just past the ticket booth indicates the location of each of the exhibits. Archaeological Park is open from 8 am to 5 pm daily in winter (and closes a little later in summer), but shuts at 4 pm on Friday. Entrance costs JD3 for a combination ticket (see Information earlier this chapter).

Church of the Apostles

As part of an overall program to rehabilitate the town's heritage, another extraordinary mosaic, dedicated to the 12 Apostles, is on view. This huge mosaic was created in 578 AD, and is one of the few instances where the mosaicist, Salamios, put his name to his work. The central portion shows a woman, Thalassa, who depicts the sea, surrounded by fish and other nasty marine creatures. Illustrated in the same mosaic are representations of more serene native animals and birds, flowers and fruits.

The walkway partially surrounding the mosaic allows a great view, and the sunlight gleaming through a stained glass window over the mosaic is quite enchanting. Opening times are supposed to be the same as the Archaeological Park, but this can be taken with a grain of salt. Entrance costs JD3 for a combination ticket (see Information earlier this chapter).

Burnt Palace & Martyr's Church

At the back of the tourist office is the Burnt Palace, a 6th century private mansion destroyed by fire about 100 years after it was built. It contains even more mosaics, with a series of walkways around them. On the same site are the remains of mosaics from the 6th century Martyr's Church, which was destroyed in the 8th century although many of the mosaics somehow survived.

Both sites were still being excavated and renovated at the time of research, but are due to open soon. The exhibits promise to be as interesting and as well displayed as the Archaeological Park. Currently, entrance is free, and it's open every day during daylight hours, even if the tourist office is closed. However, an entrance fee and regulated opening hours are likely to be introduced soon.

Madaba Museum

The Madaba Museum (☎ 544056) was created from several old Madaba homes. It contains the **Folklore Museum**, with jewellery, traditional costumes and a copy of the Mesha Stele (see the boxed text 'A Stele at Twice the Price' later in this chapter). The most interesting mosaics are the ones dating back to the 6th century in the (poorly lit) room marked **Traditional House of Madaba**; the **Byzantine Mosaic**; and the **Mosaic of the Paradise**, depicting where all the righteous hope to end up. The museum also features artefacts from Umm ar-Rasas and Machaerus castle in Mukawir (see Around Madaba).

However, the museum is not that interesting, but if you've bought the JD3 ticket, which includes entry to the museum, you might as well have a look. There are **views** of the unattractive urban sprawl of modern Madaba from the museum grounds. The museum is open every day from 9 am to 5 pm, and until 4 pm on Friday.

Places to Stay

Madaba Hotel (☎/fax 540643, Al-Jame St) is the cheapest and most central place in Madaba. The rooms downstairs are clean, but spartan, although the shared bathroom could be cleaner and the water supply is unreliable – but for a negotiable JD8/16 for singles/doubles, it's good value. The nicer rooms upstairs cost JD9/18. Breakfast is JD1 per person, and other meals can be pre-ordered. A ground floor *restaurant* was being built at the time of research.

Lulu's Pension Bed & Breakfast (☎ 543 678, fax 547617, Hamraa' al-Asd St) is a delightful place. The effusive manager offers terrific doubles (no singles) upstairs with a private bathroom and a balcony for JD25. Downstairs, the rooms share a spotless bathroom and cost JD10/20/30 for singles/doubles/triples. All rates include breakfast. There's also a convivial TV area downstairs where guests can sometimes roll out a sleeping bag (JD6) if the rooms are full, and a kitchen for guests. Tents can be set up in the grounds for JD5 per tent. Lulu's is an obvious three-storey whitewashed building just up from Al-Mouhafada Circle.

Black Iris Hotel (☎ 541959, Al-Mouhafada Circle) is a little more classy than Lulu's, and has been heartily recommended by families and single women. Very stylish rooms (some overlooking a pleasant garden), with small spotless bathrooms, cost JD18/25, including a great breakfast. The hospitable manager happily offers discounts to about JD14/20 for stays of longer than one night. It's easy to spot from Al-Mouhafada Circle.

Places to Eat

Madaba Modern Restaurant (King's Highway) offers half a chicken, humous and salad for about JD2, and is the best of the cheap eateries near the bus/minibus station.

Abu Ghassan Restaurant (King Abdullah St) is a similar sort of place where a half-chicken, tasty salad and cold drink costs JD2.200, and the *fuul* and humous are popular among locals.

Mankal Chicken Tikka (King Abdullah St) specialises in chicken meals under JD2, and has been recommended by some readers.

Coffee Shop Ayola (Talal St), opposite St George's Church, is a charming, relaxed place, thankfully far too small to attract groups from the never ending tour buses. It serves delicious toasted sandwiches (JD1), all types of coffee (about JD1) and tea (500 fils), and cans of cold beer (JD1.500).

Madaba Resthouse (☎ 544069, Talal St), just north of St George's Church, puts on an extensive all-you-can-eat buffet lunch (from 1 pm) for JD6; and JD5 for dinner (from 7.30 pm). It doesn't offer anything a la carte, although anyone is welcome inside for a cold, but expensive, drink at any time.

Dana Restaurant (☎ 545749, An-Nuzha St) is not far from the Church of the Apostles. The food is OK, the place is clean and the staff are friendly, but you're paying more than necessary just for the decor and service.

Haret Jdoudna (☎ 548650, Talal St) is a new complex of arts and craft shops and places to eat and drink. The classy *restaurant* upstairs, and the *cafe* downstairs, are expensive, but worth a splurge: starters cost about JD2, and main courses, about JD4. In the same building, the *pizzeria* (accessible from the main road) serves delicious pizzas, which one reader claimed as the 'best he's had outside Italy'. There is usually live music in the courtyard on Friday.

With the predominance of Christianity in the town, many restaurants serve alcohol and there are several liquor stores around town. The dingy, but cheap, *Sam's Cafe & Lounge Shop (King Abdullah St)* is a strictly men's only bar.

Shopping

Madaba is famous for its colourful rugs, which can be bought at a few of the workshops near the Madaba Hotel. The shops opposite St George's Church do a roaring trade in ice creams, and sell some worthwhile souvenirs among the tacky stuff; and there's even a small gift shop inside the church.

In front of the tourist office, the National Society for the Preservation of the Heritage of Madaba and its Suburbs (see the boxed text over the page) has a necessarily long sign, and a friendly manager who speaks good English. As profits from the shop fund worthwhile local projects, you may consider shopping for souvenirs there.

Opposite the Archaeological Park, Madaba Zaman handicraft centre is currently closed. The best, and most expensive, place to shop for souvenirs is the impressive Haret Jdoudna complex (☎ 548650), on Talal St. It

Long Name; Good Cause

The National Society for the Preservation of the Heritage of Madaba and its Suburbs (☎ 544679) started in 1992, and now boasts a membership of more than 150. It aims to 'conserve the heritage and excavation of mosaics' in Madaba. It is partly funded by the American Centre for Oriental Research in Amman, and by the sale of maps, books and souvenirs at its shop in front of the tourist office.

boasts 20 arts and craft shops, including a branch of the Wadi Dana shop (see the Dana Nature Reserve section later in this chapter); several workshops for weaving, mosaics and painting; occasional live music (usually Friday); and a few restaurants. The complex is worth a look around.

Getting There & Away
The grotty bus/minibus station-cum-market is just off the King's Highway, a few minutes walk down from the town centre.

To/From Amman From Raghadan, Wahadat and Al-Quds St bus stations in Amman, buses (250 fils) and minibuses (200 fils) leave every 15 minutes or so for Madaba (one hour). They sometimes also leave from the more convenient Abdali bus station in Amman, but don't count on it. The last minibuses for Amman leave Madaba at about 7.30 pm. Surprisingly, very few service taxis bother travelling this route.

To/From Karak Public transport between Madaba and Karak is currently diabolical. One or two buses leave at about 6.30 am every day from the bus/minibus station in Madaba for Mu'tah University, about 12km south of Karak, and stop at, or near, the bus/minibus station in Karak. However, this bus rarely operates when the university is on holiday, and is no good for a trip from Karak to Madaba – see Getting There & Away in the Karak section later in this chapter.

The best option is a regular minibus to Dhiban (250 fils, 45 minutes) and then a char-tered taxi across to Ariha (see the Wadi Mujib section below). From Ariha, minibuses to Karak (500 fils, 45 minutes) leave about seven times a day from the small, mud-brick bus shelter under the mosque. The mosque is at the first T-junction if coming from Dhiban (ie about 2.5km south of Trajan Restaurant).

Alternatively, charter a service taxi or private taxi to Karak from Madaba (about JD17). It may end up being quicker to catch a minibus (or hitch a ride) from Dhiban to the Desert Highway, and wave down a minibus to Karak along the Desert Highway; or even go all the way back to Amman (Wahadat station) from Madaba and catch something to Karak from there.

To/From Other Places From near the bus/minibus station in Madaba (see the Madaba map), minibuses go to Mukawir (for Machaerus castle). To Fasaliyya village (for Mt Nebo), minibuses leave from the bus/minibus station and from outside the Bank of Jordan, on the corner of Palestine and King Abdullah streets. To Ma'in and Hammamat Ma'in, minibuses leave from an informal spot on a corner along King Abdullah St.

Refer to the Around Madaba section below for more details about transport to these and other places near Madaba.

Getting Around
Central Madaba is easy to get around on foot. If you have heavy bags, charter a taxi between the bus/minibus station and your hotel. Service taxis and private taxis can easily be chartered to anywhere around Madaba, and as far as Amman and Karak. However, drivers are becoming used to big-spending foreigners worried about the difficulties of public transport to Karak, and to attractions near Madaba, so you'll have to bargain hard for a fair price.

AROUND MADABA
There are several attractions around Madaba, but most are difficult to reach by public transport. If you don't have the time to wait around for infrequent minibuses and service taxis, and don't want to hitch, consider chartering a taxi in Madaba – most visitors do.

Two worthwhile trips by chartered taxi (or rented car from Amman) are: a hurried half day to Mt Nebo, Khirbat Mukhayyat, Ayoun Musa and Hammamat Ma'in, for about JD20 per vehicle; or a full day to the places listed above, as well as Mukawir, Umm ar-Rasas and Wadi Mujib, with a possible drop-off at Ariha (for the minibus to Karak), for about JD35.

Mt Nebo جبل نيبو

Mt Nebo is where Moses apparently saw the forbidden Promised Land, and later died and was buried. Consequently, it is the most revered Christian site in Jordan.

Mt Nebo (also known as Al-Mukhayyat) features several peaks including Siyagha ('monastery' in Aramaic), on which the Moses Memorial Church was built. Scholars don't agree on the actual site of Moses' tomb.

Still, Mt Nebo is a pleasant side-trip from Madaba, even if a little overrated by local tourist authorities. The plateau commands sweeping views, and some readers rate the mosaic here better than those in Madaba.

Information Entry to the church complex at Mt Nebo costs 500 fils. The ticket in-

cludes a small map which makes little sense unless you correlate it with the display of the complex in the Basilica, or the map in this book. The complex is open every day from 7 am to 5 pm (until 7 pm in summer), and photography is permitted.

Anyone with any specific interest in Mt Nebo can buy the hefty *Town of Nebo*, by Fr Sylvester J Salter & Fr Bellarmiro Bagatti, which also details other Christian sites in Jordan. More portable and affordable (JD4) is *Mount Nebo* by Michelle Piccirillo. Both are available inside the Basilica. The two brochures published by the Jordan Tourism Board – *Madaba and Mt Nebo* and, especially, *Mount Nebo* – are very informative, and available at the tourist office in Madaba.

The *resthouse* inside the complex seems to be permanently closed, but food and soft drinks are available at *Siyagha Restaurant*, and a couple of other uninspiring places, at the turn off to Ayoun Musa.

Moses Memorial Church Information about the original church is scarce. The existence of the church was first reported by a Roman nun, Etheria, in about 393 AD; and by the 6th century, it had expanded to become a

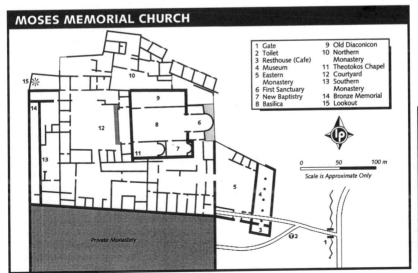

MOSES MEMORIAL CHURCH

1 Gate
2 Toilet
3 Resthouse (Cafe)
4 Museum
5 Eastern Monastery
6 First Sanctuary
7 New Baptistry
8 Basilica
9 Old Diaconicon
10 Northern Monastery
11 Theotokos Chapel
12 Courtyard
13 Southern Monastery
14 Bronze Memorial
15 Lookout

0   50   100 m
Scale is Approximate Only

Private Monastery

large Byzantine monastery. The Franciscan Brothers bought the site in the 1930s, and have excavated most of the ruins of the church and monastery. The main building open to visitors is the **Basilica**, built in the second half of the 6th century. The huge **mosaic** on the floor is another quite remarkable work of patient artistry, with scenes of wine-making and hunting, and an assortment of animals, such as panther, bear, fox, zebus and lion (all of which are now extinct in Jordan). The mosaic measures about 9m by 3m, and is very well preserved.

There is little else to see around the complex except the decrepit ruins of parts of the monastery. From the **lookout** at the back (west) of the **courtyard**, the views across the valleys to the Dead Sea and Jerusalem are superb – but often restricted by haze and pollution. Nearby, a huge **bronze memorial** symbolises the suffering and death of Jesus on the cross and the serpent which 'Moses lifted up' (John 3:14).

The map provided with the entrance ticket indicates a 'museum', but this is far from being realised. Some of the complex is part of a functioning monastery and is, therefore, off-limits to visitors.

Getting There & Away From Madaba, minibuses (150 fils, 15 minutes) leave from the bus/minibus station and from outside the Bank of Jordan building on the corner of Palestine and King Abdullah streets. The minibus stops at Fasaliyya village, from where it's a pleasant (and not too steep) 4km walk to the church complex. There are no taxis to charter in Fasaliyya, but it would be easy to hitch a ride between Fasaliyya and the church.

A return trip in a chartered service taxi or private taxi from Madaba, with about 30 minutes to look around, will cost about JD4 per vehicle; about JD5 to JD6, including a detour to, and short wait at, Khirbat Mukhayyat.

Khirbat Mukhayyat   خربة مخيط

Near the village of Khirbat Mukhayyat, the original site of Mt Nebo village, is the **Church of SS Lot and Procopius**, originally built in the late 6th century AD. Inside this unremarkable building is a remarkable **mosaic**, with representations of daily activities, such as agriculture and wine-making. The church is permanently closed, so find the gatekeeper (who lives only a few metres away) to open it for you – 500 fils is a sufficient inducement.

On top of a nearby hill lies the obvious ruins of the **Church of St George**, built in 536 AD. Very little remains, but if you're interested, ask the gatekeeper if it's OK to walk there for a look. The countryside is appealing, and nice for short **hikes**.

The turn-off to Khirbat Mukhayyat is well signposted, about 3km to the left (south) before reaching the church complex at Mt Nebo. A surprisingly good road leads into the village, but the road to the Church of SS Lot & Procopius is rough and steep. There is no regular public transport to the village or the churches, and hitching is difficult. If you have chartered a taxi to Mt Nebo, pay a little more (about JD1 to JD2 extra) for a sidetrip to Khirbat Mukhayyat.

Ayoun ('Ain) Musa   عين موسى

Ayoun Musa ('Spring of Moses') is where the great man is believed to have obtained water by striking a rock – see the special section 'Biblical Jordan' in the Facts about Jordan chapter. There is little to see except the **ruins** of a couple of churches, but the countryside is charming and there are some enticing **hiking** opportunities.

The obvious turn-off is to the right (north), about 1km before the church complex at Mt Nebo and opposite some restaurants and souvenir shops. There is no public transport in the area, and hitching will be very difficult. A trip can be combined with a visit to Mt Nebo by chartered taxi, although the road to Ayoun Musa is often treacherous and taxi drivers are reluctant to go along this road unless given substantial extra financial incentive.

Hammamat Ma'in (Zarqa Ma'in)

حمامات معن (معن الزرقاء)   ☎ 05

About 60 thermal springs have been discovered in the area south and west of Madaba. The therapeutic values of the most famous, Hammamat Ma'in (sometimes referred to as Zarqa Ma'in after the Zarqa river which feeds the springs), have been enjoyed by luminaries such as Herod the Great. The water is hot (about 45°C), and contains potassium, magnesium and calcium, among other minerals.

The complex at Hammamat Ma'in is looking forlorn these days, but is being given a well-needed facelift by a French-based consortium. Inevitably, the springs will become a bit more upmarket, and therefore probably more expensive to visit, but don't worry: the redevelopment is slated to take 30 years.

Information Visitors are not allowed to bring food or drink into the complex, but while the boots of private/rented cars and chartered taxis may be searched for large quantities of food and drink, personal bags are not. Try to avoid Friday and public holidays when this place is far too busy.

Foreigners are charged an entrance fee of JD2 just to enter the site; JD3.850 includes as much time as you want at the swimming pool and public baths. If you're clambering around the waterfalls and rocks, wear something on your feet because the ground is often hot and sharp.

Springs, Pools & Baths There are three main baths and pools in the complex. The **public baths** have clean indoor hot baths (separate for men and women), and are open from 8 am to midnight every day. It is set up mainly for locals (but foreigners are welcome), and little English is spoken.

The large, clean **swimming pool** has cold water, and is uncrowded most of the time – except for Friday, or if a particularly large tour bus arrives. The poolside *restaurant* is pleasant, and offers a set lunch for a reasonable JD3.300; and a *bar* is attached. This pool is open from 8 am to 4.30 pm every day.

Steps up from The Chalet (see Places to Stay & Eat below) lead to the warm-water **family pool**, situated under a hot waterfall. This is only for families, couples and unaccompanied women, and is the only place where women (accompanied by men or not) will feel comfortable swimming and relaxing. Entrance to this pool is not included in the ticket price of JD3.850, and costs an extra JD1.100 per person.

For a free (albeit basic) spa and sauna, walk along the road under the Ashtar Hotel to the mosque about 200m further on. Another 50m up there's a natural sulphur spa bath, and the cave to the right is a good makeshift sauna. The steps behind the mosque lead to the top of a waterfall, and to the ruins of some old **deserted houses**. This is not an area where women will feel comfortable.

Places to Stay & Eat There is nowhere cheap to stay, unless you discreetly search for a secluded camping spot away from the complex. The unexceptional *caravans* at the back of the Drop & Shop 'supermarket' were closed at the time of research. They normally offer tiny, airless cabins for about JD16.500/22 for singles/doubles, and day rates (ie not staying overnight) are about JD10 per cabin.

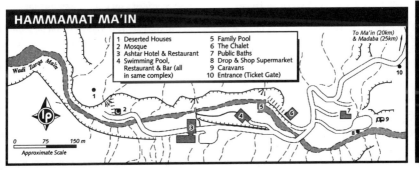

HAMMAMAT MA'IN

1 Deserted Houses	5 Family Pool
2 Mosque	6 The Chalet
3 Ashtar Hotel & Restaurant	7 Public Baths
4 Swimming Pool,	8 Drop & Shop Supermarket
Restaurant & Bar (all	9 Caravans
in same complex)	10 Entrance (Ticket Gate)

To Ma'in (20km) & Madaba (25km)

Wadi Zarqa Ma'in

0   75   150 m
Approximate Scale

KING'S HIGHWAY

The Chalet (☎/fax 545500) is also due for an overhaul. Currently, an unimpressive room, with a small bathroom and kitchen, costs JD22/33/44 for singles/doubles/triples. Day rates are about JD20 per chalet.

Ashtar Hotel (☎/fax 545500) has luxurious rooms for US$84/108, and guests have access to a private spa and health facilities. The *restaurant* on the ground floor has spectacular views overlooking the waterfall. Buffets for breakfast cost JD4.200; JD8.400 for lunch or dinner.

The Drop & Shop 'supermarket' has a basic array of cold drinks and snack food at expensive prices, but little else. Some construction work inside indicates the opening of a coffee shop sometime in the future.

Getting There & Away Although just 4km from the Dead Sea Highway, the only access road starts from the King's Highway. Hammamat Ma'in is about 27km southwest of Madaba.

Bus & Minibus From Amman, the JETT bus company offers return trips every day to Hammamat Ma'in for JD4, if returning the same day; JD7.500, if returning the following day (ie staying overnight at your own expense); and JD10 for same-day return, including entrance fee to the pools and baths, and lunch. The latter is a pretty good deal. From Hammamat Ma'in, you may be able to catch a lift on the JETT bus to Amman (about JD4), via Madaba (about JD1), which leaves at about 5 pm. For enquiries, contact the JETT domestic office in Amman (see that chapter for details), or the Ashtar Hotel.

About four minibuses (JD1.500, 1½ hours) a day travel from Wahadat bus station in Amman to Hammamat Ma'in, but be early and be patient. More regular minibuses go from Abdali bus station in Amman to Ma'in village (JD1.250, 1¼ hours), from where you'll have to organise onward transport to the springs. But remember: it's far easier to hitch a ride back from the springs to Madaba than the other way around.

From Madaba, minibuses regularly go to Ma'in village (150 fils, 15 minutes) from the spot indicated on the Madaba map – but the driver will only go to Hammamat Ma'in if there's sufficient demand (more likely on Friday), or financial incentive from passengers. The cheapest way to Hammamat Ma'in from Madaba is to catch a minibus to Ma'in village, get off at the roundabout with the carved 'gazelles' (rather than go into Ma'in itself) and hitch a ride from there. Something will come along soon enough; in fact, the JETT bus from Amman goes past at about 9 am, and may pick you up (for a negotiable fare).

Taxi A chartered service taxi or private taxi from Madaba will cost about JD4 one-way or about JD7 return, including about one hour waiting time. These taxis are best arranged at the same departure point along King Abdullah St in Madaba as the minibus to Hammamat Ma'in and Ma'in. Plenty of tourists visit the springs, so ask at hotels in Madaba about sharing the cost of a taxi ride.

Mukawir (Machaerus)

مكور(ماشيروس)

Perched on a 700m high hill, just beyond the village of Mukawir, are the ruins of Herod the Great's castle, Machaerus.

The hill was first fortified in about 100 BC, and expanded by Herod the Great in 30 BC. Machaerus is more renowned as the place where St John the Baptist was murdered – see the special section 'Biblical Jordan' in the Facts about Jordan chapter.

Machaerus is remote and difficult to reach, and there isn't a lot to see. However, the **views** of the Dead Sea from the top of Machaerus are superb, and it's serene because tour buses do not venture this far.

Castle Machaerus is known to the locals as **Qala'at al-Meshneq** ('Gallows Castle'). Past the workers' huts are some **baths** and around to the east and north are vestiges of Herod Antipas' **palace**. On the west side, parts of the **wall** and defensive **towers** can be seen, and from here are the best **views**. All of the mosaics, and the best pieces excavated, have been transferred to the museum in Madaba, and elsewhere around Jordan.

The castle is about 2km past the village, and easy to spot. The main road goes through

CHRISTOPHER WOOD

CHRISTOPHER WOOD

CHRISTOPHER WOOD

DAMIEN SIMONIS

Top: Qasr Kharana lies isolated and serene on the basalt plains of eastern Jordan.
Middle: The best preserved of the desert castles, Qusayr Amra features a fresco of a nude woman.
Bottom: The King's Highway winds precariously through the majestic Wadi Mujib.

PATRICK SYDER

The bronze memorial upon Mt Nebo

INGRID RODDIS

The glacis separates Karak castle from the town.

PAUL GREENWAY

Qasr al-Hallabat, erected under Emperor Caracalla

PAUL GREENWAY

Shobak Castle was once a Crusader stronghold.

PAUL GREENWAY

Towering gorge at Wadi Mujib

the village and ends at a car park, where the friendly caretaker can show you the start of the two tracks to the castle at the top of the hill. The longer route winds around the hill and goes past a cave where St John was apparently beheaded. Quicker (about 30 minutes), but less interesting and harder to find, is the track straight to the top.

Bani Hamida Centre At the end of the village, and the start of the road to the castle, is a women's co-operative, Weaving Project Center & Gallery, run by Bani Hamida (see the boxed text). Visitors are always welcome to look around, and it's open from 8 am to 3 pm, Saturday to Wednesday.

Places to Stay & Eat There were plans to open a small guest house in Mukawir (on the left and before the Bani Hamida Centre). It was abandoned before completion, but it may open sometime in the future. There is no reason to stay overnight in Mukawir, unless

The Bani Hamida Story

One of the several organisations in Jordan which sells goods to fund local charity projects (see Shopping in the Facts for the Visitor chapter) is Bani Hamida, named after a group of people who settled in the remote village of Mukawir.

Created under the auspices of the Save the Children fund, and with continuing assistance from the Canadian and US governments, the Weaving Project Center & Gallery was established in Mukawir to revive traditional weaving practices, raise money for the development of villages in the area and improve the independence and self-respect of local women. The project now employs about 1600 women who work in the gallery at Mukawir, or at home in one of 12 nearby villages.

Some of the items made, and available for sale, in Mukawir and Bani Hamida House in Amman include pottery, baskets, jewellery, rugs, mats, cushions and bags. Some of the stuff is created using traditional looms, and is coloured with natural dyes.

you're stuck because of infrequent public transport, although the views at night over to Israel are wonderful. There are a couple of grocery stores in the village.

Getting There & Away From just outside the bus/minibus station in Madaba (see the Madaba map), minibuses (300 fils, one hour) go to the village of Mukawir, via Libb, four or five times a day – the last at about 5 pm. Hitching from the turn-off along the King's Highway is possible, but be prepared for a long wait.

Umm ar-Rasas أم الرصاص

Umm ar-Rasas is thought to be the village of Kastron Mefaa, mentioned in the Bible as a Roman military outpost.

A light-green tin shed hangs over the ruins of the **Church of St Stephen**, one of four churches in the original village. Inside the shed are marvellous **mosaics** dating back to about 785 AD, and equally as impressive as anything in Madaba. The main mosaic clearly shows hunting, fishing and agriculture; scenes of daily life, such as boys enjoying a boat ride; and the names of those who helped pay for the mosaic. The edges of the mosaic are particularly decorative.

Close by are the limited **ruins** of Kastron Mefaa village. While nothing is labelled or signposted, it's fun to wander around. About 1.5km north of the ruins is a 15m **stone tower**, the purpose of which baffles archaeologists because there are no stairs inside but several windows at the top.

The caretaker at the church speaks little English, but can provide a photocopy of an explanation in English about the church and mosaic. Entrance is free, and it's open every day during daylight hours – but in reality, opening hours are at the whim of the caretaker. If the shed is locked, ask around for the caretaker and/or the key.

Getting There & Away A few minibuses go directly to Umm ar-Rasas, via Nitil, from the bus/minibus station in Madaba. Alternatively, catch anything going to Dhiban, and hitch a ride from there. The best option is to charter a private taxi from

A Stele at Twice the Price

The original Mesha Stele was found by a missionary at Dhiban in 1868. It was a major discovery because it not only provided historical detail of the battles between the Moabites and the kings of Israel but was also the earliest example of Hebrew script to be unearthed. After surviving intact from about 850 BC (when it was raised by King Mesha of Moab to let everyone know of his successes against Israel) to 1868 AD, it came to a rather unfortunate end.

After finding the stele, the missionary reported it to Charles Clermont-Ganneau at the French consulate in Jerusalem who then saw it, made a mould of it and went back to Jerusalem to raise the money which he had offered the locals for it. While he was away, the local families argued over who was going to get the money and some of the discontented lit a fire under the stone and then poured water on it, causing it to shatter. Although most pieces were recovered, inevitably some were lost. The remnants were gathered together and shipped off to France, and the reconstructed stone is now on display in the Louvre in Paris. Copies can be seen in the museums at Madaba and Karak.

the obvious turn-off at the roundabout in the middle of Dhiban, but the taxi drivers there are unscrupulous and demand about JD5/7 one-way/return, including some waiting time. Umm ar-Rasas is also accessible from the Desert Highway by private or chartered vehicle, but not by public transport.

The site is well signposted from the Desert and King's highways, but there is no sign whatsoever in the immediate area to indicate the actual location of the shed and ruins. The shed is about 400m behind a largish and obvious post office; take any path (accessible also by vehicle) from either side of the post office. The post office is 500m north of a T-junction at the road between the King's and Desert highways and the signposted road leading north to Nitil.

WADI MUJIB   وادي مجيب

Stretching across Jordan from the Desert Highway to the Dead Sea is the incredibly vast and beautiful Wadi Mujib valley. As well as spectacular, it's also historically known as the obvious boundary between the ancient Amorites (to the north) and the Moabites (to the south), as mentioned in the Bible. Politically, the valley now divides the governorates of Madaba (to the north) and Karak (to the south). The valley, which is about 1km deep and over 4km from one edge to another, is definitely worth seeing even if you don't intend going farther south to Karak along the King's Highway.

At the bottom of the valley, there's a bridge; a tiny, forlorn post office; and huts belonging to the hundreds of workers involved in the massive road works and the building of a dam. This construction (which can't possibly be finished before the end of 2000) is, according to local authorities, the reason why public transport between Ariha (on the southern edge) and Dhiban (to the north) has currently ceased.

Wadi Mujib Reserve
حديقة وادي مجيب الوطنية

The Wadi Mujib river and valley are now part of the vast Wadi Mujib Reserve (212 sq km). It was established in 1987 by the Royal Society for the Conservation of Nature (RSCN) for the captive breeding of Nubian ibex (which will eventually be reintroduced into the wild).

With permission from the RSCN, camping is allowed at two undeveloped places: **Wadi Mujib Campsite**, near the King's Highway; and **Radas Campsite**, closer to the Dead Sea Highway. The camp sites are open in summer (1 April to 15 October), and access costs about JD4 per person per night.

The RSCN allows hiking along two short trails, as well as the difficult 'Wadi Mujib Trail' (18km) from the King's Highway to the Dead Sea. Guides are available from the RSCN, but the region is extremely hot and dry in summer, so avoid hiking then. The RSCN is also developing trips down the river when there is enough water (ie in winter).

All permits for camping and hiking must be pre-arranged with the RSCN in Amman –

see the National Parks section in the Facts about Jordan chapter for details. There is no access into the reserve without a permit.

Dhiban ضبـان

Dhiban was once the powerful town of Dibon, the capital of an empire carved out by King Mesha in the 9th century BC, and is where the Mesha Stele was discovered (refer to the boxed text 'A Stele at Twice the Price'). There is nothing left of the ancient city, but the small, friendly village is still an important junction for transport to Umm ar-Rasas and Ariha; and it has a few dismal *eateries*.

About 3km down (south) from Dhiban is an awesome **lookout** over Wadi Mujib valley. To admire the views without crossing the valley, walk (or charter a taxi) to the lookout from Dhiban.

Ariha أريحـا

The only regular long-distance public transport north of Karak stops at Ariha. About 2.5km north of Ariha, and at the southern edge of Wadi Mujib valley, is the huge, unmissable *Trajan Restaurant*. It offers extraordinary views, as well as cold drinks, meals and souvenirs at extraordinary prices. In the future, it may be possible to stay there. It's also a good place to hitch a ride.

Ara'ir عرايـر

About 5km east of the King's Highway between Dhiban and Ariha is the village of Ara'ir. Nearby are the limited **ruins** of a Moabite village (referred to in the Bible as Aro'er), which includes one of King Mesha's fortresses. The village and ruins are best reached by rented car or chartered taxi from Madaba or Dhiban.

Getting There & Away

Dhiban is where almost all transport south of Madaba currently stops. At the moment, the only way across the mighty Wadi Mujib valley from Dhiban to Ariha (about 30km) is to charter a taxi for about JD3/6 one-way/return. (Finding a taxi in Ariha is a lot, lot harder.) Bargain hard, and be wary of drivers claiming extra payment for cleaning the car afterwards! Hitching is possible, but

will take a long time and the competition for lifts is fierce – and make sure your ride doesn't finish in the middle of the road works at the bottom of the valley.

KARAK الكرك

☎ 03

The greater part of Karak is 900m above sea level, and lies within the walls of an old Crusader city. The old city is dominated by a fortified castle – one in a long line built by the Crusaders stretching from Aqaba in the south to Turkey in the north.

Karak is harder to reach from Amman than Madaba, and is sometimes ignored by travellers speeding south to Petra, Wadi Rum and Aqaba, but the castle and charming old city are worth the effort. The downside is the lousy choice of hotels and restaurants.

History

Karak lies on the routes of ancient caravans that used to travel from Egypt to Syria in the time of the Biblical kings, and were also used by the Greeks and Romans. The city is mentioned several times in the Bible as Kir, Kir Moab and Kir Heres and later emerges as a provincial Roman town, Characmoba. The city also features on the famous mosaic in St George's Church in Madaba.

The arrival of the Crusaders launched the city back into prominence and the Crusader king, Baldwin I of Jerusalem, had the castle built in 1142 AD. This site was chosen because it was strategically placed midway between Shobak and Jerusalem and had a commanding position. It became the capital of the Crusader district of Oultrejourdain and, with the taxes levied on passing caravans and food grown in the district, helped Jerusalem prosper. The dry moat (currently being re-created) and towers were built later.

The castle was passed on to the de Milly family and through marriage fell into the hands of the rogue, Renauld de Chatillon, who delighted in torturing prisoners and throwing them off the walls into the valley 450m below; he even went to the trouble of having a wooden box fastened over their heads so they wouldn't lose consciousness before hitting the ground.

KING'S HIGHWAY

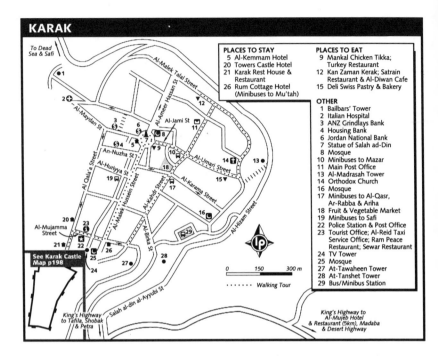

KARAK

To Dead
Sea & Safi

Al-Malek Talal Street

Al-ameer Hassan St

Al-Jami St

Al-Maydan St

An-Nuzha St

Al-Huriyya St

Al-Qala'a Street

Al-Malek Hussein Street

Al-Kahub Street

Al-Umari Street

Al-Karama Street

Al-Birka St

Al-Hizam Street

Al-Mujamma
Street

See Karak Castle
Map p198

Salah al-din al-Ayyubi St

King's Highway
to Tafila, Shobak
& Petra

King's Highway to
Al-Mujeb Hotel
& Restaurant (5km), Madaba
& Desert Highway

0　　150　　300 m

· · · · · ·　Walking Tour

PLACES TO STAY
5　Al-Kemmam Hotel
20　Towers Castle Hotel
21　Karak Rest House & Restaurant
26　Rum Cottage Hotel (Minibuses to Mu'tah)

PLACES TO EAT
9　Mankal Chicken Tikka; Turkey Restaurant
12　Kan Zaman Kerak; Satrain Restaurant & Al-Diwan Cafe
15　Deli Swiss Pastry & Bakery

OTHER
1　Bailbars' Tower
2　Italian Hospital
3　ANZ Grindlays Bank
4　Housing Bank
6　Jordan National Bank
7　Statue of Salah ad-Din
8　Mosque
10　Minibuses to Mazar
11　Main Post Office
13　Al-Madrasah Tower
14　Orthodox Church
16　Mosque
17　Minibuses to Al-Qasr, Ar-Rabba & Ariha
18　Fruit & Vegetable Market
19　Minibuses to Safi
22　Police Station & Post Office
23　Tourist Office; Al-Reid Taxi Service Office; Ram Peace Restaurant; Sewar Restaurant
24　TV Tower
25　Mosque
27　At-Tawaheen Tower
28　At-Tanshet Tower
29　Bus/Minibus Station

De Chatillon was later executed for thievery, and the castle finally fell to the Ayyubids after an eight month siege, dubbed the Battle of Hattin, in 1188 AD.

The Mamluk sultan Beybars strengthened the fortress, deepened the moat and added the lower courtyard in the late 13th century, but three towers collapsed in an earthquake in 1293. Nothing much more is known about the castle until the 1880s, when local infighting compelled the Christians of Karak to flee north to Madaba and Ma'in; peace was only restored after thousands of Turkish troops were stationed in the town.

Orientation & Information

The old city of Karak is easy to get around, although none of the streets are signposted. If you get disoriented, use the huge TV tower near the castle as a landmark. Other landmarks are the crumbling **towers** strategically placed on the edges of the old city. The town centre is around the statue of Salah ad-Din.

The area near the entrance to the castle is a bit of a tourist trap, and furtive and blatant overcharging is common in the hotels, shops and restaurants there.

The *Al Karak* map published by the Royal Jordanian Geographic Centre is mildly useful, and includes small maps of Ar-Rabba and Al-Qasr (see the Around Karak section later in this chapter), but the map in this book is detailed enough for most visitors.

The new tourist office (☎ 301 0750), above the Sewar Restaurant along Al-Mujamma St, is open from 8 am to 2 pm every day, except Friday, but is of limited use. Several banks will change money, such as ANZ Grindlays Bank and Jordan National Bank on Al-Maydan St, and the best is the Housing Bank on An-Nuzha St, which has an ATM for Visa.

A police station (☎ 191) is located along Al-Mujamma St, near the main entrance to the castle; and the well-equipped Italian Hospital is along Al-Maydan St. The main post office is along Al-Khadr St in the lower

Careering Around Karak

Other than the castle, there's little to see in Karak, but you can try this walking tour if you have the time. Allow about one hour (excluding time in the castle).

The best place to start and finish is the magnificent Karak Castle. From there head east along Al-Mujamma St, and perhaps pop into the **tourist office** and have something to eat at one of the nearby **cafes**. Then turn left (north) and walk down Al-Malek Hussein St. At the end is the chaotic square around the **statue of Salah ad-Din**. The **mosque** is worth a quick look, but be discreet.

Continue east along Al-Jami St, turn left (north) down Al-Khadr St, and then head left (north-west) along Al-Malek Talal St to **Kan Zaman Kerak**, which has an expensive **restaurant** upstairs and a charming and cheaper **cafe** downstairs. Continue south-east, and then south, along Al-Malek Talal, and enjoy the **views** from the perimeter of the old city. An interesting **orthodox church** is on a corner along Al-Malek Talal.

Turn right (north-west) along Al-Umari St, and try something at the incongruously classy (but pricey) **Deli Swiss Pastry & Bakery**. Then head left (south) up Al-Khadr St, past the **fruit & vegetable market**. Turn left (east and then south) at the corner of Al-Khadr and Al-Mujamma streets and look for **At-Tawaheen Tower**, and admire some more **views** before returning to the castle.

(northern) part of town, but a smaller, more convenient, post office is inside the police station near the entrance to the castle. The Karak Rest House and Al-Mujeb Hotel (see Places to Stay later in this chapter) have small shops selling gifts and books.

Karak can be windy, and chilly in the evening (even in summer), so come prepared.

Karak Castle

Information Surprisingly, no detailed maps of the castle are available in Karak or other places in Jordan, but the useful display in the foyer of the Karak Rest House indicates what the castle used to look like. If travelling independently, start exploring the castle before 10 am and/or after 4 pm, ie when the tour buses are absent. Bring a torch (flashlight) to explore the darker regions. Anyone over about 1m tall should constantly watch their head; the original inhabitants of the castle must have been very small.

The castle is open from 8 am to 5 pm every day; the museum, from 8 am to 4 pm. At the time of research, plenty of construction was going on at the entrance: the old dry moat was being re-created, and a few shops and restaurants were being built close by. Some Japanese funding is also helping to improve the inside of the castle.

Currently, there are no signposts or labels in any language inside the castle, which is why guides can charge JD4 per group (about five people) for a whirlwind tour (about 30 minutes).

Things to See The main entrance is known as **Ottoman's Gate**, which is at the end of a short bridge across what will be a re-created dry moat. (Another entrance, called the **Crusader Gate**, is under construction.) From Ottoman's Gate, head past the ticket office and up the stairs to the top level of the castle. To the left (east), is a long undercover building known as the **Crusader Gallery**, or **stables**, used to house horses which seemed to enjoy better living conditions than the soldiers (and certainly the prisoners).

At the far end of the gallery, in an area called the **Nabataean Church**, is a **Nabataean carving** of a body without a head. Not much is known about the carving, and it's hard to find without a guide. At the end of the gallery, an obvious passageway heads to the right (south-west). To the left (south-east) are the **soldiers' barracks**, a two-storey room with a small hole in the floor for light, and walls made of limestone and straw. The room has some **rock inscriptions** from the Byzantine period.

To the right (west) is the **kitchen**, which contains some large round stones used for grounding olives, and huge storage areas

KARAK CASTLE

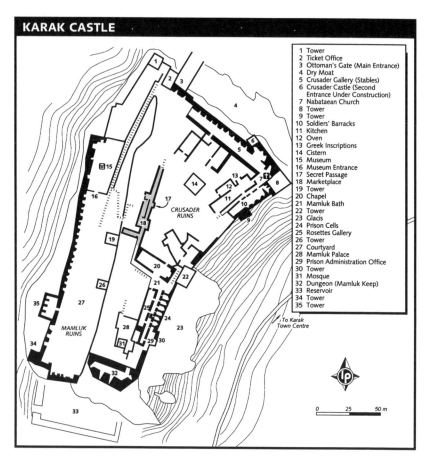

1 Tower
2 Ticket Office
3 Ottoman's Gate (Main Entrance)
4 Dry Moat
5 Crusader Gallery (Stables)
6 Crusader Castle (Second Entrance Under Construction)
7 Nabataean Church
8 Tower
9 Tower
10 Soldiers' Barracks
11 Kitchen
12 Oven
13 Greek Inscriptions
14 Cistern
15 Museum
16 Museum Entrance
17 Secret Passage
18 Marketplace
19 Tower
20 Chapel
21 Mamluk Bath
22 Tower
23 Glacis
24 Prison Cells
25 Rosettes Gallery
26 Tower
27 Courtyard
28 Mamluk Palace
29 Prison Administration Office
30 Tower
31 Mosque
32 Dungeon (Mamluk Keep)
33 Reservoir
34 Tower
35 Tower

To Karak Town Centre

0   25   50 m

for oil and wheat. In a dark tunnel (only visible with a torch) are some **Greek inscriptions** that no-one knows anything about. A door from the kitchen leads to the right (west) to the huge **oven**, a room with a chimney and even a kitchen sink.

Back up to the top level, past a **cistern**, and along the eastern edge, is the **glacis**, an incredibly steep rocky slope built so invaders could not climb up and prisoners from the prison underneath could not escape. This is where Renauld de Chatillon also delighted in expelling undesirables (see the History section earlier). The slope and attached tower were being rebuilt at the time of research.

Down some nearby steps is another underground passageway. To the left (east) are seven **prison cells**; at the end (south) is the **prison administration office**. To the right (west) is what is called (for reasons unknown) the **Rosettes Gallery**, a living area for soldiers. The walls have several **columns** and **inscriptions** from Roman times. The prison was also used by the Mamluks, who built the **Mamluk Bath**, north of Rosettes Gallery.

Further south (but only accessible by stairs from the top level) is the **Mamluk**

Palace, built in the 14th century. This was used as a small open-air school and a mosque, with an obvious *mihrab* (niche facing towards Mecca) attached.

Heading back to the entrance to the prison, bear left (west) along a small corridor which opens out to a remarkable **marketplace** with several adjoining **cellars**. One room to the right (east), but only visible with a torch, is believed to be an (unexcavated) **secret passage** used during sieges to reach a room full of food and water.

Back on the top level, look for the ruins of the **chapel** near the entrance down to the prison. Then head south to the end of the castle to the **dungeon**, a multi-storeyed building also known as the **Mamluk keep**. The main gate is unfortunately closed, but the **views** from the top are superb if you can arrange for someone to open it up. Further south, and separate from the castle, are the ruins of a **reservoir**.

Housed in a former soldiers' barracks is a small, but well presented, museum (☎ 215 1149). It has bits and pieces from the castle, and from other nearby sites such as Tafila, Ar-Rabba and Lot's Cave, as well as a copy of the Mesha Steele (see the boxed text earlier in this chapter). Everything is well labelled in English, and it's open from 8 am to 4 pm every day.

Places to Stay

Four hotels recently amalgamated into two, so the choice of places to stay is now limited and the names can be confusing. The Rum Cottage and Towers Castle hotels, as well as several nearby restaurants, are all owned by the same man, so prices are a little high and bargaining is difficult.

Al-Kemmam Hotel (☎ 351942, Al-Maydan St), formerly known as the New Hotel, is the cheapest place, and the only one in the town centre. Beds in shared rooms cost JD3 per person. Guests can use the kitchen.

Rum Cottage Hotel (☎ 351351, fax 354 293, Al-Mujamma St) was once known as the Rum Hotel, but is confusingly still signposted as the 'Ram'. The hotel officially promises (but often does not provide) a fan, and make sure the hot water is working be-

fore handing over any money. It's on a noisy corner, and near a mosque. Singles/doubles cost JD12/17, with a private bathroom; or JD5 per person for a bed in a shared room, with a grotty communal bathroom. Breakfast costs an extra JD1 per person.

Towers Castle Hotel (☎ 352489, fax 354 293, Al-Qala'a St) is a little quieter than the Rum Cottage, and you may be able to get a room with a great view for nothing extra. Large, bright and clean rooms, with a private bathroom (but unreliable hot water), cost JD12/16; less comfortable rooms, with a shared bathroom, are JD10/12. All prices include breakfast.

Karak Rest House (☎ 351148, fax 353 148) is hard to miss at the main entrance to the castle. It has great rooms with outstanding views, a fridge, satellite TV and spotless private bathroom, for JD27.500/38.500, including a great breakfast. This is one place that is worth a splurge.

Al-Mujeb Hotel (☎ 386090, fax 386091) has luxurious rooms, with a large private bathroom, fridge and satellite TV, for JD20/30, including breakfast. Readers have raved about the service, but it is inconvenient without your own transport: it's about 5km from Karak, near the junction of the roads to Madaba (along the Desert Highway) and Amman (along the King's Highway).

Places to Eat

Most people stay near the castle, where several restaurants with pleasant outdoor settings but unremarkable food are located – but all of these places to eat seem to be managed by the same guy who runs the Towers Castle and Rum Cottage hotels.

Ram Peace Restaurant (☎ 353789, Al-Mujamma St) does strange versions of western food, so it's best to stick with what the cook knows best, ie Arabic cuisine.

Sewar Restaurant (☎ 352677, Al-Mujamma St) includes soups and dips with all main courses (priced from JD2.500), but the food is very ordinary.

Karak Rest House (see Places to Stay) has splendid views over the Dead Sea on a clear day, but caters mainly to tour groups, although independent travellers are welcome.

The buffet at JD7 is pricey, but the spread is lavish. It also has a charming outdoor *cafe*, where small cans of beer cost JD2.500.

Al-Mujeb Hotel also has a huge restaurant and cafe, but it's a long way from Karak (see Places to Stay).

Overlooking Salah ad-Din's statue in the town centre, *Turkey Restaurant* and its neighbour *Mankal Chicken Tikka* get mixed reviews from readers.

Deli Swiss Pastry & Bakery (☎ 351717, Al-Umari St) is a superb French-style place, probably the best of its kind in Jordan. It offers croissants, pies and other pastries, as well as burgers and pizzas, but the prices for everything are high, eg a cup of tea and one croissant costs JD2.

Kan Zaman Kerak (☎ 355102, Al-Malek Talal St) is a pleasant tourist complex, but doesn't have the views you would expect. Inside, *Satrain Restaurant* has good service, but the food is ordinary and pricey (about JD4.200 per main course) – although the starters (about JD1) and salads (from 700 fils) are better value. It is licensed, but alcoholic drinks are expensive. *Al-Diwan Cafe* downstairs has a selection of soft and hot drinks in a cosy, traditional atmosphere.

Getting There & Away

As with anywhere along the King's Highway, getting to and from Karak is a problem. The bus/minibus station is in the lower, south-eastern part of the old city, and the entrance is at a T-junction opposite a mosque. Some buses drop passengers off along a nearby street.

Refer to Getting There & Away in the Madaba and Wadi Mujib sections earlier in this chapter for more information about travelling between Karak and Madaba.

Bus, Minibus & Service Taxi From the bus/minibus station in Karak, minibuses and buses (both 750 fils, two hours), and occasional service taxis (JD1.250), go to Amman (Wahadat station), via the Desert Highway. Minibuses also run every hour or so along the King's Highway from Karak to Tafila (600 fils, 1½ hours), the best place for a connection to Shobak and Qadsiyya (for Dana

Nature Reserve). To Wadi Mousa (near Petra), get a minibus to Ma'an (JD1.250, two hours), which leaves three times a day (currently, 7 am, noon and 1 pm) and travels along the Desert Highway. Minibuses and buses to Aqaba (JD1.750, three hours), via the Dead Sea Highway, leave about four or five times a day (the first is about 6 am); service taxis (JD2.500) are less regular.

Minibuses along the King's Highway to Al-Qasr, Ar-Rabba and Ariha (to the north) and Mu'tah and Mazar (to the south), and to Safi on the Dead Sea Highway, depart from various spots in the old city (as indicated on the map). Consequently, these minibuses clog up the city streets, and for some reason do not use the huge, half-empty bus/minibus station.

The bus back to Madaba from Mu'tah University is no good because the departure times from the university change daily, depending on student demand and schedules.

Chartered Taxi From Amman, it is possible (with bargaining) to charter a service taxi all the way to Karak, via the Desert Highway, for about JD15 per vehicle. From Amman, via the King's Highway, with a short stopover in Madaba and stops for views across the awesome Wadi Mujib valley, a chartered service taxi will cost about JD20 – and is worth considering.

However, from Karak taxi fares are higher: there is only one taxi company, so negotiation is rarely possible. Drivers demand about JD35 to Amman, via the Desert Highway; JD30 to Petra; and JD25 to Madaba.

Getting Around

The old city of Karak would be a pleasure to walk around if not for the constant congestion of pick-ups and minibuses along the narrow and steep one-way streets. If driving to Karak in your own car, try to avoid coming into the old city. There are few places to park anyway, and the traffic is usually chaotic, so leave the vehicle somewhere outside the old city, and walk up into the city centre.

There are few taxis in the old city, except Al-Reid Taxi Service (☎ 352297), near the castle entrance. Taxis don't hang around the bus station, so it's a steep walk to your hotels.

AROUND KARAK
Dead Sea
البحر الميت

It is possible to visit the Dead Sea from Karak, but it's fairly pointless because there's nothing much to see, and nowhere to wash the salt off after a swim. (The Dead Sea section in the Northern & Western Jordan chapter has information about visiting nicer and more accessible parts of the Dead Sea.)

Regular minibuses from Karak go to the phosphate-mining town of Safi, from where it's about a 3km walk to a stretch of water. If you are heading to the Dead Sea from Karak,

In Search of Sodom

There is nothing new in the assumption that the world's naughtiest town lay somewhere around the southern end of the Dead Sea, but a team of British geologists think they have found the key to its precise location. An area of the Dead Sea south of Karak produced bitumen, a saleable item in those days and probably the 'slime pits' referred to in the Old Testament. The geologists think Sodom, and neighbouring Gomorrah, could not have been far away, since their inhabitants would have made their money from the bitumen. If they're right, the site has been under water off the east bank of the sea since Biblical times.

The Book of Genesis outlines God's displeasure at the locals' behaviour, and so 'the Lord rained upon Sodom and upon Gomorrah brimstone and fire ... and he overthrew those cities, and all the plain, and all the inhabitants of the cities, and that which grew upon the ground ... ' Fanciful legends of a fevered Biblical imagination? Not necessarily. The whole area is located on a fault line, and it would not have been the first time that such a zone has been simply swallowed up when the ground collapsed in a kind of massive implosion. Also known as 'liquefaction', or collapse of the soil, the observer reporting for the Book of Genesis may well have been describing a terrible natural disaster instead of the wrath of God.

you may also want to visit **Lot's Cave** (see the Dead Sea Highway section in the Northern & Western Jordan chapter for details).

Al-Qasr
القصر

Al-Qasr is an important regional centre with **ruins** of a Nabataean temple – look for the sign to the east. Al-Qasr is easy to reach if driving between Madaba and Karak, and is well connected by public transport with Ariha, on the southern side of the Wadi Mujib valley, and Karak.

Ar-Rabba
عرابه

The holy and historical city of Ar-Rabba was, among others, under the rule of King Mesha (in the 9th century BC), Alexander the Great (in the mid-4th century BC) and the Nabataeans (from the 2nd century BC to 2nd century AD).

At the northern end of the small town are the **ruins** of a Roman temple, with two niches which contained statues of the Roman emperors Diocletian and Maximian, and other Roman and Byzantine buildings. Nothing is signposted or labelled in any language.

The ruins are permanently open, free to enter and located to the east of the main road. Ar-Rabba is worth a stopover if driving between Madaba and Karak, and is easily accessible by minibus from Karak.

Mu'tah
مؤته

Mu'tah is a nondescript town which boasts one of the best, and most popular, universities in Jordan. **Mu'tah University** is at the actual end of the King's Highway from Karak, but the highway makes a series of confusing detours around the university and eventually heads towards Tafila. If driving, look carefully for road signs in order to bypass the university.

Mu'tah is also famous as the location of a battle in 632 AD, when Byzantine forces beat the Muslims (who took revenge and beat the Byzantines four years later). At the main junction in the south of Mu'tah, a **monument** commemorates the battle.

Places to Stay & Eat Mu'tah Palace
Hotel (☎/fax 370256) is along the King's

KING'S HIGHWAY

Highway into Mu'tah, and near an entrance to the university. It offers comfortable motel-style singles/doubles, with a private bathroom, TV and air-conditioning, for a negotiable JD18/33, including breakfast. Downstairs is a huge *restaurant*. The highway nearby is lined with several *eateries*.

Getting There & Away Minibuses regularly link Karak with Mu'tah, and there are one or two buses between Madaba and the university – see Getting There & Away in the Madaba section earlier for details.

Mazar   مزار
The dishevelled village of Mazar is home to the small, and fairly uninteresting, **Mazar Islamic Museum** (☎ 215 1042). It's open from 9 am to 3 pm every day, except Tuesday, and admission is free. Minibuses regularly go to Mazar from central Karak.

HAMMAMAT BURBITA & HAMMAMAT AFRA
حمامات بربيتا / حمامات عفرا
Hammamat Burbita and Hammamat Afra are two more thermal hot springs near Wadi Hasa, but the springs and baths at Hammamat Ma'in, not far from Madaba, are far better and more accessible. Also, women are likely to feel uncomfortable at these two springs if local men are around in any numbers.

The two springs are signposted about 23km north of Tafila; from the turn-off it's about 13km to Burbita. Burbita is a green patch in the base of a wadi with a small uninviting rock pool and a makeshift galvanised iron roof. Another 6km further on, the road ends at Hammamat Afra, a more beautiful spot favoured by Jordanians on excursion.

There is no public transport to either spot. If you're driving, expect to get hopelessly lost, and always ask lots of directions, because the road signs in this area are nonexistent, ambiguous or vandalised. A chartered taxi from Tafila to Afra will cost about JD12 return, including waiting time.

TAFILA   الطفيله
Tafila is a busy market centre and transport junction. There is nothing to see, except the

very decrepit ruins of a **Crusader castle** (which is sometimes off-limits to tourists anyway). The rather pointless tourist office is close to the bus station.

Places to Stay & Eat
Afra Hotel (☎ 03-341832) in the centre of town is the only place to stay. The singles/doubles for JD5/7 are very drab, so try to get stuck somewhere else.

Plenty of cheap places sell *felafel* and *shwarma* around the town. *Adom Resthouse*, an unmistakable green building at the southern end of Tafila and on the highway to Dana Nature Reserve, is about the best place to eat.

Getting There & Away
Minibuses from Karak (500 fils, one hour) go along a back route off the King's Highway, and cross Wadi Hasa – which is nearly as dramatic as Wadi Mujib. There are also direct minibuses to/from the Wahadat bus station in Amman (JD1, 2½ hours), via the Desert Highway; Aqaba (JD1, 2½ hours), via the Dead Sea Highway; Ma'an (850 fils, one hour), via the Desert Highway; and, just down the King's Highway, to Shobak and Qadsiyya (for Dana Nature Reserve).

DANA NATURE RESERVE
حديقة دانا الطبيعية
Dana Nature Reserve (320 sq km) is an impressive attempt at environmental protection and ecotourism. However, most of the reserve is only accessible on foot, and the high prices for everything will put some visitors off. The charming, 15th century stone village of **Dana** is separate to the reserve and worth exploring: it boasts several small craft **workshops** and loads of friendly Bedouin families.

The reserve includes a variety of landscapes, including peaks over 1500m high, and the sandstone cliffs of Wadi Dana which lead to the Dead Sea about 12km to the west. The escarpments and valleys protect a surprisingly diverse ecosystem, including about 600 species of plants (from citrus trees and desert shrubs to tropical acacias); about 200 species of birds (an exceedingly high number for a desert region);

and 33 species of animals (of which 25 are endangered), including ibex, mountain gazelle, sand cat, red fox and wolf.

The reserve has almost 100 archaeological sites, mostly unexcavated. Of most interest to archaeologists, but only accessible on foot, are the ruins of **Khirbat Finan**, copper mines mentioned in the Bible and dating back to at least the 4th century BC. For the normal visitor, there's very little to see except the ruins of a few bridges, churches and cemeteries. The hills still contain copper, but despite intense lobbying from mining companies, the Jordanian government (with pressure from the RSCN) has agreed not to allow mining in the reserve.

The reserve was taken over by the RSCN in 1993, and is something of a novel experiment in Jordan – an attempt to promote ecotourism, protect wildlife as well as improve the lives of local villagers all at once. The reserve directly or indirectly employs over 40 locals, and income from tourism has helped to develop Dana village and provide education about environmental issues in local schools. Villagers also make some excellent local crafts, sold under the brand name Wadi Dana. You will find items are for sale at the Dana Nature Shop in the visitors centre, and also at shops throughout Jordan (see Shopping in the Facts for the Visitor chapter for details).

Information

The visitors centre (☎ 368497, fax 368499), in the guesthouse complex in Dana village, is open every day from 8 am to 8 pm. Visitors can get information about hiking (see below), book accommodation (preferably in advance) and buy something at the Dana Nature Shop. Silverware and pottery is made downstairs by local women, and visitors are welcome to visit the **workshops**.

The Tower Centre (known as *al-burj*), open from 8 am to 9 pm daily, is the entrance to the reserve and to Rummam camping ground. From there, a shuttle bus transfers visitors to the camping ground and hiking trails. The entrance fee of JD5 includes the shuttle bus to/from the centre, but a look at the **views** from the carpark costs nothing.

Hiking

To go beyond the four trails listed below, you'll need permission and a guide from the RSCN in Amman (see the National Parks section in the Facts about Jordan chapter), or from the visitors centre in Dana village. The trails, which all start from the Rummam camping ground, are:

* Around the Rummam camping ground (about 1½ hours)
* Up to, and around, the nearest hill (about two hours return)
* To Dana village (about three hours one-way)
* To the Finan camp site (six to seven hours one way)

The two shorter trails are easy to follow, so no guide is necessary. Guides are compulsory for the two longer hikes, and cost JD6/10 for the short/long trails, or JD30 per day (maximum of ten hikers per guide).

One of the very few companies that offers treks in and around Dana Nature Reserve is Petra Moon Tourism Services, based in Wadi Mousa (near Petra) – see the Hiking section in the Activities chapter for contact details.

Places to Stay & Eat

Anyone contemplating camping should do so for the wilderness experience, and not to save money, because camping in the reserve is expensive. The numbers of campers are limited, so bookings are essential, and you're not allowed to pitch your own tent anywhere in the reserve.

There are two camp sites with pre-set tents; both are only open in summer (1 March to 31 October). The prices for both are JD5 per four-person tent and JD7 per person for extras (ie mattress and blanket), plus the JD5 entrance fee per person – so this adds up considerably. Both camp sites have drinking (spring) water and access to kitchen facilities. You can bring your own food, or meals can be pre-ordered for about JD5.

Rummam Campground is the more developed, and is just down (but only accessible by shuttle bus) from the Tower Centre. *Finan Campground* is far more basic, used less often and only accessible on foot from

KING'S HIGHWAY

Rummam (about 10km); or from the Dead Sea Highway (about 5km) on foot, or by 4WD, with prior permission from the RSCN.

Dana Hotel (☎ *368537)* is in the middle of Dana village. Although the rooms are airless, and have no views, it's good value and atmospheric. Rooms, with a shared bathroom, cost JD5 per person, including breakfast; meals cost an extra JD3.500. The village has a handful of basic grocery shops.

Dana Guesthouse (☎ *368497, fax 368499, email rscn@nets.com.jo)* is an unpretentious place, where guests primarily pay for some of the best views in the country. The rooms feature simple, locally made furniture, and have shared bathrooms. Singles/doubles with a balcony cost JD25/35; without a balcony, JD20/25. The one family suite with a bathroom costs JD45. All prices include breakfast; other meals cost about JD6 per person. Reservations are essential.

Getting There & Away
The Tower Centre and Rummam Campground are well signposted from the King's Highway. The turn-off is about 2.5km north of Qadsiyya village, but the signs along the dirt road (5.5km) to the centre and camp site are confusing, so ask someone if you're unsure. The visitors centre and Dana Guesthouse are in Dana village, a few kilometres further south, and are also well signposted from the King's Highway; the turn-off is about 1km north of Qadsiyya.

Occasional minibuses link Wahadat station in Amman (JD1.250, about three hours) with Qadsiyya, but it's better to come via Tafila by minibus (300 fils, 30 minutes). If coming from the north on public transport, get off at the obvious turn-offs to the Tower Centre or Dana Village and walk, or hitch a ride, the rest of the way. If coming from the south, charter a taxi, or hitch a ride, from Qadsiyya. There is very little public transport further south towards Shobak, so hitching is often necessary, but be prepared for a long wait.

With permission, it is possible to hike or take a 4WD to Finan Campground from the Dead Sea Highway. At the military checkpoint along the Dead Sea Highway, turn east to Qurayqira and head along the dirt track to Finan.

SHOBAK   شــوبـك
Shobak is another Crusader castle, with a commanding position over some incredibly desolate land. The attraction for many is the remote location, which means far fewer tour groups than at the castles at Ajlun and Karak.

Shobak castle, formerly called Mons Realis (Montreal), was built by Baldwin I in 1115 AD. It suffered numerous attacks from Salah ad-Din before finally succumbing to him in 1189. Much of its present form is owed to the restoration carried out by the Mamluks in the 14th century.

Built on a small knoll right on the edge of the plateau, the castle is most imposing when seen from a distance. The inside is decrepit, although restoration work is under way. There are two **churches** in the castle, and evidence of **baths** and **cisterns**. A guide can point out a **well**, accessible along 365 (sometimes dangerous) steps cut into the rock.

The castle is about 3km west of Shobak village, a pleasant place with a few shops, a bank (which changes money) and some basic *eateries* – but nowhere to stay. Entrance to the castle is free, and it's open every day during daylight hours. Nothing is labelled or signposted in any language, so a guide (available from the entrance) does help explain things. A torch (flashlight) is useful for poking around the dark corners.

Getting There & Away
There are two well signposted roads to the castle from the highway between Tafila and Wadi Mousa (near Petra); if driving from the north, take the second turn-off because this road is far better. Both of these roads eventually join a very narrow road up the hill to a tiny car park at the main entrance. From Shobak village to the castle, you'll have to hitch a ride or charter a taxi. If walking, head straight towards the castle from the village, and you'll cut off about 1km.

Occasional minibuses (JD1.500, 2½ hours) and service taxis (JD2) link Shobak village with Amman (Wahadat bus station). The infrequent minibus between Aqaba and Karak (see either section for details) should – but double check this first – go past the turn-off to Shobak. Also, most of the irregular minibuses and service taxis between Wadi Mousa (near Petra) and Ma'an go through Shobak village. There are mini-buses between Shobak and Tafila (750 fils, one hour).

The section of the King's Highway between Shobak and Wadi Mousa has very limited public transport, and very few private vehicles, so hitching is difficult. If chartering a taxi to Wadi Mousa from anywhere to the north, arrange a detour to the castle with the driver.

KING'S HIGHWAY

Petra

بترا

PETRA

Hewn from a towering rock wall, the imposing facades of the great buildings and tombs of Petra are testament to the one-time wealth of the ancient capital of the Nabataeans – Arabs who dominated the Transjordan area in pre-Roman times. A remarkable reminder of the commercially minded Nabataean's genius, the ruins stand witness to an almost equally impressive talent for making a fast buck. Certainly the single greatest attraction in Jordan, and indeed one of the top drawcards of the entire Middle East, Petra is sadly, but inevitably, also a tourist trap.

Since Jordan and Israel ended their state of war, Petra has turned from a popular tourist destination into bedlam. The adjoining village of Wadi Mousa is expanding apace as the rush continues to erect more hotels – whole hillsides look set to disappear at any moment under a thick layer of concrete. Luckily, Petra itself is shielded from all the visual horrors, although with up to 1000 people visiting every day, fears are growing that the tourist onslaught is not sustainable.

WADI MOUSA
وادي موسى

☎ 03

The village that has sprung up around Petra is Wadi Mousa ('Moses' River'). It's a sprawling mass of hotels, restaurants and shops stretching about 5km down from 'Ain Musa to the main entrance to Petra. The village centre, with some shops and restaurants, is little more than three streets, while most hotels are spread along the main road.

Locals are aware of tourists flocking to Petra with large wallets and little time, and every visitor – Jordanian or foreign – is fair game. Many things, including hotels and some meals, are about double the price of Amman. Distance from Amman is not an excuse, because Aqaba is certainly cheaper, and further from Amman, than Wadi Mousa.

Orientation

'Wadi Mousa' refers to everywhere between 'Ain Musa and the entrance to Petra; there

HIGHLIGHTS

- **As-Siq** – this dramatic, long and narrow gorge links the entrance with the centre of the ancient city (see page 219)

- **The Treasury** – Al-Khazneh, as it's locally known, is arguably Petra's most spectacular, and most photographed, sight in Jordan (see page 220)

- **Royal Tombs** – sometimes ignored, these diverse tombs offer great views of the old city centre (see page 221)

- **The Monastery** – Al-Deir, as it's locally known, is bigger and just as impressive as the Treasury, but involves a tough slog uphill (see page 223)

- **Al-Beid** – Little Petra, as it's sometimes known, is far less dramatic than Petra itself, but entrance is free and tour buses are usually absent (see page 228)

is an obvious village centre just down from (south-west) Shaheed roundabout.

If you're on a budget, try to base yourself within a few hundred metres of Wadi Mousa village: it's the transport junction

206

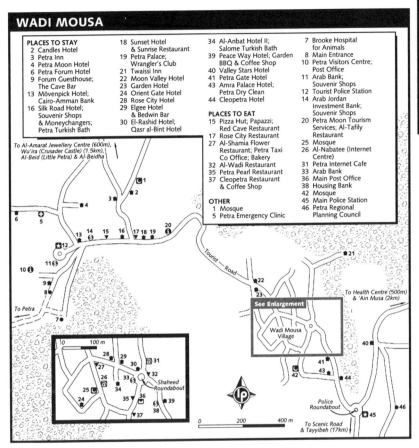

WADI MOUSA

PLACES TO STAY
2 Candles Hotel
3 Petra Inn
4 Petra Moon Hotel
6 Petra Forum Hotel
9 Forum Guesthouse;
  The Cave Bar
13 Mövenpick Hotel;
  Cairo-Amman Bank
16 Silk Road Hotel;
  Souvenir Shops
  & Moneychangers;
  Petra Turkish Bath
18 Sunset Hotel
  & Sunrise Restaurant
19 Petra Palace;
  Wrangler's Club
21 Twaissi Inn
22 Moon Valley Hotel
23 Garden Hotel
24 Orient Gate Hotel
28 Rose City Hotel
29 Elgee Hotel
  & Bedwin Bar
30 El-Rashid Hotel;
  Qasr al-Bint Hotel

34 Al-Anbat Hotel II;
  Salome Turkish Bath
39 Peace Way Hotel; Garden
  BBQ & Coffee Shop
40 Valley Stars Hotel
41 Petra Gate Hotel
43 Amra Palace Hotel;
  Petra Dry Clean
44 Cleopatra Hotel

PLACES TO EAT
15 Pizza Hut; Papazzi;
  Red Cave Restaurant
17 Rose City Restaurant
27 Al-Shamia Flower
  Restaurant; Petra Taxi
  Co Office; Bakery
32 Al-Wadi Restaurant
35 Petra Pearl Restaurant
37 Cleopetra Restaurant
  & Coffee Shop

OTHER
1 Mosque
5 Petra Emergency Clinic

7 Brooke Hospital
  for Animals
8 Main Entrance
10 Petra Visitors Centre;
  Post Office
11 Arab Bank;
  Souvenir Shops
12 Tourist Police Station
14 Arab Jordan
  Investment Bank;
  Souvenir Shops
20 Petra Moon Tourism
  Services; Al-Tafily
  Restaurant
25 Mosque
26 Al-Nabatee (Internet
  Centre)
31 Petra Internet Cafe
33 Arab Bank
36 Main Post Office
38 Housing Bank
42 Mosque
45 Main Police Station
46 Petra Regional
  Planning Council

and cheapest place to eat and shop, and Petra is still easily accessible on foot. Just about everything listed in the Wadi Mousa section below is along the main road, which doesn't really have a name, although some locals call it Tourist Rd for obvious reasons.

Information
Tourist Offices The best source of information is the Petra visitors centre near the main entrance (see the separate Petra section later). However, it's no good for general information about Wadi Mousa (eg departure times of minibuses), so ask at your hotel.

Money There are surprisingly few money-changers in Wadi Mousa. A couple of souvenir shops near the Silk Road Hotel, not far from the entrance to Petra, can change money, but if you have travellers cheques change them before you come to Petra. Most hotels will change cash (but rarely travellers cheques) at unfavourable rates, eg about US$1 = 660 fils.

The Housing Bank, up (south) from the village centre, is a quick place to change money, and has an automatic teller machine (ATM) for MasterCard, Cirrus and Visa. Near the entrance to Petra, cash and travellers cheques can be changed at the Arab Jordan Investment Bank (which also has an ATM for Visa), in the huddle of souvenir shops near the Silk Road Hotel; and at the Cairo-Amman Bank in the Mövenpick Hotel. There is also an Arab Bank inside the Petra visitors centre, and in Wadi Mousa village. All banks are open from about 8 am to 2 pm, Sunday to Thursday; and 9 to 11 am on Friday.

The representative for American Express is International Traders (☎ 215 7711), in the Silk Road Hotel complex (enter from the main road).

Post & Communications The attraction of using the small post office at the back of the Petra visitors centre is that mail is postmarked 'Petra Tur. Office'. It's open every day from 7 am to 6 pm, and on Friday from 8 am to 1.30 pm. Another small post office by the Mussa Spring Hotel ('Ain Musa) is open from 8 am to 7 pm every day, and for a couple of hours on Friday morning. The main post office in Wadi Mousa village is open from 8 am to 5 pm every day; and until 2 pm on Friday.

International telephone calls can be made from several private agencies along the main streets of Wadi Mousa village, and from the Petra Internet Cafe for about JD1.500 per minute. Several booths for Alo telephone cards are located at the entrance to Petra.

The telephone numbers in Wadi Mousa have recently changed, and all numbers now have seven digits. If you come across a six digit number, replace the first two digits (often '33') with '215'.

Currently, there are only two Internet centres in Wadi Mousa, but more will probably spring up in the future if/when Internet charges come down. Al-Nabatee is located (nabatee@joinmet.com.jo) is just up from Al-Shamia Flower Restaurant; and the Petra Internet Cafe (al-petra@index.com.jo) is close to the Shaheed roundabout. Both charge JD4 per hour, which is about twice as much as in Amman.

Bookshops The dozens of souvenir stands inside Petra, and along the main road through Wadi Mousa, sell various guide-books to Petra, but everything is more expensive than in Amman. The shops with the best range of books are around the Silk Road Hotel complex. Refer to the Petra section later in this chapter for information about books and maps relevant to Petra.

Laundry Wadi Mousa is a good place to get some washing done; most people stay a few days and will accumulate a lot of dust while hiking around Petra. One of the few places is Petra Dry Clean under the Amra Palace Hotel.

Emergency The construction of a full hospital is planned for Wadi Mousa, but until then Petra is not a great place to get sick or injured. The Petra Emergency Clinic (☎ 215 7161), set up in a make-shift trailer in the car park of the Petra Forum Hotel, does not inspire much confidence. Better is the Health Centre (☎ 215 6025), near the Acropolis Hotel and about 500m up (north) of the Police roundabout. There are a few doctors' surgeries in Wadi Mousa village.

The main police station (☎ 215 6559) is at the appropriately named Police roundabout. The tourist police station (☎ 215 6441), opposite the Petra visitors centre, is open 24 hours. A few tourist police can be found lounging around in the shade inside Petra on any given day.

Turkish Bath

A 'Turkish bath' will ease any aching muscles after traipsing around Petra. Men and women – separately – can enjoy a steam bath, massage and 'body conditioning' for JD15 per person at the Petra Turkish Bath (☎ 215 7085) in the Silk Road Hotel complex (enter from the main road). Salome Turkish Bath, near the Al-Anbat Hotel II, also charges JD15 for the 'works', but doesn't look as salubrious. The Twaissi Inn (see Places to Stay) can arrange cheaper baths (from JD8 per person, including transport) for guests.

Places to Stay

Things have changed just a little over the years in Petra. Back in 1908, Macmillan's guide to *Palestine and Syria* had the following advice:

At Petra, there is no sleeping accommodation to be found, and travellers therefore have to bring with them camp equipment, unless they prefer to put up with the inconvenience of sleeping in the Bedawin huts at Elji, half an hour distant from Petra, or spend the night in some of the numerous temples. Such a course cannot be recommended to European travellers, especially if ladies are of the party.

Until a few years ago, travellers could still sleep in the temples or camp in Petra. Visitors now have a choice of over 40 hotels in the area, mostly along the 5km stretch of road between 'Ain Musa and Petra. Camping inside Petra is strictly forbidden, and there is nowhere else to pitch a tent in the area.

Prices can fluctuate depending on the season and amount of business: the high season for hotels is generally August to October and November to February. With so much competition, tariffs are normally always negotiable, especially if you're staying for a few days. Some cheaper places advertise 'student rates', ie an invitation to bargain on rates for dorm beds, and allow a mattress on the roof.

Although many hotels offer 'half-board' (which includes breakfast and dinner) at a higher rate, you're not obliged to pay for anything but the room. Some places include breakfast, but it's often possible to negotiate a cheaper rate without breakfast and eat elsewhere. Guests can often buy breakfast, lunch or dinner at their hotel, and pay for the meals separately, but hotels that have no attached restaurant will want some notice. Promises of 'buffets' (usually in the evening) in budget and mid-range places often only eventuate if there are enough guests.

In winter, make sure there is heating – and that it works. Surprisingly few places have fans, and only the more expensive hotels have air-conditioning. While some hotels claim they have 'views', they are just vistas of Wadi Mousa valley and town; no hotel has views of Petra.

Most places more than about 1km from Petra offer free transport to – but not necessarily from – the ruins. After hours of hiking around Petra, the last thing you want is to walk uphill to your hotel, so ask if the hotel will also pick you up; ring them from the telephone booths near the main entrance, or pre-arrange a pick-up time (but allow plenty of time inside Petra). Alternatively, just charter a taxi (JD1) back to the hotel – you'll be glad you did. Some readers have also complained that the 'free transport' offered by the hotels is not as readily available as promised.

Almost every hotel listed below is along the main road between 'Ain Musa and Petra, or in Wadi Mousa village. None of the hotels have street numbers, but they will be easy to find if you use the map in this book. Most locals and taxi drivers know all the hotels anyway.

Places to Stay – Budget

There is a sameness among many budget places: as soon as one offers a gimmick, eg rooftop sleeping, free transport to Petra, buffet dinners or showing of the *Indiana Jones and The Last Crusade* video, they all do. Most rooms have private bathrooms, except if you're in a dormitory or sleeping on the rooftop. Most budget places are a fair walk to Petra, and so most include free transport to (but not necessarily from) Petra – confirm the transportation situation before agreeing to anything.

Mussa Spring Hotel (☎ *215 6310, fax 215 6910)* is in the village of 'Ain Musa; some taxi drivers may want to drop you off there to get a commission. It is pleasant, and good value for JD10/16 without/with a bathroom, and prices include a (nonsatellite) TV in the room and breakfast. Dorm-style beds cost JD4, and sleeping on the roof costs JD2. However, it's simply too far from anything.

Valley Stars Hotel (☎ *215 6059, fax 215 6914)* is well set up for backpackers, and is run by an informative and helpful manager. Singles/doubles, some being renovated at the time of research, cost JD10/15, with breakfast. Sleeping on the rooftop costs JD2.

Cleopetra Hotel (☎ *215 7090)* has helpful staff, but some of the rooms are really tiny, and the ones at the front are noisy. Still, it's good value for a negotiable JD12/16, including breakfast.

Petra Gate Hotel (☎/fax 215 6908, email petra-gate-hotel@hotmail.com) has small and simple rooms that cost JD6/8, plus JD1.500 for breakfast. It has a convivial atmosphere, pool table, restaurant for guests with great views and friendly staff, but readers have complained about smelly rooms and lack of hot water.

Peace Way Hotel (☎/fax 215 6963) is another good place which caters well to budget travellers. The rooms, JD13/18 with breakfast, are large, well furnished and have satellite TV; and staff are keen to help.

Qasr al-Bint Hotel (☎/fax 215 7115) has large rooms in a central, but quiet, location. However, it's rather characterless and while it tries to be a 'backpacker' place it doesn't succeed. Nonetheless, it's a good option for a negotiable JD8/10, plus JD1.500 for breakfast. The buffet meals (JD3) for guests have been recommended by readers.

El-Rashid Hotel (☎ 215 6800, fax 215 6801, email rashid@joinnet.com.jo) has friendly staff, and is central and quiet. Rooms with satellite TV cost JD15/25. The management is willing to negotiate down to JD12/20, which makes this terrific value.

Rose City Hotel (☎/fax 215 6440) is actually better than it looks from the outside, and staff are helpful and knowledgable. Some rooms have views, and all have a fridge and TV (not satellite). They cost JD12.500/25, including breakfast, which is particularly good value for single travellers.

Elgee Hotel (☎ 215 6701, fax 215 7002) is also central, convenient and quiet. The rooms cost JD15/20 and some have the best views in the immediate vicinity.

Twaissi Inn (☎ 215 6423) is very popular (so bookings may be required). While the rooms are similar to those in about twenty hotels nearby, it's the service, knowledgable staff and videos (other than *Indiana Jones*) every night which attract guests. Rooms cost JD10/12, and beds in a shared room, JD6 – all including breakfast. A mattress on the floor is JD2. It's about 400m up (follow the signs) from Shaheed roundabout. But please note: reports of sleazy behaviour and worse have been received from readers.

Orient Gate Hotel (☎/fax 215 7020) is convenient and quiet. Clean rooms, many with views, cost JD10/15 with breakfast and a private bathroom; or about JD8/10 without breakfast and a shared bathroom.

Garden Hotel (☎ 215 7313) is great value. It's a little off the main road, and has what could be termed as a real 'garden'. However, one reader did warn guests to be security conscious, and another complained about bed bugs. Plain rooms (some with balconies) cost JD5/8 with a shared bathroom; and dorm-style beds are JD3. Breakfast is an extra JD1, and guests can use the communal kitchen.

Moon Valley Hotel (☎ 215 6724, fax 215 8131) is also good value, especially if you can negotiate a lower price. It offers large rooms for (officially) JD8/15, plus JD1.500 for breakfast.

Sunset Hotel (☎ 215 6579, fax 215 6950) is of mid-range standard, but staff are willing to accept budget tariffs – so this is the only cheapish place close to Petra. The comfortable rooms (some are better than others) with (nonsatellite) TV and fridge cost JD15/18 with breakfast; or as little as JD12/15 without. Dorm-style beds are JD5.

Places to Stay – Mid-Range

Most places in this range offer optional 'half-board'. All have heating, but few have air-conditioning, unless stated otherwise.

Amra Palace Hotel (☎ 215 7215, fax 215 7071) caters mainly to tour groups, but good discounts for independent travellers are possible when business is quiet. The official rate for plush singles/doubles is JD20/30 with breakfast. All rooms have good views, air-con and what one reader described as the 'best bathroom in Jordan'.

Al-Anbat Hotel II (☎ 215 7200, fax 215 6888) is new and desperate for guests, so the management is quite willing to negotiate. All rooms are well furnished with satellite TV, and some have views. They cost JD15/18 with breakfast, although staff will try to convince you to take the 'half-board' for JD18/25.

Just up from the Mövenpick Hotel, a few bland places are being built. They are close to Petra, but lack any character and landscaping. However, all rates at these hotels are negotiable because there's so much competition in the immediate area.

Petra Moon Hotel *(☎/fax 215 6220)* is one of the better places. Nicely decorated rooms, with satellite TV, cost JD15/25 (negotiable), including breakfast.

Silk Road Hotel *(☎ 215 7222, fax 215 7244)* is part of a large complex with several shops. (The hotel entrance is on a side street.) It charges a reasonable JD30/45 for air-con rooms, including breakfast, and has been recommended by readers.

Petra Inn *(☎ 215 6403, fax 215 6401, email nabatee@go.com.jo)*, in a convenient but desolate location, offers bland, air-con rooms for JD24/36, with breakfast.

Candles Hotel *(☎ 215 6954, fax 215 7311)* is similar to others in the area, but has better views. Good rooms cost JD25/35, with breakfast; JD30/40 for 'half-board'.

Places to Stay – Top End

Top end hotels rarely include breakfast. The prices listed below include all the extra taxes and service charges.

Petra Palace *(☎ 215 6723, fax 215 6724, email ppwnwm@go.com.jo)* is well situated, and the cheapest place in Wadi Mousa with a swimming pool. Luxurious rooms cost JD33/47, including breakfast, and it claims to offer 'discounts to students' – ask, and you may be surprised how far they will negotiate.

Two hotels are run by the Forum company. **Petra Forum Hotel** *(☎ 215 6266, fax 215 6977, email petra@interconti.com)* has all the luxuries expected for JD108/120, and a pool with awesome views over the northern Siq. **Forum Guesthouse** *(same contact details)* is even closer to the main entrance to Petra, and surprisingly good value. At JD60/72 for quiet and comfortable rooms, it's easily the best value of the top end places.

Mövenpick Hotel *(☎ 215 7111, fax 215 7112, email petramph@go.com.jo)* is the unmistakable place on the corner of the road leading into Petra. It offers a range of rooms at different prices, depending on the season,

views and so on. The average price is a whopping US$102/180, including breakfast.

Along the Scenic Road, which starts at the Police roundabout and finishes in Tayyibeh, are numerous top end places with great views, swimming pools and high prices. They cater mainly to tour groups, and provide free transport to/from the ruins because there are very few taxis along this road.

Grand View *(☎ 215 6871, fax 215 6983)* is the first as you come from Wadi Mousa. The official rate of JD90/120 is negotiable when business is slow. **Petra Panorama** *(☎ 215 7390, fax 215 7389)* is next, and about the same standard, and charges JD120/137. **Petra Plaza** *(☎/fax 215 6407)* is farther up the road, and also charges JD120/137.

Refer to Tayyibeh in the Around Petra section later for information about the luxurious **Taybet Zaman Hotel & Resort**.

Places to Eat

The main road, especially in Wadi Mousa village, is dotted with **grocery stores** where you can stock up on food, munchies and drinks for Petra. There's a good, unnamed **bakery** in the north-west corner of Wadi Mousa village, recognisable by its pink shutters. Several **fruit and vegetable stalls** are located in the village.

Most hotels have a restaurant where guests can pre-order a buffet meal, usually dinner (the assumption is that visitors are in Petra during the day). The buffets are not necessarily great value, and anything costing more than JD3 per person is probably too much. Some hotels also have attached restaurants, which are open to the public. Most of the cheapest places to eat are in Wadi Mousa village.

Places to Eat – Budget

Surprisingly few places offer simple *felafel* and *shwarma*. The southern road through Wadi Mousa village has several cheap eateries, such as **Al-Shamia Flower Restaurant** *(☎ 215 6107)* where salads cost 500 fils, and chicken and kebab meals about JD2.500.

Garden BBQ & Coffee Shop, part of (and attached to) the Peace Way Hotel, is one of the best places in town. The seats are outside (so a little noisy and cold in winter), and the service is not always lightning fast, but the meals are large and good value, eg a delicious 'Turkish-style' chicken meal, with soup and salad, costs JD2.500.

Al-Wadi Restaurant (☎ 215 7163) offers a large number of tasty dishes, eg kebabs with a small salad for JD1.500, and the omelette and tea breakfast (JD1) is fantastic. It's open from about 7 am to midnight, and is one of the best places to find out departure times for minibuses, and to wait (downstairs) for one.

A few places in Wadi Mousa offer buffet dinners for about JD2 for salad only (good for vegetarians), or JD3 for salad with kebabs or shwarma. *Petra Pearl Restaurant* has been recommended by readers. The free tea/coffee with its simple buffet is a nice touch, and it's one of the best places in the village for breakfast. *Cleopetra Restaurant & Coffee Shop* is OK, but prices are too high.

Rose City Restaurant (☎ 215 7099) is the cheapest, and one of the best places, near the entrance to Petra. Readers have regularly praised the friendly staff and good prices for Arabic food. A three-course meal costs about JD2 per person; buffets, about JD3. It's also open early for breakfast.

Places to Eat – Mid-Range

Many places along the main road leading to Petra cater to the crowds staying at upmarket hotels nearby. Consequently, some places are just budget-style eateries (with ordinary food, decor and service) charging mid-range prices. Cold drinks sold anywhere near the entrance to Petra cost the earth.

Red Cave Restaurant (☎ 215 7099) is cavernous and cool, and offers meals from JD3, and shwarmas for about JD1. *Al-Tafily Restaurant (☎ 215 7677)* is probably the nicest of the mid-range places near Petra. Salads start from 700 fils, but main courses cost at least JD3.500. *Sunrise Restaurant*, under the Sunset Hotel (geddit?), has meals from JD4, which include soup and salad, although it doesn't advertise the fact.

Pizza Hut, near the Silk Road Hotel complex, is surprisingly good value, and therefore popular: small pizzas cost from

JD2, and a visit to the salad bar is JD1.500. It's far better than *Papazzi* next door.

For a treat and air-conditioned relief, pop into the Mövenpick Hotel and enjoy an Swiss-style ice cream (JD1) or a huge fruit cocktail (JD2.500). Either can be enjoyed in their sumptuous indoor lounge.

Entertainment

There is very little to do in the evening, but recover from aching joints and plan your next day's journey around Petra. The Petra section later has information about the 'Petra by Night' extravaganza.

Bedwin Bar in the Elgee Hotel is often closed, but staff happily serve large Amstel beers (JD3) in the hotel foyer. *Wranglers Pub*, inside the Petra Palace, has a trendy setting but is expensive: small bottles of beer cost from JD2; JD6 for a jug of beer.

The poolside bar at the *Petra Forum Hotel* has extraordinary views, and not unreasonable prices: JD2.200 for a small beer, and JD4 for cocktails. It's better than *The Cave Bar*, a converted Nabataean resthouse, right at the entrance to Petra, which looks like something from the *Flintstones.*

Shopping

It would be hard to come to Petra and not buy some sort of souvenir. The best souvenir shops are lined up along the road into Petra, and around the Petra visitors centre.

Inside the visitors centre are three shops whose profits assist worthwhile local projects: the Jordan Design & Trade Centre sells a wide selection of rugs, ceramics and wall-hangings, among other stuff, for the benefit of local women; the Society for the Development & Rehabilitation of Rural Women supports the development of local arts, preserves 'traditional heritage', helps needy families and has established a nursery for children of working women; and the Wadi Mousa Ladies' Society is similar to the other two.

About 600m up (follow the signs) from the Petra Moon Hotel, the Al-Amarat Jewellery Centre (also known as the Wadi Musa Project for Traditional Jewellery) is another shop selling high-quality but expensive stuff for the benefit of local women.

Getting There & Away

Although a large village, and the number one tourist attraction in Jordan, public transport to and from Wadi Mousa is terrible, and getting any reliable information is far from easy. The unofficial terminal for all public transport is the unsigned Shaheed roundabout in the upper (eastern) end of Wadi Mousa village. One of the best sources of information about local transport is your hotel, especially places such as the Twaissi, Cleopetra and Peace Way. Alternatively, ask the friendly guys at the Al-Wadi Restaurant, right on the roundabout.

JETT Bus The JETT bus company operates three buses a week (on Sunday, Tuesday and Friday – but schedules change regularly) in both directions (3½ hours) between its domestic office in Amman and the main gate to Petra. A one-way/return trip costs JD5.500/11, which is not a bad way of getting to or from Petra/Wadi Mousa directly. However, the full day trip, including return bus, guide, horse ride and lunch, for JD32.500 is very poor value because it excludes the (huge) entrance fee. Book at the JETT office in Amman (see that chapter for details).

Minibus Most minibuses can drop passengers off anywhere between 'Ain Musa village and the main entrance to Petra, but for departures it's best to wait at Shaheed roundabout. Most minibuses won't depart without being at least half full, so be prepared for some waiting. Tickets can only be pre-booked (ask your hotel to do this) for the 6 am departure to Amman, and the 6.30 am service to Aqaba.

Three minibuses officially travel every day between Amman (Wahadat bus station) and Wadi Mousa (JD1.650, three hours) along the Desert Highway, via Tayyibeh. These minibuses leave Amman at about 6 am, 8 am and midday – the departure times from Wadi Mousa are inexact, so ask. Minibuses leave Wadi Mousa for Ma'an (500 fils, 45 minutes) about every hour (more often in the morning); and from Ma'an, there are regular connections to Aqaba, Amman and Wadi Rum.

Minibuses also leave Wadi Mousa for Aqaba (JD3, two hours) at about 6.30 am, 8 am and 4 pm – but double check these times the day before. For Wadi Rum (JD1.500, 1½ hours), one minibus leaves Wadi Mousa at 6 am; alternatively, get a minibus to Aqaba, and get off at, and hitch a ride from, the turn-off to Wadi Rum. To Karak, a minibus sometimes leaves at about 8 am, but demand for this service is considerably less because so few locals use it. The minibus usually doesn't even bother leaving on Friday and Saturday at all, so it's probably quicker to go via Ma'an on any day.

All minibuses (except the one to Ma'an) have signs in English. If you're confused by conflicting information about departure times, just get to the Shaheed roundabout by 6 am and ask at the Al-Wadi Restaurant. Something going your way will certainly leave the roundabout between 6 and 8 am.

Service Taxi Occasional (white) service taxis run between Amman (Wahadat station) and Wadi Mousa (JD2.500, plus JD1 for luggage), via Shobak village. However, don't expect to find anything in the afternoon going either way. Most service taxis in Wadi Mousa travel to/from Ma'an, but all service taxis can be chartered to just about anywhere. Most originate from other towns, and only come to Wadi Mousa if there are enough passengers going there in the first place.

If you catch a service (or private) taxi don't accept a 'recommendation' by the driver for any hotel in Wadi Mousa. Their 'recommendation' is based solely on the amount of commission they receive from the hotel, which is usually far from Petra and, therefore, struggling for guests.

Private Taxi Private (yellow) taxis around Wadi Mousa will go anywhere for a price, but not much negotiation is possible. One-way trips to Al-Beid (Little Petra) cost about JD10; Wadi Rum, JD30; Aqaba, JD30; and Karak, JD40.

Some readers have been able to charter a private taxi all the way between Wadi Mousa and Amman, stopping off for lightning quick visits to Karak, the Dead Sea and

Madaba, for about JD80. For long distances, however, it will always be cheaper to charter a service taxi (if you can find one) rather than a private taxi. The following Getting Around section has details about private taxis in Wadi Mousa.

Hitching The best place to wait for a ride to anywhere out of Wadi Mousa is the fork in the road in 'Ain Musa, right opposite the Mussa Spring Hotel. Allow five hours to get to Karak, and about three to Aqaba. A lot of the traffic out of Wadi Mousa only goes as far as Ma'an, however, but the highway outside of Ma'an is a great place to get further rides in either direction (see the Ma'an section in the Southern Jordan chapter).

Getting Around

Plenty of unmetered private (yellow) taxis ply the main road between 'Ain Musa and the entrance to Petra, although you may have to wait a few minutes. The standard, non-negotiable fare is JD1 anywhere around the central Wadi Mousa area; a little more as far as 'Ain Musa. This is obviously too much, but the road from Petra to most hotels is steep and you'll certainly appreciate a taxi after exploring the ruins.

The two local private taxi companies are Petra Taxi Co (☎ 215 6600), which has an office just down from the Al-Shamia Flower Restaurant; and Al-Anbat Taxis (☎ 215 6777), which has no office at all. Private taxis can be chartered to just about anywhere (see the Getting There & Away section).

PETRA بترا

Match me such marvel save in eastern clime, a Rose Red City, half as old as time

Dean Burgon, 'Petra'

So many words have been written about Petra, including the much overworked poem above, but they hardly do the place justice. It's a cliche, but seeing is believing.

Much of Petra's fascination comes from its setting on the edge of Wadi Araba. The sheer and rugged sandstone hills form a deep canyon; the easiest access is through the Siq, a narrow winding cleft in the rock anything from 2m wide to 200m deep. Although the sandstone could hardly be called 'rose red', it does take on deep rusty hues interlaced with bands of grey, yellow and every shade in between. The soft rock is being eroded by wind, water and salt (see the boxed text 'Saving the Siq' later in this chapter).

Few buildings in Petra (which means 'rock' in Greek) are freestanding; the bulk are cut into the rock. Until the mid-1980s, many of these caves were home to the local Bedouin, who have since been moved to new 'villages' to the north – an arrangement they're less than happy with. However, a handful of families still pitch their black goat-hair tents inside Petra, or live in the caves. The Bedouin make their money from drink and souvenir stands, and by selling handicrafts and other artefacts – usually scraps of distinctive pottery and 'old' coins.

The best time to visit Petra is from mid-October to the end of November, and late January to the end of May. This avoids the coldest, wettest (when floods are possible) and hottest times of the year.

History

Excavations carried out in the 1950s unearthed a Neolithic village at Al-Beidha, just to the north of Petra, which dates from about 7000 BC. This puts it in the same league as Jericho on the West Bank as one of the earliest known farming communities in the Middle East.

Between that period and the Iron Age (from 1200 BC), when the area was the home of the Edomites, nothing is known. The Edomite capital, Sela (mentioned in the Bible) was thought to have been on top of Umm al-Biyara (see the relevant section under Hiking later in this chapter), although the actual site of Sela appears to lie to the north, about 10km south of Tafila.

The Nabataeans were a nomadic tribe from western Arabia who settled in the area in around the 6th century BC. They soon became rich: first by plundering and then by levying tolls on the trade caravans traversing the area under their control. The Seleucid ruler Antigonus, who came to power in Babylonia when Alexander the Great's empire was parcelled up, rode against the Nabataeans in 312 BC and attacked one day when all the men were absent. His men killed many of the women and children and made off with valuable silver and spices. The Nabataeans retaliated immediately, killing all but 50 of the 4000 raiders. Antigonus tried once more to storm Petra but his forces, led by his son Demetrius, were driven off.

Petra later became the sophisticated capital of a flourishing empire (or, more properly, a 'zone of influence') which reached Syria and Rome. As the Nabataean territory expanded , more caravan routes came under their control and their wealth increased accordingly. It was principally this, rather than territorial acquisition, that motivated them.

The Roman general Pompey, having conquered Syria and Palestine in 63 BC, tried to exert control over the Nabataean territory but the Nabataean king, Aretas III, was able to buy off the Roman forces and remain independent. Nonetheless, Rome exerted a cultural influence and the buildings and coinage of the period reflect the Graeco-Roman style.

The Nabataeans weren't so lucky when they chose to side with the Parthians in the latter's war with the Romans, finding themselves obliged to pay Rome heavy tribute after the defeat of the Parthians. When the Nabataeans fell behind in paying the tribute, they were invaded twice by Herod the Great. The second attack, in 31 BC, saw him gain control of a large slice of territory. Finally in 106 AD, the Romans took Petra and set about imposing the usual plan: a colonnaded street, baths, etc.

With the rise of Palmyra in Syria and the opening up of sea-trade routes, Petra's importance started to decline. During the Byzantine period, a Bishopric was created in Petra and a number of Nabataean buildings were altered for Christian use. By the time of the Muslim invasion in the 7th century, Petra had passed into obscurity and the only activity in the next 500 years was in the 12th century when the Crusaders moved in briefly and built a fort.

From then until the early 19th century, Petra was a forgotten city, known only to local Bedouin inhabitants. These descendants of the Nabataeans were reluctant to reveal its existence because they feared (perhaps, not without reason) that the influx of foreigners might interfere with their livelihood. Finally in 1812, a young Swiss explorer, JL Burckhardt, heard locals tell of some fantastic ruins hidden deep in the mountains of Wadi Musa valley (see the boxed text).

'Ibrahim' Burckhardt

Johann Ludwig (also known as Jean Louis) Burckhardt was born in Switzerland in 1784. To assist with what was seen in those days as a dangerous sponsored journey around the Middle East, he was taught Arabic and learned to eat, sleep and behave like a Bedouin. He lived in Aleppo (Syria) for two years, converted to Islam and lived under the alias of Ibrahim bin Abdullah.

In 1812, while en route from Damascus to Cairo, he visited Jerash, Amman, Karak and Shobak. On the way, he heard locals tell of some fantastic ruins hidden in the mountains of Wadi Musa valley. To make the detour, he had to think of a ploy so that his guide and porters were not suspicious of his interest, as he explained in his posthumous journal, *Travels in Syria and the Holy Land*:

I, therefore, pretended to have made a vow to have slaughtered a goat in honour of Haroun (Aaron), whose tomb I knew was situated at the extremity of the valley, and by this stratagem I thought that I should have the means of seeing the valley on the way to the tomb.

He was able to examine, albeit very briefly, a couple of sites including the Treasury (Al-Khazneh) and the Urn Tomb, and reported that 'it seems very probable that the ruins at Wadi Musa are those of ancient Petra'.

Burckhardt later explored Egypt and Mecca, but contracted fatal dysentery in 1817. He died at only 33 years old, and is buried in the Islamic Cemetery in Cairo.

Orientation

Books & Maps Almost nothing in Petra is signposted, labelled or captioned in any language, so a map and guidebook are essential. For most visitors planning to see the major sights over one or two days, the information and maps in this book will be more than sufficient. The *Petra: The Rose Red City* brochure, published by the Jordan Tourism Board, has an easy-to-read map, a few explanations and useful photos which help identify certain places – but try to get one before coming to Petra, because the Petra visitors centre often runs out of them (especially in English).

There are plenty of souvenir books about Petra, such as *Petra* by Iain Browning. They may be nice for the coffee table back home, but are too big to lug around Petra. One of the best guidebooks, *Petra: A Traveller's Guide* by Rosalyn Maqsood, includes lots of history and culture, and details several hikes (although the maps are poor). There's a chapter on hiking in Petra in Tony Howard and Di Taylor's *Walks, Treks, Caves, Climbs & Canyons in Pella, Ajloun, Moab, Dana, Petra & Rum*. French speakers may wish to look out for *Petra, La Cite des Caravanes* by Christian Auge and Jean-Marie Dentzer. These books are available at shops and stalls inside Petra, and around Wadi Mousa.

A more detailed map of Petra is necessary for anyone hiking long distances (see the Hiking section later in this chapter) without a guide. The best currently available is the Royal Jordanian Geographic Centre's contoured (1:5000) map, published as *The Tourist Map of Petra* and the *Map of Petra*. Both are available in Petra and Wadi Mousa.

Information

What to Bring Don't underestimate the size of Petra, and the heat in summer. Always take a good hat, sturdy footwear and, especially in hot weather, lots of water. A few mosquitoes can make life a little uncomfortable at night time in Wadi Mousa, and flies can be annoying during the day in Petra, so bring some repellent (or buy it in Wadi Mousa).

Equip yourself with supplies before entering Petra, otherwise you'll be clobbered for everything from large bottles of water (JD1.500) to the 'lunch box' (JD3), offered by the tent cafes. This generally consists of a couple of slices of dry bread, some yoghurt, cheese, tomato, cucumber and an orange; and is generally very poor value. And bring lots of film.

Tourist Offices The first stop for all visitors should be the Petra visitors centre (☎ 215 6020, fax 215 6060), just before the entrance. It's an impressive building, with an information counter; several souvenir shops (see Shopping in the Wadi Mousa section earlier); toilets; and a branch of the Arab Bank. The Jordan Tourism Board's brochure about Petra and other places in Jordan can be picked up here. The centre is open every day from 7 am to 10 pm. The information counter is the place for booking horses and carriages, and guides, and is open from 7 am to 6 pm every day.

Opposite the Theatre inside Petra is an information centre. Although it's really just another souvenir stall, staff can offer some advice, and there are useful maps for perusal (and sale).

The Petra Regional Planning Council (see the boxed text 'Petra & Tourism' opposite), just behind the main police station at the Police roundabout in Wadi Mousa, is a local development coordinating agency. It is not a tourist office, but is happy to help anyone with specific enquiries about the development of Petra and Wadi Mousa.

Entry Fees & Conditions Admission for foreigners for one day costs a staggering JD20. The passes for two days (JD25) and three days (JD30) are manifestly better deals; and a three-day ticket entitles you to a fourth day for free. (If you buy the one-day ticket and then realise you need more time to explore Petra, you may be able to pay the extra JD5 on day one for the two-day ticket – but certainly don't count on it.) If you have the time, fork out the extra to allow a leisurely exploration over two or three days. Note: no student discounts are available.

Children under 12 pay half price; and – wait for it – Jordanian citizens pay just JD1. Tickets are available from the window outside the Petra visitors centre. Keep your ticket handy because spot-checks occur inside the ruins. Multi-day tickets are not transferable because you have to sign them, and they must be used on consecutive days, starting from the day of purchase. To enter Petra twice in one day, pre-arrange it with the gatekeeper, but remember: it's a 90 minute return walk from the entrance to the Nabataean Museum area, so popping in to Petra a couple of times a day is a waste of time and energy.

We continue to hear disturbing stories about people avoiding the entrance fee by hiking into Petra. But be warned: hiking in remote areas of Petra without a guide is dangerous and entering Petra without a ticket is illegal. Tourist police are on the constant lookout for those without tickets, and woe betide you if you get caught.

It's vital to plan your trip around Petra properly to make efficient use of your time (see the boxed text 'Suggested Itineraries' later in this chapter). If you're on an organised tour, you have little choice, but independent travellers should start a full-day trip well before 9 am. Tickets are available from 6 am, and anyone with a multi-day ticket could start earlier. With a multi-day ticket, it's possible to enjoy a six-hour exploration of Petra before it gets too hot, and be back at your hotel for lunch and a siesta – and then continue early the next day. By avoiding the heat, you need to carry less water, and will feel far more motivated to explore.

Opening Times Petra is officially open every day from 6 am until about 5 pm but, in reality, it's never really closed; these times are when tickets can be bought, and the last time for the day that visitors are officially allowed in. People with multi-day tickets (bought on previous days) can enter Petra as early as 5 am, and others can stagger back through the entrance at any time. However, start the long walk back up the Siq before sunset; and always start long hikes early in the morning. Staying overnight anywhere inside Petra is strictly prohibited.

Petra & Tourism

Petra is overwhelmingly the major attraction for visitors to Jordan, and is visited by about 300,000 people a year (nearly one thousand a day!). Entrance fees to Petra are also a significant source of revenue for the government: over JD6.4 million (about US$9 million) was collected in 1997; in contrast, Jerash generated just JD851,313 (about US$1.2 million).

All revenue from entrance fees goes to the Jordanian treasury, but only about 25% filters back to the Petra Region Planning Council (PRPC). This money is not necessarily used for restoration, so grants, from organisations such as the World Bank, are vital. Established in 1966, the PRPC (☎ 03-215 7092, fax 215 7091, email prc@amra.nic.gov.jo) is responsible for developing tourism in an area of some 853 sq km, of which 264 sq km have been designated as an 'Archaeological Park'. Among the stated aims of the PRPC are 'environmental protection' and 'growth and management of sustainable forms of tourism'. It is also involved in an urgently needed urban development plan for the towns of Wadi Mousa and Tayyibeh, and the scenic road between both places.

More concerned with the direct environmental and ecological future of Petra is the Petra National Trust, or PNT (☎ Amman 06-593 0338, fax 593 2115, or email enquiries@petranationaltrust.com). You can check out their Web site at www.petra nationaltrust.com. The PNT is an independent NGO which aims to 'preserve the environment, antiquities and cultural heritage of the Petra region'. Established in 1989, the PNT helps the PRPC to identify problems, and is involved in training guides, staff and rangers; studying the impact of damage to Petra from erosion and tourism; reducing the number of drink and souvenir stalls in Petra (but finding other avenues of income for stall owners); lobbying against sound-and-light shows and 'Petra By Night' walks; and creating better, designated walking trails.

PETRA

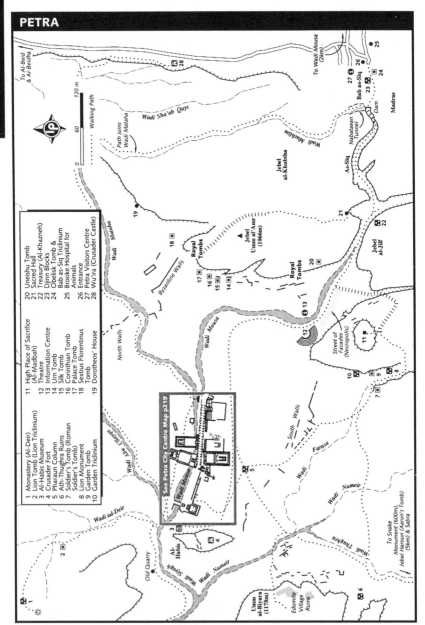

1 Monastery (Al-Deir)
2 Lion Tomb (Lion Triclinium)
3 Al-Habis Museum
4 Crusader Fort
5 Pharaun Column
6 Ath-Thughra Ruins
7 Soldier's Tomb (Roman)
8 Soldier's Tomb)
9 Lion Monument
10 Garden Tomb
10 Garden Triclinium

11 High Place of Sacrifice (Al-Madbah)
12 Theatre
13 Information Centre
14 Urn Tomb
15 Silk Tomb
16 Corinthian Tomb
17 Palace Tomb
18 Sextius Florentinus Tomb
19 Dorotheos' House

20 Uneishu Tomb
21 Sacred Hall
22 Treasury (Al-Khazneh)
23 Djinn Blocks
24 Obelisk Tomb & Bab as-Siq Triclinium
25 Brooke Hospital for Animals
26 Entrance
27 Petra Visitors Centre
28 Wu'ira (Crusader Castle)

See Petra City Centre Map p219

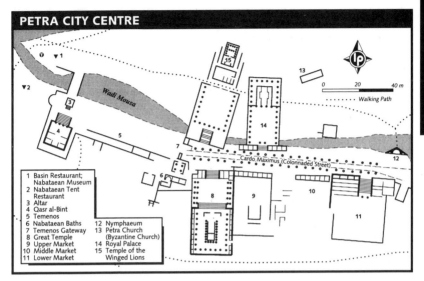

PETRA CITY CENTRE

Wadi Mousa

Cardo Maximus (Colonnaded Street)

Walking Path

0   20   40 m

1 Basin Restaurant;
   Nabataean Museum
2 Nabataean Tent
   Restaurant
3 Altar
4 Qasr al-Bint
5 Temenos
6 Nabataean Baths
7 Temenos Gateway
8 Great Temple
9 Upper Market
10 Middle Market
11 Lower Market
12 Nymphaeum
13 Petra Church
   (Byzantine Church)
14 Royal Palace
15 Temple of the
   Winged Lions

Toilets There are toilets at the Petra visitors centre at the entrance; the information centre opposite the Theatre; and very clean ones at the back of Qasr al-Bint. Refrain from taking an informal leak: some places around the ruins are starting to smell like the urinals at a football match (not helped by horse, donkey and camel droppings).

Things to See & Do

There are over 800 registered sites in Petra, including some 500 tombs, but the best things to see are easy to reach. From the main entrance, an 800m path heads downhill to the start of the Siq. The path passes the Brooke Hospital for Animals (see the boxed text later in this chapter) and through an area called the **Bab as-Siq** ('Gateway to the Siq').

Djinn Blocks Just past the entrance are three enormous monuments, known as the Djinn ('Spirit') Blocks, built by the Nabataeans. Their exact functions remain a mystery, but they could have been tombs, or built as dedications to their god, Dushara.

Obelisk Tomb & Bab as-Siq Triclinium Further along the path are four obelisks,

built as funereal symbols by the Nabataeans in the 1st century BC. Underneath is a Nabataean *triclinium* (dining room), with its three small chambers, where feasts were probably held to commemorate the dead.

As-Siq The 1.2km Siq starts at an obvious bridge, which is, in fact, part of a new **dam**. The dam was built in 1963, on top of one built by the Nabataeans in about 50 AD, to stop water from Wadi Musa river flowing through the Siq. To the right (north), Wadi Muthlim heads invitingly through a **Nabataean tunnel** – the start (or finish) of a great hike (see Hiking later in this chapter).

The Siq often narrows to about 5m (at some points to about 2m) wide, and the walls tower up to 200m overhead. The original channels cut in the walls to bring water into Petra are visible, and in some places the 2000 year old terracotta pipes are still in place. In Roman times, the path was paved and one section is still intact. The wall niches used to hold figures of the Nabataean god, Dushara.

The Siq is not a canyon (a gorge carved out by water), but is actually one block that has been rent apart by tectonic forces,

PETRA

Suggested Itineraries

If your time is limited, it is imperative to make some sort of itinerary. You may wish to follow the suggestions below:

Half-Day (about five hours) You will have little time to explore much, so concentrate on the As-Siq; the Treasury (Al-Khazneh); the Theatre; the Royal Tombs; everything along the Colonnaded Street; the temples and churches, just south and north of the Colonnaded Street; and the Nabataean Museum.

One Day (about eight hours) One day is really the minimum time needed to do Petra any justice. Try not to rush around in one day if you have time to visit for two days: pay the extra for a two-day ticket and explore the site more slowly and thoroughly. In one day, explore the places mentioned above, and allow time for a walk up to the Monastery; and to the High Place of Sacrifice, or above the Treasury on Jebel al-Khubtha, if you have any remaining time and energy.

Two Days This is an ideal amount of time, and allows leisurely exploration, hikes to more remote areas, and a long lunch on one or both days. On the first day, allow time to visit the places mentioned under 'Half-Day', and climb to the Monastery. On the second day, detour as far as you want up Wadi Muthlim and Wadi Siyagh for some different landscapes away from the masses; climb to the High Place of Sacrifice from the Theatre and go back to the city centre (or vice versa); and hike above the Treasury on Jebel al-Khubtha.

Three Days A three-day ticket allows an extra day for free (ie four days), and plenty of time to explore the sites and hike off the beaten track. For the first two days, follow the itinerary listed above. On the third and/or fourth days, hike to Jebel Haroun, via Snake Monument; hike between the dam (at the entrance to the Siq) and the Nymphaeum, along Wadi Muthlim and Wadi Mataha; and allow some time to explore Al-Beid (Little Petra) and the ruins of Al-Beidha village.

evinced at various points where the grain of the rock on one side matches the other. The entrance to the Siq was once topped by an arch built by the Nabataeans. It survived until the late 19th century, and some remains can be seen at the entrance to the Siq.

Further along (west), the walls close in still further, and at times almost meet overhead, shutting out the light and seemingly the sound as well. Just as you start to think that there's no end to the Siq, the bottleneck of visitors, horses and carriages indicate the first glimpse of one of the most impressive of Petra's monuments.

Treasury (Al-Khazneh) Tucked away in such a confined space, the Treasury (known locally as Al-Khazneh) is well protected from the ravages of the elements, and it must be from here that Petra gained its 'rose red' reputation. Although carved out of the solid iron-laden sandstone to serve as a tomb for a Nabataean king (carvings in the facade show gods and other important figures worshipped by the Nabataeans), the Treasury gets its name from the story that pirates hid their treasure here (in the urn in the middle of the second level). Some locals obviously believed this tale because the 3.5m high urn is pockmarked by rifle shots, the results of vain attempts to break open the solid-rock urn.

Barely distinguishable reliefs on the exterior of the monument have aroused much speculation (little of it conclusive) about their identification, although it is felt they represent various Nabataean gods. The date of the Treasury's construction has also been a subject of debate, and estimates range from 100 BC to 200 AD.

Like all the rock-hewn monuments in Petra, it's the facade that captivates; the interior is just an unadorned square hall with a smaller room at the back. The Treasury, which is 43m high and about 30m wide, is at its most photogenic between about 9 and 11 am (depending on the season) in full sunlight; it's also pretty (but not photogenic) late in the afternoon when the rock glows.

From the Treasury, the Siq turns off to the right (north-west), and diagonally opposite is a **sacred hall**, which may have had ritual connections with the Treasury.

Street of Facades Heading towards the centre of the city centre, and just before the Theatre, are an amazing number (over 40) tombs and houses built by the Nabataeans, but with a definite style reminiscent of the Assyrians. Colloquially called the Street of Facades, they are similar to the hundred or more tombs all around Petra, but are certainly the most accessible. It's easy to forget about these when the majestic Theatre comes in view, but the tombs are worth exploring.

Theatre Probably built by the Nabataeans in the 1st century BC, the Theatre (with an original capacity of about 3000) was somehow cut out of rock, slicing through many caves and tombs in the process. It was renovated and enlarged (to hold about 7000) by the Romans not long after they came in 106 AD. Under the stage floor were storerooms and a slot through which a curtain could be lowered at the start of a performance. Through this slot an almost-complete statue of Hercules was recovered.

The Theatre was badly damaged by an earthquake in 363 AD, and parts of it have been removed to help build other structures in Petra. The Theatre is not currently used, but plans are under way to hold events there, much to the chagrin of the Petra National Trust (see the boxed text 'Petra & Tourism' earlier in this chapter).

High Place of Sacrifice (Al-Madbah) The most accessible of the many sacrificial places high in the mountains is simply called the High Place of Sacrifice, known locally as Al-Madbah ('The Altar'). Located on top of Mt Madbah, the **altars** are fairly unimpressive, but the **views** of the city centre to the north-west, Wadi Mousa village to the east and the white shrine on top of Jebel Haroun

to the far south-west are certainly worth the effort. About 50m down (north) over the rocks from the High Place are more staggering **views**, this time of the Royal Tombs.

The steps to the High Place, which start about 200m before (south-east) the Theatre and just past a couple of souvenir stands, are fairly obvious, although not signposted. The climb up takes about 45 minutes, and is better in the early morning when the sun is behind you. It's marginally easier than the steps up to the Monastery, but is still steep and taxing at times. Donkey owners will implore you to ride one of their poor animals for a negotiable JD5/7 one way/return.

At the top, pass the two **obelisks** dedicated to the Nabataean gods, Dushara and al-'Uzza; the altars are a few metres further along and at the highest point in the immediate area. The top of the ridge was levelled to make a platform, and large depressions with drains show where the blood of sacrificial animals flowed out.

You can return the same way (ie back along the steps and finishing near the Theatre), but if you have the energy it's better to go back via Wadi Farasa and on to the city centre, or south-west towards Snake Monument and/or Jebel Haroun. See Hiking later in this chapter for more details about hiking to and from the High Place of Sacrifice.

Royal Tombs The Wadi Musa river bed widens out after the Theatre. To the right (north), carved into the face of Jebel al-Khubtha, are the impressive burial places known collectively as the 'Royal Tombs'.

The first (and most southern) is **Uneishu Tomb**, dedicated to a member of the Nabataean elite. It's virtually opposite the Theatre, and easy to miss because most visitors head to the other main tombs.

Urn Tomb, recognisable by the enormous urn on top, is accessible by stairs. It has an open terrace over a double layer of vaults, probably built in about 70 AD for King Malichos II. The room inside is enormous, measuring 18m by 20m, and the patterns in the rock are striking. It's hard to imagine how the smooth walls, sharp corners and three small chambers at the top were carved out with such precision. A Greek inscription on the back wall details how the building was used as a Byzantine church in the mid 5th century.

Further up (north) is **Silk Tomb**, the most unimpressive of the group. It has been badly damaged by earthquakes and erosion but is noteworthy for the pink, white and yellow colouring of the rocks.

Corinthian Tomb is a badly weathered monument of strange design and unknown purpose, with a top similar to the Treasury. This tomb was still being restored at the time of research, and was fenced off.

Palace Tomb is a three storey imitation of a Roman palace, and one of the largest and most recent monuments in Petra. The top left corner is built – rather than cut out – of stone, because the rock face didn't extend far enough to complete the facade. The four doors lead into small uninteresting rooms.

A few hundred metres further around (north-east) is **Sextius Florentinus Tomb**, built in 130 AD for a Roman governor whose exploits are regaled in an inscription above the entrance. This tomb is often neglected, but is worth the short walk.

There is plenty of room here for wider exploration of more photogenic tombs, and other temples and religious sites in the area. If you have the time and energy, a track between the Palace and Sextius Florentinus tombs leads to a wonderful position above the Treasury – refer to Hiking later in this chapter for details.

Colonnaded Street Further along (west) the Wadi Musa is the Colonnaded Street, where a few columns have been re-erected and the slopes of the hills either side are littered with the debris of the city centre.

Built in about 106 AD, over the remains of another thoroughfare built by the Nabataeans, the Colonnaded Street follows the standard Roman pattern of an east-west decumanus. What is puzzling is the lack of evidence of a cardo, or north-south axis, which traditionally was always the main street.

At the start of the Colonnaded Street is the **Nymphaeum**, or public fountain. Little remains to be seen today, and it's really only recognisable by the huge tree, a welcome respite from the endless sun in summer. On the left (south), are the limited remains of the market area, archaeologically divided into **Lower Market**, **Middle Market** and **Upper Market**. Further up on the right (north) are the unrecognisable ruins of the **Royal Palace**.

The street finishes at the **Temenos Gateway**, built in 2nd century AD with three arches, wooden doors and towers. It marked the entrance to the *temenos*, or courtyard, of the Qasr al-Bint. Opposite (south), are the decrepit ruins of some **Nabataean baths**.

Great Temple Excavations of the Great Temple (sometimes called the 'Large Temple' or 'Southern Temple') have been under way since 1993. Findings suggest that it was a major Nabataean temple built in the 1st century BC, but destroyed by an earthquake not long after. It's currently fenced off, but there's enough to see to justify the short walk up the hill. There is a helpful notice board with a map and explanations in English.

Qasr al-Bint This temple was built by the Nabataeans in around 30 BC, but destroyed in about the 3rd century AD. Despite the name given by local Bedouins – Qasr al-Bint al-Pharaun ('Castle of the Pharaoh's Daughter') – it was almost certainly built as a dedication to the Nabataean god, Dushara. The altar indicates that it was probably the main place of worship in the Nabataean city, and the walls were once brightly decorated with friezes and reliefs. It's 23m high, and the only freestanding structure in Petra.

Temple of the Winged Lions The newly excavated Temple of the Winged Lions is named after the carved lions that topped the capitals of the columns. The temple was built in about 27 AD, and dedicated to the fertility goddess, Atargatis, who was the partner to the main male god, Dushara.

This was a very important temple, and had a colonnaded entry with arches and porticoes that extended down to and across the wadi at the bottom. Fragments of decorative stone and plaster found on the site, and now on display in the Nabataean Museum, suggest that both the temple and entry were handsomely decorated. The area is partially fenced off, but is easy to reach. Although there's not much to see, the **views** are nice.

Petra Church (Byzantine Church) An unmistakable pale green roof covers the remains of the Petra Church (also known as the Byzantine Church). The church was originally built by the Nabataeans, and then redesigned and expanded by the Romans. It eventually burned down, and was then destroyed by various earthquakes, before being lovingly restored by the American Center of Oriental Research in Amman.

Inside the church are some exquisite **mosaics** on the floor, created in the Byzantine period. Ask someone there to open the **baptistery** at the back for a quick look around. A helpful map and explanations in English are located inside the church.

Al-Habis Just beyond the Qasr al-Bint is the small hill of Al-Habis ('The Prison'). Steps lead up the face of Al-Habis to the (free) **Al-Habis Museum**. The museum, which has a tiny collection of artefacts, is inside a cave tomb, and is probably not worth the climb unless you want more **views**. A **trail** goes past the museum for 100m or so, and overlooks Wadi Siyagh, but then becomes dangerous. (It is possible to walk along Wadi Siyagh, however: see Hiking later in this chapter.)

On top of Al-Habis are the limited ruins of a small **Crusader fort**, built in the 12th century AD as a lookout. The path (an easy 15 minutes) to the fort starts at the southern end of Al-Habis hill; look for the signs, or ask directions. The ruins are not impressive, but the **views** of the city centre certainly are.

Monastery (Al-Deir) Similar in design to the Treasury, the Monastery (known locally as Al-Deir) is far bigger (50m wide and 45m high), and just as impressive. Built in the 3rd century BC, the crosses carved on its inside walls suggest the Monastery was used as a church in Byzantine times.

Opposite the Monastery there's a strategically placed drinks stall in a cave with a row of seats outside where you can sit and contemplate the majestic sight. Up past the

Saving the Siq

The Siq, which runs along the dry Wadi Musa river bed, is under constant threat for three very different reasons. Firstly, nearly 1000 people visit every day (see the boxed text 'Petra & Tourism' earlier in this chapter), and walk up and down it at least twice (and, sometimes, vandalise it). Secondly, flash floods are not uncommon in winter, and have caused serious damage (and deaths) in the recent past.

Finally, the Nabataeans built sophisticated hydraulic systems to divert flood waters from along the Siq to other wadis, and for irrigation and storage. After centuries of neglect, erosion and earthquakes, these are ironically causing serious damage to the Siq and various monuments because their bases are now often in underground water, loaded with salt that works its way up the walls and destroys the sandstone. The perpetual damage to the Treasury (Al-Khazneh) is the most worrying.

Various foreign governments and NGOs are busy undertaking surveys, and some urgently needed restoration of the Nabataean hydraulic system has started. The main benefactor is the Swiss government which feels some kindred spirit with Petra because the 'discoverer' of Petra, Burckhardt (see the separate boxed text earlier in this chapter), was born in Switzerland.

drinks stand, and a few minutes further up the rocks, are stunning **views** of Wadi Mousa village to the south-east; Wadi Araba, which stretches from the Dead Sea to Aqaba, to the far west; and the peak of Jebel Haroun, topped by a small white shrine, to the south.

The climb to the Monastery takes about one hour, and is best started in mid-afternoon when there is welcome shade along the way (and the Monastery is at its most photogenic). The spectacular ancient rock-cut path of more than 800 steps is easy to follow (but steep and taxing at times), and is a spectacle of weird and wonderfully tortured stone. If you really don't want to

PETRA

walk, donkeys (with a guide) can be hired for about JD3/5 one way/return.

The start of the trail to the Monastery is not signposted, nor is it particularly obvious. It starts from behind (north-west) the building with the Basin Restaurant and Nabataean Museum. If in doubt, ask locals – or look for weary hikers coming down.

The path to the Monastery passes the **Lion Tomb** (or Lion Triclinium) set in a small gully. The two lions that lent the tomb its name are weather-beaten, but can still be made out, facing each other at the base of the monument.

It was possible to walk up a trail to a point above the Monastery, but this is currently not allowed – more for the sake of preserving tourists than the Monastery (one visitor fell to her death a few years ago).

Nabataean Museum In the same building as the Basin Restaurant, this museum has a small, but interesting, display of artefacts from the region. The explanations in English are comprehensive, and will help most visitors understand the history of Petra. A shop inside the main building sells detailed maps of the area.

'Petra by Night' 'Petra by Night' is a walk down the Siq (which is specially lined with candles) as far as the Treasury, where traditional Bedouin music is played and mint tea is served. It sounds rather tacky, and is very expensive, but many readers have recommended it.

The walk starts from the Petra visitors centre at 8.30 pm on Thursday night, and lasts two hours. Tickets cost JD12 (children under 12 are free), and are available from a few travel agencies in town or, better, from the information counter inside the Petra visitors centre. However, this is only reasonable value if you happen to be going to Petra on a Thursday anyway; otherwise, you have to fork out the JD20 (one-day) entrance fee, *plus* JD12.

Hiking

Anyone with enough energy, time and enthusiasm who wants to get away from the crowds, see some stunning landscapes, explore unexcavated tombs and temples and, perhaps, meet some Bedouin villagers, should go hiking. (See Hiking in the Activities chapter for some general hints.)

Guides can be hired from the information counter just inside the Petra visitors centre, and they speak English, Greek, Arabic and French. They charge JD15 for a group of up to 10 people for a basic (2½ hours) tour of Petra – but this only covers the main sights in the city centre. Guides for other places, such as the Monastery and High Place of Sacrifice, will cost a little more; a guide is essential for Umm al-Biyara and Sabra and recommended for Jebel Haroun (about JD35 for one day). For longer hikes, organise a reliable (but expensive) guide at the visitors centre one day in advance; or try to find a cheaper (and possibly less reliable) guide inside Petra.

A list of a few popular and accessible hikes around Petra follows. None of them are too strenuous or involve camping overnight (which is not allowed anyway). Serious hikers should also pick up one of the two hiking maps mentioned in the Books & Maps section earlier. Please note that the approximate hiking times do not include the time needed to explore the site and/or appreciate the views.

Wadi Siyagh

One trail starts behind (north-west) Al-Habis hill and goes along Wadi Siyagh. Once a suburban area of Petra, the wadi and the nearby slopes have some unexcavated **tombs** and **residences** to explore. The main attractions are probably the number of **shady trees** and **water pools** (and even waterfalls in the winter) along the wadi. Anywhere along Wadi Siyagh, and away from the noisy museum/restaurant area and past the quarry, is a great place for a picnic or a nap in the sun.

The trail along Wadi Siyagh is easy to follow, but becomes a bit rough in parts. Just go as far as you want, but remember that you must come back the same way. Do not walk along the wadi if rain is imminent because flash floods are a real possibility.

The centre of Petra, a remarkable ancient city carved out of rose-red rock, is accessible through the narrow Siq (top left); other attractions include the Urn Tomb (top right), reached by a vaulted stairway, and the imposing Obelisk Tomb and Bab as-Siq Triclinium (bottom).

PAUL GREENWAY

Camels are available for short rides, and photographs, near Petra's Theatre.

JEAN-BERNARD CARILLET

A triclinium (hall for religious feasts) at Petra.

CHRIS BARTON

Bottles of Petra's sand are popular souvenirs.

JEAN-BERNARD CARILLET

Petra's Monastery (Al-Deir), an enormous tomb, perches on a rocky outcrop above the main ruins.

CHRISTOPHER WOOD

SARA-JANE CLELAND

DAMIEN SIMONIS

PATRICK SYDER

Top Left: Surreal effects of eroded sandstone at Little Petra.
Middle Left: Petra's deep rusty hues are interlaced with bands of grey and yellow.
Bottom & Top Right: Bedouin still live and work around Petra.

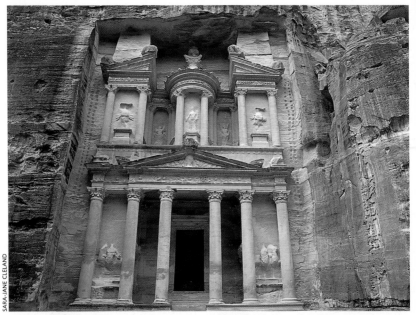

Top: Petra's world-famous Treasury (Al-Khazneh) as seen from near the Siq.
Bottom Left: One of the inheritors of Petra, a Bedouin with his camel.
Bottom Right: The Street of Facades is testament to the wealth of Petra's Nabataean population.

Qasr al-Bint to High Place of Sacrifice, and back, via Wadi Farasa. This is a two hour return trip. Most people head to the High Place of Sacrifice from the steps near the Theatre, but it's possible to start from near the city centre. From behind the Qasr al-Bint, go up the obvious path for about 300m to a four-way junction at the **Pharaun Column**. The walking (ie nonvehicular) trail heads uphill to the High Place, via Wadi Farasa. It's best to start early morning.

However, the trail up the steps from near the Theatre to the High Place, and back down to the Qasr al-Bint, via Wadi Farasa, is far easier to follow.

High Place of Sacrifice to Qasr al-Bint, via Wadi Farasa The trip to Qasr al-Bint from the High Place of Sacrifice takes one hour one way; add an extra 40 minutes if you go via Wadi Farasa. Refer to the High Place of Sacrifice section earlier for information about getting to the High Place along the steps starting near the Theatre.

As you face the drinks stand from the top of the path (which starts from near the Theatre), a trail to the left (west) heads down to Wadi Farasa ('Butterfly Valley'). The start of the trail is not immediately obvious, so look for the helpful piles of stones indicating the trail, or ask for directions at the drinks stand.

On the way down is the **Lion Monument**, where water used to run down the rock from above and out of the lion's mouth. The lion is about 5m long and 2.5m high. A stone **altar** diagonally opposite suggests the fountain had some religious function. The steps wind further down the side of the cliff to the **Garden Tomb**, which archaeologists believe was probably a temple. To the right (east), are the remains of a high wall, part of what was once a water reservoir.

A little further down on the left (west) is the **Soldier's Tomb** (also known as the Roman Soldier's Tomb), so named because of the statue over the door. Virtually opposite (east) is the **Garden Triclinium**, a hall used for feasts after the dead were placed in the Soldier's Tomb. The triclinium is unique in Petra because of the decorations on the interior walls.

A few minutes further down is a gorge

and the path then flattens out and follows Wadi Farasa, the site of ancient rubbish dumps, and ends up at the **Pharaun Column**, the only surviving column of another Nabataean temple. If disoriented, the pale green roof over the Petra Church, north of the Colonnaded Street, is a good landmark. At the start of Wadi Farasa, a trail of sorts heads west towards Snake Monument.

Snake Monument The trip from the High Place of Sacrifice to the Snake Monument and back to Qasr al-Bint takes three hours, or 2½ hours return from Qasr al-Bint. The curled stone on a rock pedestal that faintly resembles a snake is not that exciting, but there's a chance to meet Bedouin villagers (who will charge JD1 per cup of tea).

The trail at the (southern) end of Wadi Farasa (if coming from the High Place of Sacrifice) is not obvious. If you have a map and a sense of direction, head left (west) as soon as the trail heads into a gorge past the Garden Triclinium; continue west, and then south-west, past a Bedouin village to the left (south); and then down Wadi Thughra for another 45 minutes. Another Bedouin settlement with a large, brown tent marks the spot where the Snake Monument can be seen. From there, return to Qasr al-Bint.

In fact, it's far easier to reach the Snake Monument from Qasr al-Bint. Head up the obvious path behind the Qasr al-Bint until you reach the Pharaun Column; take the middle (vehicular) path down to the Snake Monument (the path to the left heads up to the High Place of Sacrifice, and the third (to the far right) goes nowhere interesting. The sign near the Pharaun Column warns not to go further without a guide, but the Snake Monument is easy to reach on foot. Follow the obvious vehicular path; the Bedouin village and monument is another 15 minutes walk south-west from the end of this path.

Umm al-Biyara The return trip from Qasr al-Bint to Umm al-Biyara ('Mother of Cisterns') takes about three hours return. Umm al-Biyara is a mountain (1178m) to the south-west of the city centre. On top may have been the Edomite capital of Sela, from where the

Judaean king Amaziah (who ruled from 796 to 781 BC) threw 10,000 prisoners to their deaths over the precipice – although the actual site is probably further north and not far from Tafila.

The mountain does have the ruins of a 7th century BC **Edomite village** on top, and many unexcavated **tombs** along the eastern cliffs. There's very little to see among the village ruins, but the **views** over the city centre and the surrounding area are probably the best you will see in Petra.

However, the trek to the top is extremely tough going. The trail starts from behind Qasr al-Bint, and initially follows Wadi Thughra (ie along the road towards the Snake Monument from Pharaun Column). The path up the rock face starts from next to the largest of the rock-cut tombs on the south-east face. Climb up the rock-strewn gully to the left of this tomb for 50m and look for, and keep following the original path cut into the rocks. At times, the steps have completely eroded away and are dangerous.

A guide is strongly recommended. Start the hike in the mid-afternoon when most of the path is in shade.

Dam to the Nymphaeum, via Wadi Muthlim and Wadi Mataha This trip takes three hours one way. At the eastern entrance to the Siq is a dam. Only a few metres north is an incredible **Nabataean tunnel**, which leads to a small and beautiful Siq along Wadi Muthlim.

At the point where Wadi Muthlim finishes and reaches **Sidd Ma'jan**, it's possible to head east and then south along Wadi Sh'ab Qays to near the **Wu'ira Crusader Castle** (see the Around Petra section later). However, it's not clear whether hiking in this eastern part of Petra is allowed; and tourist police are always on the lookout for anyone trying to get into Petra for free. It's also difficult to get bearings in this part of Petra, and getting lost is a real possibility.

It's far better to head west along Sidd Ma'jan, which soon leads into Wadi Mataha. Along this wadi is **Dorotheos' House**, the interesting ruins of a number of residences. Wadi Mataha continues west, and then

south-west, and eventually meets the Wadi Musa river bed at the Nymphaeum.

The final part is tricky, and may be impassable if it's been raining. There is a genuine possibility of flash floods along Wadi Muthlim, because the dam at the start of the Siq diverts water down this wadi. Do not start this trek if it's raining, or is likely to.

Above the Treasury This trip takes 1¼ hours return from the Palace Tomb. An obvious set of steep steps commences about 150m north-east of the Palace Tomb. The climb takes about 20 minutes and leads to the top of a ridge affording wonderful **views**. Start this hike in the mid-afternoon when some parts are in shade.

If you continue south along a less obvious dirt path at the end of the steps for another 15 minutes, and then down a small ravine, you'll come to a dramatic position about 200m above the Treasury, with fantastic (but incomplete) views of the mighty edifice. You may have the place to yourself (there's not even a drink stand in sight), and the only noise you can hear are the echoes from the people marvelling at the Treasury below. It is easy to get disoriented while finding the path back to the top of the steps, so look out for landmarks.

Jebel Haroun This trip from the Qasr al-Bint to Jebel Haroun via the Snake Monument takes five hours. Jebel Haroun (1350m) is thought to be Mt Hor from the Bible where Aaron, brother of Moses, is believed to be buried. According to the Quran, it's also where Mohammed became a prophet. The small, white **shrine** on top of Jebel Haroun, which can be seen from Wadi Mousa village and even the Dead Sea, was built in the 14th century, apparently over Aaron's tomb.

The trail to Jebel Haroun starts at the Pharaun Column, and goes past the Snake Monument. Simply continue to the south-west towards the obvious white shrine (which can look deceptively close); the trail is not steep until the last bit. At the bottom of the mountain, find the caretaker if you want to see inside the shrine. A guide is recommended. Alternatively, go on a donkey (with a guide) from the Qasr al-Bint or even the High Place of Sacrifice.

However, the views of Petra are just as good, and far more accessible, from the Monastery and the High Place of Sacrifice, and the shrine on Jebel Haroun is not that impressive, so most hikers may want to give this pilgrimage site a miss.

Sabra This trip from Qasr al-Bint to Sabra takes five hours return. South of the Snake Monument are the remains of the Nabataean village, Sabra, with some ruins of walls, temples, bridges and a theatre. A guide is needed to even find the trail from Snake Monument.

Horse, Donkey & Camel
Horses with guides can only be rented for the 800m stretch between the main entrance and the start of the Siq. The going price down to the start of the Siq is a hefty JD7 (one way) per person, but can be negotiated down to as little as JD2 going back up to the entrance (which some weary visitors gladly pay).

Horses and carriages with guides are only allowed between the main entrance and the Treasury (2km). These are officially for the disabled and elderly, but are often rented by tired hikers. They cost JD20 (return) for a two-person carriage.

Donkeys with guides are also available all around Petra for negotiable prices. They can go almost to the top of the Monastery (about JD3 one way), and all the way to the High Place of Sacrifice (about JD5 one way), and can be rented for trips as far as Snake Monument and Jebel Haroun. Leading donkeys is a genuine occupation for local Bedouin, but animal lovers may think twice about hiring one of these poor animals to climb the incredibly steep and narrow paths to the Monastery or High Place.

Camel rides are more for the novelty value, and are available for short rides and photographs near the Theatre and Qasr al-Bint. A trip between the Qasr al-Bint and the Treasury, for example, costs about JD7.

If you see any animal being cruelly (rather than just harshly) treated, please report it to the Brooke Hospital for Animals (see the boxed text).

Brooke Hospital for Animals

Just to the left of the main entrance to Petra is a large expanse of ground dotted with horses. At the back is the Princess Alia Horse Clinic (☎ 215 6379, fax 215 6437), affiliated with the London-based Brooke Hospital for Animals (Web site www.brooke-hospital.org.uk), which has a number of animal hospitals in Egypt, Pakistan and India.

Founded in 1987, the clinic in Petra aims 'to improve the condition and well being of working equine animals'. It cares for abused horses; educates locals and children in the area about the treatment of animals; provides free preventive measures against disease; and operates mobile clinics to remote regions. It also provides sun shelters and water troughs for horses; and gives (second-hand) saddles and other equipment to owners of working animals. Over 20,000 horses, and 250 other animals, were treated by staff in 1997.

If you see a genuine case of any animal being badly treated (rather than being worked hard), please ring the number (operating 24 hours a day) listed above. (See Treatment of Animals in the Society & Conduct section of the Facts about Jordan chapter for more information.)

While the staff at the clinic are friendly, they are not interested in being a 'tourist attraction', but anyone with a genuine interest in their work – and, especially, anyone wishing to make a donation – can visit the clinic any day between 8 am and 3 pm.

Places to Eat & Drink
At the far western end of Wadi Musa, and past the end of the Colonnaded Street, two restaurants offer similar all-you-can-eat hot and cold buffets. The upmarket *Basin Restaurant* charges JD7.200, and the more informal *Nabataean Tent Restaurant*, JD6.

At most attractions inside Petra, and a few places in between, stands sell cold drinks, bottled water and some basic foodstuffs, as well as souvenirs, but prices are horrendous

PETRA

and it's best to stock up in Wadi Mousa. Note that restaurants and shops in Petra remain open during Ramadan, but be discreet when drinking, eating or smoking in front of locals.

Getting There & Away
Refer to Getting There & Away in the Wadi Mousa section earlier for information about getting to and from Petra; and to Getting Around in the same section for details about travelling between Wadi Mousa and Petra.

Organised Tours One of the few established agencies in Wadi Mousa which arranges trips inside Petra, and to other places such as Aqaba and Wadi Rum, is Petra Moon Tourism Services (☎ 215 6665, fax 215 6666, PO Box 129, email petram@go.com.jo), which has an office on the road into Petra. You can find their Web site at www.petra moon.com. Zaman Tours & Travel (☎ 215 7723, fax 215 7722, PO Box 158, email zamantours@joinnet.com.jo) has also been recommended by readers.

Most of the mid-range and top end hotels in Amman and Aqaba can arrange day trips to Petra by bus or chartered taxi for about JD32, including transport, lunch and perhaps a horse ride – but does not include the entrance fee. The JETT bus company also runs frequent bus trips from Amman – see Getting There & Away in the Wadi Mousa section earlier.

AROUND PETRA
☎ 03
If you have more time (and energy) there are a few other worthwhile attractions in the vicinity, although they pale into insignificance compared to Petra itself.

Getting to some of the places near Petra is difficult by public transport. Some hotels (eg the Qasr al-Bint, Twaissi, Sunset and Peace Way hotels), and some travel agencies in Wadi Mousa can arrange tours to take in some – and even all – of the places listed below, as well as very quick trips to Wadi Rum, Dana and Shobak castle, for about JD10 per person (minimum of four). Invariably, however, you will have to find other passengers to share the cost; all the

hotel or agency does is find the taxi and driver. It may be cheaper (and certainly more flexible) to charter a service or private taxi yourself for the day, although taxi drivers in and around Wadi Mousa blatantly overcharge tourists, and are loathe to negotiate too much (see Getting Around in the Wadi Mousa section earlier).

Wu'ira (Crusader Castle)   وعره
Built by the Crusaders in the early 12th century AD, Wu'ira was abandoned less than 60 years later. A precarious bridge leads to the limited ruins.

Look for the poorly signed turn-off, about 1.5km north of Mövenpick Hotel, and on the left (west) side of the road leading to Al-Beid (Little Petra). Entrance is free, and it's open every day during daylight hours. Refer to Hiking earlier in this chapter for information about hiking to the castle.

Al-Beid (Little Petra)   البيد
Al-Beid ('The Cold') is colloquially known as Little Petra, though, of course, it's not nearly as dramatic or extensive. The advantages are that entrance is free, and if you get there early (say, before 8 am), there may not be another person, tour bus or souvenir stall in sight.

From the car park, an obvious gate leads to the 400m-long Siq, which occasionally expands out into larger areas. The first open area has a **temple**, which archaeologists know little about. Four **triclinium** – one on the left and three on the right – are in the second open area, and were probably once used as dining rooms to feed hungry travellers. About 50m further along the Siq is the **Painted House**, which is another small dining room.

At the end of the Siq are some steps. If you squeeze past these and go about 100m further on there are some great **views** of the rocky landscape, ideal for short **hikes**.

Getting There & Away Tours to 'Little Petra' are offered at some hotels in Wadi Mousa for about JD10 per vehicle, while a chartered private (yellow) taxi charges about JD10 one way. There is no need for a guide, so don't bother paying extra for one.

If you're driving, head up (north) the road from the Mövenpick hotel and follow the signs to 'Beda' and then to the 'Baida Ruins'. There is little traffic along this road, but most hitchhikers will get a ride soon enough – wait at the junction with the sign to 'Beda' about 300m up from the Mövenpick. The entrance to Al-Beid is only a few hundred metres from the main road. If in a rented car or chartered taxi, check out the Wu'ira castle either on the way there or on your return.

Al-Beidha   البيدا

The ruins of Al-Beidha village date back some 9000 years and, like Jericho, constitute one of the oldest archaeological sites in the Middle East. The remains are unremarkable, however, and will only excite archaeology buffs. The Petra National Trust (see the boxed text 'Petra & Tourism' earlier in this chapter) hopes to continue excavations and, in the future, set up trails and signs for visitors.

To get there, follow the trail starting to the left of the entrance to 'Al-Beid' for about 20 minutes.

'Ain Musa   عين موسى

If you arrive by public transport from most places, you'll pass a small building on the right with three white domes. This is not a mosque, but 'Ain Musa ('Moses' Spring'), where Moses supposedly struck the rock with his staff and water gushed forth to the appreciation of the thirsty masses (see the special section 'Biblical Jordan' in Facts about Jordan for more details). Opposite, is the Mussa Spring Hotel (see Places to Stay in the Wadi Mousa section earlier).

The road then winds down about 2km to the village of Wadi Mousa, and a further 3km to the main entrance to Petra.

Tayyibeh   الطيبه

The so-called Scenic Road from Wadi Mousa to Tayyibeh, about 17km south of Wadi Mousa, is spectacular for sunsets, and worth driving along at dusk if you have access to your own vehicle or are able to charter a taxi.

Tayyibeh is the home of *Taybet Zaman Hotel & Resort* (☎ 215 0111, fax 215 0101), a recreation of a typical stone village, with modest little flat-roofed houses with brightly painted doors, for which guests pay JD102/127. It's certainly an interesting – and highly successful – experiment in tourism, and is definitely a tasteful way to set up a hotel. In addition, the complex has a terrace *restaurant* with magnificent views, handicraft shops and an inviting swimming pool.

Local minibuses (400 fils) from Shaheed roundabout in Wadi Mousa village go to Tayyibeh. A taxi will go there for about JD3 one way.

Southern Desert

This chapter mainly deals with two of Jordan's most popular attractions: Wadi Rum, a magnificent moonscape of sand and rocks, with a tantalising historical link to the enigmatic Lawrence of Arabia, and Aqaba, which boasts the only beach and resort area in Jordan, and has enough diving and snorkelling, restaurants and bars to satisfy most visitors.

The Desert Highway is the main route between Amman and Aqaba: the highway passes through monotonous desert for about 300km as far as Ras an-Naqb, from where it winds down off the plateau past the turn-off to Wadi Rum and on to Aqaba. Public buses (but not the private ones run by JETT and Trust), minibuses and service taxis between Amman and Aqaba, Petra and Karak all use the Desert Highway, but the quickest way between Amman and Aqaba is the Dead Sea Highway (see the Northern & Western Jordan chapter), while the King's Highway (see that chapter for details) has the most attractions.

QATRANA　　　　القطرانـه

One of the few towns along the Desert Highway is Qatrana, a couple of kilometres north of the turn-off to Karak. The only reason to stop here is to have a look at the **Qatrana castle**, built in 1531 by the Ottomans. It has been nicely restored, but nothing is explained and it's neglected. There's been a token effort made to fence it off, but the gaps are large enough to drive a truck through, so it seems anyone is welcome to have a look around.

Qatrana has some uninspiring *diners* for truckies. Most tourists head for the *Ba'al-baki Tourist Complex* (☎ 03-398 080, fax 398 156), about 8km north of Qatrana on the highway. It has souvenir shops; a *restaurant* where buffets cost from JD3.300 to JD6.600; and motel-style *rooms* for JD33 per double (no single rates), including breakfast.

MA'AN　　　　معان
☎ 03

Ma'an has been a transport junction and trading centre for many centuries, and is now the

HIGHLIGHTS

- **Wadi Rum** – this desolate area offers some extraordinary desert scenery, and silent nights with a stunning blanket of stars (see page 232)

- **Camel Treks** – travelling by camel from Wadi Rum to Aqaba or Petra is an interesting alternative to the service taxi and minibus (see page 239)

- **Aqaba** – Jordan's one and only 'resort' has a balmy winter climate and an idyllic setting (see page 242)

- **Diving & Snorkelling** – remarkable marine life and coral are just waiting to be explored off the coast of Aqaba, and most is accessible to snorkellers (see page 254)

- **Pharaoh's Island** – although officially part of Egypt, day trips can be organised from Aqaba for diving, snorkelling and exploring the Crusader castle (see page 256)

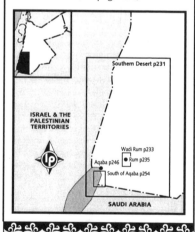

biggest town, and administrative centre, of southern Jordan. There is nothing of interest in Ma'an, but some travellers may have to

230

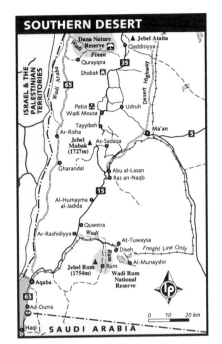

SOUTHERN DESERT

(Map labels:)
Dana Nature Reserve
Finan
Jebel Ataïta
Qaddisiyya
Qurayqira
Shobak
Desert Highway
ISRAEL & THE PALESTINIAN TERRITORIES
Wadi Araba
Petra
Wadi Mousa
Udruh
Tayyibeh
Ar-Risha
Ma'an
Jebel Mubak (1727m)
As-Sadaqa
Gharandal
Abu al-Lasan
Ras an-Naqb
Al-Humayma
al-Jadida
Quweira
Ar-Rashidiyya
Wadi
At-Tuwaysa
Diseh
Freight Line Only
Jebel Rum (1754m)
Rum
Al-Munayshir
Wadi Rum National Reserve
Aqaba
Ad-Durra
Haql
SAUDI ARABIA
0   10   20 km

stay overnight while before getting transport to Wadi Rum, Wadi Mousa (near Petra) and Aqaba. The people of Ma'an are friendly – probably because they see so few tourists – and there is one decent hotel and several good places to eat.

Orientation & Information
Ma'an has all the usual facilities, including an Internet centre for a large town; many shops and restaurants are near the corner of King Hussein (the main thoroughfare) and Palestine streets. Horizon Internet Centre (email hor-pc@go.com.jo), on King Hussein St, charges JD2 per hour; half that in the evening. The Arab Bank, on King Hussein St, has an ATM for Visa and MasterCard, but the Housing Bank, on the same street, is the place to change money and has an ATM for Visa.

Places to Stay
Kreashan Hotel (☎ 213 2043, Al Bayyarah St) – also signposted as *Krishan Hotel* – has

clean, simple and sunny rooms, each with a private balcony, in a good part of town. Singles/doubles/triples cost JD7/12/16 with a shared bathroom and hot water; JD3 per person for a dorm-style bed.

On a main road west of the town centre, *Shweikh Hotel* (☎ 213 2427) charges JD6 for a double with a bathroom and about JD2 for a bed in a dorm. *Hotel Tabok (no telephone)*, just up the road, charges similar prices, but is slightly better than the Shweikh – which should be a last resort.

Places to Eat
National Restaurant, under the Kreashan Hotel, offers fine food, including breakfast, in a clean and hospitable setting. Along King Hussein St, and near the two banks, are several outstanding *restaurants* which serve delicious barbecued and grilled chicken. The *pastry shop* on King Hussein St has a huge range of tasty treats, and there are a few *cafes* in the bus station.

Khoury Resthouse, about 600m along the feeder road when you come off the Desert Highway from the north, is normally worth visiting for a drink – the bar is a truly psychedelic experience. However, the building was closed at the time of research because the manager was ill, and he didn't know if or when the bar would re-open.

Getting There & Away
Ma'an is a junction for transport to Wadi Mousa (near Petra), Aqaba and (indirectly) Wadi Rum.

Bus, Minibus & Service Taxi The station for buses, minibuses and service taxis is an easy 10 minute walk south of Kreashan Hotel; charter a taxi to/from the other two hotels. Most public transport departures from Ma'an start to slow down by about 2 pm, and virtually stop at about 5 pm.

To Wahadat bus station in Amman, there are regular minibuses (JD1.050, three hours) and faster service taxis (JD2). To Aqaba, minibuses (JD1.200, 1 hour 20 minutes) and service taxis (JD1) are also reasonably regular. To Wadi Rum, catch the minibus to Aqaba and hitch a ride from the turn-off.

Minibuses (500 fils, 45 minutes) leave for Wadi Mousa (near Petra) about every hour (more often in the morning). A service taxi (JD1) to Wadi Mousa would be quicker, and probably easier to find. To Karak, there are occasional service taxis (JD1.500), and three minibuses (JD1.250, two hours) a day.

Chartered Taxi It seems that every second vehicle in Ma'an is a private (yellow) taxi. These can be chartered to just about any-where in southern Jordan, and drivers are always on the lookout for long-distance trips. Fares are reasonably standard, but slightly negotiable: to Wadi Mousa, about JD7; and to Karak or Aqaba, about JD15.

Hitching The Desert Highway actually by-passes the western side of Ma'an, so if you're hitching to places further south or north there's no need to go into Ma'an. If you're staying in Ma'an, and then hitching, charter a taxi to the turn-off along the Desert Highway, about 4km north-west of the town centre.

WADI RUM وادي رم
☎ 03

Wadi Rum offers some of the most extraor-dinary desert scenery you'll ever see and, along with Petra, is a 'must' for most vis-itors. Although more and more people flock here, the area has lost none of its forbidding majesty – yet. Thankfully, there is still no hotel, so those who decide to stay overnight are a blessed minority.

Wadi Rum deserves at least three days. The silent nights with a stunning blanket of stars are unforgettable – have fun watching meteors and other fireworks as Orion chases Scorpio across the sky. Equally memorable are the sunrises and sunsets, best observed from one of the *jebels* (mountains) – the colour changes are dramatic and rapid.

The jebels of Wadi Rum completely dom-inate the small settlement of Rum, which has a few concrete houses, a school, some shops and the 'Beau Geste' fort, headquarters of the much-photographed Desert Patrol Corps.

Wadi Rum was first possibly mentioned in Ptolemeus' Geography as 'Aramaua', and according to Islamic scholars (and

Desert Patrol

The camel-mounted Desert Patrol was set up to keep dissident tribes in order, and to patrol the border. Today, they have ex-changed their camels for blue armoured pa-trol wagons – with heavy machine guns mounted at the back – especially adapted for the desert. They can achieve speeds of over 100 km/h through the desert as they pursue their prey (drug smug glers on the Saudi border, or so they say), and occasion-ally rescue tourists who have lost their way.

The men of the Desert Patrol can be quite a sight in their traditional full-length khaki robes, dagger at the waist, pistol and rifle slung over the shoulder – but mostly they wear khaki uniforms like anywhere else. Even their value as a tourist attraction seems unable to halt the tide of modern-isation. Inside the compound, the officer and men on duty (who are not always ne-cessarily Bedouin) sit under the shady eu-calyptus trees and while away the time en-tertaining visitors with traditional Arabic coffee or tea.

hopeful local tourist authorities) mentioned in the Quran as 'Ad'. Excavations have confirmed that the area was inhabited be-tween 800 and 600 BC, and popular with travellers because of the abundance of springs and animals (for hunting). By about the 4th century BC, Wadi Rum was settled by the Nabataeans who built temples and wrote many inscriptions on the rocks – many of which can still be seen.

The region is probably more famous be-cause the indefatigable TE Lawrence (see the 'Lawrence of Arabia' boxed text on the next page), stayed here in 1917. The seren-dipitous discovery of a Nabataean temple (behind the Government Rest House) in 1933 again put Wadi Rum on the world map, but the temple was not completely excavated until 1997 by the Institut Français d'Archeo-logie du Poche-Orient (French Institute of Archaeology of the Near East).

The region known as 'Wadi Rum' is ac-tually a series of valleys about 2km wide,

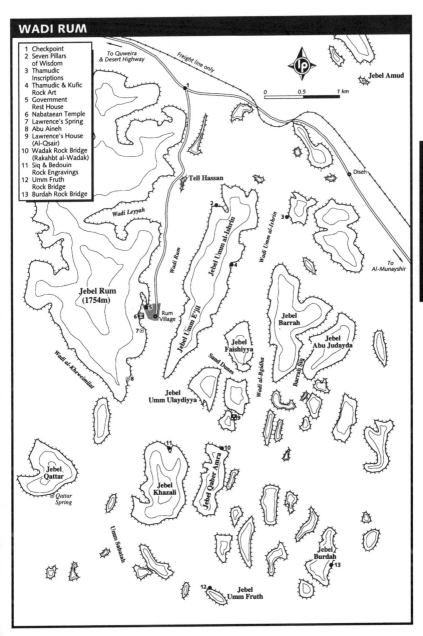

WADI RUM

1 Checkpoint
2 Seven Pillars
  of Wisdom
3 Thamudic
  Inscriptions
4 Thamudic & Kufic
  Rock Art
5 Government
  Rest House
6 Nabataean Temple
7 Lawrence's Spring
8 Abu Aineh
9 Lawrence's House
  (Al-Qsair)
10 Wadak Rock Bridge
   (Rakahbt al-Wadak)
11 Siq & Bedouin
   Rock Engravings
12 Umm Fruth
   Rock Bridge
13 Burdah Rock Bridge

To Quweira
& Desert Highway

Freight line only

Jebel Amud

0   0.5   1 km

Tell Hassan

Diseh

SOUTHERN DESERT

Wadi Leyyah

Wadi Rum

Jebel Umm al-Ishrin

Wadi Umm al-Ishrin

To
Al-Munayshir

Jebel Rum
(1754m)

Jebel Umm E'jil

Rum
Village

Jebel Barrah

Jebel
Abu Judayda

Barrah Siq

Jebel
Faishiyya

Wadi al-Khweimilat

Wadi al-Bajdha

Sand Dunes

Jebel
Umm Ulaydiyya

Jebel
Qattar

Qattar
Spring

Jebel
Khazali

Jebel Qaber Amra

Umm Sahatah

Jebel
Burdah

Jebel
Umm Fruth

SOUTHERN DESERT

Lawrence of Arabia

Born in 1888 into a wealthy English family, Thomas Edward Lawrence ('TE' to his friends) studied archaeology, which led him in 1909 and 1910 to undertake excavations in Syria and Palestine. With the outbreak of WWI, Lawrence became an intelligence agent in Cairo. In 1915 he recorded his ideas on the Arab question and these were taken into consideration by British intelligence. Supporting the cause of the Arab Revolt and manifesting his own hostility towards French politics in Syria, Colonel Lawrence favoured the creation of a Sunni and Arab state. He also became the main architect of the English victory against the Turks.

But it was the desert revolt of October 1918 that etched Lawrence's name into legend. At the side of Emir Faisal and the English general Allenby, Lawrence conquered Aqaba. He entered Damascus in triumph, marking the final defeat of the Ottoman Turks. Syria then became a joint Arab-English state.

Returning to England, Lawrence defended his ideas at the peace conference and served as the special interpreter of the Hashemites. It was at this time that he started his principal work, *The Seven Pillars of Wisdom*, which recounts his adventures. (He apparently wrote it twice, because he lost the first manuscript in a train station in London.)

In 1921, following the conference in Cairo at which both Lawrence and Churchill participated, he was sent to Transjordan to help Emir Abdullah formulate the foundations of the new state. He later left this position and enrolled in 1922 with the Royal Air Force (RAF), under the assumed name of Ross, first as a pilot, then as a simple mechanic.

In 1927, he left on a mission to India but returned home because of rumours that he had encouraged an uprising of Afghan tribes. He left the RAF in February 1935 and died on 19 May after a motorbike accident.

KATE NOLAN

stretching north to south for about 130km. Among the valleys is a desert landscape of sand and rocks, punctuated by majestic jebels which have been eroded into a soft sandstone over a period of up to 50 million years. The valley floors are about 900m above sea level, and the highest peak in Jordan is Jebel Rum (1754m), near the Government Rest House.

Although conveniently and collectively known as 'Bedouin', the major tribe of Wadi Rum is the Huweitat, who claim to be descended from the Prophet Mohammed. Villagers and desert nomads throughout the Wadi Rum area number about 5000. Despite the onset of full-scale tourism, the local people maintain traditional lifestyles, and many still live in tents in the desert and travel on camels. The local people are also incredibly friendly, particularly to foreigners who make the effort to get out into the desert and away from the masses at the Government Rest House.

Despite its barren appearance, Wadi Rum is home to a complex ecological system. Dotted among the desert are small plants which are used by the Bedouin for medicinal purposes, and during the infrequent rains parts of the desert can turn into a colourful sea of flowers.

With the extreme heat and lack of water, not many species of animals exist, and sensibly most only venture out at night. With a lot of luck, you may see Nubian ibex, jackals, wild goats and the strictly nocturnal Arabian sand cat. Rodents, such as jerboas and gerbils, are more common. A few birds of prey, such as vultures and eagles, as well as more genteel sparrows and larks, can be found. And watch out for scorpions, snakes and the scary (but harmless) camel spider.

Wadi Rum recently came under the management of the Royal Society for the Conservation of Nature (RSCN). To assist the RSCN and the local people to preserve the fragile ecosystem of Wadi Rum, please ensure that everything you take into the desert you take out, and that you encourage your guides and drivers to do the same.

When to Go

The coolest months to visit are early spring (March and April) and late autumn (October and November). In winter (December to February) it can rain, and snow on the mountains is not uncommon in the hot season (May to September) daytime temperatures often soar past 40°C. Throughout the year (including summer), however, night time temperatures can often plummet to 0°C, so come prepared if you're camping or watching the sun set or rise.

Bring some insect repellent: flies during the day can be tiresome and the mosquitoes at night (especially if you're sleeping out in the open) can be voracious.

Information

The centre of Wadi Rum is Rum village, and the hub of the village is the Government Rest House. Facilities for tourists throughout Wadi Rum are very limited, eg there is no post office and nowhere to change money. Although the prices and range of goods at the two tourist-oriented shops just across from the Rest House are not bad, it makes sense to stock up on food and water

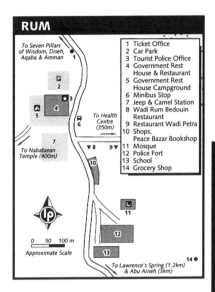

RUM

To Seven Pillars of Wisdom, Diseh, Aqaba & Amman

To Health Centre (350m)

To Nabataean Temple (400m)

0   50   100 m
Approximate Scale

To Lawrence's Spring (1.2km) & Abu Aineh (3km)

1 Ticket Office
2 Car Park
3 Tourist Police Office
4 Government Rest House & Restaurant
5 Government Rest House Campground
6 Minibus Stop
7 Jeep & Camel Station
8 Wadi Rum Bedouin Restaurant
9 Restaurant Wadi Petra
10 Shops; Peace Bazar Bookshop
11 Mosque
12 Police Fort
13 School
14 Grocery Shop

elsewhere, eg Aqaba. Another grocery shop, with cheaper prices but a poorer range, is behind (south-east) the police fort, but it mainly caters to locals. The Peace Bazar Bookshop has a range of books and maps about Wadi Rum.

The JD1 per person entrance fee to Wadi Rum entitles you to one – and only one – tiny cup of tea or coffee behind (but not inside) the Government Rest House. (This is apparently so the Rest House can take its share of the revenue, although most of the takings are funnelled back to the village, evinced by the new health centre.) To bring in a 'touristic car' costs JD5 and a 'private car', JD4 – although the difference is not entirely clear to the visitor or ticket seller.

The tourist police (☎ 201 8215) is in a small office in the Rest House complex. Go there if you have any questions or problems; the English-speaking officers can also help arrange guides and jeeps. The office officially opens every day at about 7.30 am and closes at about 10 pm – but nothing much gets going at the Rest House until after 8 am.

A new health centre (no telephone as yet) is located about 500m east of the Rest House. The police station (☎ 201 7050) in the old police fort will not receive general complaints (go to the tourist police at the Rest House instead), but they will come looking for you if you get lost.

If you're coming for the day, bring a hat, sunscreen, sturdy footwear and water (also available at the shops and Rest House). If camping anywhere, including the Rest House, bring a torch (flashlight); something to read or do, because the entertainment in the evening is far from riveting; and, if possible, a padlock (the tents are lockable).

The Bedouin are a conservative people, so please dress appropriately. Loose shorts and tops for men and women are fine around the Rest House and village, but baggy trousers/skirts and modest shirts/blouses will, besides preventing serious sunburn, earn you more respect from the Bedouin, especially out in the desert.

Books & Maps If you plan to do any short hikes and scrambles, pick up a detailed guidebook and search for a good map; if you intend to do some serious hiking and rock climbing, organise a guide from the tourist police office.

The British climber, Tony Howard, has spent a lot of time exploring Wadi Rum, and has co-written (with Di Taylor) the excellent and detailed *Treks & Climbs in the Mountains of Wadi Rum & Petra*. The 3rd edition was updated in 1997, and costs JD20. The condensed, pocket-sized and more affordable (JD3) version of this is called *Walks & Scrambles in Rum* (published by Al-Kutba). Treks and climbs around Wadi Rum are also mentioned in Howard and Taylor's new *Walks, Treks, Caves, Climbs & Canyons in Pella, Ajloun, Moab, Dana, Petra & Rum*. These books are available in some bookshops throughout Jordan and (normally) at the Peace Bazaar Bookshop in Rum village.

The Wadi Rum brochure published by the Jordan Tourism Board is colourful and has a map showing the major sites. The 1997 *Map of Rum* is contoured and detailed of a small section of northern Wadi Rum, ie around Rum village. The most detailed and informative map is *Wadi Rum Tourist Plan*, published by Int Traditional Services Corp,

Wadi Rum National Reserve

The popularity of Wadi Rum is starting to take its toll: 4WD tracks crisscross the desert; rubbish is left by tourists and Bedouin guides; rock art is damaged, often deliberately; and safety bolts are left on the jebels by rock climbers.

In an attempt to stop the continuing damage to the fragile landscape of Wadi Rum, the Royal Society for the Conservation of Nature (RSCN) has taken over the region and plans to implement a proper balance between promoting tourism and protecting the environment.

At the time of research, the RSCN had not fully established the Wadi Rum National Reserve, but by about mid-2001 the RSCN will probably have turned Wadi Rum into a reserve similar to Dana Nature Reserve.

This will probably mean:

• The number of visitors, campers, trekkers and rock climbers will be limited.
• Prices for everything, including entrance and camping fees, will increase.
• A network of jeep, camel and hiking trails will be created.
• Guides and jeep drivers will be trained.
• An informative visitors centre (near the Seven Pillars of Wisdom) will be built.

but unfortunately it's not widely available in Jordan (and not for sale at the Peace Bazar Bookshop).

Excursions
Short Excursions Most of the attractions around Wadi Rum can only be reached in a 4WD vehicle, on a camel or by hiking. Anyone with less money, more time and limited energy can see a few things on foot in the immediate vicinity of the Government Rest House; or hitch a ride along the road to Diseh.

On a small hill about 400m behind (south-west) the Rest House (follow the telephone poles) are the limited ruins of a

1st century BC **Nabataean temple**. An interesting explanation (in English and French) of the temple and its excavation is on a wall inside the Rest House. Near the temple are some **inscriptions** by hunters and nomads dating back to the 2nd century BC.

Lawrence's Spring is named after TE Lawrence because he wrote about it in *The Seven Pillars of Wisdom*, but it's more properly known locally as 'Ain ash-Shallaleh. Head south from the Rest House and follow the eastern side of Jebel Rum for about 1.2km. From the obvious water tank at ground level, a rather steep, 20-minute scramble up some rocks (follow the line of green shrubs) brings you to a small, pleasant pool with startling **views** to Jebel Khazali and beyond. Near the tank are several **Nabataean inscriptions**, as well as some written by camel drivers of the Saudi Arabian Thamud tribe.

About 3km south of the Rest House, and past Lawrence's Spring, is Abu Aineh, which has another spring and a temporary camp site (but only for tour groups). To get there, keep following the eastern side of Jebel Rum.

Long Excursions Most of the major attractions, nicer landscapes and better rock formations are further away from the Government Rest House, but you will need to have rented a 4WD and a knowlegable guide in order to find them. The tourist police and jeep drivers, for some strange reason, believe that tourists would rather see Lawrence's House (in fact, just a pile of stones) than a beautiful spring such as the one at Jebel Qattar.

The following list of major sites are the ones featured in the tourist police itineraries and at the tourist police station. Some of the places have more than one name, so we have included alternative names. The distance by jeep or on foot from the Rest House in Rum village is included in brackets.

Barrah Siq (14km) This long (about 5km) siq is worth exploring, but be very careful if it's raining, or if rain is imminent, because flash floods are possible.

Burdah Rock Bridge (19km) This is a narrow piece of rock precariously perched about 80m

above the ground. It can be climbed (up the western side) without gear by anyone who has experience in rock climbing; otherwise a guide is recommended. (One climber fell to his death here in early 1999.)

Jebel Faishiyya/Anfaishiyya (10km) Boasts the best Nabataean and Thamudic inscriptions in Wadi Rum, but they're probably of more interest to archaeologists than ordinary travellers.

Jebel Khazali (7km) This serene spot has some welcome shade. There is a narrow siq which can be explored on foot for about 150m until some rocks, which can only be surmounted by rope, block the way.

Lawrence's House/Al-Qsair (9km) This is little more than a heap of bricks, apparently once part of a house occupied by you-know-who, and built on the foundations of a Nabataean temple. There is nothing to see, but the remote location and supreme views of the red sands are the prime attraction.

Qattar Spring (8km) Although not on the normal itineraries offered by jeep drivers, this spring is worth trying to find (especially during the rainy season); the immediate area offers some short hikes.

Sand Dunes/Red Sands (6km) While there are sand dunes in several places around (but certainly not all over) Wadi Rum, the place designated as 'sand dunes' on the tourist trail is a small section of beautiful red sand up the slope of Jebel Umm Ulaydiyya. It's a great area for scrambling around and falling over (harmlessly).

Seven Pillars of Wisdom (8km) Named after Lawrence's book, this large rock formation is easy to see and reach from the main road into Wadi Rum, just south of the junction to Diseh. Because it is so accessible, it's not included on jeep tours from the Rest House, but can be negotiated as an extra. Otherwise, hitch a ride or walk along the main road from the Rest House.

Sunset & Sunrise (11km) Dusk and dawn are magical (and cooler) times to be in the desert. The best vantage points differ according to the time of the year; the most common is Umm Sabatah . Jeep drivers can take you there and wait; drop you off and pick you up later (they are reliable about these things); or provide a 'sunset tour' with a 'traditional' Bedouin dinner for about JD20 per person.

Umm Fruth Rock Bridge (13km) This is another small, but fairly remote, rock bridge which can be easily climbed without gear or a guide.

Wadak Rock Bridge/Rakahbt al-Wadak (9km) This rock formation is easier to climb and more accessible than Burdah Rock Bridge but is not as impressive. However, the views across the valley are superb.

4WD

Most places can only be visited by a 4WD vehicle. If you have a private car which isn't a 4WD, or don't mind hitching, the road to Diseh from the turn-off to Rum has some spectacular jebels and landscapes.

Hiring a Jeep with a Driver Most places listed in the Long Excursions section earlier could be visited, albeit quickly, in about six hours. However, jeeps with a driver rented from Rum village will not take you everywhere, even if you rent the jeep for what is ostensibly a 'full day tour'. All rates offered by drivers depend entirely on the number of places visited, rather than the amount of time the vehicle is rented.

Most jeeps hold about six people. The common, older types are pick-ups which can hold two (preferably one) passenger in the front, and up to six (preferably four) on bench seats at the back. The jeeps in Rum are generally uncomfortable and never air-conditioned, but they are great fun. The drivers are genuinely reliable when it comes to dropping off and picking up passengers, and most speak some English.

The official costs of jeep rental from Rum village and back are listed below according to pre-arranged itineraries on the wall inside the tourist police office. The 'times' also listed on the wall are exaggerated, so you may feel disappointed and ripped-off if a 'four hour' tour (according to the itineraries listed on the wall) only takes two hours. A refund for unused time is not possible: you won't be able to convince the driver to use the extra time to visit other places, unless you pay considerably more; and any detours or different itineraries to those listed in the tourist police office will involve complicated negotiations and more dinars.

See Excursions earlier for details about each place listed below:

Lawrence's Spring	(JD6)
Jebel Khazali	
Via Lawrence's Spring.	(JD15)
Umm Sabatah	(JD18)
Or any other vantage spot for a sunset – negotiate for a pick up later.	

Burdah Rock Bridge	(JD32)
Via Lawrence's Spring, Jebel Khazali, Sand Dunes and Lawrence's House, and possibly via Jebel Faishiyya and Wadak Rock Bridge for no extra charge.	
Barrah Siq	(JD45)
Via the Sand Dunes and Jebel Faishiyya, and anything else you can negotiate with the driver.	
'Full Day'	(JD45)
Although this is actually about 8 am to 6 pm, the fare will still only include a select number of places, all open to negotiation with the driver.	

Remember the price is per vehicle, so obviously the more people you can round up to share the cost the better – and don't accept an increased price per vehicle just because you've found some extra people to come along. The prices listed above are the upper limit in bargaining, and the drivers at the jeep station in Rum village will negotiate a little; if you go further into Rum, you may find that negotiation is easier. However, there is some sort of cartel operating among jeep drivers in Rum, so going from one driver to another and haggling may prove difficult.

The tourist police are happy to advise about which tours to take, find a reliable jeep driver (but there is a roster system of sorts), write down in Arabic the places you want to visit (if your driver has limited English) and act as an arbitrator. But in the end, negotiation is between you and the driver – and drivers are now used to big-spending tourists.

One alternative is the Wadi Rum Eco-Tourism Project (☎ 03-201 9216, fax 201 9217) which rents out its 4WDs (with drivers) to help fund local projects (eg a mobile health clinic). These 4WDs are not cheap – eg a two hour return trip from the Rest House to three nearby sites is at least JD20 per vehicle – but the vehicles are more comfortable than the battered old jeeps in Rum; air-conditioned 4WDs are available for 10% extra. They also offers day trips from Aqaba to Wadi Rum for about JD50 per vehicle, and from Aqaba to Petra for about JD70. Their office is signposted along the Desert Highway, about 1.5km north of the turn-off to Wadi Rum.

Renting Your Own 4WD There is nowhere to rent a self-drive 4WD in Wadi Rum, but it is possible to rent a 4WD in

Aqaba (see Getting Around in the Aqaba section later for details of rental agencies and costs). This obviously allows you considerably more freedom and flexibility than an organised jeep tour, but driving to anywhere more than about 5km from the Government Rest House without a guide is not recommended. A guide will cost about JD5 per hour from the tourist police office.

Petrol is sold by the can at the grocery shop south-east of the police fort. And, finally, remember that it's very easy to get lost around Wadi Rum and getting bogged in soft sand in 40°C is no fun.

Camels

Camels are more authentic and ecologically sound than a jeep, but the poor animals don't cover much distance – about 20km per day – and only carry one passenger at a time. The going rate for long trips is JD20 per day. One-way trips from Rum village to near Aqaba can take anything from three to six nights, depending on the route; and to near Wadi Mousa (for Petra), about five nights. (Camels obviously do not travel all the way into larger towns.) Add to this the cost of hiring tents from the camel driver (alternatively, bring your own tent or sleep under the stars); food; and returning the camels back to Rum.

The official rates (per person/camel) for short return trips around Wadi Rum are also on the wall of the tourist police office, and are listed below. The prices for camel trips are more negotiable than for jeep trips, especially if you deal directly with the camel owners and drivers (usually boys) at the jeep and camel station in Rum.

Nabataean Temple (JD2)
Only about 800m return, but worth it for the novelty.
Lawrence's Spring (JD7)
A more interesting trip to really get the feel of a camel ride. About 1½ hours return.
Jebel Khazali (JD16)
Via Lawrence's Spring. Possibly getting a sore backside by now. About 6 hours return.
Burdah Rock Bridge (JD40)
Via Lawrence's Spring, Jebel Khazali and Umm Sabatah. This is an overnight trip, so you must hire or bring a tent, or sleep under the stars; and bring food and water.

Hiking

Although some adventurous travellers and experienced hikers do trek around Wadi Rum for a day or two without a guide, it's recommended that one be employed if you're planning on going to anywhere listed under Long Excursions earlier. One popular hike is a circumambulation of Jebel Rum (eight hours).

Remember that it's very easy to get disoriented; temperatures can be extreme; natural water supplies are uncommon and not always drinkable; passing traffic is nonexistent; and maps are fairly inadequate. Hiking should not be attempted in the hotter months (May to September) when temperatures are extreme, and dehydration and exhaustion are real dangers. The local police are sick and tired of rescuing stupid foreigners who think they can walk hours in the midday sun with little protection and inadequate water supplies. Five-litre water containers can be bought at the shops in Rum, and should be enough water for one person for two days.

The books written by Tony Howard and Di Taylor (see Books & Maps earlier in this chapter) list a number of hikes in the region.

Rock Climbing

Wadi Rum offers some challenging rock climbing, nearly equal to anything in Europe. There is a vast array of climbs ranging from Grade 3 to Grade 6. The most accessible and popular climbs are detailed in books written by Tony Howard and Di Taylor (see Books & Maps earlier in this chapter).

Rock climbing is still a nascent industry in Wadi Rum, however, so you need to bring your own gear. Bolts have been hammered into a few rock faces, but be very careful if you intend to go your own way – there have been several bad accidents. The rocks are soft and can be treacherous, and the starting points for climbs are not signposted, so a guide is recommended. To find a qualified guide who specialises in rock climbing, contact the tourist police in the Government Rest House in Rum village a few days in advance so that equipment and transport can also be organised.

One of the more popular climbs for amateurs is up Jebel Rum, because minimal gear

SOUTHERN DESERT

is needed and it's close to the Rest House, although a guide is still required to find the best route and to help with the climb. Nothing is cheap: climbers have been quoted about JD70 for the more difficult route, which is closer to the Rest House; or about JD110 for the easier route from the western side of Jebel Rum, which involves hiring a jeep.

Organised Tours

Most visitors come on organised day trips, often on huge buses from Wadi Mousa, Aqaba and Amman. These sorts of tours are, of course, expensive and inflexible; and are normally only part of a pre-paid package tour. One of the few bus tours run by a company in Aqaba is Aquamarina Tours (☎ 03-201 6250, fax 201 4271, email aquam@ go.com.jo), which offers half-day trips, including sunset viewing and dinner, for US$60 per person. Bookings can be made at any of the hotels formerly known as Aquamarina I, II and II in Aqaba.

An increasing number of companies do offer cheaper, and more flexible, jeep tours from Aqaba. These are definitely worth considering because organising your own 4WD tour in Rum may end up being more expensive than organised jeep tours from Aqaba. These tours use the desert road to or from Aqaba; offer a better standard of tent and food than the Rest House; and avoid the hassle of public transport to/from Wadi Rum.

The following agencies in Aqaba (☎ 03) offer day trips, which normally leave Aqaba at about 1.30 pm and include dinner; and overnight trips, which usually leave at about 10.30 am and include tent accommodation, dinner and breakfast. Both types of tour visit most of the important sites listed under Long Excursions earlier in this chapter.

Al-Khouli Tourism & Travel Agency
   (☎/fax 203 0682) in the Al-Khouli Hotel; runs overnight trips for JD45 per person.
Peaceway Tours
   (☎/fax 202 2665, email peacewaytours@index .com.jo) in the Housing Bank Centre next to the Crystal Hotel. It is about the best place around, and offers day trips for JD35, and overnight trips for JD45.
   Web site www.peaceway.com

Qutaish & Sons
   (☎/fax 201 2295, fax 201 4679), down a lane between Raghadan and Zahran streets and opposite the Al-Shami Restaurant; organises overnight trips for JD50.

Places to Stay

Surprisingly (and thankfully) there is still no hotel in Rum village, or anywhere in Wadi Rum. So, at the moment all accommodation is in tents – either yours, or one provided by the Government Rest House or set up by local Bedouin. Camping anywhere in the desert is permitted, but facilities (shops, toilets, showers etc) are nonexistent anywhere away from Rum village.

Rum Village *Government Rest House* *(☎ 201 4240)* has six two-person tents in a dusty camp site at the back. These tents cost JD3 per person, and include a thin mattress and grotty blanket. Sleeping on the roof of the Rest House for JD2, including mattress, sheet, pillow and blanket, is cooler but noisy, and mosquitoes can be bad. Deals including breakfast (JD5/6 per person if on the roof/in the tent) and 'half board' including breakfast and buffet dinner (JD12.100/ 13.200), are not great value.

The Rest House has showers (with an unreliable water supply); adequate toilets (the nicer ones are kept locked at night, and only used by tour groups during the day!); and somewhere to safely store luggage. The tents can be locked, so bring a small padlock. If you already have a tent, head out into the desert because you're not allowed to pitch it in the Rest House camp site.

In the Desert Experiencing the legendary hospitality of the Bedouins and sleeping out under the stars are great reasons for heading out into the desert. If you have a tent, just head south from the Rest House and find a secluded spot somewhere. If you want to sleep without a tent, remember that it can get very cold at night, and mosquitoes can be a problem. If you don't have a tent but still want to sleep in the desert, or you're really keen to meet some Bedouin, ask at the Rest House, tourist police or jeep and camel drivers in Rum village about sharing a tent

Wadi Rum is a magnificent example of desert scenery. It features some of Jordan's best hiking and is one of the country's most popular tourist destinations, along with Petra and Jerash.

Bedouin goat-hair tents (top), sprouting desert plants (bottom left) and timeless rock formations (bottom right) are some of the memorable sights of Wadi Rum.

The small settlement of Rum which, thankfully, still has no hotels.

The towering, soft sandstone cliffs of Wadi Rum have been eroded over 50 million years.

Top: Waiter service at Aqaba, Jordan's only beach resort.
Middle: Stopping for petrol on the Desert Highway, a main route from Amman to Aqaba.
Bottom: Glass-bottom boats are a popular way to view Aqaba's underwater treasures.

with, or sleeping under the stars near, some Bedouin. Local families occasionally rent out space in their tent, and provide basic meals, for a negotiable price of anything from JD2 to JD8 per person per day. Although the facilities are basic (ie no toilets or showers anywhere) and not private, and the accommodation and food is simple, it's worth it for the hospitality and experience.

There is usually some wood around for a fire, but please use it sparingly: supplies are very limited and needed by the Bedouin. It's better to bring a stove or eat uncooked foods (eg fruits, breads, canned meat etc) – and, of course, please take out everything you bring in. Some travellers recently reported that their tents (even those which were padlocked) set up in the desert were ripped open, and some valuables, including food but not camping equipment, were stolen. It's best to leave valuables at a hotel in Aqaba or Petra, or at the Rest House in Rum village, and to carry anything else of value with you when you leave your tent for the day.

Places to Eat

Government Rest House has an overpriced restaurant with a limited menu, but it does try hard. A plate of kebabs, chips (French fries), salad and *humous* costs JD3.600, but the sandwiches are fairly ordinary. Salads usually cost about 800 fils, and an omelette, JD1.200. When tour groups arrive, a buffet breakfast (JD4.400), and lunch and dinner (both JD6.600), is usually served. The buffets are normally available to independent travellers, but aren't great value. The Rest House also serves alcohol, and a large Amstel beer (not unreasonably priced at JD2.500) while watching the sun's rays light up Jebel Umm al-Ishrin is a perfect way to finish off a tough day.

Two obvious restaurants just down from the Rest House serve basic food and drinks, but don't open for breakfast until after 8 am: *Wadi Rum Bedouin Restaurant* and *Restaurant Wadi Petra*.

For those on a budget, the best advice is to buy your own food. The two shops just down from the Rest House has a range of canned food, biscuits and mineral water;

probably adequate for most people staying a day or two. If you're trekking or camping for longer, or are particularly fussy, bring supplies from somewhere else, eg Aqaba or Wadi Mousa (near Petra).

Getting There & Away

Public transport is very limited because Rum village has a small population, and most visitors come on organised tours. To find out the current timetables of public transport – the day before you want to leave – contact staff at the Government Rest House (if staying there), or the tourist police (if you're not). Private (yellow) taxis hang around the car park, and all public transport stops in front of the Rest House.

Minibus To Aqaba (JD1.500, one hour), minibuses leave at about 7 am and 12.30 pm; but only at 7 am on Friday and public holidays. To Wadi Mousa, for Petra (JD1.500, 1 hour 30 minutes) a minibus leaves at about 8.30 am. Either one will take you to the turn-off along the Desert Highway (750 fils), from where it's easy enough to hail a bus to more distant places, such as Ma'an, Karak and Amman.

Service Taxi & Private Taxi Occasional service taxis hang around Rum and the Rest House waiting for a fare back to wherever they came from – normally Aqaba, Wadi Mousa or Ma'an. To charter a service taxi or private taxi count on about JD20 to Aqaba, and about JD30 to Wadi Mousa and Ma'an.

Hitching Because of the dire lack of transport to and from Rum village, most travellers (including locals) are forced to hitch – a normal form of transport in this part of Jordan anyway.

The well-signed turn-off to Wadi Rum is along the Desert Highway, about 5km south of Quweira. From Aqaba, take a minibus or hitch to either Quweira (500 fils) or Ma'an (JD1.200); and from Wadi Mousa (near Petra), take a minibus, service taxi or hitch to Aqaba. Then disembark at the turn-off to Wadi Rum, and wait for a lift directly to Rum or as far as the turn-off to Diseh, from where you can ask the guys at the check-point to hail down a passing vehicle.

Hitching along these roads is rarely free, however, and you may be asked an absurd amount for a lift. Don't pay more than about JD3 between the Desert Highway and Rum, and about JD1 between the turn-off to Diseh and Rum – unless you hail down an empty taxi (not as unlikely as it sounds).

At Rum, ask around the car park for a lift, or hail something down from outside the ticket office.

DISEH   الدسيه

Diseh is north-west of Rum village, about 12km (as the vulture flies) but 22km by road. This town is trying – unsuccessfully – to become a small-scale alternative to Rum, but its surrounding terrain is not as breath-taking, and the facilities are even more un-developed than in Rum.

Things to See
The paved road to Diseh from the turn-off to Rum offers a few accessible jebels and land-scapes, which are easy to explore. The local Bedouin are keen to get some of the tourist biscuit and will happily drive you out into the desert area north of the railway line. The area is dotted with **Nabataean and Roman dams**, artificial **rock bridges** and **rock carvings** and **inscriptions**. The landscape around **Jebel Amud** is the most interesting.

Places to Stay & Eat
There are no hotels or restaurants in Diseh, but there are a few basic *shops* with a slightly better range of goods than in Rum. *Camping* out in the desert is possible, but find a se-cluded spot and lock your tent, if possible. Alternatively, ask around about staying with one of the local Bedouin families – for a ne-gotiable fee of about JD5 to JD8 per person per night, including basic meals.

Getting There & Away
Minibuses between Aqaba and Diseh are ir-regular, so it is better to catch anything going along the Desert Highway, or to Rum directly, and get off at the turn-off to Diseh. A lot more traffic goes along the road all the

way to Diseh, so hitching is easy enough. From Rum, hitch to the turn-off to Diseh and look for anything going your way.

Getting Around
Bargain hard if you want to rent a jeep (with a driver). Don't pay more than JD40 per ve-hicle for a full day, which is a little cheaper than in Rum, but the drivers in Diseh are also very reluctant to take the 'full day' rental to its logical conclusion. Also, there seems some division about where jeep dri-vers in Diseh can't (or won't) take tourists around Wadi Rum – and vice versa.

AQABA   العقبة
☎ 03
The balmy winter climate and idyllic setting on the Gulf of Aqaba make this Jordan's aquatic playground. While Amman shivers in winter with temperatures around 5°C and the occasional snowfall, the mercury hovers steadily around 25°C in Aqaba. In summer, the weather is uncomfortably hot, however, with daytime temperatures over 35°C, but it's often bearable because of the sea breezes, and more manageable if you enjoy the mandatory siesta between 1 and 4 pm.

Aqaba is popular with Jordanians from the north, and with Saudis from the across the border, and is an obvious place for trav-ellers to break up a journey to/from Israel or Egypt. Although the diving and snorkelling is not as good as in Egypt, and the beaches are not as accessible as those in Israel, Aqaba is a relaxed place, and there is a good range of hotels and restaurants. However, anyone looking for resort-style atmosphere and facilities may be disappointed, and the line of tankers less than 500m from the beaches are far from picturesque.

History
Excavations at Tell al-Khalifa, 4km west of central Aqaba and right on the Jordan-Israel border, have revealed copper smelters thought to be the site of Ezion Geber as mentioned in the Bible. Smelting was also carried out here from the 10th to the 5th century BC with ore coming from mines in Wadi Araba.

As trade with southern Arabia and Sheba (present-day Yemen) developed, the area around Aqaba thrived because the great road from Damascus came through, via Amman and Petra, and then headed off west to Egypt and Palestine. The main town was occupied by Ptolemies from Egypt, during the 3rd and 2nd centuries BC, and then the Nabataeans, from about the 3rd to the 1st centuries BC, and during Roman times it was renamed Aqabat Ayla ('Pass of Alia') – from which the modern name of Aqaba originated.

At the time of the Muslim invasion in 636 AD, there was a church and even a Bishop of Ayla. The Crusaders occupied the area in the 12th century and fortified a small island nearby – then called Ile de Graye, but now known as Pharaoh's Island (see the South of Aqaba section later in this chapter). By 1170, both the port and island were in the hands of the Ayyubids, under Salah ad-Din. In 1250, the Mamluks took over, followed by the Muslims in about 1320. By the beginning of the 16th century the town had been swallowed up by the Ottoman Empire, and lost much of it's significance when the main trading area of the region was moved to Baghdad in the middle of the 16th century.

For about 500 years, until the Arab Revolt during WWI, Aqaba remained an insignificant fishing village. Ottoman forces occupied the town but were forced to withdraw after a raid by TE Lawrence and the Arabs in 1917. From then on, the British used Aqaba as a supply centre from Egypt for the push up through Transjordan and Palestine regions.

After WWI, the Transjordan-Saudi Arabian border had still not been defined, so Britain arbitrarily drew a line a few kilometres south of Aqaba. The Saudis disputed the claim but took no action. As the port of Aqaba grew, the limited coastline proved insufficient, so in 1965 King Hussein traded 6000 sq km of Jordanian desert for another 12km of coastline with Saudi Arabia.

Orientation

King Hussein St (also known as the Corniche) is the main axis of Aqaba. It runs more-or-less north-south along the coast through the centre of town, and follows the Aqaba Gulf around to the west as far as Israel and to the south as far as Saudi Arabia. In the city, a walking path parallels King Hussein St but it only hugs the coast in small sections because of the private beaches owned by the upmarket hotels to the north-west and the marina and navy docks in the city centre.

Most of the charmless urban sprawl in Aqaba is taking place in the north and west of the town, and the massive port facilities start a few kilometres south of the city centre. Consequently, central Aqaba has been spared the ravages of development and maintains some charm. Most of the cheap hotels, restaurants, banks and other facilities are clustered together in the city centre, with the more expensive hotels at the north-western end of the beach.

Maps The maps of Aqaba in this book are enough for most visitors. The Royal Jordanian Geographic Centre publishes a detailed street map, but it's of little use to tourists. The Aqaba brochure printed by the Jordan Tourism Board, available at the tourist office, is worth picking up.

Information

Tourist Office The tourist office (☎ 201 3731) is in the visitors centre on Prince Mohammed St – look for the door marked 'Information'. Staff are friendly enough, but can offer little more than the usual range of brochures published by the Jordan Tourism Board. The office is open every day from 7.30 am to 1.30 pm, and 4 to 6 pm, but hours are less stringently enforced on Friday.

Visa Extensions The police station (☎ 201 4211), opposite the bus station, is the only place in Jordan (other than Amman) where visas can be reliably extended. A two-month extension is possible within one hour. The visa section of the police station is open from 8 am to 1 pm, and 5 to 7 pm, every day but Friday.

SOUTHERN DESERT

Money There are numerous banks around the city; many are located along the southern side of Al-Hammamat al-Tunisieh St. The best are: the Arab Bank, which has an automatic teller machine (ATM) for Visa and MasterCard, near the park; Jordan National Bank, on Zahran St; and the Housing Bank (with an ATM for Visa and Plus cards) along the Corniche. There is also an ATM for Visa and Plus cards outside the General Post Office.

If you're stuck without cash on a Friday or public holiday, try the Cairo-Amman Bank inside the Arab Bridge Maritime Co building on Al-Petra St. The bank is open every day so that people can change money into US dollars to pay for ferry tickets to Egypt.

Numerous moneychangers are also dotted around the city centre; many are located around the corner of Zahran and Ar-Razi streets. They are open for far longer than banks, and most change travellers cheques without commission.

The agent for American Express is International Traders (☎ 201 3757), situated on Al-Hammamat al-Tunisieh St. It can generally hold mail for clients, but does not change travellers cheques.

Post & Communications The General Post Office is open from 7.30 am to 7 pm every day (but closes at 1.30 pm on Friday), and has a poste restante service.

Outside the post office is a gaggle of Alo and JPP telephone booths, and several stalls nearby sell telephone cards for both Alo and JPP. Other private telephone agencies are located on the main streets, and some moneychangers also offer telephone services.

There is no local Internet Service Provider (ISP) in Aqaba, so the cost of using the Internet in Aqaba is prohibitively expensive because the ISPs are in Amman (and must be reached using long-distance telephone rates). The following places in central Aqaba charge from JD7 to JD8 per hour: Mecca Exchange (mecca@index.com.jo), on Ar-Razi St; Al-Cazar Hotel (tourist@alcazar.com.jo), An-Nahda St, but evenings only; and Universal Services (cec.aqaba@firstnet.com.jo), near the General Post Office.

The telephone numbers in Aqaba have recently changed. If you come across an old six-digit number, replace the first '3' with '20' (eg 313 757 becomes 201 3757).

Bookshops The Yamani Library bookshop on Zahran St has a great range of titles about Jordan and the Middle East. A few doors away (south-west), the Redwan Library bookshop stocks an impressive selection of novels in English, and other European languages, as well as books about Jordan and Lonely Planet guides to other places in the region. Both sell magazines and newspapers from the USA, UK and Europe. Several stalls on Zahran St sell the English-language newspapers published in Amman.

Electricity In a touching reminder of Britain's influence in the region, the sockets in Aqaba are mostly of the three-prong UK variety – so come prepared.

Laundry Most visitors stay long enough in Aqaba to get some laundry done – especially useful if you've gathered layers of dust and sand from Wadi Rum. Frindes Laundry on Al-Petra St is the cheapest place; Rana Dry Clean on An-Nahda St is better, but more expensive.

Emergency The Princess Haya Hospital (☎ 201 4111) is well equipped – and has great views. It also offers decompression chambers, and staff are trained to deal with diving accidents. The most convenient police station (☎ 201 4211) is the one opposite the bus station.

Dangers & Annoyances Women travellers have reported varying degrees of harassment from local lads on the public beaches. This may even happen on the beaches belonging to the major hotels, but if it does at least you can complain to the hotel management. On the public beaches, foreign women will feel far more relaxed (but not necessarily more comfortable) wearing loose shirts and baggy shorts. See Beaches in the following Activities section for more details.

Ayla (Old Aqaba)

Along the Corniche, and incongruously squeezed between the marina and the Mövenpick Resort (under construction), is the site of old Aqaba, the early medieval port city that bore the name of Ayla. The ruins are limited, but worth a quick look if you're in the area. Helpful noticeboards in English clearly pinpoint items of interest and put the place in some perspective. The site is free to enter, permanently open and accessible from the beach or the main road.

At the back of the parking space behind the JETT bus office is another small section of the old city, but this is fenced off while excavations continue.

Aqaba Castle (Mamluk Fort)

Aqaba Castle (sometimes called 'Mamluk Fort') is certainly worth a look, especially if you're visiting the tourist office. The castle was built in the early 14th century AD by the Crusaders, and then rebuilt by the Mamluks in the 16th century as a resting place for Egyptian pilgrims travelling to and from Mecca. It has been renovated several times, including in 1587 and 1628, but was substantially destroyed by shelling from the British Royal Navy in WWI. The Hashemite Coat of Arms above the main entrance went up during WWI after the Turks were thrown out by combined British-Arab forces in 1917.

A helpful map and explanation in English is on a notice board in the courtyard. Entrance is free, and the castle is open 8 am to 5 pm every day (but less reliably so on Friday).

Aqaba Museum (Museum of Aqaba Antiquities)

This small museum is inside the visitors centre, once the home of Sherif Hussein bin Ali, the great-great-grandfather of the present king (King Abdullah II), who lived here for a while after WWI.

The museum has some coins from other countries, such as Iraq and Egypt, a few interesting ceramics and information about the excavations of Ayla (Old Aqaba). All captions are in English. The collection is of minimal interest, however, and many vis-

itors may not feel inclined to fork out the JD1 entrance fee when it's free to enter the Aqaba Castle nearby. The museum is open from 7.30 am to 1 pm, and 4 to 6 pm, every day but Tuesday.

Beaches

Aqaba, while promoting itself as a 'resort' (most brochures feature pictures of people happily water-skiing and lazing on the beach), is not nearly as developed as it pretends to be. The stretch of public beach between the marina and the Aqaba Hotel is reasonable, but the mammoth Mövenpick Resort, which is currently under construction and straddles both sides of the main road, plans to 'privatise' most (and possibly all) of this public beach for the exclusive use of guests. If so, the only public beaches in Aqaba will be between the navy docks and Aqaba Castle (and half of this beach is covered with cafes); and just south of the Mina House Restaurant, which is the quietest and safest public beach for women.

The best beaches are along the coastline south of Aqaba (see the South of Aqaba section later), although most spots have little shade and are only accessible by public transport. The most popular for locals is the beach at the National Touristic Camp. Far, far better, however, are the beaches run by the Royal Diving Centre and Club Murjan.

The beaches run by the upmarket hotels in the north-west part of Aqaba are clean and available to the public – but normally at a cost. Coral Beach Hotel and Aquamarina Beach Hotel officially charge the public a ludicrous JD6 to use their beach, while the Aqaba Hotel officially charges JD2.200. (Some hotels in central Aqaba sell 'beach passes' to the Aqaba Hotel for JD1.500.)

Glass-Bottom Boats

If you can't go diving or snorkelling, the next best thing is a ride in a glass-bottom boat. The boat ride is fun, but the amount of fish and coral that can be seen is usually disappointing. The going rate is about JD5/10 per boat (holding about ten people) for 30/60 minutes, but this can be negotiated down to about JD5 per hour if business is

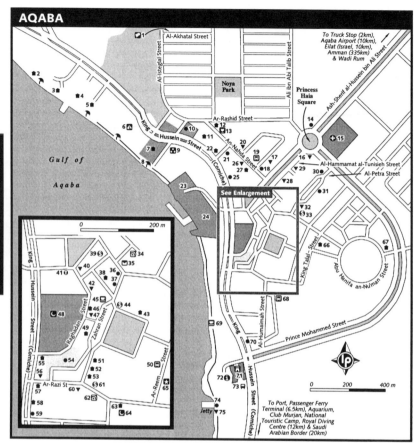

slow or competition is fierce (especially so on Friday). Ask around at your hotel about sharing costs with other passengers, or wait around for a boat to fill up. The guys who run these boats are shrewd, so bargain hard.

Most boats are currently lined up along the public beach between the marina and the Aqaba Hotel, and a few others moor near the Mina House Restaurant – which is where they'll probably stay if/when the Mövenpick Resort commandeers the other beach.

The glass-bottom boats can also be rented for longer trips if you want to go swimming or snorkelling (bring or rent your own equip-

ment); this is a great day out if you can get a group together. Count on about JD50 per day for a boat holding ten people, or about JD35 for a smaller boat holding about six.

Water Sports

Both the Al-Cazar Hotel and the Diving Club at the Aquamarina Beach Hotel (see Places to Stay) are well set up for water sports. Nothing is cheap, of course: about JD3 for a short burst of water-skiing; JD4 for wind surfing; and about JD2 for the use of a 'banana boat'. Another place to hire jet-skis, and ask about expensive yacht trips, is

AQABA

PLACES TO STAY
2 Coral Beach Hotel; German Honorary Consulate
3 Radisson SAS Hotel & Coral Bar
4 Aquamarina Beach Hotel
5 Aqaba Hotel
6 Camp Juhani
7 Mövenpick Resort
11 Miramar Hotel; Oryx Rent-a-Car
12 Al-Cazar Hotel
22 Aqaba Gulf Hotel
27 City Hotel
38 Red Sea Hotel; Dweikh Hotel 1; Nairoukh Hotel 1; Amira Hotel
43 Qasr al-Nil Hotel
46 Al-Shuala Hotel; Al-Amer Hotel; Syrian Palace Restaurant
49 Al-Khouli Hotel; Al-Khouli Tourism & Travel Agency; National Restaurant
51 Jordan Flower Hotel
52 Petra Hotel
53 Jerusalem Hotel
55 Beach Hotel
57 Crystal Hotel; Avis Car Rental; Peaceway Tours; Housing Bank
58 Nairoukh Hotel 2
63 Al-Naher al-Khaled Hotel
66 Al-Zatari Hotel
67 Royal Hotel

PLACES TO EAT
16 Mr Cool Cafe

17 Gelato Uno
20 Pizza Hut
26 Chili House; Captain's Restaurant; Rana Dry Clean
28 Bakery
29 Al-Mohandes Cafeteria
32 China Restaurant
40 Ali Baba Restaurant
42 Hani Ali Ice Cream
47 Al-Shami Restaurant; Qutaish & Sons Travel Agency
56 Pearls Fast Food
60 Juice Stands
75 Mina House Restaurant

OTHER
1 Egyptian Consulate
8 Public Beach; Cafes; Glass-Bottom Boats
9 Ayla (Old Aqaba) Ruins
10 JETT Bus Office; Part of Ayla Ruins
13 Harley Place
14 Royal Jordanian Airlines Office
15 Princess Haya Hospital
18 Hertz Car Rental; Coffee Shops
19 Trust International Transport Bus Office
21 Red Sea Diving Centre
23 Marina; Romero Restaurant; Royal Yacht Club of Jordan
24 Navy Docks
25 Aqaba International Dive Centre

30 Frindes Laundry
31 Arab Bridge Maritime Company; Cairo-Amman Bank; Humam Supermarket
33 ANZ Grindlay's Bank
34 Universal Services (Internet Centre)
35 General Post Office; Telephone Booths; ATM
36 Yamani Library (Bookshop)
37 Redwan Library (Bookshop)
39 International Traders (American Express)
41 Public Toilets
44 Arab Bank
45 Al-Fardos Coffee Shop
48 Sherif al-Hussein bin Ali Mosque
50 Main Bus/Minibus Station
54 Produce Souq
59 Moon Rent-a-Car; Aqaba Turkish Baths
61 Jordan National Bank
62 Mecca Exchange Booth (Internet Centre); Moneychangers
64 Mosque
65 Police Station
68 Minibus/Service Taxi Station (to Karak & Safi)
69 Cafes; Paddle Boats
70 Dolphin Centre
71 Aqaba Castle (Mamluk Fort)
72 Visitors Centre; Tourist Office; Aqaba Museum
73 Minibuses (to Saudi Arabia)
74 Speedboat Dock

SOUTHERN DESERT

around the marina. Locals prefer the more sedate paddle boats, available near the cafes north of the Aqaba Castle. Any of the dozens of faster speedboats docked around the Mina House Restaurant can also be rented for very negotiable prices. (For diving and snorkelling information, see the Activities chapter.)

Turkish Baths

Aqaba Turkish Baths (☎ 203 1605) on King Hussein St offers the full works – massage, steam bath and scrubbing – for a negotiable JD8. Women are welcome to attend, but need to make a reservation in advance so that 'special' arrangements (ie female attendants) can be found.

Organised Tours

Most people come to Aqaba for the beaches and diving/snorkelling, but Aquamarina Tours (☎ 201 6250, fax 201 4271, email aquam@go.com.jo) offers 'city tours' for US$10 per person. However, the sites of Aqaba (with the exception of the Aquarium) can be visited on foot very easily. Also popular are trips to Pharaoh's Island (see the South of Aqaba section later).

Aqaba is close enough to Petra for a quick trip, but very few agencies bother organising anything because they realise that a day trip can do no justice to Petra. A more popular and worthwhile short side trip is to Wadi Rum – see Organised Tours under

Getting There & Away in the Wadi Rum section earlier for more details.

One of the better local agencies for tours, and general advice, is Peaceway Tours (☎/fax 202 2665, email peacewaytours@ index.com.jo) in the Housing Bank Centre. For more information check out their Web site at www.peaceway.com.

Places to Stay

Aqaba is a popular place for Jordanian and Saudi tourists in winter (October to March), but when this peak season actually starts and finishes depends on the whims of individual hotel staff. People also flock to Aqaba from northern Jordan during long weekends and public holidays, and just before and after the *haj* (pilgrimage to Mecca). At these times, prices may increase by up to 30%, and finding a good budget or mid-range room for a reasonable price is more difficult – but certainly not impossible. Prices listed below are for the low season (April to September).

Just about all hotels, including the budget places listed below, have air-conditioning, and sometimes a fan also. In summer, do not stay in a room without air-conditioning, and always make sure that it's working properly before forking out any money. In summer, those on a tight budget may find it cooler to sleep on the roof of one of the budget hotels, or on the beach (see the South of Aqaba section later in this chapter).

Places to Stay – Budget

Camping Camping in Aqaba has little to recommend itself, except the low price and the possibility of sea breezes in summer.

Camp Juhani (no telephone, King Hussein St) can offer a piece of dirty ground in a grotty setting for JD1 per person. There are toilets and a simple *restaurant* is attached, but the main advantage is its proximity to the private hotel beaches.

Aqaba Hotel (☎ 201 4090, fax 201 4089) has the gall to charge JD6 per person for a noisy piece of turf, likely to be shared with an overland truck company. The area is nevertheless shady, and guests have access to toilets, showers and the hotel beach.

National Touristic Camp (☎ 201 6750) is the best place for camping, but not for swimming or snorkelling. Your own tent can be pitched on the beach for JD1 per person, plus 500 fils entrance fee. Otherwise, a basic pre-set tent for two people costs JD2 per tent; and a tent for three or four people, JD3. There are sun shelters, showers, snorkelling gear to rent and a few basic restaurants on the beach, but the area is desolate and uninviting. Refer to the South of Aqaba section later for more details.

Hotels Unless stated otherwise, most places listed below have (nonsatellite) TV, air-conditioning and a private bathroom with hot water (not always reliable). Many places do not offer breakfast (unless stated otherwise), but can rustle up something simple for JD1 to JD1.500 extra. Tariffs in most budget and mid-range hotels are negotiable by JD1 to JD3 per person per night, especially in quieter times.

Qasr al-Nil Hotel (☎ 201 5177), near the park in the city centre, is the cheapest and grubbiest place in town. Basic singles/doubles cost JD3/5, and most have balconies (with reasonable views) and fans (but no air-con or TV). The communal bathroom facilities are none too enticing, however.

Three cheapies are next to each other along Zahran St; it's worth checking out all three before deciding. All have communal bathrooms. Beds in a shared room cost about JD2.500 per person, and sleeping on the roof, about JD2.

Jordan Flower Hotel (☎ 201 4377) is probably the best of the three. The furniture is the newest, the guys who run it are the friendliest and the shared bathrooms are the cleanest. Rooms cost JD5/7.

Petra Hotel (☎ 201 3746) has rooms for JD5/7, but the toilets and showers are substandard. One advantage is that it has a lift to the rooms.

Jerusalem Hotel (☎ 201 4815) is the most basic, and the staff know it, so discounts to about JD4/6 are possible.

Four places which border on the mid-range price and standard are all close to each other at the northern end of Zahran St.

They are located in a quiet off-street court-yard, and many rooms have balconies and views.

Dweikh Hotel I and *Nairoukh Hotel I* (☎ *201 9284, fax 201 2985)* are in the same building and somehow share the same telephone and fax numbers. The Dweikh charges JD13.200/16.500, and has the added advantage of satellite TV in every room, but doesn't include breakfast. The Nairoukh charges JD15.400/19.800 including breakfast, and has nice bathrooms.

Amira Hotel (☎ *201 8849, fax 201 2559)* is slightly better, and more expensive, than the Dweikh and Nairoukh. Nicely furnished rooms with huge double beds go for JD15.500/19.800.

Red Sea Hotel (☎ *201 2156, fax 201 5789, email redsea@firstnet.com.jo)* has large, well-furnished rooms which are a bargain if you can negotiate (not hard) the price down from JD10/15 to JD7/10. The cheaper rooms for JD7/10 are dingy, have no air-conditioning and should be avoided.

Al-Khouli Hotel (☎/*fax 203 0152, Zahran St)* is an increasingly popular alternative. The hotel is central and clean, and was undergoing some (needed) renovation at the time of research. The rooms are sunny, and good value for JD8/12.

Al-Naher al-Khaled Hotel (☎ *201 2456, fax 201 2457, Ar-Razi St)* officially charges JD15.400/19.800, but the cluey manager realises this is too much and readily discounts to about half, ie JD7.700/11. For this price, the rooms, which are old-fashioned but clean, comfortable and have balconies, are very good value.

Beach Hotel (☎ *201 5108)*, in the souq area, caters more to Jordanians, but foreigners are welcome. It's central, pleasantly furnished and good value for JD8/12.

Al-Amer Hotel (☎ *201 4821, Raghadan St)* has unreliable hot water and no breakfast, but is good value if you can negotiate down to JD10/15. The rooms are nicely furnished with huge beds, and some have balconies with great views.

Al-Shuala Hotel (☎ *201 5153, fax 201 5160, Raghadan St)* is very similar to the Al-Amer, but more expensive. Rooms cost JD15.400/23.200, so try to negotiate by pointing out the lower tariffs offered by the nearby Al-Amer.

Places to Stay – Mid-Range

Every place listed below has a fridge (useful for keeping drinks cold); air-conditioning (vital); TV (but rarely satellite); telephone (fairly useless); and a private bathroom with hot water (usually reliable). Mid-range places are slightly more comfortable, and usually offer better views, than most hotels in the budget range, but are often not particularly good value unless you can negotiate a better price. Unless stated otherwise, all places include breakfast.

Crystal Hotel (☎ *202 2001, fax 202 2006, Ar-Razi St)* is a top end place with mid-range tariffs, and is convenient, clean and friendly. Singles/doubles start from a reasonable JD30/48.

Nairoukh Hotel 2 (☎ *201 2980, fax 201 5749, King Hussein St)* has smallish but well-furnished rooms, some with great views, for JD19.800/27.500. It's better value than the Crystal.

Al-Zatari Hotel (☎ *202 2970, fax 202 2974, King Talal St)* is the unmistakable new place just up from (east) the bus station. The hotel is spacious and new, and most rooms, which offer satellite TV and terrific views of Aqaba, cost from a negotiable JD15/22.

Three hotels, known formerly as Aquamarina I, II and III, are under the same management. Each hotel charges identical prices – JD48/66, without breakfast – for almost identical rooms with satellite TV, as well as swimming pools and other mod cons, which is good value compared to the other top end places.

Aquamarina Beach Hotel (☎ *201 6250, fax 201 4271, King Hussein St)* – also still known as Aquamarina I – is, well, on the beach to the north-west.

City Hotel (☎ *201 5165, fax 201 9028, An-Nahda St)* – aka Aquamarina II – is centrally located.

Royal Hotel (☎ *201 9425, fax 201 3569, Abu Hanifa an-Nu'man St)* – aka Aquamarina III – is not as popular as the other two, because it's nowhere near the beach.

Aqaba Hotel (☎ 201 4090, fax 201 4089, King Hussein St) has unremarkable rooms for JD40/58, but does boast its own private beach.

Al-Cazar Hotel (☎ 201 4131, fax 201 4133, email alcsea@alcazar.com.jo, An-Nahda St) charges a reasonable JD35/45 for pleasant rooms, and has a swimming pool. It's also set up for water sports and diving, and has a pub and Internet centre – refer to Activities, Entertainment and Post & Communications for more details about these.

Miramar Hotel (☎ 201 4340, fax 201 4339, King Hussein St), another top end beach-type 'resort', is struggling to keep up with the Aquamarinas etc, so it does offer surprisingly good rates: JD20/25. It also has a swimming pool because it's not on – but is still close to – the public beach.

Places to Stay – Top End

All the top end places are along King Hussein St in the north-western part of the city. The Radisson and Coral Beach have their own private beaches. All tariffs listed below include breakfast.

Aqaba Gulf Hotel (☎ 201 6636, fax 201 8246) is not on the waterfront, but compensates with a good-sized swimming pool. It charges US$98/120 for singles/doubles.

Radisson SAS Hotel (☎ 201 2426, fax 201 3426) is probably the most luxurious and, therefore, the most expensive. A room in the older part of the hotel is good value for JD84; rooms with city views cost JD108 whilst those with sea views cost JD132.

Coral Beach Hotel (☎ 201 3521, fax 201 3614) is the most northern of the bunch; it's poorly signed and was undergoing some renovation at the time of research. It doesn't attract tour groups, so discounts from the official rate of US$80/100 are possible.

Places to Stay – Rentals

The owner of Peaceway Tours (see Organised Tours earlier) rents out a furnished two-bedroom apartment with kitchen for JD10 per night (low season) and JD20 (high season). There is no restriction on the length of stay.

Other apartments can be rented, but most are only available for a minimum of one

week and must be pre-booked in the high season. Look out for ads in the windows of travel agents. Several places for rent can be found along Abu Hanifa an Nu'man and An-Nahda streets.

Places to Eat

Aqaba has a large range of places to eat, but it is becoming harder to find value for money. While most travellers will welcome seafood as a tasty change to kebabs and *shwarmas*, the bad news is that seafood is expensive.

A few small *grocery stores* are dotted around central Aqaba, so stock up here if you're heading to Wadi Rum (although there are a couple of shops in Rum village). The best *bakery* (unsigned in any language) is along Al-Hammamat al-Tunisieh St. The best supermarket is *Humam Supermarket*, next to the Arab Bridge Maritime Co building on Al-Petra St. The *produce souq*, at the back of the southern end of Raghadan St, is where all manner of meat, chicken, fish, fruit and vegetables can be bought.

Places to Eat – Budget

Al-Mohandes Cafeteria (Al-Hammamat al-Tunisieh St) is a very popular place for cheap and tasty shwarma and *felafel* in a clean setting in a more upmarket part of town.

Pearls Fast Food (☎ 201 5057, Ar-Razi St) has good food, but the flies may put some people off. Main courses start at JD1.500. It's open 24 hours, and good for breakfast.

Syrian Palace Restaurant (☎ 201 4788, Raghadan St), upstairs above the Al-Amer Hotel, offers good food at moderate prices, eg fish from JD5, *koftas* for about JD1.500 and salads, about 500 fils. The service is good, if a little slow, and the views from the few tables by the window are worth getting there early for.

Al-Shami Restaurant, in a lane between Zahran and Raghadan streets, is another popular place recommended by several readers. The menu (in English outside) offers a wide range of tasty dishes, including a delicious kofta (JD2.500), and the salads (about 500 fils) are almost a meal in themselves. Guests can dine alfresco or in the air-conditioned section upstairs with stunning views.

Altar Boosh Restaurant (Raghadan St), a few metres north of the Al-Amer Hotel, has also been recommended by readers, not least for the entertaining way the owner makes shwarmas. (He claims to have made 250 in one hour!)

National Restaurant (Zahran St), under the Al-Khouli Hotel, is one of the best in town, and open for breakfast from about 7.30 am. The menu (in English) offers a range of Arabic and western food; specials, such as a half-chicken, salad, humous and chips cost JD2.200. It's about the cheapest place around for fish meals (about JD3.500).

Mr Cool Cafe (Princess Haia Square) offers tasty burgers for about 900 fils, salads for 450 fils and cheap hot and cold drinks in a friendly atmosphere – also see Cafes & Ice Cream Parlours in the Entertainment section.

Pizza Hut (☎ 201 6947, An-Nahda St) is good value, with small pizzas from JD1.850, and cheese and salami 'submarine sandwiches' for about JD1.500. The soft drinks are expensive, however.

Chili House (☎ 201 2435, An-Nahda St) is arguably the best place for burgers (about JD1.500), and offers the usual fries and soft drinks, as well as pasta dishes for about JD2.

Places to Eat – Mid-Range & Top End

Ali Baba Restaurant (☎ 201 3901, Raghadan St) has tables set up outside, and an air-conditioned room inside. Patrons pay more for the setting than the meals, which include Indian *biryanis* for JD5, fish dishes for about JD7, and a set-price continental breakfast, JD3.500. Alcohol is available, but not cheap: a can of Amstel will cost about JD2.

China Restaurant (☎ 201 4415, Al-Petra St) offers tasty meat and rice dishes (around JD3), great soups (JD1), and a substantial *chow mein* (JD2.200). The cook is Chinese, and his restaurant has long maintained a high standard. It's one of the few independent restaurants (ie not linked to an upmarket hotel) that actually sells alcohol: a large beer costs JD2.200.

Captain's Restaurant (☎ 201 6905, An-Nahda St) has a predictable nautical theme. Pasta dishes cost a reasonable JD2, but steaks are pricey at JD5. It is also open for breakfast.

Mina House Restaurant (☎ 201 2699) is in a boat moored south of the Aqaba Castle. It's not as expensive as you may think, especially if you – ironically – avoid the pricey fish meals. Mina obviously specialises in fish (about JD7 per dish), but the chicken dishes are a more affordable JD4.

Han Ali (☎ 201 5200, Raghadan St) serves fish (about JD5), salads (about 600 fils) and other meals from JD3. Breakfast is served from about 8 am, and the alfresco setting is ideal for morning or afternoon tea.

Romero Restaurant (☎ 202 2404), at the Royal Yacht Club of Jordan in the marina, is a charming but expensive place to watch the sun set and mingle with the nouveaux riches. Main courses cost from JD4 to JD7, and burgers about JD2. A bar is also attached – see Bars in the Entertainment section below.

Entertainment

Cafes & Ice Cream Parlours There are *cafes* along the two public beaches, ie near the ruins of Ayla (Old Aqaba) and north of the Aqaba Castle (where the front row seats of the cafes are so close to the water that you can wet your toes while you whet your whistle). No alcohol is served at these public places.

The *juice stands* on Ar-Razi St are popular places for travellers to hang out at and meet others. *Al-Fardos Coffee Shop*, just off Zahran St and close to the Red Sea Hotel, is a traditional cafe where local men sip coffee and play backgammon and chess. It has a pleasant outdoor setting, and foreign women are welcome.

To help alleviate heatstroke, head for anywhere that sells ice cream, eg *Mr Cool Cafe (Princess Haia Square)*, about which one reader raved about the ice cream and friendly staff; *Hani Ali (Raghadan St)*, an unmissable, garish purple and yellow place, and a sugar-addict's paradise of traditional sweets and delicious ice cream; or *Gelato Uno*, just off An-Nahda St behind the Hertz car rental office.

Bars All the top end hotels have bars, and most offer 'happy hours', eg the Crystal Hotel has the *Romantic Bar*. Popular with expats is the *Dolphin Bar*, downstairs in the Al-Cazar Hotel, which has pool tables and a friendly atmosphere. About the only authentic, independent bar in Aqaba is *Harley Place (An-Nahda St)*, near the Al-Cazar, which has regular 'happy hours'. There's often live music after about 9 pm.

The upmarket crowd go to the *Royal Yacht Club of Jordan* in the marina. It's a great place to unwind, enjoy the sunset and catch some late afternoon breezes. Large beers cost JD3 and spirits, without mixers, about JD3. Sadly, the inviting pool behind the restaurant is strictly for members only.

For traditional Arabic dancing, and more modern stuff, head to the *nightclub* in the Aquamarina Beach Hotel. The *Coral Bar* at the Radisson SAS Hotel has a nightclub with an entertaining resident piano player.

Shopping

Plenty of shops sell tacky 'I wuz in Aqaba'-type souvenirs, although more interesting mementos are available: packets of spices, such as cardamom and saffron, from JD1; cassettes of western music (and dubious legality); delicious roasted nuts; and a better standard of the sand-in-the-bottle. (The guys who painstakingly place the coloured sand in the tiny bottles set up tables along Zahran St.). We urge you not to buy anything made of coral; besides harming the marine environment, selling and buying the stuff is highly illegal.

Getting There & Away

Air Aqaba is the only other place in Jordan with an airport. Royal Wings, a subsidiary of Royal Jordanian Airlines, flies between Aqaba and Amman at least four times a day for JD30/60 one-way/return. These flights depart and/or arrive at either the Marka airport (in north-eastern Amman) or the larger Queen Alia international airport, south of the capital.

Royal Wings (☎ 201 4474) has an office at the Aqaba airport, but it's far more convenient to buy tickets at the Royal Jordanian Airlines office (☎ 201 4477), on Ash-Sherif al-Hussein bin Ali St, where tickets for other Royal Jordanian flights can be bought, confirmed and changed. The Royal Jordanian office is open every day from 8 am to 6 pm, and until 2 pm on Friday.

Bus For travel between Amman and Aqaba it's worth paying extra for the comfortable and air-conditioned JETT and Trust private buses. Private buses are also quicker (about 3½ hours) because they travel along the Dead Sea Highway, whereas the cheaper public buses (and minibuses) go along the more populated Desert Highway (about five hours) in order to pick up and drop off passengers.

Try to book tickets for JETT or Trust buses at least a day in advance, and as soon as possible at peak times. Buses for both companies leave from outside their respective offices. From the JETT office (☎ 201 5222), on King Hussein St, buses run three or four times a day in both directions. Tickets costs JD4/8 one-way/return. Trust International Transport (☎ 203 2300), on An-Nahda St, offers about five departures a day in both directions for the same price.

Ordinary public buses (and minibuses) travel between Amman (Wahadat bus station) and the main bus/minibus station in Aqaba (JD3, five hours) about every hour between 7 am and 3 pm. The best company for public buses is probably Afneh (also known as Afana), which has services (JD3.300) about every hour between 7 am and 10 pm from its office at Wahadat, as well as the more convenient Abdali bus station in Amman.

To Israel, Trust International Transport has daily services to Nazareth (JD10.500); and to Tel Aviv (JD14), via Haifa (JD10.500), every day but Saturday.

No buses link Aqaba with anywhere in Saudi Arabia. All public transport to Saudi now leaves from Amman, and does not use the border at Ad-Durra, south of Aqaba.

Minibus To Wadi Mousa (for Petra), minibuses (JD3, two hours) leave at about 8 am, 10 am and 12.30 pm, but the exact departure times depend on the number of passengers going in both directions. Otherwise, get a connection in Ma'an (JD1.200, 1 hour 20 minutes).

Two minibuses go to Wadi Rum (JD1.500, one hour) early in the morning, but only once on Friday and public holidays, and again the departure time from Aqaba depends on when the minibus arrives from Wadi Rum in the first place. It's probably easier to catch a minibus to Ma'an, disembark at the obvious turn-off to Wadi Rum and then hitch a ride to Rum village from there.

Minibuses to Wadi Mousa, Wadi Rum and Ma'an, and public buses and minibuses to Amman, leave from the main bus/minibus station along Ar-Reem St. Minibuses to Karak (JD1.750, three hours) leave several times a day from the small station next to the mosque on Al-Humaimah St; and to Safi at the southern end of the Dead Sea – both via the Dead Sea Highway.

Service Taxis From the main bus/minibus station, service taxis head to Amman (JD3.250, five hours), but far less regularly than buses and minibuses; and sometimes to Ma'an (JD1). To Karak (JD2.500), they leave from the terminal on Al-Humaimah St. Service taxis start lining up at both stations at about 6 am, and many have left by 8 am – so get an early start. They can be chartered to other places such as Wadi Mousa (Petra) for about JD25, and Wadi Rum for about JD12 – but bargain hard.

From the main bus/minibus station, service taxis also go to the nearby Israeli border (about JD1), but more often in the early morning. The taxis are normally marked 'Southern Passing Service' (or something similar), and often have the number '8' on the door. Chartering a service taxi or private taxi between central Aqaba and the border costs about JD5. For more information about crossing the southern border to/from Israel, see the relevant section in the Getting There & Away chapter.

Hitching If you've hitched a ride to Aqaba on a truck, you may be dropped off at the enormous truck park about 3km north of the city centre. A service taxi into the centre shouldn't cost more than about 500 fils;

a private taxi, about JD2. For hitching north from Aqaba, the truck park is also a good place to start.

Boat Although several agencies along the Corniche sell ferry tickets to Nuweiba (Egypt), you're better off dealing directly with the ferry company: Arab Bridge Maritime Co (☎ 201 3235), on Al-Petra St. The office is open every day for ticket sales from 8 am to 2.30 pm and 5.30 to 7.30 pm, but does not reopen in the evening on Friday. The Cairo-Amman Bank in the same building is open at the same time, and will change dinars into US dollars for ferry tickets (which must be paid for in US dollars).

Refer to the Sea section in the Getting There & Away chapter for information about travelling between Jordan and Egypt on the ferry.

Getting Around
To/From the Airport The Aqaba airport, which is all but deserted when no flights are coming or going, is about 10km north of town, and close to the border with Israel. There is no public bus or minibus to the airport, so take a shared taxi marked 'Southern Passing Service' (or something similar) from the main bus/minibus station. However, many have left by mid-morning so you may have to take a private taxi (JD3 to JD5). Be wary of taxi drivers trying to fleece unsuspecting tourists who have just arrived in Aqaba.

To/From the Ferry Terminal Minibuses leave from near the entrance to Aqaba Castle along the Corniche for the Saudi border, and pass the terminal (250 fils) for ferries to Egypt. A private taxi between the ferry terminal and central Aqaba should not cost more than about JD2.

Car Aqaba has several car rental agencies but, like in Amman, they are far from cheap. If you want to rent a car for any length of time and wish to cover the whole country that way, it's cheaper in Amman. However, hiring a car from Aqaba makes some sense because there are more attractions in southern Jordan (and some, like Shobak, are hard to reach) and Aqaba is far easier to drive around than Amman.

The prices listed below include insurance and often unlimited kilometres – but exclude petrol and the recommended 'collision damage waiver' (CDW) fee of about JD7-8 per day for normal cars, and about JD10-12 for 4WDs:

Avis
   (☎ 202 2883) Housing Bank Centre, King Hussein St. Charges from JD28.500 per day for normal cars, and can arrange returns to Amman for an extra JD30. 4WDs have to be pre-ordered from Amman, and cost from JD55.
Hertz
   (☎ 201 6206, fax 201 6125) An-Nahda St. Charges from JD33; a return to Amman is an extra JD35. 4WDs cost JD66, but only the first 150km is free.
Moon Rent-a-Car
   (☎/fax 201 9734) King Hussein St. An unimpressive outfit, but prices here are more negotiable than at other agencies. Normal cars cost about JD38.500; 4WDs cost from JD49.500.
Oryx Rent-a-Car
   (☎ 201 3133, fax 201 8288) Miramar Hotel, King Hussein St. Specialises in 4WDs, but these are often booked out for weeks ahead and don't come cheap at about JD65. Only 150 to 200km are free, and there is a JD300 excess (ie no CDW is available). It also rents out small cars from JD27.500, plus JD300 excess.

Taxis Hundreds of private (yellow) taxis cruise the streets beeping at any tourist (Jordanian or foreign) who is silly enough to walk around in the infernal heat rather than take an air-conditioned taxi. Taxis are unmetered, so prices are negotiable, and the drivers in Aqaba are often unscrupulous. Try to get an idea of an approximate fare from one of the locals or a hotel staff member; and, of course, agree to a price before getting in.

SOUTH OF AQABA
The road south of Aqaba stretches about 18km to the Saudi Arabian border at Ad-Durra. Much of the coastline is taken up by the massive port facilities, but there are a few beaches and diving and snorkelling spots. See Diving & Snorkelling in the Activities chapter for details. All the following

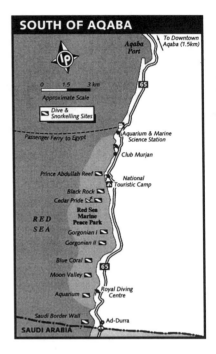

SOUTH OF AQABA

places (except Pharaoh's Island) are accessible by the minibus which leaves from near the Aqaba Castle along the Corniche.

Aquarium المربى المائي
Part of the Marine Science Station complex, the aquarium (☎ 201 5145) is worth a visit. The displays are well labelled in English and provide a glimpse of the Gulf's marine life, eg coral, moray eels, turtles and the dangerous stone fish. The aquarium is about 7.5km south of central Aqaba, and about 500m south of the passenger terminal for ferries to Egypt. It's open every day from 8 am to 5 pm, and entrance costs JD1.

Club Murjan نادي المرجان
About 1.3km south of the Aquarium is Club Murjan, the beach and diving centre run by the Al-Cazar Hotel in Aqaba. Guests of the hotel, and divers using the diving centre run by the hotel, can enjoy the facilities at Club Murjan for free, while the public can use the

Red Sea Marine Peace Park

Jordan's only stretch of coastline is the northern part of the Gulf of Aqaba, and is home to over 300 types of coral and numerous species of fish and marine life. Aqaba is also Jordan's only port (and a major shipping lane for the region), and resort, both of which cause real problems for the fragile marine environment.

In an attempt to halt the damage, the Red Sea Marine Peace Park (☎ Aqaba 03-201 9405, fax 201 4206) was established in 1997. The park stretches for about 8.5km, from the Marine Science Station to the Royal Diving Centre, and extends about 350m off-shore and 50m inland. The park contains about 80% of Jordan's public beaches, and most of the decent diving and snorkelling spots, so the park managers are trying to find the right balance between promoting tourism and preserving the marine environment.

Local and foreign environmentalists have managed to ban fishing and limit boating in the park; establish jetties into the sea so that divers and snorkellers can jump into the water rather than wade out over coral from the beach; and ensure that no hotels will be built within the park. A visitors centre is planned, and park rangers will ensure that visitors and locals obey the strict environmental protection laws.

The park managers also hope to conduct a public awareness campaign for locals (particularly children) and all divers and snorkellers; lobby the government to enforce local environmental laws; and conduct further research into the damage caused by tourism and pollution. The Marine Science Station, south of Aqaba, is also deeply involved in the preservation of the marine environment, and recently received a US$2.5 million grant, in tandem with Israel, from the US.

excellent **beach, swimming pool** and toilets/showers during the day for JD3, including return transport from the Al-Cazar. Snorkelling gear costs an extra JD4 per day;

and watersports gear, such as canoes and paragliders, are also available. There is a *bar* and a *restaurant* on site.

National Touristic Camp مخيم السياحة الوطني

This forlorn place is almost completely devoid of any character and shade, but it is one of the few places where the public are welcome for beach-oriented activities. There's some coral offshore for **snorkelling**, but pollution is a problem. The **beach** can get uncomfortably crowded on Friday, and it's a bit of a hangout for young local men, so find a secluded place if you're camping (see Places to Stay earlier in this chapter) or swimming (if female).

Entrance to the site (500 fils) allows visitors to use the beach and sit under a sun shelter. There are a few basic eateries, such as *Mohammed Sea Bedouin Cafe*, and places to buy cold drinks, but it's worth bringing your own food and drink from Aqaba.

The beach is about 1km south of Club Murjan, and about 10km from central Aqaba. The entrance is not clearly signposted in any language, so look for the obvious large space of ground where the sandy desert meets the sandy beach.

Royal Diving Centre مركز الغوص الوطني

About 6km further south (16km from central Aqaba), and close to the Saudi border, is the Royal Diving Centre (RDC), the best place for swimming, diving and snorkelling. It also has a gorgeous **swimming pool** and **beach**, where women can feel relaxed. Shade is available.

The entrance fee of JD2 allows guests to use the facilities, ie beach and pool for the day; and the *restaurant* serves simple snacks, drinks and alcohol. Snorkelling gear costs an extra JD3 per day. Entrance and transport is free for anyone scuba diving with the RDC.

The minibus (500 fils one-way) provided by the RDC picks up guests from outside most mid-range and top end hotels in Aqaba (eg the Crystal and Miramar hotels, but not the Aquamarina hotels) at about 9 am and returns at about 5 pm. Tee up the minibus with one of the hotels or, better, ring the RDC the day before. A private taxi costs about JD3 one-way, but will be difficult to arrange going back to Aqaba.

Pharaoh's Island   جزيرة فرعون

This picturesque island, also known as Fara'un and Coral islands, is about 15km south of Aqaba, but only a few hundred metres from Taba, in Egypt. It is actually in Egyptian waters, but travelling to or from Egypt this way is not permitted.

Excavations suggest that the island was inhabited as far back as the Bronze Age. The fantastic Crusader **Salah ad-Din Fort** is fun to explore; and there is really good **swimming** and **snorkelling** in the lagoon and **diving** further out, which is accessible only by boat.

Aquamarina Tours (☎ 201 6250, fax 201 4271, email aquam@go.com.jo) seems to have the monopoly on trips to the island. The price is about JD24 per person (depending on the number of passengers aboard), which includes the entrance fee to the island, Egyptian visa, lunch and transport – but boats only leave when there are enough passengers (about ten) to make the trip feasible.

Tickets can be bought at most of the travel agencies in Aqaba, or at the hotels formerly known as Aquamarina I, II and III. Take notice that at least two days notice is required to allow enough time for visas to be processed.

Aqaba, Jordan's water playground, features some of the world's best diving and snorkelling sights including the Red Sea Lion fish (middle left) and colourful coral.

Activities in Jordan include helping at an archaeological dig such as this at Wadi Finan (top right & top left), and hiking at Wadi Dana (middle) and Wadi Rum (bottom).

Activities

Some people come to Jordan for the history and the archaeological sites, still others come for the diving and snorkelling near Aqaba. The more energetic and adventurous can even try hiking and rock climbing.

Diving & Snorkelling

Although more spectacular off the coast of Sinai in Egypt, the diving and snorkelling at the top end of the Gulf of Aqaba is still some of the best in the world. The advantages are that all sites are accessible from a major town (Aqaba); most sites are easy to reach for snorkellers; and most are accessible from a jetty or the beach, so a boat is not required (which reduces the cost considerably). Also, visibility in the gulf is usually excellent (as much as 40m, although it's usually closer to 20m); the tides are minimal; the water is shallow; and drop-offs are often found less than 50m from shore.

Most of the coastline south of Aqaba has remained pristine despite the inevitable pollution and damage caused by the huge port facilities, and the popular resort of Aqaba – thanks mainly to the far-sighted Red Sea Marine Peace Park (see the boxed text in the Southern Desert chapter). Some of the reefs near Aqaba were affected by an earthquake in 1995, but damage was minor and not permanent, and the coral is already starting to regenerate.

Information

When to Go Diving is possible all year, but January is the coldest month and July and August are the hottest. The best time is early February to early June for water and outside temperatures, visibility and marine life, although March and April are not good because of algae bloom. The other factors to consider are the higher prices and possible lack of decent rooms in Aqaba during winter. Despite the outside temperature in summer, however, the cold stream in the gulf makes the water temperature bearable.

Marine Life & Coral The northern end of the Gulf of Aqaba enjoys high salinity, and the winds from the north and minimal tides mean the water stays clear. The temperature of the water is warm (average of 22.5°C in winter and 26°C in summer), attracting a vast array of fish, and helping to preserve the coral.

According to the Jordan Royal Ecological Society (☎/fax Amman 06-567 9142, email jreds@nets.com.jo), the gulf has over 110 species of hard coral, 120 species of soft coral and about 1000 species of fish. These include colourful goat fish, leopard flounder and clown fish; various species of butterfly fish, parrot fish and angel fish; the less endearing spiky sea urchin; poisonous stone fish, scorpion fish and lion fish; sea snakes; jellyfish; and moray eels. Green turtles and hermit crabs are also to be found.

The Redwan Library bookshop in Aqaba (see Bookshops in the Southern Desert chapter) sells the plastic 'Red Sea Fishwatchers Field Guide', which can be taken under water to identify species of fish and coral.

Books The two major bookshops in Aqaba (see Bookshops in the Southern Desert chapter) have a good range of books about diving, such as the *Introduction to the Marine Life of Aqaba*. Lonely Planet's *Diving and Snorkeling Guide to The Red Sea* concentrates mainly on sites along the Egyptian coast, but does have a small detailed, section about diving around the Gulf of Aqaba.

Health If you're cut by coral, or stung by a stonefish, refer to the Health section in the Facts for the Visitor chapter for advice and remedies. The Princess Haya Hospital in Aqaba is well equipped for diving mishaps, and even has a decompression chamber.

ACTIVITIES

Local Regulations Some of the local regulations (which will be rigorously enforced in the future) are fairly obvious:

- Do not touch or feed the fish.
- Do not touch or remove any marine life or coral, dead or alive, from the sea or beach.
- Do not walk on the reef – use a jetty (or boat) to reach the water.
- Do not throw any rubbish into the sea, or leave it on the beach.
- Ensure that boat anchors are on buoys, and not attached to precious coral.

Diving & Snorkelling Sites

The coast between Aqaba and the Saudi Arabian border boasts about 30 diving and snorkelling sites. Of these, about 25 can be enjoyed by snorkellers and all but one is accessible from a jetty or beach.

The names of the sites do change from time to time, and from one diving agency to another, and several sites have been subdivided and given even more names. Please remember that none of the sites are signposted in any language, nor are they even remotely obvious from the road: if you want to dive or snorkel independently you'll have to ask for directions, or take pot luck. Snorkellers will find it far better to pay the extra and use the private beaches run by the Royal Diving Centre or Club Murjan (refer to the South of Aqaba map in the Southern desert chapter).

The more popular sites (listed in order from Aqaba) are:

Prince Abdullah Reef Offshore from the National Touristic Camp, it has good visibility and decent but unspectacular coral. It's easily accessible from the beach, and the coral starts about 20m offshore.

Black Rock Although located at the southern end of the National Touristic Camp and inconvenient for anyone staying at the camp it does boast diverse species of soft coral.

Cedar Pride This ship was deliberately sunk to create a diving site in 1985. It's only 200m offshore, and in water about 20m deep. The wreck is covered with bright, soft coral and is home to schools of colourful fish. The waves can be a bit harrowing at times, however, and the sea urchins can be a pain. Sadly, this is also the site with the most litter.

Gorgonian I This reef is probably the best place for snorkelling, although the waves can be difficult. The coral is superb, and there's plenty of marine life and the chance to see sea turtles.

Gorgonian II Similar in size, accessibility and standard to Gorgonian I, but the coral is not as good and there are numerous moray eels.

Blue Coral This is another sloping reef, with hard and soft coral at shallow depths.

Moon Valley Accessible from the beach, about 800m north, and run by the Royal Diving Centre (RDC), this is a sandy area with a sloping reef and a varied, but unremarkable, array of fish and coral.

Aquarium Not to be confused with the aquarium at the Marine Science Station, this is the name given to the reef accessible from the jetty at the RDC. There are enough colourful fish, and soft and hard coral, to impress all divers and snorkellers.

Saudi Border Wall The coral is perfectly preserved, but because it's only about 300m north of the Jordan/Saudi border, independent divers and snorkellers should stay away.

Pharaoh's Island Offshore from, and part of, Egypt, this island is only accessible by boat on a day trip from Aqaba (see the South of Aqaba section in the Southern Desert chapter). Snorkelling is great in the lagoon, but the best diving is only accessible by boat.

Diving Centres in Aqaba

While it is tempting to choose the cheapest diving centre, it's wise to use one of the reputable and well-established agencies listed below. Always check the equipment and talk to staff before deciding anything, and get recent recommendations from other travellers.

Prices listed below include a full tank and weight-belt (unless stated otherwise), but a wetsuit and fins will cost extra. Transport is always included. None of the agencies listed below will accept divers without one of the usual diving certificates.

Aqaba International Dive Centre
(☎/fax 203 1213) King Hussein St. This popular and well-equipped centre charges JD10 for one dive, plus JD8 for gear. Prices are cheaper for more than one dive, and are negotiable.

Aquamarina Diving Club
(☎ 201 6250, fax 201 4271, email aquam@go .com.jo) King Hussein St. Based at the Aquamarina Beach Hotel. Prices were unavailable at the time of research.

Red Sea Diving Centre
(☎ 202 2323, fax 201 8969) Between King Hussein and An-Nahda streets. Charges about JD24 for two dives, plus equipment hire; JD40 for two dives with equipment. There are some exceptionally good photos of marine life and coral inside the shop.

Royal Diving Centre
(☎ 201 7035, fax 201 7097) In operation since 1986, the RDC is located about 16km south of Aqaba (refer to the South of Aqaba section later for more information). One/two dives cost JD10/17; a night dive is JD20. One reader did complain about faulty equipment, tattered wetsuits and unprofessional staff, but most other divers have recommended the place.

Sea Star
(☎ 201 4131, fax 201 4133) Based at the Al-Cazar Hotel in Aqaba, which also has a private beach called Club Murjan south of Aqaba (see the South of Aqaba section in the Southern Desert chapter). One or two dives cost JD30 per dive; JD18 per dive for more than three dives.

Extras All of these diving centres can organise night dives. Camera enthusiasts should note that no dive centres have marine cameras for hire, so bring your own. Other costs include: an underwater torch (flashlight), about JD5 per trip; wetsuits, about JD3.300/6.600 for a short/long one; and fins, about JD1.500.

Diving Courses Most of these diving centres run courses for BSAC, PADI or CMAS. Costs range from about JD25 for a basic one-dive 'introductory' course to about JD200/300 for a four/six-day PADI course. Other courses include 'advanced diver'; 'wreck diver course'; and 'dive master'. Courses are often run by Europeans who speak English, French, German and/or Italian.

Snorkelling

Snorkelling equipment is usually expensive, so bring your own. Full gear – ie snorkel, mask and fins – can be rented from the National Touristic Camp (JD2-3 per day); Dolphin Centre (☎ 201 6511, King Hussein St) for JD5; Aquamarina Beach Hotel (JD6); and the Aqaba International Dive Centre (JD8). Snorkelling gear can also be bought from the Redwan Library (see Bookshops in the Southern Desert chapter).

It's often worth paying extra for a package deal which includes full gear, transport and/or use of a decent beach, eg the Aqaba International Dive Centre charges JD10 for gear and transport (accompanying a scuba diving trip); the Royal Diving Centre charges JD5, including gear and use of its beach and swimming pool, but excluding transport (500 fils one way); and Club

---

Safety Guidelines for Diving & Snorkelling

Before embarking on a diving or snorkelling trip, careful consideration should be given to a safe, as well as an enjoyable, experience. You should:

• Possess a current diving certification card from a recognised scuba diving instructional agency.

• Be sure you're healthy and feel comfortable diving.

• Obtain reliable information about physical and environmental conditions at the dive site (eg from a reputable local dive centre).

• Be aware of local laws, regulations and etiquette about marine life and the environment (see the Local Regulations section).

• Dive only at sites within your realm of experience; if available, engage the services of a competent, professionally trained dive instructor or dive master.

• Be aware that underwater conditions vary significantly from one region, or even site, to another. Seasonal changes can significantly alter any site and dive conditions. These differences influence the way divers dress for a dive and what diving techniques they use.

• Ask about the environmental characteristics that can affect your diving and how local trained divers deal with these considerations.

Murjan charges JD7 for gear, transport and use of its beach and pool.

Dweikh Hotel I and the Dolphin Centre also offer snorkelling trips, which includes transport and gear, for JD8 and JD10 respectively, but these are not good value because they use the less appealing public beaches, such as the National Touristic Camp.

If you have your own gear and want to snorkel away from the beach, ask the diving agencies about the cost of accompanying a scuba diving trip. The cheapest place to snorkel is the National Touristic Camp (see the South of Aqaba section in the Southern Desert chapter), which only costs 500 fils to enter, is accessible by public transport and has cheap snorkelling gear for hire. Ask the staff there to point out the best spots.

Considerations for Responsible Diving & Snorkelling

The popularity of diving and snorkelling off the coast of Aqaba is placing immense pressure on the fragile marine ecosystem. To help preserve the ecology and beauty of the reefs, please consider the following tips when diving or snorkelling:

- Don't use anchors on the reef, and take care not to ground boats on coral.
- Avoid touching living marine organisms with your body or dragging equipment across the reef. Polyps can be damaged by even the gentlest contact. Never stand on corals, even if they look solid and robust. If you must hold on to the reef, only touch exposed rock or dead coral.
- Be conscious of your fins. Even without contact the surge from heavy fin strokes near the reef can damage delicate organisms. When treading water in shallow reef areas, take care not to kick up clouds of sand. Settling sand can easily smother the delicate organisms of the reef.
- Practise and maintain proper buoyancy control. Major damage can be done by divers descending too fast and colliding with the reef. Make sure you're correctly weighted and your weight-belt is positioned so that you stay horizontal. If you haven't dived for a while, have a practice dive in a pool before trying the reef. Be aware that buoyancy can change over the period of an extended trip: initially you may breathe harder and need more weight; a few days later you may breathe more easily and need less weight.

- Resist the temptation to collect or buy corals or shells. Aside from the ecological damage, taking home marine souvenirs depletes the beauty of a site and spoils the enjoyment of others – and is highly illegal in Jordan.
- Ensure that you take out all your rubbish and any litter you may find as well. Plastics in particular are a serious threat to marine life. Turtles can mistake plastic for jellyfish and eat it.
- Resist the temptation to feed fish. You may disturb their normal eating habits, encourage aggressive behaviour or feed them food that is detrimental to their health.
- Minimise your disturbance of marine animals. In particular, do not ride on the backs of turtles as this causes them great anxiety.

Digging up the Past

What is Archaeology?

If you have ever watched archaeologists on a dig, handling with meticulous care what to the outsider seems little more than discarded rubbish, you may have asked yourself how archaeology works. Contrary to popular belief, archaeology is not so much the study of lovingly excavated objects in themselves, but more what they tell us about the human past.

Questions asked about the past vary with time and place, but many are constant. When did permanent settled life begin, and how? When did complex city-based civilisation arise? If civilisations ended suddenly, why? From Graeco-Roman times onwards, more and more written records became available, but relating the written and archaeological record is often far from easy.

Middle Eastern archaeology began around 1830, prompted by a desire to know how the recorded traditions of the Bible related to the archaeological remains discovered in the Biblical lands. The results of such comparisons rarely satisfy more than a minority.

Today, archaeologists concentrate on questions which lend themselves to more or less unambiguous results. They are better at determining when and how things have happened, but they're less confident about determining why. Ever more sophisticated scientific techniques are employed in the analysis of archaeological remains.

Multidisciplinary studies have become standard practice. So, for instance, when investigating the first permanent settlements, archaeologists study the remains of animals and plants, as these provide them with information on foraging patterns and the time of year in which they took place, as birth, migration and harvest patterns have remained nearly constant for the past 10,000 years. Carbon dating gives us an approximate time, osteology a fair idea of the physical condition of the settlers, lithic and bone tool analyses some idea of the technology of settlers, and chemical analysis of flaked stone tools (like obsidian), ground stone bowls (like fine basalt), and stone ornaments (greenstone and carnelian), coupled with shell ornament sourcing (dentalium and cowrie) gives an idea of trade routes and the extent of interregional contact at any given time.

Studying these features across 20 sites should allow a more general picture to emerge, but this is not always so. The more archaeologists explore the past, the harder it becomes to see general laws. They're learning that a variety of paths can lead to the same result. Studying the human past is always fascinating, because like travelling, you're confronted by differing values and ways of doing things, prompting a reassessment of your own culture and achievements.

A History of Exploration in Jordan

Biblical concerns fuelled the first explorations of Mesopotamia and Palestine, although what is today Jordan was largely ignored. Only after the Napoleonic Wars was any organised exploration undertaken.

1860-1920 Jordan was first explored by a collection of American, French and German surveyors, seeking to emulate the formidable and exemplary (not to say militarily useful) British Survey of Western Palestine. Apart from the discovery in 1868 of the Mesha Stele, raised by King Mesha of Moab (as described in the boxed text in the King's Highway chapter), there was little progress

Books & Magazines

Before you get started, you might like to do a little reading. There are several popular periodicals, including the American *Expedition* and *Archaeology*; the French *Le Monde du Bible*; and the German *Antike Welt*.

For a detailed look at the main archaeological sites, a number of books are available in Jordan. *Petra* and *Jerash & the Decapolis* (both about JD15), by Iain Browning, are well illustrated and detailed. Refer to Books in the Petra and Jerash sections for details about other titles relating to these sites.

The excellent series of guides written by Rami Khouri are small and cheap (about JD3), eg *Petra – A Guide to the Capital of the Nabataeans* and *Jerash – A Frontier City of the Roman East*. Each guide gives full details of the sites, and has good maps.

Written in 1959, *The Antiquities of Jordan*, by G Lankester Harding, is dated, but still the most comprehensive guide to archaeological sites in Jordan and the West Bank. The author was director of the Department of Antiquities in Jordan for 20 years.

A more academic approach to the whole subject are the two volumes published by the Jordanian Department of Antiquities called *Studies in the History and Archaeology of Jordan*.

as the Ottoman hold over Jordan was unsteady at best, and locals were not terribly partial to foreigners poking around.

1920-60 Under cautious British rule, modest excavation projects got under way from the mid-1920s, aimed above all at consolidation of the main standing monuments, ie the 'desert castles' of eastern Jordan, castles at Ajlun, Karak and Shobak, and the Roman-Islamic ruins of Amman.

Research-oriented projects focused on the Graeco-Roman cities of the Decapolis, ie ten cities of ancient Palestine. See the boxed text 'The Decapolis' in the Amman chapter.

Anglo-American excavations began at Jerash, the best preserved Roman provincial city in the Middle East; and a German team returned to Roman Gadara (Umm Qais).

In the 1930s, a Franco-German team began excavations at prehistoric Teleilat Ghassul (3km north-east of the Dead Sea), the first great prehistoric site (circa 4000 BC) discovered in Jordan; and the Franciscans began to uncover remarkable mosaics at Madaba and Mt Nebo, among the best in the Levant.

Unrest at the time, WWII and the first Arab-Israeli wars greatly curtailed archaeological work in Jordan for nearly 20 years, although major Canadian-American excavations at Dhiban (between Madaba and Karak), and renewed British work at Petra, commenced early in the 1950s.

From 1960 The Six Day War in 1967, and subsequent unsettled conditions, interrupted large-scale archaeological projects across the country for a few decades, but since the mid-1970s activity has steadily increased.

Major British work in southern Jordan concentrated on the ancient Edomite capital of Buseirah (west of Tafila). The British also investigated the Roman legionary fortress at Udhrah and the Byzantine-Islamic city at Khirbat Faris, and continued work on the Ammonite-Islamic Citadel in Amman, the North Theatre at Jerash, the 'desert castles' to the east, and Tell as-Saidiyeh in the Jordan Valley.

American presence grew steadily in the 1970s, but since the early 1980s has spread throughout the country taking up projects far too numerous to cite here. Among the most spectacular are the excavations at prehistoric 'Ain Ghazal (near Amman), where a number of 8500 year old life-size plaster statues were discovered; the Amman Citadel, where parts of the monumental Roman Temple of Hercules have been re-erected; the Nabataean-Byzantine excavations at Petra, including a Greek manuscript library; Roman-Islamic Ayla (now Aqaba) and Umm al-Jimal; and Byzantine-Islamic Madaba.

Australian archaeologists have been working in Jordan for more than 30 years, with particular emphasis on the Jordan Valley – first at prehistoric Teleilat Ghassul (where a temple complex and a stunning wall painting were discovered); and Pella. Activity has gradually spread to Jerash, Hawran and other places in southern Jordan.

German teams continue to focus on the Decapolis cities, eg the Roman-Byzantine Umm Qais; several Bronze Age sites east of Irbid; important early mining sites in Wadi Finan (now in the Dana Nature Reserve); and the well-preserved early Neolithic village site of Basta (near Petra).

French work has grown steadily from the 1970s, most notably on the stunning Temple of Zeus and South Gate excavations at Jerash; and projects at prehistoric Abu Hamid (Jordan Valley), the enigmatic Hellenistic mortuary temple site of Iraq al-Amir (near Amman); and Petra.

Getting Involved

If you're interested in working on archaeological excavations, plan ahead. No dig director will welcome an inquiry two weeks before a season begins. Many permits and security forms may have to be completed, so allow time for all possible bureaucratic niceties. Opportunities are growing as field project leaders realise the advantages of taking on energetic and motivated amateurs, often willing to pay for the privilege of working on a dig.

When you write to dig directors, tell them what you can do. If you have special skills (eg photography or draughting), have travelled in the region, or worked on other digs (or similar group projects), let them know.

Archaeological Schools & Organisations in Jordan

To get an idea of what is going on, and where and when, contact one of the organisations listed below. All are based in Amman.

Deutsches Evangelisches Institut für Altertumswissenschaft des Heiligen Landes, Zweigstelle Amman (☎ 534 2924, fax 533 6924) PO Box 183, Amman 11118.

American Center for Oriental Research (ACOR) (☎ 534 6117, fax 584 4181) PO Box 2470, Jebel Amman, Amman 11181. ACOR is part of the

Archaeological Institute of America (AIA), and prepares an extensive annual listing of field-work opportunities in the Middle East. Write to: AIA, 135 William St, New York NY 10038.

British Institute at Amman for Archaeology & History (☎ 534 1317, fax 533 7197) PO Box 519, Al-Jubeiha, Amman 11941.

Institut Français d'Archéologie du Proche Orient (☎ 464 0515, fax 461 1170) PO Box 5348, Amman, 11181.

Friends of Archaeology (☎/fax 593 0682, email foa@nets.com.jo) PO Box 2440, Amman 11181. Established in 1960, this Jordanian-run, nonprofit organisation aims to 'protect and preserve the archaeological sites and cultural heritage of Jordan'. FoA operates educational field trips – but for members only. Web site www.arabia.com/FOA

University of Jordan: Archaeological Department (☎ 535 5000, ext 3739).

Archaeological Schools Overseas

Among universities that send teams to the Middle East are:

Australia	Universities of Melbourne & Sydney, Australian National University (Canberra)
Canada	University of Toronto
France	CNRS Lyon & Paris I
Germany	DAI Berlin, Tübingen & Heidelberg
Holland	Universities of Amsterdam & Leiden
UK	Universities of Cambridge, London & Edinburgh
USA	Chicago, UCLA & Yale.

Digging up the Past was written by Dr Stephen Bourke, Department of Archaeology, University of Sydney

Hiking

For most visitors, hiking is not high on the list of things to do in Jordan. Several areas are worth exploring on foot, but the rocky hills to the north, cities in the centre and deserts of the south are far from inviting. One advantage is that distances are small, but the downside is the heat, and scarcity of water. Also, hiking trails are mostly non-existent, and no organisations in Jordan are specifically involved in hiking or trekking. Most available hiking trails are short, and

Prehiking Safety Guidelines

Before embarking on a hiking trip, careful consideration should be given to a safe – as well as enjoyable – experience. Please:

- Pay fees and possess any permits required by local authorities.
- Be sure you're healthy and feel comfortable hiking.
- Obtain reliable information about physical and environmental conditions along the route you intend to take (eg from park authorities).
- Be aware of local laws, regulations and etiquette about wildlife and the environment.
- Hike in regions and on tracks or trails within your experience level; if available, engage the services of a competent, professionally trained guide.

take less than one day, while long-distance and overnight trekking is rarely possible.

Any hike will take longer, and take more out of you, than you think – walking in sand is not easy, nor is going uphill in the hot sun. Allow yourself plenty of time, and also give yourself time to linger and enjoy the view, chat with passers-by, or simply sit in the shade during the heat of the day.

Information

When to Go The best time for hiking is undoubtedly the middle of spring (mid-March to late April), when it's not too hot, the rains should have finished, the flowers should be in bloom and the wells and springs should be full. At this time, however, trips through Wadi Mujib, or some of the wadis in Petra, may still be flooded or impassable in places. Late September to mid-October is also good: dry but not excessively hot.

Rain and floods can occur throughout the months of November to March. This is not a good time to hike or camp in narrow wadis and ravines because flash floods can sweep unheralded out of the hills. Such instances are, fortunately, rare: the most usual problem with water is a lack of it.

ACTIVITIES

What to Bring A lightweight wind-proof top is recommended, as is a thin fleece jacket for the evening. Lightweight waterproofs are rarely needed, except perhaps for some of the wetter mid-winter days – unless you're spending time from October to April in the north, which is undoubtedly colder and wetter than the south. Most people walk in lightweight cotton clothes or the modern equivalent and trainers are the usual footwear, although some prefer lightweight walking boots which give more ankle support.

It's not advisable to wear shorts or sleeveless tops – it's inappropriate dress for conservative villages in the countryside, and you may get burnt to a crisp anyway. Don't forget a hat, sunscreen, medical kit, knife, torch (flashlight) and matches. Water purifiers and insect repellent will also be very useful.

Books The British climbers, Tony Howard and Di Taylor, have spent a lot of time exploring the hiking, trekking and rock climbing possibilities in Jordan. The results are the 3rd edition (1997) of the excellent and detailed *Treks & Climbs in the Mountains of Wadi Rum & Petra* (JD20); the condensed, pocket-sized and more affordable (JD3) *Walks & Scrambles in Rum*, published by Al-Kutba; and the recent *Walks, Treks, Caves, Climbs & Canyons in Pella, Ajloun, Moab, Dana, Petra & Rum* (JD22). These books are available in major bookshops in Jordan.

Maps Knowing precisely where you're going can often be a problem, and anything other than road maps are hard to come by. For short hikes without guides, the maps in this book will be sufficient, but buy a decent map (available in Jordan) if hiking around Wadi Rum or Petra – see under Maps in the relevant sections for details.

Hiking Agencies Only a tiny fraction of the plethora of travel agencies throughout Jordan offer any hiking or trekking:

Discovery
   (☎ 06-569 7998, fax 569 8183, email discovery@nets.com.jo) PO Box 3371, Amman 11118. Web site www.discovery1.com

Petra Moon Tourism Services
   (☎ 03-215 6665, fax 215 6666, email petram@go.com.jo) PO Box 129, Wadi Mousa (near Petra). Offers treks of up to six days around Petra, Dana Nature Reserve, Wadi Rum and Shobak. Web site www.petramoon.com
Zaman Tours & Travel
   (☎ 03-215 7723, fax 215 7722, zamantours@jo innet.com.jo) PO Box 158, Wadi Mousa (near Petra). Also runs camping and camel treks

Places to Go

Wadi Rum This uniquely beautiful desert area has become acknowledged as one of the world's foremost desert climbing areas, and offers the visitor a remarkable variety of venues from a short stroll up to Lawrence's Spring to wonderful scrambles up Burdah Rock Bridge and Jebel Rum (1754m), Jordan's highest mountain. More difficult routes need a guide and a safety rope.

To get into the desert experience, you can walk for days among superb scenery as the rock domes and sandscapes change from the ghostly colour of a full moonlit night to the hot furnace hues of late afternoon. Despite a recent move to Rum village, the Bedouin still retain most of their camps out in the desert. They welcome visitors, but please offer some payment in return (which may be refused). As more tourists come and go, however, charging for food and tea, and certainly accommodation, is now common. As always, the further off the road you get the more sincere your welcome is likely to be.

Although some adventurous travellers and experienced hikers do hike around Wadi Rum for a day or two without a guide, a guide is strongly recommended for any long-distance trekking. Remember that it's very easy to get disoriented, temperatures can be extremely hot during the day and cold at night, natural water supplies are uncommon and not always drinkable, passing traffic is nonexistent and maps are fairly inadequate. Hiking should not be attempted in summer (May to September) when temperatures are extreme, and dehydration and exhaustion are real dangers.

Wadi Rum will soon become fully under the control of the Royal Society for the Conservation of Nature (RSCN), which may limit the number of hikers, establish hiking trails and enforce the hiring of guides. More details about this, and general information about hiking and rock climbing in Wadi Rum, can be found in the Wadi Rum section of the Southern Desert chapter. For more details about the RSCN, refer to the Ecology & Environment section and the boxed text 'RSCN', both in the Facts about Jordan chapter.

Petra To explore Petra properly is a major undertaking in itself. In addition to walking around the main site, there are several tough climbs, mostly up steep steps, to lookouts and other extraordinary places, such as the Monastery. Anyone with enough energy, time and enthusiasm can hike off the beaten track in and near Petra (eg Al-Beid, also known as Little Petra) to escape the crowds, see some stunning landscapes, explore un-excavated tombs and temples and, perhaps, meet some Bedouin villagers.

However, there are some areas in Petra – mainly the wadis – which are potentially dangerous during the rainy season, and regions which may be officially off limits, because the tourist police may think you're trying to get into Petra for free (ie illegally). Women should not venture too far into remote areas on their own.

Refer to Hiking in the Petra chapter for further details and information.

King's Highway The area around the castle at Shobak is great for hiking, and trails head south through the hills, and past ancient stands of oak, to Al-Beid (Little Petra).

Dana Nature Reserve is primarily a nature reserve, so hiking is limited to four recognised hiking trails. Beyond these trails you'll need permission, and a guide, from the RSCN or the visitors centre in Dana village. More information can be found in the Dana Nature Reserve section of the King's Highway chapter.

North of Dana, and all the way to Amman, the high hills of the desert rise from the abyss of Wadi Araba and are slashed by huge canyons such as Wadi Hasa and Wadi Mujib. Over these hills and down the steep sides of

Some Tips

There are a few things to remember before you head off into the countryside:

Camping
The Jordanian authorities don't look too kindly on camping or sleeping out away from recognised camping areas, so stick to the few designated camping sites – see Camping in the Accommodation section of the Facts for the Visitor chapter for more information.

Food & Water
Just about any basic food is available in any of the larger towns and villages, including fresh bread and dehydrated foods; the smaller ones are only likely to have pasta, rice and tinned foods, however. Small camping gas cylinders tend only to be available in large towns. Drink more than you need before starting and carry plenty: two litres each per day is a minimum. Take more if you can, unless you're absolutely certain it is available along the way.

Wildlife
You may be lucky enough to see anything from tortoises through to ibex or fox, and plenty of birds. More obnoxious are the hyenas which prowl the gorges and hills above the Dead Sea, mainly at night – they can be dangerous, although fortunately they are very reclusive. In the desert regions, there are snakes and scorpions, so tread gently – or, rather, noisily.

these dramatic gorges, the thin ribbon of the King's Highway winds its way and forms the starting point for some short walks and great hikes – a few of which emerge on the Dead Sea Highway.

For example, from the start (eastern end) of Wadi Hasa is a short climb up a conical hill to the ruins of the once magnificent Nabataean temple at Khirbat Tannur. Considerably more strenuous is the trek down Wadi Mujib, 'The Grand Canyon of Jordan', which takes two or three days. However, this does require special permission from the RSCN.

North of Wadi Mujib, Machaerus (in the village of Mukawir) is connected by seldom trodden paths to the hot springs at Hammamat Ma'in. From Hammamat Ma'in, it's possible to hike (10km) down to the Dead Sea. This hike takes about five hours, and involves some scrambling down rock faces (2 to 3m high) and walking along the narrow wadi. Don't do this in the rainy season.

Local guides are recommended for all long-distance hikes in this area, and permission is required to enter any reserve run by the RSCN.

Around Amman If you have any energy left after walking up and down the *jebels* (hills) of Amman, and dodging the traffic in Downtown, head for some nearby villages. From the bus station in Salt, the main road leads into Wadi She'ib, a refreshing valley with some interesting caves. Fuheis is another great area for short hikes: just head down the road from the main roundabout where the bus from Amman eventually stops. From Wadi as-Seer, an easy walk (about 10km) leads past some caves and ends up at the fascinating Iraq al-Amir castle.

Northern & Western Jordan The cooler, forested hills around Jerash, Ajlun and Dibbeen National Park offer a different, and almost unexpected, terrain. In the spring, carpets of red crown anemones fill the meadows beneath the pine forested and sometimes snow-capped rolling hills. Here, numerous short hikes are possible along marked (but unmapped) trails through the woods and into quiet valleys where you may meet local farmers tending their crops. Flowers and birdlife are plentiful and it can be a relaxing way to while away a few hours. All this northern area is, in general, easy walking country usually on small roads or stony trails between villages that are rarely too far apart.

To the west, the hills drop into the Jordan Valley, now no longer the dust-bowl of Wadi Araba but a fertile agricultural valley cradling a tightly knit patchwork of fields dotted with plastic greenhouses. Tucked in a side valley are the ruins of Pella which can be reached on foot from the hills above by small trails leading into the valley. To the north, the area around the expansive ruins of Gadara at Umm Qais offers short walks and views of the Golan Heights with the Sea of Galilee and the Yarmouk River below.

Responsible Hiking
The popularity of hiking is placing some pressure on the natural environment. Please consider the following tips when hiking and help preserve the ecology and beauty of the Jordanian landscape.

Rubbish Carry out all your rubbish. Don't overlook those easily forgotten items, such as silver paper, orange peel, cigarette butts and plastic wrappers. Empty packaging weighs very little anyway and should be stored in a dedicated rubbish bag. Make an effort to carry out rubbish left by others. Never bury your rubbish. Digging disturbs soil and ground-cover and encourages erosion. Buried rubbish will more than likely be dug up by animals, who may be injured or poisoned by it. It may also take years to decompose, especially at high altitudes.

Minimise your waste. Take minimal packaging and taking no more food than you'll need. If you can't buy in bulk, unpack small-portion packages and combine their contents in one container before your trip. Take reusable containers or stuff sacks. Don't rely on bought water in plastic bottles. Disposal of these bottles is creating a major problem: use iodine drops or purification tablets instead. Sanitary napkins, tampons and condoms should also be carried out, despite the inconvenience. They burn and decompose poorly.

Human Waste Disposal Contamination of water sources by human faeces can lead to the transmission of hepatitis, typhoid and intestinal parasites such as giardia, amoebas and roundworms. It can also cause severe health risks to local residents and wildlife. Where there's a toilet, please use it. Where there is none, bury your waste. Dig a small hole 15cm deep and at least 100m from any watercourse. Consider carrying a light-weight trowel for this purpose. Cover the waste with soil and a rock. Always use your toilet paper sparingly and then bury it with the waste.

Washing Don't use detergents or toothpaste in or near watercourses, even if they're biodegradable. For personal washing, use biodegradable soap and a water container at least 50m away from the watercourse. Disperse the waste-water widely to allow the soil to filter it fully before it finally makes it back to the watercourse. Wash cooking utensils 50m from watercourses using a scourer or sand instead of detergent.

Erosion It is important to stick to existing tracks and avoid short cuts that bypass a switchback. If you blaze a new trail straight down a slope, it will turn into a watercourse with the next heavy rainfall and eventually cause soil loss and deep scarring. If a well-used track passes through a mud patch, walk through the mud: walking around the edge will increase the size of the patch. Avoid removing the plantlife that keeps topsoil in place.

Fires & Low-Impact Cooking The cutting of wood for fires can cause rapid deforestation. Cook on a light-weight kerosene, alcohol or Shellite (white gas) stove and avoid those powered by disposable butane gas canisters. If you're hiking with a guide and porters, supply stoves for the whole team. If you light a fire, use an existing fireplace rather than creating a new one. Don't surround fires with rocks as this creates a visual scar. Use only dead, fallen wood. Ensure that you fully extinguish a fire after use.

Wildlife Conservation Do not engage in or encourage hunting – it is illegal in all parks and reserves in Jordan. Don't buy items made from endangered species. Discourage the presence of wildlife by not leaving food scraps behind you. Place gear out of reach and tie packs to rafters or trees. Do not feed the wildlife as this can lead to animals becoming dependent on hand-outs, to unbalanced populations and to diseases such as 'lumpy jaw'.

Park Regulations Take note of and observe the rules and regulations of the national or state reserve that you are visiting.

Language

Arabic is Jordan's official language. English is also widely spoken but any effort to communicate with the locals in their own language will be well rewarded. No matter how far off the mark your pronunciation or grammar might be, you'll often get the response (usually with a big smile): 'Ah, you speak Arabic very well!'.

Learning a few basics for day-to-day travelling doesn't take long at all, but to master the complexities of Arabic would take years of consistent study. The whole issue is complicated by the differences between Classical Arabic *(fus-ha)*, its modern descendant MSA (Modern Standard Arabic) and regional dialects. The classical tongue is the language of the Quran and Arabic poetry of centuries past. For long it remained static, but in order to survive it had to adapt to change, and the result is more or less MSA, the common language of the press, radio and educated discourse. It is as close to a lingua franca (a common language) as the Arab world comes, and is generally understood, if not always well spoken, right across the Arab world – from Baghdad to Casablanca. An educated Iraqi would have no trouble shooting the breeze about world politics with a similarly educated Moroccan, but might have considerably more difficulty ordering lunch.

Fortunately, the spoken dialects of Jordan are not too distant from MSA. For outsiders trying to learn Arabic, the most frustrating element nevertheless remains understanding the spoken language. There is virtually no written material to refer to for back-up, and acquisition of MSA in the first place is itself a long-term investment. An esoteric argument flows back and forth about the relative merits of learning MSA first (and so perhaps having to wait some time before being able to communicate adequately with people in the street) or focusing your efforts on a dialect. If all this gives you a headache now, you'll have some inkling of why so few non-Arabs, or non-Muslims, embark on a study of the language.

Pronunciation

Pronunciation of Arabic can be tongue-tying for someone unfamiliar with the intonation and combination of sounds. Pronounce the transliterated words slowly and clearly.

This language guide should help, but bear in mind that the myriad rules governing pronunciation and vowel use are too extensive to be covered here.

Vowels

Technically, there are three long and three short vowels in Arabic. The reality is a little different, with local dialect and varying consonant combinations affecting their pronunciation. This is the case throughout the Arabic-speaking world. More like five short and five long vowels can be identified:

a	as the 'a' in 'had'
e	as the 'e' in 'bet'
i	as the 'i' in 'hit'
o	as the 'o' in 'hot'
u	as the 'oo' in 'book'

A macron over a vowel indicates that the vowel has a long sound:

ā	as the 'a' in 'father'
ī	as the 'e' in 'ear', only softer
ū	as the 'oo' in 'food'

Consonants

Pronunciation for all Arabic consonants is covered in the alphabet table on the following page. Note that when double consonants occur in transliterations, both are pronounced. For example, *al-Hammam* (toilet/ bath), is pronounced 'al-ham-mam'.

Other Sounds

Arabic has two sounds that are very tricky for non-Arabs to produce, the 'ayn and the glottal stop. The letter 'ayn represents a sound with no English equivalent that comes even close. It is similar to the glottal

The Arabic Alphabet

Final	Medial	Initial	Alone	Transliteration	Pronunciation
ا			ا	ā	as the 'a' in 'father'
ـب	ـبـ	بـ	ب	b	as in 'bet'
ـت	ـتـ	تـ	ت	t	as in 'ten'
ـث	ـثـ	ثـ	ث	th	as in 'thin'
ـج	ـجـ	جـ	ج	g	as in 'go'
ـح	ـحـ	حـ	ح	H	a strongly whispered 'h', almost like a sigh of relief
ـخ	ـخـ	خـ	خ	kh	as the 'ch' in Scottish *loch*
ـد			د	d	as in 'dim'
ـذ			ذ	dh	as the 'th' in 'this'
ـر			ر	r	a rolled 'r', as in the Spanish word *caro*
ـز			ز	z	as in 'zip'
ـس	ـسـ	سـ	س	s	as in 'so', never as in 'wisdom'
ـش	ـشـ	شـ	ش	sh	as in 'ship'
ـص	ـصـ	صـ	ص	ş	emphatic 's'
ـض	ـضـ	ضـ	ض	ḍ	emphatic 'd'
ـط	ـطـ	طـ	ط	ţ	emphatic 't'
ـظ	ـظـ	ظـ	ظ	ẓ	emphatic 'z'
ـع	ـعـ	عـ	ع	'	the Arabic letter 'ayn; pronounce as a glottal stop – like the closing of the throat before saying 'Oh oh!' (see Other Sounds on p.268)
ـغ	ـغـ	غـ	غ	gh	a guttural sound like Parisian 'r'
ـف	ـفـ	فـ	ف	f	as in 'far'
ـق	ـقـ	قـ	ق	q	a strongly guttural 'k' sound; in Egyptian Arabic often pronounced as a glottal stop
ـك	ـكـ	كـ	ك	k	as in 'king'
ـل	ـلـ	لـ	ل	l	as in 'lamb'
ـم	ـمـ	مـ	م	m	as in 'me'
ـن	ـنـ	نـ	ن	n	as in 'name'
ـه	ـهـ	هـ	ه	h	as in 'ham'
ـو			و	w	as in 'wet'; or
				ū	long, as the 'oo' on 'food'; or
				aw	as the 'ow' in 'how'
ـي	ـيـ	يـ	ي	y	as in 'yes'; or
				ī	as the 'e' in 'ear', only softer; or
				ay	as the 'y' in 'by' or as the 'ay' in 'way'

Vowels Not all Arabic vowel sounds are represented in the alphabet. See Pronunciation on p. 268.
Emphatic Consonants Emphatic consonants are similar to their nonemphatic counterparts but are pronounced with greater tension in the tongue and throat.

stop (which is not actually represented in the alphabet) but the muscles at the back of the throat are gagged more forcefully – it has been described as the sound of someone being strangled. In many transliteration systems 'ayn is represented by an opening quotation mark, and the glottal stop by a closing quotation mark. To make the transliterations in this language guide (and throughout the rest of the book) easier to use, we have not distinguished between the glottal stop and the 'ayn, using the closing quotation mark to represent both sounds. You'll find that Arabic speakers will still understand you.

Transliteration

It's worth noting here that transliteration from the Arabic script into English – or any other language for that matter – is at best an approximate science.

The presence of sounds unknown in European languages and the fact that the script is 'defective' (most vowels are not written) combine to make it nearly impossible to settle on one universally accepted method of transliteration. A wide variety of spellings is therefore possible for words when they appear in Latin script – and that goes for places and people's names as well.

The whole thing is further complicated by the wide variety of dialects and the imaginative ideas Arabs themselves often have on appropriate spelling in, say, English

The Transliteration Dilemma

TE Lawrence, when asked by his publishers to clarify 'inconsistencies in the spelling of proper names' in The Seven Pillars of Wisdom – his account of the Arab Revolt in WWI – wrote back:

'Arabic names won't go into English. There are some "scientific systems" of transliteration, helpful to people who know enough Arabic not to need helping, but a washout for the world. I spell my names anyhow, to show what rot the systems are.'

(and words spelt one way in Jordan may look very different again in Syria, heavily influenced by French); not even the most venerable of western Arabists have been able to come up with a satisfactory solution.

While striving to reflect the language as closely as possible and aiming at consistency, this book generally spells place, street and hotel names and the like as the locals have done. Don't be surprised if you come across several versions of the same thing.

Pronouns

I	*ana*
you	*inta* (m)/*inti* (f)
he	*huwa*
she	*hiyya*
we	*naHnu/eHna*
you	*ento*
they	*humma*

Greetings & Civilities

Arabs place great importance on civility and it's rare to see any interaction between people that doesn't begin with profuse greetings, inquiries into the other's health and other niceties.

Arabic greetings are more formal than in English and there is a reciprocal response to each. These sometimes vary slightly, depending on whether you're addressing a man or a woman. A simple encounter can become a drawn-out affair, with neither side wanting to be the one to put a halt to the stream of greetings and well-wishing. As an *ajnabi* (foreigner), you're not expected to know all the ins and outs, but if you come up with the right expression at the appropriate moment they'll love it.

The most common greeting is *salām alaykum* (peace be upon you), to which the correct reply is *wa aleikum as-salām* (and upon you be peace). If you get invited to a birthday celebration or are around for any of the big holidays, the common greeting is *kul sana wa intum bi-khīr* (I wish you well for the coming year).

After having a bath or shower, you will often hear people say to you *na'iman*, which roughly means 'heavenly' and boils down to an observation along the lines of 'nice and clean now, huh'.

Arrival in one piece is always something to be grateful for. Passengers will often be greeted with *al-Hamdu lillah al as-salāma* – 'thank God for your safe arrival'.

Hi.	*marHaba*
Hello.	*ahlan wa sahlan* or just *ahlan* (Welcome)
Hello. (response)	*ahlan bēk*
Goodbye.	*ma'a salāma/ Allah ma'ak*
Good morning.	*sabaH al-khayr*
Good morning. (response)	*sabaH 'an-nūr*
Good evening.	*masa' al-khayr*
Good evening. (response)	*masa 'an-nūr*
Good night.	*tisbaH 'ala khayr*
Good night. (response)	*wa inta min ahalu*

Basics

Yes.	*aiwa/na'am*
Yeah.	*ay*
No.	*la*
Please. (request)	*min fadlak* (m)/ *min fadlik* (f)
Please. (formal)	*law samaHt* (m)/ *law samaHti* (f)
Please. (come in)	*tafaddal* (m)/ *tafaddali*(f)/ *tafaddalū* (pl)
Thank you.	*shukran*
Thank you very much.	*shukran jazīlan*
You're welcome.	*'afwan/ahlan*
Pardon/Excuse me.	*'afwan*
Sorry!	*āsif!*
No problem.	*mish mushkila/ mū mushkila*
Never mind.	*maalesh*
Just a moment.	*laHza*
Congratulations!	*mabrouk!*

Small Talk

Questions like 'Is the bus coming?' or 'Will the bank be open later?' generally elicit the inevitable response: *in sha' Allah* – 'God willing' – an expression you'll hear over

and over again. Another common one is *ma sha' Allah* – 'God's will be done' – sometimes a useful answer to probing questions about why you're not married yet.

How are you?	*kayf Hālak?* (m)/ *kayf Hālik?* (f)
How are you?	*shlonak?* (m)/ *shlonik?* (f)
Fine.	*al-Hamdu lillah* (lit: Thanks be to God)
What's your name?	*shu-ismak?* (m)/ *shu-ismik?* (f)
My name is ...	*ismi ...*
Pleased to meet you. (departing)	*furṣa sa'ida*
Nice to meet you.	*tasharrafna* (lit: you honour us)
Where are you from?	*min wayn inta?*

I'm from ...	*ana men ...*
Algeria	*al-jazīr*
Australia	*ustrālya*
Canada	*kanada*
Egypt	*masir*
Europe	*oropa*
Japan	*yaban*
Libya	*libya*
Morocco	*maghreb*
New Zealand	*nyu zīlanda*
South Africa	*afrika el janubiya*
Tunisia	*tūnes*
the USA	*amerka*

Are you married?	*inta mutajawwiz?* (m)/ *inti mutajawwiza?* (f)
Not yet.	*mesh Halla*
How old are you?	*ay 'amrak?/ kam sana 'andak?*
I'm 20 years old.	*'andī 'ashrīn sana*
I'm a student.	*ana tālib* (m)/ *ana tāliba* (f)
I'm a tourist.	*ana sa'iH* (m)/ *ana sa'iHa* (f)
Do you like ...?	*inta batHib?*
I like ...	*ana baHib ...* (m)/ *ana uHib...* (f)
I don't like ...	*ana ma baHib ...* (m)/ *ana lā uHib ...* (f)

Language Difficulties

Do you speak English?	*bitiHki inglīzi?/ Hal tatakallam(i) inglīzi?*
I understand.	*afham*
I don't understand.	*ma bifham la afham*
I speak ...	*ana baHki .../ ana atakallam ...*
English	*inglīzi*
French	*faransi*
German	*almāni*
I speak a little Arabic.	*ana behke arabe shway*
I don't speak Arabic.	*ana ma behke arabe*
I want an interpreter.	*urīd mutarjem*
Could you write it down, please?	*mumkin tiktabhu, min fadlak?*
What does this mean?	*yānī ay?*
How do you say ... in Arabic?	*kayf taqul ... bil'arabi?*

Getting Around

Where is ...?	*wayn ...?*
airport	*al-maṭār*
bus station	*maHaṭṭat al-bāṣ/ maHaṭṭat al-karaj*
railway station	*maHaṭṭat al-qiṭār*
ticket office	*maktab at-tazākar*
What time does ... leave/arrive?	*sa'a kam biyitla'/ biyuṣal...?*
aeroplane	*ṭīyara*
boat/ferry	*al-markib/as-safīna*
bus	*al-bāṣ*
train	*al-qiṭār*
I want to go to ...	*ana badeh rūh ala ...*
Which bus goes to ...?	*aya otobīs beh rūh ala ...?*
Does this bus go to ...?	*hal otobīs beh rūh ala ...?*
How many buses per day go to ...?	*kam otobīs be rūh ben wa'har ...?*
How long does the trip take?	*kam as-sa'a ar-raHla?*

Please tell me when we get to ...	*omol mārūf elleh hamma nūsal ...*
Stop here, please.	*wakef, omal mārūf*
Please wait for me.	*ntov, omal mārūf*
May I sit here?	*feneh ekād Hon?*
1st class	*daraja ūla*
2nd class	*daraja thāni*
ticket	*at-tazkarah*
to/from	*ila/min*
Where can I hire a ...?	*wayn feneh esta'jer ...?*
bicycle	*al-'ajila*
car	*as-sayyāra/ārabeye*
motorcycle	*motosaikul*
guide	*ad-dalīl*

Directions

How do I get to ...?	*kīf būsal ala ...?*
Can you show me (on the map)?	*wayn (fil kharīṭa)?*
How many kilometres?	*kam kilometre?*
What ... is this?	*shū ... hey?*
street/road	*ash-sharia*
village	*al-qariyya*
on the left	*'ala yasār/shimāl*
on the right	*'ala yamīn*
opposite	*muqābil*
straight ahead	*'ala ṭūl/sawa/dugri*
at the next corner	*tanī zarūb*
this way	*min hon*
here/there	*hon/honāk*
in front of	*amām*
near	*qarīb*
far	*ba'īd*
north	*shimāl*
south	*junub*
east	*sharq*
west	*gharb*

Around Town

I'm looking for ...	*ana abHath ...*
Where is the ...?	*wayn ...?*
bank	*al-maṣraf/al-bank*
beach	*ash-shāti'*
chemist/pharmacy	*as-ṣayidiliyya*

city/town	al-medīna	Can I see it?	mumkin atfarraj-ha?
city centre	markaz al-medīna	It's very noisy/	fī khēr dajeh/waṣaq
customs	al-jumruk	dirty.	
entrance	ad-dukhūl	How much is it	qad aysh li kul
exchange office	masref	per person?	waHid?
exit	al-khuruj	How much is it	adeh bel leil?
hotel	al-funduq	per night?	
information	isti'lāmāt	Where is the	wayn al-Hammam?
market	as-sūq	bathroom?	
mosque	al-yamā'/al-masjid	We're leaving	eHna musafirīn
museum	al-matHaf	today.	al-youm
old city	al-medīna qadīma		
passport & immi-	maktab al-jawazāt	address	al-'anwān
gration office	wa al-hijra	air-conditioning	kondishon
police	ash-shurṭa	blanket	al-baṭāniyya
post office	maktab al-barīd	camp site	mukhaym
restaurant	al-maṭa'am	electricity	kahraba
telephone office	maktab at-telefon	hotel	funduq
temple	al-ma'abad	hot water	mai Harra/sākhina
tourist office	maktab as-siyaHa	key	al-miftaH
		manager	al-mudīr

I want to change ... baddeh sarref ...
  money   maṣāri
  travellers cheques   sheket msefrīn

shower	dūsh
soap	sabūn
toilet	twalet/mirhad

What time does it aymata bteftah/
  open/close?   byeftah?
I'd like to make a fene talfen omol mārūf
  telephone call.

Paperwork

date of birth	tarīkha al-mūlid
name	ism
nationality	jensīya
passport	jawaz as-safar
permit	tasrīH
place of birth	makan al-mūlid
visa	sima

Accommodation

I'd like to book feneh ehjuz ...
  a ...
Do you have a ...? fī ...?
  (cheap) room   ghurfa (rkīsa)
  single room   ghurfa mufrada
  double room   ghurfa bi sarīrayn

for one night la leile waHde
for two nights leiltēn

Food

I'm hungry/thirsty. ana ju'ān/atshān
What is this? ma hādha?/
    shu hādha?
I'd like ... bheb ...
Another ... please. ... waHid kamān, min
    fadlak

breakfast	al-fuṭūr
dinner	al-'ashā
food	al-akl
grocery store	al-mahal/al-baqaliyya
hot/cold	harr/bārid
lunch	al-ghada
restaurant	al-maṭ'am
set menu	tabak

Vegetarianism is a nonconcept in the Middle East. Even if you ask for meals without meat, you can be sure that any gravies, sauces etc will have been cooked with meat or animal fat. See Food in the Facts for the Visitor chapter for more information.

Shopping

Where can I buy ...?	*wayn feneh eshtereh ...?*
What is this?	*shu hadha?*
How much?	*qad aysh/bikam?*
How many?	*kam waHid?*
How much money?	*kam fulūs?*
That's too expensive.	*mayda ghalī khēr*
Is there ...?	*fī ...?*
There isn't (any).	*ma fī*
May I look at it?	*feneh etallā 'alaya?*

chemist/pharmacy	*farmasiya*
laundry	*gaşīl*
market	*sūq*
newsagents	*maktaba*

big	*kabīr*
bigger	*akbar*
cheap	*rakhīs*
cheaper	*arkhas*
closed	*maghlūq/musakkar*
expensive	*ghāli*
money	*al-fulūs/al-maşāari*
open	*maftūH*
small/smaller	*şaghīr/as-ghar*

Time & Date

What's the time?	*as-sā'a kam?*
When?	*matā/emta?*
now	*Halla'*
after	*bādayn*
on time	*al waket*
early	*bakīr*
late	*ma'qar*
daily	*kil youm*
today	*al-youm*
tomorrow	*bukra/ghadan*
day after tomorrow	*ba'ad bukra*
yesterday	*imbārih/ams*
minute	*daqīqa*
hour	*sā'a*
day	*youm*
week	*usbū'*
month	*shahr*
year	*sana*
morning	*soubeh*
afternoon	*bād deher*

Emergencies

Help me!	*sā'idūnī!*
I'm sick.	*ana marīd* (m)/ *ana marīda* (f)
Go away!	*imshi!*
doctor	*duktūr/tabīb*
hospital	*al-mustash-fa*
police	*ash-shurta/al-bolis*

evening	*massa*
night	*leil*

Monday	*al-itnein*
Tuesday	*at-talata*
Wednesday	*al-arbi'a*
Thursday	*al-khamīs*
Friday	*al-jum'a*
Saturday	*as-sabt*
Sunday	*al-aHad*

Months

The Islamic year has 12 lunar months and is 11 days shorter than the western (Gregorian) calendar, so important Muslim dates will fall 11 days earlier each (western) year. There are two Gregorian calendars in use in the Arab world. In Egypt and westwards, the months have virtually the same names as in English (January is *yanāyir*, October is *octobir* and so on), but in Jordan, Syria and eastwards, the names are quite different. Talking about, say, June as 'month six' is the easiest solution, but for the sake of completeness, the months from January are:

January	*kanūn ath-thani*
February	*shubāt*
March	*azār*
April	*nisān*
May	*ayyār*
June	*Huzayrān*
July	*tammūz*
August	*'āb*
September	*aylūl*
October	*tishrīn al-awal*
November	*tishrīn ath-thani*
December	*kānūn al-awal*

Numbers

Arabic numerals are simple to learn and, unlike the written language, run from left to right. Pay attention to the order of the words in numbers from 21 to 99.

0	•	şifr
1	١	waHid
2	٢	itnayn/tintayn
3	٣	talāta
4	٤	arba'a
5	٥	khamsa
6	٦	sitta
7	٧	saba'a
8	٨	tamanya
9	٩	tis'a
10	١•	'ashara
11	١١	Hid-'ashr
12	١٢	itn-'ashr
13	١٣	talat-'ashr
14	١٤	arba'at-'ashr
15	١٥	khamast-'ashr
16	١٦	sitt-'ashr
17	١٧	saba'at-'ashr
18	١٨	tamant-'ashr
19	١٩	tisa'at-'ashr
20	٢•	'ashrīn
21	٢١	waHid wa 'ashrīn
22	٢٢	itnein wa ashrīn
30	٣•	talātīn
40	٤•	'arba'īn
50	٥•	khamsīn
60	٦•	sittīn
70	٧•	saba'īn
80	٨•	tamanīn
90	٩•	tis'īn
100	١••	mia
101	١•١	mia wa waHid
200	٢••	miatayn
300	٣••	talāta mia
1000	١•••	alf
2000	٢•••	alfayn
3000	٣•••	talāt-alaf

Ordinal Numbers

first	awal
second	tanī
third	talet
fourth	rabeh
fifth	khames

The Hejira months, too, have their own names:

1st	MoHarram
2nd	Safar
3rd	Rabi' al-Awal
4th	Rabei ath-Thāni
5th	Jumāda al-Awal
6th	Jumāda al-Akhira
7th	Rajab
8th	Shaban
9th	Ramadan
10th	Shawwal
11th	Zuul-Qeda
12th	Zuul-Hijja

Glossary

This glossary is mostly a list of Arabic (A) and French (F) words commonly used in Jordan, plus some archaeological (arch) terms and abbreviations.

abu (A) – 'father of ...'
agora (arch) – open space for commerce and politics
'ain (ayoun) (A) – spring or well
Alo – one of the two private telephone companies in Jordan
amir (A) – see *emir*
Ayyubids – the dynasty founded by Salah ad-Din (Saladin) in Egypt in 1169

bab (abwab) (A) – gate
beit (A) – house
beit ash-sha'ar (A) – goat-hair Bedouin tent
benzin (A) – regular petrol
burj (A) – tower

caliph (A) – Islamic ruler
caravanserai – large inn enclosing a courtyard, providing accommodation and a marketplace for caravans
cardo maximus (arch) – Roman main street, from north to south
centraal (F) – telephone office

Decapolis – literally 'ten cities'; this term refers to a number of ancient cities in the Roman Empire, including Amman and Jerash
decumanus (arch) – Roman main street, from east to west
deir (A) – monastery
donjon (F) – dungeon
duwaar (A) – circle

Eid al-Fitr (A) – Festival of Breaking the Fast, celebrated throughout the Islamic world at the end of *Ramadan*
emir (A) – Islamic ruler, leader, military commander or governor; literally 'prince'
ewan – vaulted hall opening into a central court

haj (A) – the pilgrimage to Mecca
Haji (A) – one who has made the haj to Mecca
hammam(at) (A) – natural hot springs; sometimes refers to a Turkish steam bath, and toilet or shower
hijab (A) – woman's head scarf

IAF – Islamic Action Front, the largest political party in Jordan
ibn (A) – 'son of ...'
il-balad (A) – 'downtown', ie the centre of town
imam (A) – religious leader

jalabiyyeh (A) – man's full-length robe
janub(iyyeh) (A) – south(ern)
jazira (A) – island
jebel (A) – hill or mountain
JETT – Jordan Express Travel & Tourism, the major private bus company in Jordan
jisr (A) – bridge
JPP – one of the two private telephone companies in Jordan
JTB – Jordan Tourism Board

khutba (A) – Islamic sermon
khirbat (A) – ruins of an ancient village
kufic (A) – a type of highly stylised old Arabic script

madrassa (A) – theological college that is part of a noncongregational mosque; also a school
malek (A) – king
malekah (A) – queen
Mamluks – literally 'slaves'. This Turkish slave and soldier class was characterised by seemingly unending blood-letting and intrigue for the succession.
masjid (A) – mosque
matar (A) – airport
medina (A) – old walled centre of any Islamic city
midan (A) – town or city square
mihrab (A) – niche in the wall of a mosque that indicates the direction of Mecca

minaret (A) – tower on top of a mosque
minbar (A) – pulpit in a mosque
MSA – Modern Standard Arabic
muezzin (A) – mosque official who calls the faithful to prayer five times a day, often from the *minaret*
muhafaza(t) (A) – governorate(s)
mukhabarat (A) – secret police
mumtaz (A) – 'super' petrol or '1st class' (especially on trains); literally 'excellent'

nargila (A) – water pipe used mainly by men to smoke tobacco
necropolis (arch) – cemetery
NGO – nongovernment organisation
nymphaeum (arch) – literally 'temple of the Nymphs'; a place with baths, fountains and pools

PLO – Palestine Liberation Organisation
PNA – Palestine National Authority
PNT – Petra National Trust
praetorium (arch) – military headquarters
propylaeum (arch) – grand entrance to a temple or palace
PRPC – Petra Region Planning Council

qala'at – (A) castle or fort
qasr (A) – castle or palace
qibla (A) – direction of Mecca
Quran (A) – holy book of Islam
Qusayr (A) – small castle or palace

rababah (A) – traditional single-string Bedouin instrument

Ramadan (A) – Muslim month of fasting
ras (A) – cape, point or headland
RDC – Royal Diving Centre (near Aqaba)
RSCN – Royal Society for the Conservation of Nature

servees – service taxi
shamal(iyyeh) (A) – north(ern)
Sharq al-Awsat (A) – Middle East
sheikh (A) – officer of the mosque or venerated religious scholar
sherif (A) – descendent of the Prophet Mohammed (through his daughter, Fatima); general title for Islamic ruler
sidd (A) – dam
siq (A) – gorge or canyon
souq (A) – market
stele – stone or wooden commemorative slab or column decorated with inscriptions or figures

tell (A) – ancient mound created by centuries of urban rebuilding
temenos (arch) – a sacred courtyard or similar enclosure
tetrapylon (arch) – an archway with four entrances
triclinium (arch) – dining room

Umayyads – first great dynasty of Arab Muslim rulers
umm (A) – 'mother of ...'

wadi (A) – valley or river bed formed by watercourse, dry except after heavy rainfall

Acknowledgments

THANKS

Many thanks to the following travellers who used *Jordan & Syria* and wrote to us with helpful hints, useful advice and interesting anecdotes about travelling in Jordan.

Abdul Hadi Hamed Yassin, Adrian Bickley, Akel Biltaji, Alf Sandberg, Alfred Heuperman, Alistair McBride, Amanda Harvey, Ambrogio Radaelli, Anders W Frederiksen, Andrew Graham, Andrew Knowlman, Andrew Osborne, Andrew Radford, Andrew Sargeant, Andrzej Bielecki, Angeline van Hout, Antonio Sanchez, Arnold Barlow, Avraham Hampel, Balazs Garamvolgyi, Barry Aitken, Betsy Guelcher, Bettina Dalgard Rasmussen, Bill & Joan Hamerman Robbins, Brian Kuhn, Bronwyn Hughes, Bruce Kilby, Bruno Hasler, Bryan & Alison Bluck, C & W Yee, C Hoad, Carlos Gajardo-Gallardo, Carol Kiecker, Caroline Logan, Carolyn deRoos, Carsten Hyld Iversen, Chad Thomson, Charles Brown, Charlotte Volund, Chris Caul, Chris De Voecht, Chris Dixon, Christelle Dain, Christine & Andrew Mayer, Cies Pierrot, Clavien Mireille, Cor Breukel, DJ Graham, Damien Galanaud, Dan Stacey, Dan Tamir, Daniel & Veronique Vuille, Dave O'Brien, Dave Sismey, David Birtles, David Grant, David Halford, David Martin, David Roberts, David & Bettina Roth, Dawn Davids, Deepa Vasudevan, Dene Brosnan, Diny Sijm, Dirk Leman, Dominique Brooks, Domique De Bast, Dr Andrea Eggenstein, Dr Annette Prelle, Dr Ghassan Ramadan-Jaradi, E Christyham, Ed Raw, Eddy Veraghtert, Edo Plantingo, Elaine Dalton, Eleonora Humphreys, Elizabeth Bostock, Ellen van Geest, Emily Peckham, Eric Linder, Erica Sigmon, Etienne Scheeper, Evelyn Wang, Filip Lundberg, Fiona Dent, Fiona Kelcher, Fionna Baker, Flash Moore, Fletcher Simpkins, Frank Ellsworth, G Kennedy, Gary Young, Georgette van Schotherst, Gerard Braun, Gerard Ferlin, Gianna Tortoli, Gillian & Mike Finnie, Gordon Breckenridge, Gustav Jahnke, Hilvert Timmer, Imran Khan, Indira Rosenthal, Ismail Akinay, J Josey, J Keith Mercer, Jacques Demagny, James Rix, Jamie Doman, Jamil van der Linde, Jan & Sandra Vanseveren-Defleyt, Jan LH Ippen, Jan Tielemans, Jane McKenzie, Jane Pennington, Jason McLoughlin, Jasper Van Den Brink, Jeffrey Skinner, Jenni Fleming, Jenny Arkell, Jenny Wardall, Jeremy Moses, Jeroen & Nicole Bergers Heerlen, Jerry Vegas, Jesmond Dubbin, Jesper Bergmann Hansen, Jo Kennedy, Joan Stokes, Joanna & Darek Grzymkiewicz, Joanne Laird, Joel Swain, Johan Olsson, Johannes Dobler, John & Bev Treacy, John J Hayward, John Langdon, John Shalalo, Jose Pras, Joshua Barnes, Joy Pelton, Karim Mubarak, Karin & Libor, Karl Jeffery, Karri Goeldner, Kathryn Dally, Kees Botshuijver, Ken & Ros Taylor, Kennet & Pernille Foh, Khalid F Bandak, Kieran Donovan, Kirstie William, Kristina Kavaliunas, Kristy Williams, Lara Cooke, Laura Hansgen, Laurie Faen, Len Keating, Leo Bouwman, Leone Marsdon, Lisa Marie Gonzales, Lorenzo Caselli, Lya den Hartogh, Lytton John Musselmen, M Caroe, M Holloway, M Jackson, Maggie Armstrong, Major Eric Bouwmeester, Makis & Dimitris Aperghis, Marc Louvrier, Marco Saracino, Marie-Lise Quaradeghini, Mark Conrod, Mark Tinker, Martin Lockett, Mary Shyng, Massimo Laria, Matevz Zgaga, Matthew Schiltz, Matthias Korth, Megan Sutton, Michael Decker, Michael Nightingale, Michael Phelan, Michael Ward, Mohammed Atich, Mojmir Kucera, Musa Twaissi, Na Choo, Nadia Graham, Naser & Sharifeh Sagheer, Nic Lowe, Nick Picton, Nicky McLean, Norman Sheppard, Odile Rouzin, Ola Lindmark, Pascale De Schinkel, Patrick Wullaert, Patrick & Nelleke, Patrick Philip, Paul Fahy, Paul Werne, Pernille Eiholm Kjaer, Peter Holm, Peter Van De Velde, Petr Hruska, Phil Bramley, Phil Mowatt, Philip Coggan, Pierre Beland, Puk Breeman, RJ Collie, Remco Oostelaar, Rita Fernsler, Rob Abbott, Robert Benford, Robert E Friedenberg, Robert Vetters, Robin Mackay, Rod Leard, Rolland Csomai, Ron Neeleman, Rosita Bernstein, Ruth Ward, Sabina Cavicchi, Sally Bothroyd, Sarah Michael, Silvano Baraldi, Simon Wheeler, Sonia Peressini, Sophia Lambert, Steve Mabey, Steve Walker, Stuart Dutson, Sue Bellamy, Sue Cannon, Sue Haines, Susan ver Ploey, Tanya & John Hortop, Ted & Anne Last, Theo Borst, Tina Calov, Tommy Malmspren, Ton de Kruyff, Trine Marott, Trish Moffitt, Veronica Vervaeck, Vincent S Smith, Wael Nawafleh, Wendy Bijwaard, Wolf Gotthilf, Yasmina Volet, Yee Chun-hing, Zahid Ali, Zoe & Scott.

LONELY PLANET

Phrasebooks

L onely Planet phrasebooks are packed with essential words and phrases to help travellers communicate with the locals. With colour tabs for quick reference, an extensive vocabulary and use of script, these handy pocket-sized language guides cover day-to-day travel situations.

- handy pocket-sized books
- easy to understand Pronunciation chapter
- clear & comprehensive Grammar chapter
- romanisation alongside script to allow ease of pronunciation
- script throughout so users can point to phrases for every situation
- full of cultural information and tips for the traveller

'... vital for a real DIY spirit and attitude in language learning'
                                                        – *Backpacker*

'the phrasebooks have good cultural backgrounders and offer solid advice for challenging situations in remote locations'
                                                        – *San Francisco Examiner*

Arabic (Egyptian) • Arabic (Moroccan) • Australian *(Australian English, Aboriginal and Torres Strait languages)* • Baltic States *(Estonian, Latvian, Lithuanian)* • Bengali • Brazilian • British • Burmese • Cantonese • Central Asia (Uyghur, Uzbek, Kyrghiz, Kazak, Pashto, Tadjik • Central Europe *(Czech, French, German, Hungarian, Italian, Slovak)* • Eastern Europe *(Bulgarian, Czech, Hungarian, Polish, Romanian, Slovak)* • Ethiopian (Amharic) • Fijian • French • German • Greek • Hebrew • Hill Tribes • Hindi & Urdu • Indonesian • Italian • Japanese • Korean • Lao • Latin American Spanish • Malay • Mandarin • Mediterranean Europe *(Albanian, Croatian, Greek, Italian, Macedonian, Maltese, Serbian, Slovene)* • Mongolian • Nepali • Pidgin • Pilipino (Tagalog) • Quechua • Russian • Scandinavian Europe *(Danish, Finnish, Icelandic, Norwegian, Swedish)* • South-East Asia *(Burmese, Indonesian, Khmer, Lao, Malay, Tagalog Pilipino, Thai, Vietnamese)* • South Pacific Languages • Spanish (Castilian) *(also includes Catalan, Galician and Basque)* • Sri Lanka • Swahili • Thai • Tibetan • Turkish • Ukrainian • USA *(US English, Vernacular, Native American languages, Hawaiian)* • Vietnamese • Western Europe *(Basque, Catalan, Dutch, French, German, Greek, Irish, Italian, Portuguese, Scottish Gaelic, Spanish (Castilian), Welsh)*

LONELY PLANET

Lonely Planet Journeys

Journeys is a unique collection of travel writing – published by the company that understands travel better than anyone else. It is a series for anyone who has ever experienced – or dreamed of – the magical moment when they encountered a strange culture or saw a place for the first time. They are tales to read while you're planning a trip, while you're on the road or while you're in an armchair in front of a fire.

These outstanding titles explore our planet through the eyes of a diverse group of international writers. JOURNEYS books catch the spirit of a place, illuminate a culture, recount a crazy adventure or introduce a fascinating way of life. They always entertain, and always enrich the experience of travel.

MALI BLUES
Traveling to an African Beat
Lieve Joris (translated by Sam Garrett)
Drought, rebel uprisings, ethnic conflict: these are the predominant images of West Africa. But as Lieve Joris travels in Senegal, Mauritania and Mali, she meets survivors, fascinating individuals charting new ways of living between tradition and modernity. With her remarkable gift for drawing out people's stories, Joris brilliantly captures the rhythms of a world that refuses to give in.

THE GATES OF DAMASCUS
Lieve Joris (translated by Sam Garrett)
This best-selling book is a beautifully drawn portrait of day-to-day life in modern Syria. Through her intimate contact with local people, Lieve Joris draws us into the fascinating world that lies behind the gates of Damascus. Hala's husband is a political prisoner, jailed for his opposition to the Assad regime; through the author's friendship with Hala we see how Syrian politics impacts on the lives of ordinary people.

THE OLIVE GROVE
Travels in Greece
Katherine Kizilos
Katherine Kizilos travels to fabled islands, troubled border zones and her family's village deep in the mountains. She vividly evokes breathtaking landscapes, generous people and passionate politics, capturing the complexities of a country she loves.

'beautifully captures the real tensions of Greece' – *Sunday Times*

KINGDOM OF THE FILM STARS
Journey into Jordan
Annie Caulfield
Kingdom of the Film Stars is a travel book and a love story. With honesty and humour, Annie Caulfield writes of travelling in Jordan and falling in love with a Bedouin with film-star looks.

She offers fascinating insights into the country – from the tent life of traditional women to the hustle of downtown Amman – and unpicks tight-woven western myths about the Arab world.

Lonely Planet Online

Whether you've just begun planning your next trip, or you're chasing down specific info on currency regulations or visa requirements, check out Lonely Planet Online for up-to-the-minute travel information.

As well as miniguides to more than 250 destinations, you'll find maps, photos, travel news, health and visa updates, travel advisories and discussion of the ecological and political issues you need to be aware of as you travel. You'll also find timely upgrades to popular guidebooks that you can print out and stick in the back of your book.

There's an online travellers' forum (The Thorn Tree) where you can share your experience of life on the road, meet travel companions and ask other travellers for their recommendations and advice.

There's also a complete and up-to-date list of all Lonely Planet travel products including travel guides, diving and snorkeling guides, phrasebooks, atlases, travel literature and videos, and a simple online ordering facility if you can't find the book you want elsewhere.

Lonely Planet Diving & Snorkeling Guides

Beautifully illustrated with full-colour photos throughout, Lonely Planet's Pisces books explore the world's best diving and snorkeling areas and prepare divers for what to expect when they get there, both topside and underwater.

Dive sites are described in detail with specifics on depths, visibility, level of difficulty, special conditions, underwater photography tips and common and unusual marine life present. You'll also find practical logistical information and coverage on topside activities and attractions, sections on diving health and safety, plus listings for diving services, live-aboards, dive resorts and tourist offices.

LONELY PLANET

Guides by Region

L onely Planet is known worldwide for publishing practical, reliable and no-nonsense travel information in our guides and on our Web site. The Lonely Planet list covers just about every accessible part of the world. Currently there are thirteen series: travel guides, shoestring guides, walking guides, city guides, phrasebooks, audio packs, city maps, travel atlases, diving & snorkeling guides, restaurant guides, first-time travel guides, healthy travel and travel literature.

AFRICA Africa on a shoestring ● Africa – the South ● Arabic (Egyptian) phrasebook ● Arabic (Moroccan) phrasebook ● Cairo ● Cape Town ● Cape Town city map● Central Africa ● East Africa ● Egypt ● Egypt travel atlas ● Ethiopian (Amharic) phrasebook ● The Gambia & Senegal ● Healthy Travel Africa ● Kenya ● Kenya travel atlas ● Malawi, Mozambique & Zambia ● Morocco ● North Africa ● South Africa, Lesotho & Swaziland ● South Africa, Lesotho & Swaziland travel atlas ● Swahili phrasebook ● Tanzania, Zanzibar & Pemba ● Trekking in East Africa ● Tunisia ● West Africa ● Zimbabwe, Botswana & Namibia ● Zimbabwe, Botswana & Namibia travel atlas
Travel Literature: The Rainbird: A Central African Journey ● Songs to an African Sunset: A Zimbabwean Story ● Mali Blues: Traveling to an African Beat

AUSTRALIA & THE PACIFIC Auckland ● Australia ● Australian phrasebook ● Bushwalking in Australia ● Bushwalking in Papua New Guinea ● Fiji ● Fijian phrasebook ● Healthy Travel Australia, NZ and the Pacific ● Islands of Australia's Great Barrier Reef ● Melbourne ● Melbourne city map ● Micronesia ● New Caledonia ● New South Wales & the ACT ● New Zealand ● Northern Territory ● Outback Australia ● Out To Eat – Melbourne ● Out to Eat – Sydney ● Papua New Guinea ● Pidgin phrasebook ● Queensland ● Rarotonga & the Cook Islands ● Samoa ● Solomon Islands ● South Australia ● South Pacific Languages phrasebook ● Sydney ● Sydney city map ● Sydney Condensed ● Tahiti & French Polynesia ● Tasmania ● Tonga ● Tramping in New Zealand ● Vanuatu ● Victoria ● Western Australia
Travel Literature: Islands in the Clouds ● Kiwi Tracks: A New Zealand Journey ● Sean & David's Long Drive

CENTRAL AMERICA & THE CARIBBEAN Bahamas, Turks & Caicos ● Bermuda ● Central America on a shoestring ● Costa Rica ● Cuba ● Dominican Republic & Haiti ● Eastern Caribbean ● Guatemala, Belize & Yucatán: La Ruta Maya ● Jamaica ● Mexico ● Mexico City ● Panama ● Puerto Rico
Travel Literature: Green Dreams: Travels in Central America

EUROPE Amsterdam ● Amsterdam city map ● Andalucía ● Austria ● Baltic States phrasebook ● Barcelona ● Berlin ● Berlin city map ● Britain ● British phrasebook ● Brussels, Bruges & Antwerp ● Budapest city map ● Canary Islands ● Central Europe ● Central Europe phrasebook ● Corsica ● Croatia ● Czech & Slovak Republics ● Denmark ● Dublin ● Eastern Europe ● Eastern Europe phrasebook ● Edinburgh ● Estonia, Latvia & Lithuania ● Europe on a shoestring ● Finland ● France ● French phrasebook ● Germany ● German phrasebook ● Greece ● Greek Islands ● Greek phrasebook ● Hungary ● Iceland, Greenland & the Faroe Islands ● Ireland ● Italian phrasebook ● Italy ● Krakow ● Lisbon ● London ● London city map ● London Condensed ● Mediterranean Europe ● Mediterranean Europe phrasebook ● Norway ● Paris ● Paris city map ● Poland ● Portugal ● Portugal travel atlas ● Prague ● Prague city map ● Provence & the Côte d'Azur ● Romania & Moldova ● Rome ● Russia, Ukraine & Belarus ● Russian phrasebook ● Scandinavian & Baltic Europe ● Scandinavian Europe phrasebook ● Scotland ● Slovenia ● Spain ● Spanish phrasebook ● St Petersburg ● Switzerland ● Trekking in Spain ● Ukrainian phrasebook ● Vienna ● Walking in Britain ● Walking in Ireland ● Walking in Italy ● Walking in Spain ● Walking in Switzerland ● Western Europe ● Western Europe phrasebook
Travel Literature: The Olive Grove: Travels in Greece

INDIAN SUBCONTINENT Bangladesh ● Bengali phrasebook ● Bhutan ● Delhi ● Goa ● Hindi & Urdu phrasebook ● India ● India & Bangladesh travel atlas ● Indian Himalaya ● Karakoram Highway ● Kerala ● Mumbai (Bombay) ● Nepal ● Nepali phrasebook ● Pakistan ● Rajasthan ● Read This First: Asia & India ● South India ● Sri Lanka ● Sri Lanka phrasebook ● Trekking in the Indian Himalaya ● Trekking in the Karakoram & Hindukush ● Trekking in the Nepal Himalaya
Travel Literature: In Rajasthan ● Shopping for Buddhas

LONELY PLANET

Mail Order

Lonely Planet products are distributed worldwide. They are also available by mail order from Lonely Planet, so if you have difficulty finding a title please write to us. North and South American residents should write to 150 Linden St, Oakland, CA 94607, USA; European and African residents should write to 10a Spring Place, London NW5 3BH, UK; and residents of other countries to PO Box 617, Hawthorn, Victoria 3122, Australia.

ISLANDS OF THE INDIAN OCEAN Madagascar & Comoros ● Maldives ● Mauritius, Réunion & Seychelles

MIDDLE EAST & CENTRAL ASIA Arab Gulf States ● Central Asia ● Central Asia phrasebook ● Hebrew phrasebook ● Iran ● Israel & the Palestinian Territories ● Israel & the Palestinian Territories travel atlas ● Istanbul ● Istanbul to Cairo ● Jerusalem ● Jordan & Syria ● Jordan, Syria & Lebanon travel atlas ● Lebanon ● Middle East on a shoestring ● Syria ● Turkey ● Turkey travel atlas ● Turkish phrasebook ● Yemen
Travel Literature: The Gates of Damascus ● Kingdom of the Film Stars: Journey into Jordan

NORTH AMERICA Alaska ● Backpacking in Alaska ● Baja California ● California & Nevada ● Canada ● Chicago ● Chicago city map ● Deep South ● Florida ● Hawaii ● Honolulu ● Las Vegas ● Los Angeles ● Miami ● New England ● New Orleans ● New York City ● New York city map ● New York, New Jersey & Pennsylvania ● Pacific Northwest USA ● Puerto Rico ● Rocky Mountain ● San Francisco ● San Francisco city map ● Seattle ● Southwest USA ● Texas ● USA ● USA phrasebook ● Vancouver ● Washington, DC & the Capital Region ● Washington DC city map
Travel Literature: Drive Thru America

NORTH-EAST ASIA Beijing ● Cantonese phrasebook ● China ● Hong Kong ● Hong Kong city map ● Hong Kong, Macau & Guangzhou ● Japan ● Japanese phrasebook ● Japanese audio pack ● Korea ● Korean phrasebook ● Kyoto ● Mandarin phrasebook ● Mongolia ● Mongolian phrasebook ● North-East Asia on a shoestring ● Seoul ● South-West China ● Taiwan ● Tibet ● Tibetan phrasebook ● Tokyo
Travel Literature: Lost Japan

SOUTH AMERICA Argentina, Uruguay & Paraguay ● Bolivia ● Brazil ● Brazilian phrasebook ● Buenos Aires ● Chile & Easter Island ● Chile & Easter Island travel atlas ● Colombia ● Ecuador & the Galapagos Islands ● Healthy Travel Central & South America ● Latin American Spanish phrasebook ● Peru ● Quechua phrasebook ● Rio de Janeiro ● Rio de Janeiro city map ● South America on a shoestring ● Trekking in the Patagonian Andes ● Venezuela
Travel Literature: Full Circle: A South American Journey

SOUTH-EAST ASIA Bali & Lombok ● Bangkok ● Bangkok city map ● Burmese phrasebook ● Cambodia ● Hanoi ● Healthy Travel Asia & India ● Hill Tribes phrasebook ● Ho Chi Minh City ● Indonesia ● Indonesia's Eastern Islands ● Indonesian phrasebook ● Indonesian audio pack ● Jakarta ● Java ● Laos ● Lao phrasebook ● Laos travel atlas ● Malay phrasebook ● Malaysia, Singapore & Brunei ● Myanmar (Burma) ● Philippines ● Pilipino (Tagalog) phrasebook ● Singapore ● South-East Asia on a shoestring ● South-East Asia phrasebook ● Thailand ● Thailand's Islands & Beaches ● Thailand travel atlas ● Thai phrasebook ● Thai audio pack ● Vietnam ● Vietnamese phrasebook ● Vietnam travel atlas

ALSO AVAILABLE: Antarctica ● The Arctic ● Brief Encounters: Stories of Love, Sex & Travel ● Chasing Rickshaws ● Lonely Planet Unpacked ● Not the Only Planet: Travel Stories from Science Fiction ● Sacred India ● Travel with Children ● Traveller's Tales

Index

Text

Boxed Text

MAP LEGEND

CITY ROUTES

Freeway	Freeway	= = = =	Unsealed Road
Highway	Primary Road	→—→	One Way Street
Road	Secondary Road		Pedestrian Street
Street	Street	⊓⊓⊓⊓⊓	Stepped Street
Lane	Lane	→⇒ = =	Tunnel
	On/Off Ramp		Footbridge

REGIONAL ROUTES

- .... Tollway, Freeway
- .... Primary Road
- .... Secondary Road
- .... Minor Road

BOUNDARIES

- —·—·—·— .... International
- —··—··—·· .... State
- — — — .... Disputed
- ▬▬▬▬ .... Fortified Wall

HYDROGRAPHY

- .... River, Creek
- .... Canal
- .... Lake
- ⊙ ⤳ .... Spring; Rapids
- .... Dry Lake; Salt Lake
- .... Waterfalls

TRANSPORT ROUTES & STATIONS

- ⊢——●—— .... Train
- ⊢ + + + -.. .... Underground Train
- ▬ ▬ ⓜ .... Metro
- ▬▬▬ .... Tramway
- ▸—⊩—⊩—▸.. .... Cable Car, Chairlift
- - - - - 🛱 .... Ferry
- - - - - - .... Walking Trail
- · · · · · · · .... Walking Tour
- .... Path
- ————— .... Pier or Jetty

AREA FEATURES

- .... Building
- ❀ .... Park, Gardens
- .... Market
- .... Sports Ground
- 🐾 .... Beach
- + + + ... Cemetery
- .... Campus
- ⌐¬ .... Plaza

POPULATION SYMBOLS

◎ CAPITAL	.... National Capital	● CITY	.... City	● Village	.... Population Small
◉ CAPITAL	.... State Capital	● Town	.... Population Large		.... Urban Area

MAP SYMBOLS

♠ .... Place to Stay	▼ .... Place to Eat	● .... Point of Interest

✈ .... Airport	⊞ .... Cinema	☾ .... Mosque	▢ .... Pub or Bar
⊖ .... Bank	◲ .... Dive Site	▲ .... Mountain	🔟 .... Ruins
⊅ .... Beach	▢ .... Embassy	🏛 .... Museum	⊗ .... Shopping Centre
⊕ .... Border Crossing	⊕ .... Golf Course	◙ .... National Park	◙ .... Synagogue
▤ .... Bus Terminal	⊕ .... Hospital	← .... One Way Street	◙ .... Taxi Rank
◙ 🅿🅿 .... Camping/Caravan	ⓓ .... Internet Cafe	🅿 .... Parking	◙ .... Telephone
⌂ .... Cave	☀ ⛰ .... Lookout	✪ .... Police Station	⊕ .... Toilet
✚ ⊕ .... Church	⚱ .... Monument	▭ .... Post Office	❶ .... Tourist Information

Note: not all symbols displayed above appear in this book

LONELY PLANET OFFICES

Australia
PO Box 617, Hawthorn, Victoria 3122
☎ 03 9819 1877 fax 03 9819 6459
email: talk2us@lonelyplanet.com.au

USA
150 Linden St, Oakland, CA 94607
☎ 510 893 8555 TOLL FREE: 800 275 8555
fax 510 893 8572
email: info@lonelyplanet.com

UK
10a Spring Place, London NW5 3BH
☎ 020 7428 4800 fax 020 7428 4828
email: go@lonelyplanet.co.uk

France
1 rue du Dahomey, 75011 Paris
☎ 01 55 25 33 00 fax 01 55 25 33 01
email: bip@lonelyplanet.fr
www.lonelyplanet.fr

World Wide Web: www.lonelyplanet.com *or* AOL keyword: lp
Lonely Planet Images: lpi@lonelyplanet.com.au